1000
Questions
About
Canada

1000
Questions
About
Canada

Places, People, Things and Ideas
A Question-and-Answer Book on Canadian
Facts and Culture

John Robert Colombo

A HOUNSLOW BOOK
A MEMBER OF THE DUNDURN GROUP
TORONTO · OXFORD

Publisher: Anthony Hawke
Editor: Julian Walker
Design: Bruna Brunelli
Printer: Friesens Corporation

Canadian Cataloguing in Publication Data

Colombo, John Robert, 1936-
    1000 questions about Canada

ISBN 0-88882-232-4

1. Canada — Miscellanea. I. Title. II Title: One thousand questions about Canada.

FC61.C648 2001   971'.002   C2001-930649-0
F1008.3.C65 2001

1 2 3 4 5   05 04 03 02 01

THE CANADA COUNCIL | LE CONSEIL DES ARTS
FOR THE ARTS | DU CANADA
SINCE 1957 | DEPUIS 1957

Canada

ONTARIO ARTS COUNCIL
CONSEIL DES ARTS DE L'ONTARIO

We acknowledge the support of the **Canada Council for the Arts** and the **Ontario Arts Council** for our publishing program. We also acknowledge the financial support of the **Government of Canada** through the **Book Publishing Industry Development Program** and **The Association for the Export of Canadian Books**, and the **Government of Ontario** through the **Ontario Book Publishers Tax Credit** program.

Dundurn Press
8 Market Street
Suite 200
Toronto, Ontario, Canada
M5E 1M6

Dundurn Press
73 Lime Walk
Headington, Oxford,
England
OX3 7AD

Dundurn Press
2250 Military Road
Tonawanda NY
U.S.A. 14150

Jonathan and Suzanne
Catherine and Stuart
Theo and Annie

May they know their country's greatness

Contents

Preface

In this book you will find one thousand entries, some long, some short, devoted to subjects of Canadian interest. The entries are loosely grouped into four categories – People, Places, Things, Ideas – but other than that they are arranged in no particular order. (As merchandiser Ed Mirvish always says, "Messy sells better than neat.") Each entry consists of a straight-forward question followed by an informative answer. The work is a question-and-answer book, not a quiz book. A question-and-answer book bears the same relationship to a quiz book that a general-interest magazine does to a daily newspaper: It tells little stories. It does not dwell on current events but on curious events of lasting interest. Nor is the present book an almanac or a fact book. Instead it is a work that has been prepared to be of interest to the general reader with a taste for Canadian subjects and topics. In fact, it is my hope that the unlikely questions will be answered in such a way as to surprise the reader and from time to time astonish him or her.

This book is not the first question-and-answer book that I have researched and written. There are two earlier books, both published by Doubleday Canada. *1001 Questions about Canada* appeared in 1986; *999 Questions about Canada* appeared in 1989. They sold quite well in trade paperback editions and were reprinted a number of times. The first book featured mostly facts and figures about Canada, the kind of basic information that turns up in reference works and news stories in newspapers. The second book consisted of what are called feature stories, stories like those encountered in magazines, stories of human interest. For a number of reasons, including lean publishing years, these two works were not immediately followed by *1000 Questions about Canada*. After all, a question-and-answer book, though it might be noteworthy, is hardly newsworthy. It is unlikely to be widely reviewed, to make the headlines, to win a book award, to be optioned for a major motion picture, or to be translated into Japanese. Such a book is its own reward.

The book was researched and written with the general reader in mind, yet it is my hope that the specialist reader will find something in the field of his or her specialty that is offbeat and surprising through the use of the invaluable Index. The indexing is reasonably inclusive – not every reference could be recognized, of course – so my advice to the reader or browser is to spend some time with it. It is surprising how many users forget that the numbers in the index refer to question numbers, not page numbers.

Two maxims have guided me throughout the research and writing of this work. One maxim is only three words long and it goes like this: "Facts are fun." There is a lot of pleasure to be had from reading and learning. It is like a game: What do I know? What can I learn? As pupils and students in school we were seldom encouraged to look at a body of information from the point of view of how it can be put to good and playful use. Too often facts and figures had to be committed to memory. Not so with this book. Nothing has to be memorized. There are no tests and no final examinations.

My other maxim is only two words long. It goes like this: "Deep Fun." Fun may be foolishness and clowning around, but having fun is also one of mankind's most rewarding and engrossing activities. The activity should be deeply informative and enlightening. The information that is being presented may be basic, or it may be offbeat, even off-the-wall, but if it is presented in a funny, provocative, or thoughtful manner, it will be exciting to read, memorable to recall, and perhaps even useful.

So facts are fun, deep fun.

There are two other points that should be made. One of them concerns Canada, the other Canadians. Marshall McLuhan once said, "Cigarette smokers are not interested in tobacco." What he had in mind is that people are generally not interested in their addiction or their environment. They prefer to think about other matters for reasons of escapism from present realities. It could be said that people who live in this country have, generally, in the past at least, not paid much attention to the country itself. They prefer to learn about foreign places. This too is escapism. McLuhan also observed, "Ignorance is learned." Some people take as much pride in their lack of knowledge and information as do others in their possession of knowledge and information. It takes an effort to be stupid, almost as much as to be informed.

Being informed about Canadiana may be frivolous for a Cambodian or a Colombian, but it remains foundational and functional for a Canadian. Self-knowledge is fundamental to maturity. National knowledge is the buttress that supports the retaining wall of citizenship and personal well-being. To be competitive domestically and globally, one must know where one stands and one must understand oneself and the world. There are other forms of knowledge, but they rest on the firm foundation of self-knowledge and national knowledge.

In previous books I have quoted one of my favourite mottos: "Canada only needs to be known in order to be great." I firmly believe that. The key word is "known," and the essential words are "to know." The notion of "greatness" flows from knowing. There are many measures of "greatness." Some countries have it thrust upon them (in the form of the abundance of natural resources, remoteness from warlike neighbours, resources of an educated population, respect for essential institutions, encouragement from inspirational, ambitious or influential people, etc.). Other countries, with seemingly few advantages, excel through the use of reason, general resourcefulness, respect for tradition, or sense of reserve. (One thinks here of countries like Sweden and Japan as well as constitutional anomalies like Luxembourg and Switzerland.) Canada has far to go in this regard. We need to begin to use our brains; our brawn took us only so far. We cannot continue to squander our natural heritage and accidental advantages forever. The time is now to begin to make reasonable arrangements to ensure the long-range well-being of the inhabitants of this country. It is high time to invest in ideas and innovation. The time is ripe to begin to think about what Canada was, is, and should be. We should determine the ideal destiny of our citizens and their regions, otherwise the necessities of fate will overtake us. Unless we assume that responsibility, other people will do it for us.

"Canada only needs to be known in order to be great." It is a great big wonderful country. That is certain. Whether or not the land will ever support a great people, a people as great as it is, we do not know. All we know is that we should act in such a way that we make use of the opportunities at hand so the peoples of the world will recognize that we are a people who are fit to inhabit so great a country.

Acknowledgements

The research and writing of the present work proceeded over a period of more than ten years. There is no way I am able to acknowledge the assistance I received from everyone who made a contribution to its pages, but I must express my appreciation for the contributions that were made by the following people: researcher Alice Neal, librarian Philip Singer, editor Julian Walker and the rest of the staff at Dundurn, investigators Dwight Whalen and W. Ritchie Benedict, correspondents Tom Williams of Calgary and Ion Will of Ivory Coast, colleagues Cyril Greenland, David A. Gotlib, Kamala Bhatia, Suparna Ghosh, and last but not least my wife Ruth Colombo.

People

001. Who is the most widely known Canadian of all time?

There are a number of ways to answer this question. Hiawatha is probably the most widely known Canadian of all time, but the semi-legendary Indian warrior and lawmaker is not generally regarded as a person or as a Canadian. Nor is the Icelandic colonist Leif the Lucky considered to be a Canadian, although his name is internationally recognized because he was an early colonist. Two movie personalities, Nanook of the North from the Belcher Islands, Nunavut, and Toronto-born Mary Pickford were once globally recognized. Norman Bethune was known throughout the Communist half of the world for his humanitarian internationalism. Among currently living people, the statesman Pierre Elliott Trudeau is as widely known as any single Canadian. Sprinter Ben Johnson captured the headlines of the world for two feats: running faster than anyone on Earth and using banned steroids during Olympic competition. So it is a toss-up who is the most widely known Canadian of all time. The most widely known fictional Canadian is Anne Shirley – Anne of Green Gables. Perhaps the most widely known stock character is The Mountie.

002. Are Canadians the world's wealthiest people?

No. According to a study undertaken by the World Bank, Canadians are on average the second-wealthiest people on Earth.

According to Drew Fagan, writing in "Canada Ranked Second Richest," *The Globe and Mail*, 18 September 1995, Australians come first and Canadians second, followed by citizens of Luxembourg, Switzerland, and Japan. The evaluations are based on estimates of natural capital (surface and subsurface resources), produced assets (production equipment), and human resources (education, nutrition, etc.). In an independent survey, the World Bank found that with respect to GNP per capita, Canada ranks seventeenth in the world.

003. Who were "the half-million"?

"The half-million" is the phrase used by a military historian and an archivist to refer to the invasion of Britain by Canadian soldiers during the Second World War. Some five hundred thousand military personnel (that is, half a million men and women) spent some or all of the war years in various locations throughout Britain.

The effect of the Canadians on the British and the influence of the British on the Canadians is the subject of *The Half-Million: The Canadians in Britain, 1939-1946* (1987) by the military historian C.P. Stacey and the archivist Barbara M. Wilson. Their conclusions? "A community of feeling between peoples does live on. The fact that in 1939-46 half a million Canadian service men and women spent long periods in the United Kingdom and formed warm connections there, and that some 45,000 of the men brought British wives back with them, had its due effect, which is felt to this day."

004. Who was the first professional full-time book reviewer in Canada?

It marks a stage in the evolution of a country's literature when it may boast that there is a person who is fully and gainfully employed by a newspaper or a periodical to write reviews of current books and to edit a regular review page or section in a publication.

William Arthur Deacon is generally considered the first professional full-time book reviewer in Canada. Although his tastes and own prose style were not the most modern, even for his day, he undertook the task or practised the trade with high seriousness; indeed, he did so with prophetic earnestness because he saw literature as the expression of nationalism. He reviewed full-time for *Saturday Night* (1922-28), *The Mail and Empire* (1928-36), and *The Globe and Mail* (1936-60). Among the authors whose books he recommended to the attention of a national audience were Hugh MacLennan and Gabrielle Roy.

005. Who is the worst Canadian poet of all time?

There is no agreement on the correct answer to this question. But the literary cognoscenti would place their bets on an unselfconscious versifier who displayed no talent whatsoever, but plenty of ambition. His name was James Gay (1810-1891) and he called himself "Poet-Laureate of Canada and Master of All Poets."

Gay lived in Guelph, Ontario's "Royal City," where he worked as a hotelkeeper and then as an umbrella repairer. Upon the death of Longfellow, he wrote in familiar terms to Lord Tennyson: "Dear Sir, Now Longfellow is gone there are only two of us left. There ought to be no rivalry between us two." Needless to say, no rivalry was experienced, as Tennyson unaccountably failed to acknowledge Gay's missive. Unperturbed, Gay wrote: "A poet's mind is clear and bright, / No room for hatred, malice or spite." A selection of Gay's good-bad verse appears in William Arthur Deacon's satire *The Four Jameses* (1927, 1953, 1974).

006. Who is the worst writer of prose in Canada?

The laurels for writing the worst prose should be awarded to James D. Gillis (1870-1965), a native of Cape Breton Island and a long-time schoolteacher, who penned a series of booklets and published and sold them himself. Generations of readers have found his prose inadvertently amusing so Gillis should be awarded a retroactive Leacock Medal for Humour. Today all his booklets are collectors' items; some of them, in reprint editions, are sold in Nova Scotia as souvenir items. Gillis's best-known publication is *The Cape Breton Giant* (1899), his brief hagiography of Angus MacAskill. The story of Gillis is told by William Arthur Deacon in his amusing literary and subliterary study, *The Four Jameses* (1927, 1953, 1974).

007. Who was the first native-born novelist?

Major John Richardson (1796-1852) is accorded the honour of being the first native-born novelist. He was, coincidentally, the fledgling country's least successful author.

As the literary critic William Arthur Deacon wrote: "Looking down that long avenue of time, one sees Major John Richardson, our first native-born novelist, after making a reputation in London and Paris, returning to Canada, here trying futilely to make a living by writing; and then going to New York in 1852, selling his beloved dog to buy his last meal, and lying down to die of starvation because he was too proud to beg."

Richardson, born at Queenston, Upper Canada, fought with distinction in the War of 1812 and wrote about his military experiences in works of fiction and non-fiction. Richardson completed, in all, some twenty books, but only one is in print in the 1990s. That book is a three-volume novel called *Wacousta: or, The Prophecy; A Tale of the Canadas* (1832), which tells a sensational and heroic version of Pontiac's Indian uprising. The book is studied – rather than read – by students of early Canadian literature.

008. What is the difference between an Indian and a native?

An Indian is a person registered or entitled to be registered as an Indian according to the Indian Act, that is, a status Indian. A native is a Canadian of aboriginal descent. A native may be a status or non-status Indian, a Métis, or an Inuk.

009. What was the native population of the New World at the time of contact?

There is no way of knowing for sure the size of the resident native population of North and South America at the time of contact. Contact is taken to be when Christopher Columbus made his historic landing in the Caribbean in 1492, or when Jacques Cartier made his landfall farther north in 1497. The estimate of demographers, ethnologists, historians, and others is that the total native population of the Americas in the 1490s was 15 million. South and Central America and Mexico accounted for the majority of natives; the territory now occupied by the United States and Canada accounted for one million or fewer natives.

010. Did a Canadian design the Australian flag?

It seems so. Not much is known of Captain Charles Ross. (Indeed, he is sometimes referred to as Lieutenant Ross.) But it is known that he was a Canadian from Toronto and that he was a gold miner at the Eureka camp near Ballarat in the New South Wales district of Australia. He was present when the miners barricaded themselves in and defied the government troops. On 3 December 1854, the troops attacked, killing a number of the miners, among them Charles Ross. Before the act of defiance, Ross designed the makeshift, home-made flag that briefly flew above the Eureka Stockade. The simple design of this flag depicted the constellation known as the Southern Cross, which dominates the sky of the Southern Hemisphere the way the North Star and the Big Dipper dominate the sky of the Northern Hemisphere. It became the basis of the official Australian flag. One would like to know more about Charles Ross. Was he, one wonders, related to Betsy Ross, the housewife who sewed the American Stars and Stripes?

011. Who was the first non-Nordic European to set foot on the American continent proper?

The Anglo-Italian navigator John Cabot set foot on the American continent on 24 June 1497. Although the site of the landfall is debated, many feel Cabot stepped ashore and raised a cross at some point on the eastern coast of Cape Breton Island, Nova Scotia, which he mistakenly believed to be the eastern coast of Asia.

Cabot is the first known non-Nordic European to set foot on the American continent proper. He was preceded by the Norsemen who settled L'Anse aux Meadows around 1000 A.D., but not by the Italian navigator Christopher Columbus, who in 1492 set foot on the Caribbean island of Hispaniola, not on the American continent proper.

012. Who was Oak Island's most distinguished treasure-hunter?

The distinction of being Oak Island's most distinguished treasure-hunter belongs to Franklin Delano Roosevelt, the President of the United States.

Young Franklin summered on Campobello Island, New Brunswick, where there was much talk of the fabulous Money Pit on Oak Island in

Mahone Bay off the east coast of Nova Scotia – both tall tales of pirate treasure and details of extensive excavations. In 1896, when he was fourteen years old, Franklin devoted four days of his summer vacation to the task of digging up another Maritime island for a treasure trove which was never found. In 1909, as a 27-year-old law clerk in New York City, he became a minor shareholder in one of the companies engaged in digging and drilling on Oak Island. As late as 1939, as U.S. President, despite the worsening international scene, he took time to keep up with developments on Oak Island, even to the extent of corresponding with the leading prospectors who were hopeful that they would uncover the fabled Money Pit.

013. What is the curse of Oak Island?

Tradition holds that Oak Island in Nova Scotia's Mahone Bay will yield its treasure only after the last of its oak trees has fallen and seven of its prospectors have perished. The curse of Oak Island was recalled by D'Arcy O'Connor in *The Big Dig: The $10 Million Search for Oak Island's Legendary Treasure* (1988). As O'Connor noted in 1988, only three of an immense stand of oak trees remain on the island, and as of 1996, six people have met accidental deaths while searching for the fabled Money Pit.

014. Who was the first Canadian to play a starring role at the Stratford Festival?

The first Canadian performer to play a starring role at the Stratford Festival was Don Harron. Artistic director Tyrone Guthrie offered Harron the role of Bertram in *As You Like It* in 1953, the year the Festival opened. Harron accepted and did not betray the director's trust.

In the Festival's early years, all the principal parts were offered to performers from Britain and the United States. Since then Canadian actors and actresses have played the majority of the leading roles, so Harron was a pioneer. And since then he has become widely known as a comic and author, virtually indistinguishable from Charlie Farquharson, the wisecracking farmer from Parry Sound.

015. What is the full name of Pierre Trudeau?

Pierre Elliott Trudeau's full and legal name is Joseph Philippe Pierre Yves Elliott Trudeau. Québécois journalists irritatingly referred to him as Elliott Trudeau, drawing attention to the fact though his father was French, he had a Scottish mother. Following in the footsteps of American headline writers who wrote about LBJ, Canadian headline writers reduced Trudeau's name to three initials: PET. More correct would have been the following initials: JPPYET.

016. Who were the Lords of the Line?

The Lords of the Line is a wonderful phrase. It refers to the six powerful men – strong personalities, every one of them – who were the first heads (presidents or chairmen) of the Canadian Pacific Railway. Together they ran the CPR for a total of ninety years. The CPR was established as a railway line in 1871. Since 1971 the conglomerate has been known as Canadian Pacific Limited. Here are the names of the men who served as the Lords of the Line: Sir George Stephen, Sir William C. Van Horne, Thomas G. Shaughnessy, Edward Beatty, Buck Crump, and Ian Sinclair. Their stories were told by David Cruise and Alison Griffiths in *Lords of the Line* (1988).

017. Who was the last Prime Minister to authorize the awarding of knighthoods?

R.B. Bennett was the last Prime Minister to authorize the awarding of knighthoods to Canadians. Thereafter no Canadian citizen, although yet a British subject, could receive a British title. Bennett did so during his tenure as Prime Minister (1930-35). Yet, curiously, Bennett was the sole Prime Minister of Canada to ever be created a Viscount, a distinction superior to that of a Knight.

Embittered by his years in public life, Bennett settled in Britain where in 1941 his influential friends secured for him a viscountcy. Thereafter he was known as Viscount Bennett of Mickleham, Calgary, and Hopewell. His title refers to three places close to his heart: his birthplace, Hopewell Hill, Nova Scotia; his old constituency, Calgary East and Calgary West in Alberta; and the British village where he lived (and eventually died).

018. Was Lester B. Pearson the sole Canadian to be awarded the Nobel Prize for Peace?

The answer to this question depends on what is meant by the word "Canadian." Everyone knows that Lester B. Pearson was awarded the Nobel Prize for Peace. That event occurred in 1957. Two years later the Nobel Prize for Peace was awarded to Philip Noel-Baker, British diplomat, socialist, cabinet minister in Labour governments. He received the coveted award for the international role he played in the promotion of peace. But was Noel-Baker a Canadian? He was born in London, England, to Canadian-born Quaker parents, educated at Cambridge, and he became an influential member of the British Labour cabinet. He was a British subject but remained proud of his Canadian – and Quaker – connection.

019. Who was the first Québécois to be appointed Governor General?

Georges P. Vanier was the first French Canadian or Québécois to be appointed Governor General of Canada. He was appointed to the highest office in 1959 and served until his death in 1967. Vanier followed in the wake of Vincent Massey, who was the first Canadian – and hence the first English Canadian – to be appointed to that office, all previous appointees having been titled Britishers.

020. Who is the famous American who became Deputy Postmaster General of British North America in 1753?

Benjamin Franklin, the American statesman, became Deputy Postmaster General of British North America in 1753. He established post offices in Quebec City, Trois-Rivières, and Montreal, thereby initiating the first attempt to streamline the colony's antiquated postal service. He resigned his post in 1774. Postal affairs were handled by provincial authorities until 1851, when the Canadian Post Office – the Royal Mail – came into being.

021. Whose automobile bore the licence plate "47 U 1"?

Barbara Ann Scott, after winning the European figure-skating championship in Davos, Switzerland, and the world championship in

Stockholm, Sweden, returned home to Canada to thunderous enthusi-
asm. The Mayor of Ottawa publicly presented her with a gift: a yellow
Buick convertible with the licence plate "47 U 1." This alphanumeric
code could be read in rebus fashion: 1947 you won.

The young skater was delighted. But delight turned to dismay when
Avery Brundage, head of the International Olympic Committee, stated
that accepting the gift was in contravention of the Olympic rules of ama-
teurism. If the skater wished to compete in next year's Olympics at St.
Moritz, she would have to return the automobile.

Brundage was called Avery "Umbrage" in Toronto and his effigy was
burnt in Brandon, Manitoba. But displaying no anger, Barbara Ann Scott
returned the keys, competed in the Olympics, took the gold medal, and
then reclaimed the car with the licence plate that read "47 U 1," as noted
by Trent Frayne in *The Best of Times: Fifty Years of Canadian Sport* (1988).

022. Is there a decline in the Anglophone population of Quebec?

Yes. The Anglophone population of Quebec is on the decline. In 1971,
Anglophones in Quebec numbered 789,185, or 13.1% of the population.
In 1986, Anglophones numbered 678,785, or 10.4%. The decline can be
attributed to a series of separatist governments in Quebec and the exodus
of Quebeckers to such cities as Brockville (which lies just across the
Quebec-Ontario border), Toronto, and Vancouver.

023. Is there a decline in the Francophone populations of New Brunswick and Ontario?

Statistics published in the journal *Language and Society*, Summer 1989,
show clearly that there was a decline in the francophone populations of
New Brunswick and Ontario, and indeed in all of Canada, at least in so
far as the percentage of Francophones compares to the population as a
whole. New Brunswick's francophone population declined from 34% of
the population (215,724 Francophones) in 1971 to 33.6% (237,570
Francophones) in 1986. Similarly the decline in Ontario was from 6.3%
(482,040 Francophones) in 1971 to 5.5% (484,265 Francophones) in
1986. In Canada as a whole – excluding Quebec, where the francophone
population also showed an increase – the decline in Francophones as a percentage of the population was roughly from 6% in 1971 to 5% in 1986.

024. Who played Anne in *Anne of Green Gables?*

Megan Follows, the teenage actress (who was born in Toronto in 1969), was cast by director Kevin Sullivan as the red-headed moppet Anne Shirley in the 1985 made-for-television movie based on *Anne of Green Gables* (1908). Three years later she appeared in the first of its sequels. It was an ideal casting.

However, Miss Follows, the daughter of actors Ted Follows and Dawn Greenhalgh, was filmdom's second Anne, not its first. The first Anne was a young, otherwise unknown Hollywood actress who renamed herself Anne Shirley, after the appealing character, and appeared in the 1934 movie *Anne of Green Gables* as well as in its 1940 sequel *Anne of Windy Poplars.*

025. Who were the Four Lads?

The Four Lads were Frank Busseri, Bernard Toorish, James Arnold, and Corrado "Connie" Codarini. These four young Torontonians formed a singing group in the early 1950s and succeeded in making a name for themselves as performing and recording stars. Their hit singles included "Mocking Bird" and "Standing on the Corner."

026. Was the actor Michael J. Fox born in Burnaby, British Columbia?

No. The television and movie actor Michael J. Fox was raised in Burnaby, which is part of Vancouver, British Columbia, but his birthplace was Edmonton, Alberta, in 1961. He rose to stardom with NBC's *Family Ties* and he has starred in the *Back to the Future* series and in many other Hollywood movies which have made good use of his comic talents.

027. Was *Fraggle Rock* filmed in Canada?

Fraggle Rock, the popular children's television show, was filmed in Toronto. It was produced by the CBC in conjunction with Henson Associates, the organization founded and headed by Jim Henson, the inventor of the *Muppets*. The association, begun in 1977, ended in 1983 after a successful run of light entertainment for children.

028. Who created Mr. Canoehead?

Mr. Canoehead had a cult following across Canada and the northern United States in the early 1980s. The character, who wore a long canoe like an immense hat, was created by The Frantics, a Toronto-based comedy group. First heard on CBC Radio, they moved to CBC Television in 1986. The Frantics were a talented group made up of Paul Chato, Peter Wildman, Rick Green, and Dan Redican.

029. Who is Quebec's most famous impressionist?

André-Phillipe Gagnon came to fame as an impressionist following an appearance on *The Tonight Show* in November 1986. Gagnon's tour-de-force was his imitation of all eighteen voices heard on the U.S. famine relief record "We Are the World." Gagnon was born in Loretteville, Quebec.

030. Which Canadian singer has "very sexy shoulders" according to Prince Charles?

Patsy Gallant, the singer who was born in Campbellton, New Brunswick, was told by Prince Charles, who danced with her at a ball held at Rideau Hall in Ottawa on 6 April 1976, that she had "very sexy shoulders." What was Gallant's response? "I told him my husband thinks so too."

031. Who was "the hairdresser to the stars"?

MGM's Sidney Guilaroff, a hair stylist born in Montreal in 1910, has been called "the hairdresser to the stars." He worked as the studio stylist at MGM in Hollywood in the 1930s and 1940s. The hairdresser was "discovered" in New York by Claudette Colbert for whom he devised a special wave and cut for the 1934 movie *It Happened One Night*.

032. Clive Barnes called him "the greatest illusionist I have ever seen." Who is he?

Clive Barnes, influential drama critic of The New York Times, described the late Doug Henning, the Winnipeg-born illusionist, as "the greatest illusionist I have ever seen. Better than Houdini." Barnes had in mind the mind-boggling illusions of Henning's *The Magic Show* in the 1970s.

033. What hit song did Walter Huston sing in *Knickerbocker Holiday?*

Walter Huston, the Toronto-born actor, father of the late director John Huston, intoned Kurt Weill's moving "September Song" in the 1944 movie *Knickerbocker Holiday*. The story goes that while composer Weill and playwright Maxwell Anderson were working on the movie script they telegraphed Huston in California asking for his vocal range. Huston responded: "No range." Despite that – or perhaps because of that – he was offered the part and sang that song most memorably and movingly.

034. Who are the Irish Rovers?

The Irish Rovers are a singing group formed in Calgary in 1964. The original members were: Will Millar (leader), George Millar (brother), Joe Millar (cousin to Will and George), Jimmy Ferguson, and Wilcil McDowell. All are natives of Antrim County, Northern Ireland. Their big break came at the Purple Onion in San Francisco in 1964 and their major hit was "The Unicorn" (1968). Their novelty number "Grandma Got Run Over by a Reindeer" was released in time for major Christmas sales in 1982.

035. Who is the actress who introduced the cakewalk and the song "After the Ball is Over"?

Credit goes to May Irwin, the vaudeville, stage, and silent-screen performer. She was born in Whitby, Ontario. The darling of Broadway and the Gay Nineties, she is credited with the introduction of the fancy step known as the cakewalk, and also with the first performance of the sentimental song "After the Ball is Over."

036. What do the initials k.d. stand for in the name k.d. lang?

k.d. lang (who prefers her names to appear in lower-case letters) is a singer and songwriter with a unique style and manner (sometimes called "torch with twang") who was born in 1962 in Consort, Alberta. The initials stand for Kathryn Dawn (or kathryn dawn).

037. Does k.d. lang believe she is the reincarnation of Patsy Cline?

The torch-and-twang singer k.d. lang has a strong emotional connection with the Nashville singer Patsy Cline who died in a plane crash in 1963. But it is unlikely that the Canadian singer literally holds that she is the incarnation of the American singer.

According to Don Gillmour, "The Reincarnation of Kathryn Dawn," *Saturday Night*, June 1990, it began in 1981 when lang was cast as a Patsy Cline-ish character in the musical *Country Chorale* by Raymond Storey produced in Edmonton and Red Deer. "The playwright Raymond Storey gave the nineteen-year-old lang some Cline records and made suggestions as to character. During the play's run, lang remembered childhood dreams of a plane crash (Cline died in a plane crash in 1963) and felt there was a spiritual bond between them, that her career was being guided by Cline. On an early visit to Nashville, she went to the Country Music Hall of Fame, which opened its vaults so she could touch Cline's stage costumes." Thereafter she affected her distinctive manner of dress and deportment as well as her distinctive torch-and-twang singing style.

038. Who was the world's first movie star?

Florence Lawrence, the vaudeville actress who was born in 1886 in Hamilton, Ontario, was the world's first movie star. That is, she was the first "player" to be identified by name on the screen or on a playbill. In the early days of the movies, all the performers were anonymous. Lawrence was originally identified as the "Biograph Girl" and then as "The Imp Girl." Finally, she was given credit as plain and simple Florence

Lawrence. She died in 1938, by which time Hollywood had its "star system" firmly in place.

039. Are the McGarrigle sisters English or French?

The McGarrigle sisters – Anna and Kate – were born in Montreal in 1944 and 1946 respectively. They wrote "Heart Like a Wheel" for Linda Ronstadt and other popular songs for other popular singers. They bear an Irish surname but they are French in background. They are also bilingual and perform effectively in both French and English. In fact, some of their albums are all-French; others are all-English.

040. Who wrote "Put Your Hand in the Hand?"

Gene MacLellan, the singer and songwriter who was born in Val d'Or, Quebec, is best remembered as the composer of Anne Murray's signature song "Snowbird." But he composed any number of popular songs, including the modern spiritual, "Put Your Hand in the Hand."

041. Who was the lead singer with the Sons of the Pioneers?

Bob Nowlan. The singer and songwriter was christened Robert Clarence Nobles, following his birth near Saint John, New Brunswick. In the 1940s he appeared in more than sixty Westerns with Roy Rogers and Dale Evans. Among his many Western favourites were "Cool Water" and "Tumbling Tumbleweeds." Nolan died in 1980, but his group, the Sons of the Pioneers, continues to perform.

042. Who wrote the jazz composition called "The Canadiana Suite"?

Oscar Peterson, the Montreal-born jazz pianist, composed "The Canadiana Suite." The jazz composition for piano and orchestra was initially released in 1964 with Peterson at the keyboard, Ray Brown on double bass, and Edmund Thigpen on drums, and was re-released in 1984. It has eight parts: Ballad to the East, Laurentide Waltz, Place St. Henri, Hogtown Blues, Blues of the Prairies, Wheatland, March Past, and Land of the Misty Giants.

043. Who was Lottie Pickford?

Lottie Pickford was a silent-screen performer who had the fortune – or the misfortune – to be the younger sister of Mary Pickford. She was born, like Mary, in Toronto. She appeared with Mary and her older brother Jack in the 1910 silent film *A Gold Necklace*. She died at the age of thirty-six in 1936, after an undistinguished career in silent and sound movies in Hollywood.

044. Who played Will Cole in *The Rowdyman*?

The Newfoundland-born actor Gordon Pinsent played Will Cole, the wild rascal from the Great Island, in the popular movie *The Rowdyman* which was released in 1972. Pinsent, in addition to playing Cole's part, wrote the screenplay, directed the production, and based a novel on the script.

045. Which Canadian actress was famous for her smile?

Marie Prevost, a screen comedienne of the silent era, was famous for her smile. The 1924 silent movie *The Marriage Circle* ends with Prevost giving the viewer a smile that is so enigmatic it seems to sum up a life of sexual indiscretion. It was much commented upon at the time. Prevost was a native of Sarnia, Ontario. Her real name was Marie Bickford Dunn.

046. Who "nationalized" the Dionne Quintuplets?

The birth of the Dionne Quintuplets was such a sensation that there was the likelihood that the infants and their parents would be exploited by promoters, advertisers, and the curious public. Mitch Hepburn, Premier of Ontario, passed the Guardianship Act in 1934. He later extended it for seventeen years, which placed the five girl babies under the protection of the Crown – in effect "nationalizing" them. With World War II, press attention moved away from the sisters. In 1998 the three surviving Dionnes were successful in their application to the Ontario government for reimbursement.

047. Who played Papa Dionne in the Hollywood movies about the Dionne Quintuplets?

John Qualen, a Vancouver-born actor, created the role of Papa Dionne. He appeared alongside the Dionne Quintuplets (who played themselves) in Hollywood's three "bio-pics" which capitalized on the sentimental appeal of the famous Quints from Northern Ontario. The movies are *The Country Doctor* and *Reunion* (both released in 1936) and *Five of a Kind* (1938). John Qualen was the professional name of the character actor who was born John Oleson in Vancouver in 1899. Before his death in 1986, he had appeared in more than 120 movies, including such familiar ones as *Casablanca* and *The Grapes of Wrath*, as well as on numerous television programs.

048. What movie has outgrossed all other Canadian-made movies?

National Lampoon's Animal House has outgrossed all other Canadian movies. It tells the story of fraternity life at a New England college in 1962, and it stars Donald Sutherland and John Vernon as well as the late John Belushi. It was an early directorial credit for the Canadian producer-director Ivan Reitman, whose career in Hollywood continued to rise with successive hit movies. *Animal House* began a long series of National Lampoon films.

049. Who are the Canadian actors who have played American presidents on the screen?

At least three Canadian actors have played American presidents in Hollywood films. Walter Huston appeared as the president in *Abraham Lincoln* in 1930. Raymond Massey played the role in *Abe Lincoln in Illinois* in 1940. Alexander Knox created the part of Woodrow Wilson in the 1944 movie *Wilson*. Gordon Pinsent assumed the character of an unnamed American president (modelled on John F. Kennedy) in the 1970 science-fiction suspense film *Colossus: The Forbin Project*. On television, the part of a future American president in the 1988 series *Amerika*, which told of a Soviet takeover of the United States, was given to the Montreal-born actor Allan Royal.

050. Who are the two actors who appeared as lovers in the film *Forbidden Journey* and then in real life were married?

Forbidden Journey, an independently produced espionage thriller, was set and shot in Montreal in 1949. The two principals, Czech-born singer and actor Jan Rubes and the American actress Susan Douglas, met for the first time on the set, played doomed lovers in the film, and married shortly thereafter. They were not cast again in the same movie until they accepted parts in *The Outside Chance of Maximilian Glick* which was filmed in Winnipeg in 1987.

051. What are the names of the members of Rush?

Rush is the longest-lasting of the country's rock bands. It was formed in the Toronto suburb of Willowdale in 1974. Singer Geddy Lee leads the three-man group with guitarist Alex Lifeson and drummer/lyricist Neil Peart. Their albums are released by their own record company, Anthem, and internationally by Atlantic Records.

052. Who played Polly in the Andy Hardy movies?

The Toronto-born actress Anne Rutherford created the role of Polly Benedict in the Andy Hardy movies. MGM produced seventeen of these juvenile comedies in the 1930s and 1940s. Rutherford as Anne played opposite the immensely popular Mickey Rooney who was the impish Andy Hardy.

053. Who is the Canadian-born correspondent and news reporter who was known for his interviews on *60 Minutes?*

Morley Safer, the Toronto-born broadcaster, is remembered for his interviews on *60 Minutes*, CBS's Sunday evening public-affairs program beginning in 1970.

054. Which Canadian-born film producer discovered the actor Michael Caine?

Michael Caine, playing a bit part in a forgettable movie called *Zulu*, was spotted by Harry Saltzman, the London-based film and television producer. Saltzman signed Caine to a seven-year contract but generously revoked it when Caine went on to film fame, and when Saltzman himself went on to co-produce the James Bond films with great profit. Saltzman, a successful producer, was a native of Saint John, New Brunswick.

055. Who is the Canadian-born actor who appeared opposite Jane Fonda in *They Shoot Horses, Don't They?*

Michael Sarrazin, who was born in Quebec City, received his Hollywood break when he was cast opposite Jane Fonda in the 1969 movie *They Shoot Horses, Don't They?* The movie captures the spirit of the marathon dances of the 1930s.

056. Who won the Supermodel of the World title in Los Angeles in 1986?

The title of Supermodel of the World was won by Monika Schnarre, a fourteen-year-old high school student from Scarborough, Ontario. The model contest was held in Los Angeles in 1986. Ed Gould, writing in *Entertaining Canadians: Canada's International Stars 1900-1988* (1988), had this to say about the tall model: "She was carefully groomed to follow such beauties as Suzy Parker in the 1950s, Jean Shrimpton in the 1960s, and Lauren Hutton in the 1970s."

057. Which Quebec-born film producer and director was known as "the father of motion picture comedy"?

The title belongs to Mack Sennett, the film pioneer who was born Michael Sinnott in Richmond, Quebec. His career was given assists by fellow Canadians Marie Dressler and David Belasco. Sennett made a name for himself as a vaudeville performer. A chance meeting with W.D. Griffith led to work in the silent pictures. Encouraged by Mary Pickford, he established the Keystone Kops which specialized in slapstick comedy. He won an Oscar (his second) in 1937 for "his lasting contribution to the comedy technique of the screen, the basic principles of which are as important today as when they were first put into practice."

058. Who created the ballet called *Gladly, Sadly, Badly, Madly?*

That was the lively title of the ballet created by Lynn Seymour, the prima ballerina who was born in Wainwright, Alberta. She choreographed *Gladly, Sadly, Badly, Madly* and danced the lead for the London Contemporary Dance Theatre in 1975.

059. Who is the bandleader on *The Late Show with David Letterman?*

The appealing bandleader on David Letterman's late-night talk show on NBC is Paul Shaffer, a musician, comedian, writer, and actor who was born in Thunder Bay, Ontario. He began his stint with Letterman in 1982. According to Ed Gould in *Entertaining Canadians: Canada's International Stars 1900-1988* (1988), Shaffer represents "the latest thing in New York hip – as a sort of counterbalance to the sceptical mid-Western stance of the host."

060. Who is the actress who gave Oliver Reed his comeuppance on *The Merv Griffin Show?*

"When portly, over-the-hill British actor Oliver Reed told Helen Shaver on the *Merv Griffin Show* she was very pretty but didn't have many brains, Shaver clobbered him with more *bon mots* and intellectual broadsides than he had received since his last verbal defeat by Peter O'Toole," according to Ed Gould in *Entertaining Canadians: Canada's International Stars 1900-1988* (1988). Helen Shaver, the beautiful and brainy actress, was born in St. Thomas, Ontario. She has appeared in a number of Canadian and American motion pictures, including *In Praise of Older Women* in 1978 and *The Colour of Money* in 1986.

061. Who is the actress who posed as *Miss Lotta Miles* before she became a film star?

Norma Shearer appeared in newspaper advertisements for automobile tires as *Miss Lotta Miles*. She did such work before she launched her Hollywood career as a film star and married MGM producer Irving Thalberg in 1927. She became a leading lady in that studio's productions, retiring from the film world in 1942. Shearer, born in Montreal in 1900, died in Beverly Hills in 1983.

062. Which Canadian-born film personality has received more Academy Awards than any other?

Although not well known except to film technicians and historians, Douglas Shearer made a substantial technical contribution to the production of sound films. He founded MGM's sound department, developed an advanced "sound head," and was honoured by the Academy of Motion Picture Arts and Sciences with a total of twelve Oscars plus a thirteenth Oscar that he shared with the MGM research department over a career that lasted from 1925 to 1968. No Canadian-born film personality has rivalled this number of awards, and it is unlikely that anyone ever will. His well-known sister, actress Norma Shearer, received only two Oscars. On the memorable Academy Awards night of 1930, he received the Oscar for excellence in sound and she for Best Actress in *The Divorcee*.

063. Which Canadian-born film personality designed the bombsight used to drop atomic bombs on Hiroshima and Nagasaki?

The Montreal-born film technician Douglas Shearer (1899-1971), the brother of MGM star Norma Shearer, designed the bombsight for dropping the atomic bombs. "U.S. President Franklin Roosevelt presented him with a special award for his work in designing the bombsight to drop the atomic bombs on Japan in World War II," according to Ed Gould in *Entertaining Canadians: Canada's International Stars 1900-1988* (1988).

064. Who is the comedian best known for his character Ed Grimley?

Martin Short, the comedian, writer, and actor who was born in Hamilton, Ontario, created the character Ed Grimley in 1977. Grimley was described by show business writer Ed Gould as "a frantically nervous twit who came alive on SCTV and graduated to *Saturday Night Live*." Grimley is easily recognized: his hair rises to a point above Short's head.

065. Whose singing career was launched with the hit song "I'm Movin' On"?

The singer and songwriter Hank Snow, who was born Clarence Eugene Snow in Brooklyn, Nova Scotia, made a splash in 1950 with the song he wrote and performed called "I'm Movin' On." It was on the National Hit Parade for more than a year, and it launched his career as a popular country and western singer.

066. Who appeared semi-naked as Playmate of the Month in the August 1979 issue of *Playboy?*

Dorothy Stratten, the Vancouver-born actress and model, launched her career when she appeared in the buff in the August 1979 issue of *Playboy.* She established a friendship with publisher Hugh Hefner and then with film director Peter Bogdanovich. These relationships threatened Paul Snider, her husband and manager, who in 1980, at her Los Angeles bungalow, murdered her and then shot himself to death. Jay Robert Nash wrote *Murder among the Mighty* (1983) about the murder-suicide. Bogdanovich, who did the same with his book *The Killing of the Unicorn* (1983), proceeded to marry Dorothy's kid sister in 1988. Movies about Stratten's short tragic career include *Star 80* with Mariel Hemingway and *The Death of a Centerfold: The Dorothy Stratten Story* which starred Jamie Lee Curtis.

067. Who is the host of the TV game show *Jeopardy?*

Alex Trebek is both the host and the producer of the phenomenally successful NBC game show *Jeopardy.* Trebek was born in Sudbury, Ontario. The show was originally created by Merv Griffin. *Jeopardy* offers answers and requires contestants to supply questions. The weekly show premiered in 1964.

068. Who was Halifax's authority on vampires?

Devendra Varma, a Professor of English at Dalhousie University in Halifax, was a recognized authority on the Gothic romance novel. The genre includes fiction based on the vampire legend such as Bram Stoker's novel *Dracula* (1897).

Born in India in 1924, Varma taught and lectured around the world, but in later years made Halifax his home. A technical advisor on unearthly effects to film producers, he has a screen credit for the 1971 horror film *The House that Dripped Blood.* He died in Halifax in 1994 – presumably of natural causes.

069. Which one of the Warner Bros. was born in Canada?

Jack L. Warner, the film producer, was head of production at the Warner Bros. studio in Hollywood. He launched the talkies with *The Jazz Singer.* He was born in 1892 in London, Ontario, the youngest of twelve children of Jewish immigrants who had come from Poland. The eleven other brothers were born outside Canada. Jack and his three older brothers – Harry, Sam, and Albert – became film exhibitors in New Castle, Pennsylvania. Ultimately they established the Warner Bros. studio, which in its day was the largest studio in Hollywood. It is said they released 5000 movies. Today the company is the flagship of the conglomerate known as Warner Communications, Inc.

070. Which well-known actor appeared in the movie *My Business Is My Pleasure?*

Al Waxman, the Toronto-born actor, starred in the 1974 film *My Business Is My Pleasure.* The film co-starred Xaviera Hollander, notorious as "the Happy Hooker," who was at the time a Toronto resident. In 1975, Waxman created the title role of CBC's popular series *The King of Kensington* and, later, portrayed the New York police lieutenant on the popular American television series *Cagney and Lacey.*

071. Was Fay Wray born in "Wrayland"?

She was actually born on "Wrayland" in 1907. That is the name of the Wray family farm located outside Cardston, Alberta. Although Fay Wray played many parts in silent and sound films in Hollywood, the public remembers her as the object of the giant ape's interest in the movie *King Kong*. Screams heard on the soundtrack were not her own but those of another actress, Julie Haydon.

072. Who appeared opposite Mr. Ed?

Mr. Ed was the name of the gruff-talking horse on the television series of the same name seen from 1961 to 1966. Alan Young played the nag's straight man. Born in England, Young was raised in Vancouver where he worked in radio before moving to Los Angeles. At one time he had his own radio and television shows to which he introduced such characters as the stuffy Mrs. Buff Orpington, the pretentious Mr. Hoffenpepper, and the wealthy Hubert Updike. Playing opposite Mr. Ed the talking horse eclipsed them all in fame.

073. Who is the Canadian television star who played the Lucky Strike "bull's-eye girl"?

Dorothy Collins, the Windsor-born singer and television entertainer, played the part of the Lucky Strike "bull's-eye girl" on American television commercials in the 1950s. She "wore" a giant cigarette pack (with its trademarked bull's-eye design) and danced. As it happened, Collins was a non-smoker.

074. Who are some second generation Hollywood stars?

The children of a number of Canadian-born movie stars have gone on to make names for themselves. Hart Bochner is the son of Lloyd Bochner. Rae Dawn Chong is the daughter of Tom Chong. Kiefer Sutherland is the son of Donald Sutherland and Suzanne Douglas. Megan Follows is the daughter of Ted Follows and Dawn Greenhalgh. The list could be extended to include members of the illustrious Massey family.

075. Who is the director who received an Oscar for cinematography but was not awarded it by the Academy of Motion Picture Arts and Sciences?

The Winnipeg-born cinematographer Osmond Borradaile worked in the 1930s for Alexander Korda's London Films. He is credited with the discovery of Sabu, the Elephant Boy. He was director of photography on Korda's *The Thief of Bagdad* (1940). With the outbreak of World War II, Borradaile enlisted, and Korda shifted the balance of production to Hollywood. The American cinematographer George Perinal completed the photography and received full screen credit as well as the Oscar the following year for best cinematography. Upon Perinal's death, his family forwarded the Oscar to Borradaile who had done so much to deserve it.

076. Who is the Canadian animator who created the near-sighted Mr. Magoo?

Stephen Bosustow, the producer and animator who was born in Victoria, British Columbia, created the movie cartoon character known as the near-sighted Mr. Magoo. The myopic character, who appeared in hundreds of theatrical cartoons beginning in 1949, had his own television series in 1960-2, 1965-5, and 1977-8. The character's full name was Quincy Magoo. His dog, also near-sighted, was called McBaker. All the voices were supplied by the actor Jim Backus.

077. Who wrote Sophie Tucker's theme song?

"The Last of the Red-Hot Mamas," Sophie Tucker's theme song, was written by Shelton Brooks who was born in Amherstburg, Ontario. The composer and entertainer is known for other popular songs including "Some of These Days" (1910) and "The Darktown Strutter's Ball" (1917).

078. Who composed the popular song "The Strawberry Roam"?

"The Strawberry Roam" was written in the 1930s by Wilf Carter, the country and western singer who is a native of Gysboro, Nova Scotia. He performed as "Montana Slim" in the United States, first as a rodeo performer, then as a radio singer, finally as a recording artist.

079. How many members of the Canadian Armed Forces have served on peacekeeping operations?

Members of the Canadian Armed Forces have participated in peacekeeping operations since the role was defined in 1949. They have served in the following areas: Kashmir, Egypt, Israel, Jordan, Lebanon, Syria, Cambodia, Laos, Vietnam, Congo, West New Guinea, Yemen, Cyprus, Dominican Republic, India, Pakistan, Nigeria and South Vietnam. A complete list with dates appears in Fred Gaffen's study *In the Eye of the Storm: A History of Canadian Peacekeeping* (1987). Gaffen, an historian with the Canadian War Museum, estimated that between 1949 and 1987, 45,000 Canadian military men and women have been involved in peacekeeping operations throughout the world. In a later estimate, some 80,000 members of the Canadian Armed Forces have served from the 1940s to the 1990s as international peacekeepers. Approximately eighty have died in peacekeeping operations.

080. Name the distinguished Ontario-based novelist who wrote trilogies.

Robertson Davies is the distinguished novelist whose most popular novels fall into groups of three.

The Salterton Trilogy bears the name of the fictional Ontario college-town of Salterton, which is the setting of *Tempest-Tost, Leaven of Malice*, and *A Mixture of Frailties*. The Deptford Trilogy was named after the fictional Ontario community of Deptford, and the trilogy consists of *Fifth Business, The Manticore*, and *World of Wonders*. The Cornish Trilogy is the general name – and also the surname of the principal character – of the three novels *The Rebel Angels, What's Bred in the Bone*, and *The Lyre of Orpheus*.

Readers curious about Davies' trilogies should not overlook the fact that there are, in addition, three Marchbanks books. These present the opinions of a curmudgeon named Samuel Marchbanks. Their titles are *The Diary of Samuel Marchbanks, The Table Talk of Samuel Marchbanks*, and the *Samuel Marchbanks' Almanack*. They have been collected and published as *The Papers of Samuel Marchbanks*.

It seemed that Robertson Davies had a partiality for groups of three.

081. Who was the teller of "Tales Told under the Old Town Clock"?

The Old Town Clock refers to the landmark that was erected in Halifax in 1803. It remains a popular meeting place to this day. "Tales Told under the Old Town Clock" refers to a series of radio talks and then to a series of books based on these talks. The series, replete with local lore and history, helped to popularize Maritime history and customs, first among Maritimers and then among other Canadians. The broadcasts were written and delivered by William C. Borrett, a popular Halifax broadcaster, writer, and local historian. Ultimately seven book-length collections of "Tales Told under the Old Town Clock" were published between 1944 and 1957.

082. Who is the artist who illustrated in watercolour the entire Gospel according to St. Matthew?

There are 160 verses in the Douay or Roman Catholic Version of the Gospel according to St. Matthew, and each separate verse is the subject of a watercolour conceived and executed by William Kurelek (1927-1977). The self-taught, Ukrainian-Canadian artist dispatched the 160 watercolours at the rate of one panel a week over a period of three years, following a visit to Israel in 1959 to see the sites in the Holy Land associated with the life of Jesus of Nazareth.

The complete series has served as the centrepiece of the Niagara Falls Art Gallery Kurelek Collection. It has been reproduced in full colour in the album *The Passion of Christ According to St. Matthew* (1975). Kurelek was scrupulous about historical accuracy – except when he deliberately introduced anachronisms into the illustrations to draw attention to his conviction that the Gospel speaks to all people everywhere all the time.

083. Did Buster Keaton ever star in a movie based on a stage play written by a Canadian?

As it happened, Buster Keaton, the deadpan comedian, stared in a movie based on a stage play written by a Canadian. He played the leading role in the movie *Parlour, Bedroom and Bath* (1931) which was directed in Hollywood by the expatriate French director Claude Autant-Laura. The movie was adapted from the 1917 Broadway "bedroom farce" of the same name which had been written by Charles William Bell, a lawyer and playwright who resided in his native city of Hamilton, Ontario. It has been argued that Bell's *Parlour, Bedroom and Bath* was the original "sex farce," the first of the light-weight suggestive comedies that became the mainstay of the Broadway stage. It is a broad farce about a youthful husband whose impressionable wife loves him for his lurid past.

084. Is it true that Buster Keaton made two movies in Canada?

Yes, and they are the last two movies made by the comic performer.

Buster Keaton (1895-1966) is affectionately remembered for the deadpan expression on his face and the porkpie hat on his head. One of the legends of the silent screen, he found few outlets for his talent in Hollywood in the days of sound. Nevertheless, the National Film Board of Canada made brilliant use of his comic manner in two films released in 1965.

These are *The Railrodder* and *Buster Keaton Rides Again.* The first film follows Keaton as he travels across Canada from east to west on a railway-track scooter. The twenty-five minute movie was directed by Gerald Potterton, and although not a single word is spoken, there are sight gags aplenty. Conversation is one of the mainstays of the second film, one hour in length, directed by John Spotton, which captures Keaton off camera, rehearsing scenes for the first film and reminiscing for the film crew about his career in the movies.

085. Who is the film star whose debut was marked by a Special Award at the 1969 Canadian Film Awards?

Margot Kidder made her screen debut in *The Best Damn Fiddler from Calabogie to Kaladar.* The movie was produced by the National Film Board and directed by Peter Pearson in 1968. The lovely young actress played the eldest daughter of an Ottawa Valley family; her father was played by Chris Wiggins, her mother by Kate Reid. A Special Award at the Canadian Film Awards in 1969 acknowledged Kidder's outstanding performance and screen debut. That was the first of a number of international awards for the screen star who was raised in Yellowknife, Northwest Territories.

086. Who played the part of Terry Fox in the film *The Terry Fox Story?*

The Terry Fox Story was produced in 1984 by Robert Cooper and directed by R.L. Thomas. The film honoured Terry Fox, the young athlete who despite the loss of a leg through cancer became a long-distance runner. His cross-Canada Marathon of Hope earned him the respect of millions of Canadians. The lead role was taken by Eric Fryer who had no previous acting experience. Like Fox, Fryer was a West Coast athlete who had lost a leg through cancer; like Fox, he was determined that his handicap would never dampen his desire to excel. He played the part to perfection.

087. Who is the Montreal-born director who worked on *Citizen Kane* and received screen credit as editor on *Journey into Fear?*

Director and producer Mark Robson joined RKO as a film editor and worked on Orson Welles's 1941 classic *Citizen Kane* without receiving screen credit. But two years later he was given screen credit for work as editor on Welles's *Journey into Fear*. The director, born in Montreal, went on to direct Kirk Douglas in *Champion*, Ingrid Bergman in *The Inn of the Sixth Happiness*, and Barbara Parkins in *Peyton Place*.

088. Are people of Scottish ancestry in Canada called Scottish or Scotch?

In Scotland the correct term is the Scots or the Scottish, certainly not the Scotch. There the word Scotch is reserved for Highland whisky. But in Canada people of Scottish background have always referred to themselves as either the Scottish or the Scotch. With some force John Kenneth Galbraith made this point when he titled his memoirs of life in rural Ontario *The Scotch* (1964), adding in the text that he found "the Scottish" something of an affectation. That was the North American title of his memoirs. His British publishers, not so easily convinced of the propriety of the term, insisted on retitling the book *Made to Last*.

089. Who served successively as a member of a provincial Parliament, a member of the federal Parliament, and a member of the British Parliament?

The political figure with the three-tiered career was the lawyer and politician Edward Blake. He served in the Ontario legislature (1867-1872), in the federal legislature (1873-1882), and in the British legislature (1892-1906). These are but a few of his elected positions. At one point he served simultaneously as the Premier of Ontario and as a member of the federal legislature – until dual representation was abolished in 1872.

090. Whose profile may be discerned in the marble floor of the Supreme Court of Canada building in Ottawa?

It is a little-known fact that a profile resembling former Prime Minister Pierre Elliott Trudeau may be discerned in the marble floor of the foyer of the Supreme Court of Canada building in Ottawa. The "found art" image is entirely accidental, but the caricature is so vivid it might well be the work of a political cartoonist. It is about the size of a grapefruit and is located not far from the concierge's station. At one time it was kept under a moveable carpet.

091. What was the confusion surrounding Pierre Elliott Trudeau's age?

Someone wrote that Pierre Elliott Trudeau arrived on the federal political scene "like a rock thrown through a stained-glass window." That was in the 1960s, and at the time much fuss was made of his relative youth. He became Prime Minister on 20 April 1968 – the first holder of that office to be born in the twentieth century. He was also the youngest to that date, being then but forty-nine years old.

The press and the public believed that he was only forty-seven years old. The misunderstanding was caused by an incorrect listing for his year of birth in the *Canadian Parliamentary Guide*, the standard reference book, which gave the year as 1921. Playfully Trudeau capitalized on the confusion. The press eventually ferreted out the fact that Trudeau was born in Montreal on 18 October 1919.

092. Who were the "twenty-one millionaires"?

The "twenty-one millionaires" were the wealthy merchants of Newfoundland whose offices and businesses were located on Water Street, the business section of St. John's, Newfoundland. Joey Smallwood in the 1940s maintained that the "twenty-one millionaires" or "Water Street millionaires" controlled Newfoundland's Commission Government, kept the Newfoundland people in poverty, and resisted his attempts to further union with Canada.

Here is what the journalist and author Harold Horwood had to say about these capitalists and Smallwood's obsession with them in his biography *Joey* (1989):

> Those millionaires were another of his inventions. He had decided on twenty-one as a nice, convincing figure. No one really knew how many of the Water Street merchants were millionaires, but no one ever challenged Joey's statement. The twenty-one pre-confederate millionaires became a fixed part of Newfoundland mythology. (By the time Joey got around to writing his political memoirs in the 1970s, he had forgotten the figure himself, and reduced the millionaires to twenty.)

093. Who are the people who appear on Peter Gzowski's list of the eight most difficult interviews on *Morningside?*

Peter Gzowski, as host of CBC Radio's *Morningside*, interviewed thousands of people from all walks of life. He is a past master of the art of the interview. The secret of the good interview, he revealed in *The Private Voice: A Journal of Reflections* (1988), is that the interviewee does the paddling while the interviewer does the steering.

Gzowski admitted to having failed with the following personalities: talkative comedian Martin Short, feminist author Betty Friedan, novelist and personal friend Mordecai Richler, taciturn literary critic Northrop Frye, guarded politician and later head of state Ray Hnatyshyn, withdrawn author Mavis Gallant, New Age personality Shirley MacLaine, and film producer Elvira Lount.

094. Who was the world's most-cited living author in 1977-78?

As surprising as it might seem, the world's most-cited living author during those two years was Northrop Frye, the Toronto-based literary philosopher.

Scholars and scientists are able to track the dissemination of ideas and influences through the tabulation of citations (specific references) that appear in specialist publications. This is the gauge used by the Institute of Scientific Information in Philadelphia which annually lists the "most-cited authors in the Arts and Humanities." By that measurement the most-cited living author for the years 1977-78 was Northrop Frye. In fact, in a list of most-cited authors of all time, Frye ranked eighth. Ahead of him were the following authorities: Marx, Aristotle, Shakespeare, Lenin, Plato, Freud, and Roland Barthes. The most-cited twentieth-century book was Frye's key work *Anatomy of Criticism* (1957).

095. Who is "underwater man"?

"Underwater man" sounds like the name of a splashy, comic-book superhero. But the epithetical description applies to Dr. Joseph MacInnis, marine scientist and undersea explorer. It is also the title of his memoirs published in 1971.

096. Which world-famous movie star was born at 175 University Avenue, Toronto, Ontario?

Mary Pickford, the silent-film star known as "America's Sweetheart," was born on 8 April 1893 in a modest house that once stood at 175 University Avenue. The land is now occupied by part of the Hospital for Sick Children. The site is marked by a lovely bust of Pickford which bears the inscription "Cinema's First Superstar." In the 1920s and 1930s, Mary Pickford resided with her husband Douglas Fairbanks Sr. at their stately home named Pickfair in Hollywood.

097. Did Sir Wilfrid Laurier have a mistress?

Sir Wilfrid Laurier served as Prime Minister of Canada from 1896 to 1911. Although happily married throughout his adult years, without a hint of scandal to tarnish his private or public life, he conducted a relationship of some sort (no one is certain of what sort) with Emilie

Lavergne, the wife of his former law partner. He addressed letters to her as "my dearest friend" at the time she lived with her husband in Arthabaska and he resided in Ottawa. They wrote to each other in English rather than in French, curiously. At the time (1891-93) he was Liberal leader and not yet Prime Minister; he was in his fifties and she in her late forties. Their relationship may have been playful, romantic, or sexual; historians and biographers remain uncertain to this day; the question remains more of social than political interest.

098. Who was the Lise of *Appelez-Moi Lise?*

Appelez-Moi Lise (or "Call Me Lise") was the title of the most popular talk show on any Francophone television network. Aired by Radio-Canada for only two years, between 1972 and 1974, it attracted an immense viewership, and it made the reputation of its host, Lise Payette, a Quebec writer and broadcaster. She stood for election for the Parti Québécois in 1976 and, as Minister of Consumer and Financial Affairs, was the sole woman in the Quebec cabinet. Her political undoing was referring to the wife of politician Paul Ryan as an "Yvette," a kind of Plain Jane. Later she bounced back as a columnist, commentator, and creator of *télé-romans.*

099. Who is – or was – Canada's worst Prime Minister?

There is no easy answer to that question, but most historians and political observers include on any list of the worst P.M.s the following three gentlemen: John Abbott (an avowed annexationalist who was implicated in the Pacific Scandal); Robert Borden (who divided the country over the conscription issue); R.B. Bennett (who incurred the hostility of the working class during the Depression); John G. Diefenbaker (who raised and then dashed the hopes of the electorate).

In 1990, nationalist and publisher Mel Hurtig argued with some success that Brian Mulroney, then in power, was the country's worst ever Prime Minister, having foisted on the Canadian people the Free Trade Agreement, the Meech Lake Accord, the GST, etc.

100. Who was Canada's Betsy Ross?

All American and some Canadian school children know that Betsy Ross was the American patriot who, at the behest of George Washington, on 14 June 1777, sewed the colours on the first American flag "Old Glory." Few school children know or care who sewed the first Maple Leaf Flag.

The first Maple Leaf Flag was sewn by a young Ottawa housewife, Joan O'Malley, who undertook the assignment free of charge at the request of her father, Ken Donovan, an official with the Department of Trade and Commerce. The date of the sewing is not recorded. The design was finally approved by Parliament on 15 December 1964.

The story of Canada's Betsy Ross is recalled by Walter Stefaniuk in *The Toronto Star*, 1 July 1990.

101. In what Hollywood film did actress Jane Wyman receive an Oscar for playing the part of a Canadian girl?

The Hollywood actress Jane Wyman received an Academy Award for her portrayal of Johnny Belinda in the film *Johnny Belinda* (1948). Belinda is a deaf mute and rape victim who gives birth to a baby. The movie was shot on the Northern California coast. It was based on a play by the noted Broadway playwright Elmer Rice who based it on an incident that took place on Prince Edward Island where he summered. For some reason known only to Hollywood, the locale of the movie was shifted to Nova Scotia.

102. Who taught the Mounties how to dance?

Members of the Prairie Detachment of the Royal Canadian Mounted Police were taught to dance by the young girl named Susannah (played by actress Shirley Temple) in the 1939 movie *Susannah of the Mounties*. The movie was based on Muriel Denison's charming children's novel *Susannah: Little Girl with the Mounties* (1936), in which she joins the North West Mounted Police in Regina in 1896.

103. Do physicians have a greater degree of professional autonomy in Canada than they do in the United States?

The eleven authors of the article "Controlling Health Expenditures – The Canadian Reality" published in *The New England Journal of Medicine*, 2 March 1989, concluded that physicians in Canada have a greater degree of "professional autonomy" under Medicare than do physicians in the United States working with managed care in the free-enterprise system.

104. Who was awarded the Nobel Prize for Physics in 1990?

The Nobel Prize for Physics was awarded jointly to three physicists – two American scientists associated with MIT, and one Canadian-born scientist associated with Stanford University in California. The award, announced in October 1990, recognized contributions to experimental work that proved the existence of the sub-atomic particle known as the quark.

The American scientists are Jerome Friedman and Henry Kendall; the Canadian-born scientist is Richard Taylor, who was born in Medicine Hat and who undertook both undergraduate and graduate work at the University of Alberta before continuing his scientific work at a succession of American universities.

105. Who received the 1993 Nobel Prize for Chemistry?

The 1993 Nobel Prize for Chemistry was awarded to Rudolph Marcus. The scientist was born in Montreal, he holds a doctorate from McGill University, and he has conducted his work for decades at the California Institute of Technology.

Recent Canadian-born Nobel laureates include: Richard Taylor (physicist, Alberta-born, Stanford-based, 1990) and Richard Altman (chemist, Montreal-born, Yale-based, 1989).

106. Who was the principal teacher of the young Glenn Gould?

Alberto Guerrero, music teacher and founder and conductor of Santiago's first symphony orchestra, was the principal teacher of the youthful Glenn Gould. After leaving his native Chile, Alberto Antonio de Garcia y Guerrero lived in New York and then settled in Toronto. From 1919 until his death in 1959, he taught at the Toronto Conservatory of Music (now the Royal Conservatory of Toronto). His most talented pupil was Glenn

Gould who studied under him from the age of nine to the age of nineteen. It is felt that Gould acquired his playing style, particularly the flat placement of his fingers, from his teacher. As musicologist John Beckwith once noted, "People will remember Gould as Guerrero's pupil as well as remembering Guerrero as Gould's teacher."

107. Who is the commoner who gave King Edward an order that he immediately obeyed?

The amusing description fits Ed Davis who has been called "the man who bossed a king." On his visit to Niagara Falls in 1860, the Prince of Wales (later Edward VII) was guided around the attractions by Ed Davis, son of Saul Davis, the proprietor of Table Rock House. At one point the Prince made a move to step out onto a slippery ledge about sixty feet above the Niagara River. "No, you don't," said Davis, grabbing His Royal Highness by the lapels and yanking him back onto the safety of the trail. As reported by Niagara historian Dwight Whalen, "When the group returned to the top of the bank, the Prince shook hands with Davis and went on his way."

Davis never forgot the incident and liked to boast that he was "the only man who ever gave King Edward an order that he obeyed." Nor did the King forget the act of his guide. When the King's brother, the newly appointed Governor General, toured the Falls and visited Table Rock House, he asked for Ed Davis, adding the following explanation: "King Edward told me to find you, shake hands with you, and give you his best compliments, and to tell you that he has never forgotten the order that you gave him." Davis died at the age of eighty-four in 1928.

108. Who was the luckiest military tactician who has operated in Canada since General Wolfe?

C.P. Stacey, the military historian, suggested that Prime Minister W.L. Mackenzie King "was probably the luckiest tactician who has operated in Canada since General Wolfe." Stacey had in mind Mackenzie King's assault on Minister of National Defence James Ralston in 1944 over the issue of overseas construction, calling it a case "flawless and typically deadly."

109. Who was the regional historian who titled his books "From – to –"?

William Perkins Bull (1870-1948) gave his books "from – to –" titles. He was a prominent lawyer and businessman in Toronto and his avocation was researching, writing, and publishing books on the history of Ontario's Peel County. He called them "The Perkins Bull Historical Series." They are lively compendia of local lore described in an eccentric manner. Here are the titles of his books with their years of publication:

M 'n N Canadiana (1931), *From Medicine Man to Medical Man* (1934), *From Rattlesnake Hunt to Hockey* (1934), *From Brock to Currie* (1935), *From Paganism to Davenport United* (1935), *Spadunk* (1935), *From the Boyne to Brampton* (1936), *From Hummingbird to Eagle* (1936), *From Strachan to Owen* (1937), *From Spring to Autumn* (1937), *From Amphibians to Reptiles* (1938), *From Macdonell to McGuigan* (1939), *From Oxford to Ontario* (1941).

110. Who was the youngest hockey player in Stanley Cup records?

The youngest hockey player in Stanley Cup history was Albert Forest, an enthusiastic goalkeeper with the Klondikers. He was seventeen years old in 1904-05 when he accompanied his team on its 4,400-mile trek from Dawson City, Yukon Territory, to Ottawa to play three challenge games in the Stanley Cup championship hockey series against the fabled Ottawa Silver Seven, and lost all three. As sports personality Dick Beddoes noted, "The Klondikers, beaten in their ludicrous challenge, sank in the limbo of hockey history without leaving a trace." Not quite. Fellow sports personality Brian McFarlane, after researching young Albert's story, wrote *The Youngest Goalie: The Adventures of a Hockey Legend* (1989). There are plans to turn it into a made-for-television movie.

111. Did Cyclone Taylor score a goal skating backwards?

Some amazing stories are told of the semi-legendary hockey player Frederic (Cyclone) Taylor. One of the best is how in Ottawa on 12 February 1910 he scored a goal for the Renfrew Creamery Kings "after skating backwards through an entire team of bewildered Ottawa Senators."

These are the words of sports personality Dick Beddoes who in his book *Best Hockey Stories* (1990) studied the story, interviewed Taylor before his death in Vancouver in 1979 at the age of 96, and found that the tale turned on Taylor's joking boast, carried by the *Ottawa Citizen*, that "he would skate through the Ottawa defence backwards and score a goal." The truth is Taylor never got a clear shot on the Ottawa goal and his team lost. As Beddoes concluded, "The myth's persistence made Taylor a natural-born hitching post for other legends."

112. How did Foster Hewitt rank the three top hockey players in 1944?

The Montreal Canadiens defeated the Toronto Maple Leafs in the 5-1 game of a Stanley Cup semi-final on 23 March 1944. All five of the winning team's goals were scored by Maurice (Rocket) Richard. As usual, Foster Hewitt, the veteran broadcaster, covered the game. Afterwards, asked to rank its three star players, Hewitt quipped: "First star ... Maurice Richard; second star ... Maurice Richard; third star ... Maurice Richard."

113. Did E.B. White and James Thurber attend a summer camp in Ontario?

They did.

E.B. White and James Thurber, the distinguished contributors to *The New Yorker*, attended a summer camp in Ontario. White was a counsellor for the summers of 1920 and 1921 at Camp Otter, on Otter Lake northeast of Dorset, Ontario. Eight years later he became part-owner of the camp but lost his investment in the Great Depression. The camp itself survived until the 1960s.

In mid-July 1930, White invited his friend and fellow writer James Thurber to visit him. Thurber, having domestic problems in New York at the time, spent two relaxed weeks at Camp Otter. There he sketched wild animals for the *Otter Bee*, the camp paper. These inimitable sketches are reproduced by Patricia Bradbury in *Cottage Life*, June 1989.

White recalled his experiences in fictional form in *The Trumpet of the Swan* (1970), his last children's book, in which he described a Camp Kookooskoos as "a wilderness lake just right for boys."

114. Was Sarah Bernhardt popular in Canada?

Sarah Bernhardt was France's greatest dramatic actress. She made numerous "farewell" tours of North America. In Quebec, the public, both French and English, flocked to her performances. Yet she was unpopular with the Quebec clergy who judged her to be an immoral woman. On her first visit to Montreal in 1880, Bishop Fabre urged Roman Catholics to refrain from attending her production of *Adrienne Lecouvreur*, and requested that the City Council prohibit her Christmas Day program. He was unsuccessful, according to Ramon Hathorn, writing in *The Oxford Companion to Canadian Theatre* (1989), "because existing legislation pertained only to Sunday performances, not to those on weekdays that happened also to be holy days." In the same vein, Bernhardt's visits to Quebec City and Montreal in 1905 caused Archbishop Bruchési's to issue pastoral letters that denounced the stage as an occasion of sin.

115. Who was the first woman to be appointed a K.C. in the British Empire?

Helen Alice Kinnear (1894-1970), a graduate in law from Osgoode Hall, was appointed a King's Counsellor (now a Queen's Counsellor, a designation for a senior advocate) in 1934, the first woman in the British Empire to be so appointed.

116. Who was the first woman to serve as a provincial premier?

The first woman to serve as the premier of a province was Rita Johnson. A member of the British Columbia. Legislature, Johnson was chosen by the Social Credit caucus to succeed Premier William Vander Zalm when, under the pressure of scandal, he resigned the premiership. On 2 April 1991, Johnson assumed her duties and was duly sworn in by the Lieutenant-Governor.

117. Who was the first woman elected provincial premier?

Catherine Callbeck, a lawyer and leader of the Liberal Party of Prince Edward Island, was the first woman elected provincial premier. She led her party to victory in Prince Edward Island on 29 March 1993.

118. Were the Beatles refused entry to Canada?

As odd as it might seem, they were. Beatlemania was characteristic of their first whirlwind tour of the United States in 1964. After a sell-out concert in Seattle, Washington, the Fab Four were flown in their rented jet to Vancouver. "As the Beatles' jet neared the border, it was refused entry to Canada. In the rush to get out of Seattle one small detail had been forgotten – U.S. Customs. The pilot turned the craft around and headed back to the Seattle-Tacoma Airport, where the Beatles and their entourage completed customs inspection in about twenty minutes. At 4:50 p.m., they were Vancouver-bound again," according to journalist A.J.S. Rayl and photographer Curt Gunther in *Beatles '64: A Hard Day's Night in America* (1989). Later that day, 22 Aug. 1964, they played to a sold-out house of 20,261 at Vancouver's Empire Stadium.

119. Did a Canadian poet write "The Night before Christmas"?

No. The poem "The Night before Christmas" was written in 1823 by an American versifier named Clement Clarke Moore (1779-1863). However, the versifier was the godson of Jonathan Odell, the Loyalist bard of Fredericton, who owned a handwritten copy of the popular poem that was dated 1825. A prominent Loyalist, Jonathan Odell served as physician, clergyman, provincial secretary, and poet.

120. Who is the Anna who helped to found the art school and gallery in Halifax?

One of the founding patrons of the Victoria School of Art and Design in Halifax 1887 was Anna Leonowens. Today the school is known as the Nova Scotia College of Art and Design, and Anna Leonowens is remembered as the Anna of the musical *Anna and the King of Siam* and the movie *The King and I*. The Anna Leonowens Gallery is devoted to contemporary art by the College's faculty, students and visiting artists.

121. Who was the last surviving member of the Fathers of Confederation?

Sir Charles Tupper became one of the thirty-six Fathers of Confederation in 1867. He served as Prime Minister of Canada – for ten weeks in 1896. He died in England on 30 Oct 1915 at the age of ninety-four. He was the last surviving Father of the Fathers of Confederation, observing his handiwork for a period of forty-eight years.

122. Did Mesrine have a Canadian connection?

France's most wanted man was a gangster known by his last name, Mesrine. After a two-continent manhunt, Jacques Mesrine was finally apprehended in Quebec and returned to France where he was imprisoned for life. For some time he lived at Percé in the Gaspé region with his companion, a Montrealer named Jocelyne Deraiche, who recalled her months with the dashing but deadly murderer in the memoir *J'ai Tant Aimé Mesrine* (1979).

123. Did Havelock Ellis have a Canadian lover?

It seems that he did. Havelock Ellis (1859-1939) was an English writer and a sexual counsellor and therapist who scandalized many readers with his autobiography, *My Life and Loves* (1939), which was frank (for the day) about sexual mores. In 1931, a Canadian woman named Gloria Neville visited the seventy-two-year-old Ellis and became his last lover.

124. Did a Canadian invent the jock strap?

The jock strap – the support worn by male athletes – may or may not have been devised in 1920 by John Joseph (Jack) Cartledge, a manufacturer, inventor, and native of Guelph, Ontario. It is often said that Cartledge patented the jock strap in 1923, but there is no record of this in the Canadian Patent Office Record. It is further maintained that his Elastic Hosiery Company sold the product as Protext 13. What is known for certain is that Cartledge filed for a patent on 24 March 1923 for an Elastic Knee Bandage for Athletes.

125. Who was Dale of the Mounted?

Dale of the Mounted was a fictional member of the Royal Canadian Mounted Police. This brave and resourceful officer featured as the hero of adventure novels for young readers. They were the work of Toronto writer Joe Holliday. Twelve novels in the series, published in Toronto and Cleveland, appeared between 1950 and 1962:

Dale of the Mounted; Dale of the Mounted on the West Coast; Dale of the Mounted in Newfoundland; Dale of the Mounted: Dew Line Duty; Dale of the Mounted: Submarine Hunt; Dale of the Mounted: Atlantic Assignment; Dale of the Mounted: Atomic Plot; Dale of the Mounted in Hong Kong; Dale of the Mounted in the Northwest; Dale of the Mounted in the Arctic; Dale of the Mounted on the St. Lawrence; Dale of the Mounted at the U.N.

126. Did Lon Chaney ever play a Mountie?

Movie-goers recall Lon Chaney as "the man with a million faces," and one of the versatile actor's faces was that of a stern Mountie in the silent Universal-Gold Seal movie *Bloodhounds of the North* released in 1913. A plot synopsis runs: "An embezzler and his daughter are pursued by the Mounties in the Northwestern wilderness." One of the pursuers is the Mountie played by Lon Chaney. The two-reeler was directed by a former Canadian, Allan Dwan.

127. What was the "head tax" on the Chinese?

The "head tax" on the Chinese was the levy by which a provincial government and the federal government attempted to reduce the Chinese population of Canada and to limit Chinese immigration to Canada. In 1884, the government of British Columbia imposed a $10 head tax on all Chinese living in the province. Then the federal government imposed a $50 head tax on all Chinese entering Canada after 1 January 1886. It raised the tax to $100 in 1900, and to $500 in 1904. The passage of The Chinese Immigration Act of 1923 effectively curtailed Chinese immigration until its repeal in 1947. Such taxes are now seen as a racist violation of civil liberties and an embarrassment of the first order.

128. Is Shreve a Canadian?

The full name of the character known as Shreve in William Faulkner's novel *Absalom, Absalom!* (1936) is Shrevlin McCannon who is described as being born in Edmonton in 1890 and a student at Harvard from 1909 to 1914 where he was the roommate of Quentin Compson. Shreve, knowing little about life in the U.S. South, acted as Quentin's catalyst: "Tell about the South. What's it like there? What do they do there? Why do they live there? Why do they live at all...."

129. Did Alexis Carrel ever work in Canada?

Alexis Carrel, the famous experimental surgeon who received the Nobel Prize in 1912 and wrote the best-selling book *Man the Unknown* (1938), briefly worked in Canada. Born in Lyon, France, he qualified as a physician and surgeon. Encountering professional reverses, he resolved to establish a colony of *émigrés* from France in Canada where they would farm in the West. He himself emigrated and settled in Montreal in 1904 where he joined the staff of the Montreal General Hospital. Within a year he left for the University of Chicago and then the Rockefeller Institute for Medical Research where he made an immense reputation for himself.

130. Did a French Canadian accompany Lewis and Clark?

The Lewis and Clark Expedition of 1804-06 effectively opened the American West to settlement. One member of their expedition was a French-Canadian translator named Toussaint Charbonneau. His name is spelled Charbonneau in *Travels to the Source of the Missouri River and Across the American Continent to the Pacific Ocean* (reprint 1914). Charbonneau travelled with his wife and two young children and acted as one of the expedition's interpreters.

131. Did Raymond Chandler serve with the Canadian Corps?

"It is still natural for me to prefer a British uniform," Raymond Chandler told friends when they asked him why he enlisted to serve in the Great War with the Canadian Corps rather than with the U.S. Army.

The Philip Marlowe detective novels for which Chandler is famous were ahead of him. In August 1917, he travelled to Victoria, British Columbia, where he enlisted with the Gordon Highlanders of Canada. He trained for three months in Victoria, which he found to be "dullish, as an English town would be on a Sunday, everything shut up, churchy atmosphere and so on." On 26 November, he embarked on a troopship which left from Halifax for England and there he was transferred to the British Columbia Regiment. On 18 March 1918, he was assigned to the Seventh Battalion of the Canadian Expeditionary Force (the Canadian Corps) and sent to France where his battalion served at Arras. Chandler rose to acting sergeant but was never commissioned.

Back in England, he transferred to the Royal Air Force, like many young Canadians before him. With the Armistice, he was sent back to Canada and discharged in Vancouver on 20 February 1919. As one of his biographers noted, "His military career had lasted almost exactly eighteen months."

132. Did Lewis Carroll correspond with two Canadian girls?

It is widely recognized that Lewis Carroll had a tender regard for young girls. Through a mutual friend, Mrs. Edwin Hatch, Carroll received a photograph of two of her young nieces, Mabel and Emily Kerr, who lived in Hamilton, Ontario. Their names inspired Carroll to write a sixteen-line verse called "A Double Acrostic" at Oxford on 20 May 1871. The girls then sent him a larger photograph of themselves. Carroll's complicated verse is included by Morton N. Cohen, editor of Volume One of *Letters of Lewis Carroll* (1979). There are four stanzas. The first runs as follows: "Thanks, thanks, fair Cousins, for your gift / So swiftly borne to Albion's isle – / Though angry waves their crests uplift / Between our shores, for many a league [mile]!"

133. Who is Canada's best-known fictional personage?

The journalist Robert Fulford has suggested that Anne Shirley, better known as the hero of the novel *Anne of Green Gables*, is the country's best-known fictional personage. Indeed, he suggested that she might be the best-known character, real or imagined, in Canadian history. "People in other countries might not know the name of our prime minister, but they've heard of Anne," he noted, according to Patricia Orwen in "Kindred Spirits," *The Toronto Star,* 18 Aug. 1991.

134. Whose dancing was better known than Isadora Duncan's?

History applauds Isadora Duncan as the most famous of the free-form dancers. Yet for much of her stage career, Duncan ranked second in popularity to Maud Allan, the Toronto-born, free-form dancer whose salad days extended from 1903 to 1936. Allan's most popular dance number was called "The Vision of Salome." She performed the evocative dance in Europe and America, in bare feet, clad only in gauze and jewellery, according to Felix Cherniavsky in *The Salome Dancer: The Life and Times of Maud Allan* (1991).

135. Who were the *skraelings?*

Skraelings is an Old Norse word for "weaklings." The Vikings used this word to refer to the native people who lived near their colony in the vicinity of L'Anse aux Meadows, Newfoundland. The native people were Inuit. Far from being weak, the *skraelings* defended their territory and defeated the Vikings in a number of battles, finally driving the Vikings from their shores a thousand years ago.

136. What year did the English first outnumber the French?

French Canadians were the majority in Canada until the year 1850 when English Canadians overtook them in sheer numbers.

137. Who is the lone Canadian member of the Baseball Hall of Fame?

The sole Canadian to be inducted into the Baseball Hall of Fame in Cooperstown, New York, is Ferguson (Fergie) Jenkins. Born in Chatham, Ontario, the fourth-generation black Canadian enjoyed an outstanding pitching career with the Chicago Cubs baseball team in 1966-73 and 1982-83.

138. Was Charles A. Lindbergh Jr. a Canadian?

No. Charles A. Lindbergh Jr. (1902-1974), the aviator who became the first person to fly solo across the Atlantic, doing so in his aeroplane *The Spirit of St. Louis*, 20-21 May, 1927, was an American citizen, born in Melrose, Minnesota. His father, Charles Sr., had been born in Stockholm, Sweden, and had immigrated to the American Midwest in 1881. Charles Sr. married (in the words of a newspaper account of the late 1920s) "the daughter of Dr. C.H. Land, who was born in Hamilton, Ontario, and whose grandfather, Col. John Land, a British subject, is generally credited with having founded Hamilton." Lindberg Jr.'s mother was Evangeline Land, a woman of Canadian birth.

139. Did Amelia Earhart learn to fly in Toronto?

It is often said that Amelia Earhart, the adventurous aviatrix who disappeared on a daring, clandestine flight over the South Pacific in 1937, learned to fly in Toronto. Rumour has it that she "earned her wings" at the military field at Armour Heights, now North York. Research has established that her sojourn in Toronto kindled her desire to fly.

After graduating from high school in Chicago, Earhart joined her sister in Toronto in 1918 where she trained and worked as a nurse's aid in the Spadina Military Hospital with casualties of the Great War and victims of the Great Influenza Epidemic. The aviation display occasioned by the Armistice delighted her. "What a day!" she wrote in her memoirs, *The Fun of It* (1932).

She noted: "I believe it was during the winter of 1918 that I became interested in airplanes. Though I had seen one or two at county fairs before, I now saw many of them, as the officers were trained at the various fields around the city. Of course, no civilian had the opportunity of going up. But I hung around in spare time and absorbed all I could. I remember the sting of the snow on my face as it was blown back from the propellers when the training planes took off on skis."

She wrote in more detail of her Toronto experiences in her book *Last Flight* (1937).

140. Who are Canada's Top 10 Female Athletes of the twentieth century?

A survey conducted of newspaper editors and radio and TV broadcasters by The Canadian Press/Broadcast News produced a list of the top ten female athletes of the twentieth century. Here is the list, in order of choice:

1. Nancy Greene
2. Silken Laumann
3. Barbara Ann Scott
4. Myriam Bédard
5. Marnie McBean
6. Bobbie Rosenfeld
7. Catriona Le May Doan
8. Sandra Post
9. Marilyn Bell
10. Elaine Tanner

Source: "Canada's Female Athletes of the Century," *The Globe and Mail*, 23 November 1999.

141. Who are Canada's Top 10 Male Athletes of the twentieth century?

A survey conducted of newspaper editors and radio and TV broadcasters by The Canadian Press / Broadcast News produced a list of the top ten male athletes of the twentieth century. Here is the list, in order of choice:

1. Wayne Gretzky
2. Gordie Howe
3. Bobby Orr
4. Lionel Conacher
5. Maurice Richard
6. Donovan Bailey
7. Fergie Jenkins
8. Mario Lemieux
9. Larry Walker
10. Gaetan Boucher

Source: "Male Athlete of the Century," *The Globe and Mail*, 30 November 1999.

142. Who is the first woman to have a public monument raised in her honour in Canada?

The monument to Laura Secord, the heroine of the War of 1812, was unveiled on Drummond Hill, Niagara Falls, Ontario, on 22 June 1901. It was the first public monument to a woman ever erected in Canada. The sponsors were the Lundy's Lane Historical Society and the Ontario Historical Society. The statue is the work of Mildred Peel, a sculptor from London, Ontario. Any earlier monuments raised to women were erected by individuals or non-governmental associations.

143. Did Mark Twain ever visit Canada?

Mark Twain, the American humourist, crossed the border at least half a dozen times. He gave talks and readings in Windsor, Niagara Falls, and Toronto in 1871. In 1881, to secure British Empire copyright for one of his books, he enjoyed a lengthy stay in Montreal, where he was the guest of honour at a civic banquet. In 1883, he was the guest of Governor General Lord Lorne in Ottawa and stayed in Rideau Hall. In 1885, he visited Toronto. He lectured in Winnipeg, Victoria, and Vancouver in 1895. So he knew Canada quite well. Twain made some jottings in his notebooks about some of his Canadian experiences, but it is apparent the country did not greatly excite him.

The following story is told about his arrival at a Canadian hotel. Glancing over the register, he took note of the signature of the last arrival: "Baron ... and valet." Twain signed: "Mark Twain and valise."

144. What were Chief Crowfoot's dying words?

It is widely believed that Crowfoot, Chief of the Blackfoot, as he lay dying at Blackfoot Crossing on the Bow River on 25 April 1890, uttered the following moving words:

A little while and I will be gone from among you, whither I cannot tell. From nowhere we come, into nowhere we go. What is life? It is a flash of a firefly in the night. It is a breath of a buffalo in the winter time. It is as the little shadow that runs across the grass and loses itself in the sunset.

As Robert S. Carlisle observes in his investigative article "Crowfoot's Dying Speech," *Alberta History*, Summer 1990, the eloquence is not Crowfoot's. Somebody adapted it from the speech of the African chieftain Umbopa in Sir H. Rider Haggard's popular and widely read novel *King Solomon's Mines* (1885). Umbopa's speech runs like this:

> What is life? ... It is the glow-worm that shines in the night-time and is black in the morning; it is the white breath of the oxen in winter; it is the little shadow that runs across the grass and loses itself at sunset.

No one reported Crowfoot's dying words. But his last message to his people was probably practical rather than poetic. He directed his people to obey the government and not to mourn him.

145. Was there an "Eskimo Lear"?

Shakespeare's classic play *King Lear* was given a novel, Arctic setting by director David Gardner for the Canadian Player's production at the Crest Theatre in Toronto on 24 October 1961. William Hutt played "the Eskimo Lear" wearing a parka. Gloucester's blindness was suggested by snow-goggles. Instead of the "blasted heath," the setting was the tundra of the North. In keeping with the Inuit theme, actors wielded harpoons instead of swords; dogs replaced horses in the text. The scene is described in the program as "On top of the world in the Arctic castles of Lear, Albany, Gloucester...." Although widely discussed, reviewers failed to warm to the production.

146. Was an American with a French name ever Governor General?

In a way, yes. Sir George Prevost, soldier and administrator, served as Governor-in-Chief of British North America from 1812 to 1814. The office is now that of the Governor General of Canada. Prevost, with his French name, was born in New Jersey at the time when it was a British Colony.

147. How many lawyers are there in the country?

There were more than 40,000 lawyers and law students in the country in 2000. Such, at least, is the membership of the Canadian Bar Association. Thus there is one lawyer for every 700 or so Canadians.

148. Who is hockey's Golden Jet?

Robert Martin Hull, better known as hockey's Bobby Hull, born in Point Anne, Ontario, was a fast skater and high scorer, so he was picturesquely known as Golden Jet.

149. Did Mary Livingstone come from Plainfield, New Jersey?

Radio listeners remember the tired-sounding voice of Mary Livingstone, the actress who played Jack Benny's secretary on *The Jack Benny Show*, the popular program which was heard (and then seen) Sunday evenings between 1934 and 1965.

Livingstone, a distant relative of the Marx Brothers, was born Sadie Marx in Seattle, Washington. She was raised in Vancouver where, at the age of fourteen, she met Jack Benny who was at the time a vaudeville performer. Then and there she vowed they would wed, and so they did in 1927 in Waukegan, Illinois. They lived in Hollywood, and she was such a success as a replacement for an ailing actress on the radio show that she legally changed her name to Mary Livingstone and specialized in playing Benny's secretary. It was always maintained that "Mary Livingstone came from Plainfield, New Jersey." The truth is she had never even visited Plainfield. She really came from Vancouver.

150. Who was Zaneth of the Mounties?

This is the grandiose name of Frank Zaneth (1890-1971), the Italian-born member of the Royal Canadian Mounted Police who specialized in undercover work on the Prairies and intelligence work in Montreal. As an operative he infiltrated the ranks of the Communist Party of Canada, the One Big Union, mobsters, counterfeiters, bootleggers, etc. A master of disguises, he acted as an *agent provocateur* in the Winnipeg General Strike. He signed his reports "Operative No. 1" and ultimately attained the rank of Superintendent. Zaneth's story is told in

Undercover: Cases of the RCMP's Most Secret Operative (1991) by James
Dubro and Robin Rowland.

151. Who was La Bolduc?

La Bolduc was Quebec's first female singing star, a combination of Edith
Piaf and Gracie Fields. She was born Mary Travers in the Gaspésie, married a Montrealer named Bolduc, and bore thirteen children. Yet she
found time to compose, perform, and record her own moving and often
amusing songs on topical subjects. Although her career was short (going
from her professional debut in 1928 to her death in 1941), La Bolduc
was immensely popular in her day, is nostalgically remembered in
Quebec today, and remains virtually unknown outside the province.

152. Did a royal poet explore early Canada?

A royal poet explored lands and waters that are now part of Canada
around the year 980, at least according to an early Norse epic narrative
poem. The poem recalls how in the 10th century a perilous expedition
was made to an inhospitable Arctic region by the poet Snaebjörn, a member of the early Irish royalty. In the epic the lands and waters he visited are
called variously Gunnbjörn's Reef, White Man's Land, and Great Iceland.
Details may be found in *Hamlet's Mill* (1977), a work of speculative
scholarship written by Giorgio de Santillana and Hertha von Dechend.

153. Was the Real McCoy a Canadian?

The Real McCoy is a slang expression for something genuine or authen-
tic. It may have originated in Scotland in the late nineteenth century as
"the real Mackay." It could also derive from an American pugilist named
Kid McCoy.

"But here's our real McCoy," wrote "You Asked Us," *The Toronto
Star*, 22 October 1991. "In the early 1870s, Elijah McCoy invented a
lubricator cup that continuously oiled moving parts of machinery.
Without his device, machines had to be shut down frequently for manual
lubrication. That was time-consuming and costly. Machine buyers soon
began insisting on McCoy lubricators on new equipment. They'd accept

nothing but 'the real McCoy.'" Apparently he was a black engineer and inventor born about 1844 in Colchester, Ontario, of parents who had fled form slavery in Kentucky. He died in 1929. "In his youth, McCoy was apprenticed to a mechanical engineer in Scotland. Was he also the real Mackay?" The authors cite *The World Book Encyclopaedia* which suggests that he was.

154. Did Graham Greene set one of his novels in Canada?

No. Graham Greene set his novels in many parts of the world, but Canada is not the setting of even one of them. But he did visit the country.

Calgary is the setting of one of the short works of fiction included in Greene's *Collected Stories* (1967). The story "Dear Dr. Falkenheim" (1963) is set in a place called Kosy Nuick, a bungalow on the outskirts of Calgary. It concerns an abused child who watches as Santa Claus loses his head to a helicopter blade. Greene wrote it in Calgary during a visit to a relative who was living in that city.

155. Were actors Trevor Howard and Melvyn Douglas born in Canada?

Each of these character actors of stage and screen has a slight Canadian connection, but place of birth is not one of them. Trevor Howard (1916-1988), the distinguished British leading man, was born in England, but spent some youthful years in Brantford, Ontario. Melvyn Douglas (1907-1981), the American actor, attended Upper Canada College in Toronto as a youngster. Both actors were distinguished for their suave manner and their polite manners.

156. Who was Mr. Dithers?

Newspaper readers will know Mr. Dithers to be the name of the autocratic boss of Dagwood Bumstead in the daily comic strip *Blondie*. Filmgoers of the past will recall that Mr. Dithers was played to perfection in the Blondie movies (1938-50) by the character actor, Jonathan Hale (1892-1966). Hale, born Jonathan Hatley in Hamilton, Ontario, appeared in over two hundred movies, often typecast as the exasperated businessman.

In the Blondie movies he is Dagwood's bossy boss. He crops up in the Charlie Chan and Saint movies, not to mention in *Johnny Belinda* (1948) and *Strangers on a Train* (1951). Hale committed suicide in Hollywood.

157. Who developed the semi-automatic rifle?

The first effective semi-automatic military rifle was developed by the Quebec-born toolmaker Jean C. Garand. He was raised in the United States where he anglicized his first name to John. In 1933 he devised the Garand or M1 (for Model No. 1) for the U.S. Army's armoury in Springfield, Massachusetts. He developed an effective way for the gas generated by an exploding cartridge to eject the used shell and line up a fresh one in the firing chamber of the rifle. According to "You Asked Us," *The Toronto Star*, 21 November 1991, he died in Springfield in 1974 at the age of 88.

158. What is Canadian about the Lee-Enfield rifle?

The "Lee" has a Canadian connection. James Paris Lee (1831-1904) was a Scottish-born, Canadian-raised gunsmith and firearms designer. When Lee was seven years old, the family moved to Galt and then Chatham where his father opened a jeweller's shop. Like his father, Lee had a mechanical bent. In 1862 he patented and built his first rifle, and a Lee rifle from this period is on display at the Wallaceburg and District Museum. Lee subsequently moved to Wisconsin and became a naturalized American citizen.

Lee invented the bolt-action repeating rifle – the so-called magazine rifle capable of thirty shots a minute. From the Boer War to the Korean War, Lee's rifles were in use as principle service weapons by British and American troops. According to one estimate, almost ten million of his rifles were manufactured. The history of his firearms is a complex story of modifications, but here are a couple of generalizations. In 1888, the British Army adopted the Lee-Enfield (named after the location in England of the manufacturing plant) as its main infantry weapon. In 1895, the U.S. Navy adopted the Lee, known as either the Remington-Lee or Winchester-Lee, after its U.S. manufacturers. Today Lee's rifles are highly prized by firearms collectors.

People

159. Who are the Barenaked Ladies?

The Barenaked Ladies is the catchy name of a modern rock music group. The five performers are all male. They perform fully clothed, of course, and have become a huge success both at home and in the United States. The group was formed in Toronto in 1988.

160. Was an American "action painter" born in Montreal?

Philip Guston, the American "action painter," as the "abstract expression-ists" are sometimes called, was born in Montreal in 1913. His parents took him to Woodstock, New York, in 1916, and he was raised in the United States. So to all intents and purposes, he was an American "action painter," not a Canadian one. He died in 1980.

161. Who wrote the popular song "Seasons in the Sun"?

It seems that three songwriters contributed to the popularity of the love song "Seasons in the Sun." In 1961, Jacques Brel wrote the French words and music of "Le Moribond," which told of an old man dying of a broken heart after his best friend stole his wife. In 1974, Rod McKuen translated the lyrics into English, and as "Seasons in the Sun" the song became a widely recorded hit single. Then Terry Jacks, the Vancouver writer-performer, adapted the lyrics to reflect the plight of a dying youth. His 1974 version outsold all singles worldwide that year. Curiously, Jacks receives no printed credit in such reference books as *Reader's Digest Canadian Family Songbook* (1978) and *Great Songs of the 70's* (1964) edited by Milton Okum.

162. Who was Mike Merry?

The Druze Canadian reported to me under the name of Mike Merry but that was only the anglicized version of Ismail Me'ereh. He was a cheerful soul with strikingly large brown eyes and a burly figure. He had migrated as a boy with his parents from the Jebel Druze in Syria to Canada and he was now the owner of a grocer's shop in Winnipeg. In spite of the fact that he had never been back to his native land since then, he spoke Arabic as a Druze should do and had in his possession a list of his kinsmen in the Jebel. He was a phenomenally good shot with a rifle.

So recalled the British military officer Sir Alec Kirkbride in his memoir, *An Awakening: The Arab Campaign 1917-18* (1971). At the time Sir Alec was stationed in Cairo and he enlisted Mike Merry to serve as an intelligence officer with Lawrence of Arabia in 1918.

163. Did a Canadian write the song "Far Away Places"?

The Montreal-born pianist and songwriter Alex Kramer moved to New York in 1938. He wrote the music and his American wife Joan Whitney wrote the words for the popular romantic song "Far Away Places" (1948). Other compositions by the husband-and-wife team include "High on a Windy Hill" (1940), "Ain't Nobody Here But Us Chickens" (1947), and "No Other Arms, No Other Lips" (1952).

164. Who was the first Hollywood star to sign the cement in the forecourt of Graumann's Chinese Theatre?

Hollywood's grandest movie premieres were held at Graumann's Chinese Theatre, now known as Mann's Chinese Theatre. In 1927, showman Sid Graumann began asking leading movie personalities to inscribe their names and greetings in wet cement. The first stars so honoured were Hollywood's reigning couple, Mary Pickford and Douglas Fairbanks Sr. The first signature was that of Toronto-born Mary Pickford, America's Sweetheart.

165. Was the Sundance Kid a Canadian cowboy?

No. *Butch Cassidy and the Sundance Kid*, the popular Western movie released in 1969, starred Paul Newman as the outlaw Butch Cassidy, and Robert Redford as his sidekick Harry Longbaugh, nicknamed the Sundance Kid. Longbaugh was a likeable American cowboy who kept brushing against the law. In the 1880s, he worked briefly for the North West Cattle Company, the famous Bar U Ranch, in Southern Alberta. Returning to Montana, he fell in with an outlaw gang, blew up an express train, claimed $600,000, and crossed into Mexico with Butch Cassidy, the gang's leader. It is believed that he and Butch Cassidy died in a shootout with federal troops at San Vincente, Bolivia, in 1909. A forensic anthropologist claimed in 1992 to have found their bones. Yet the legend persists that both Butch and Sundance survived the shootout and in the early 1900s returned to the United States and lived under aliases in the Western U.S. They may be buried somewhere in Wyoming, as noted by Mitchell Smyth in "Whatever Happened to ... Butch and Sundance?" in *The Toronto Star*, 19 January 1992.

166. Did a Canadian serve as Henry Miller's secretary?

Yes. The Quebec-born writer Gérald Robitaille served as secretary and general factotum to the novelist Henry Miller. This occurred in the late 1960s and early 1970s when Miller had moved from Big Sur and Pacific Palisades. The relationship between Robitaille and Miller was mentioned in passing by Mary V. Dearborn in *The Happiest Man Alive: A Biography of Henry Miller* (1991):

> The Miller entourage also included a young Canadian, Gérald Robitaille, and his wife, Diane. Robitaille was acting as Miller's secretary, companion, and chauffeur. An ardent admirer of his employer, Robitaille saw himself as a sort of son. According to Robitaille, Miller wanted him to write his biography. For the time being, however, Robitaille acted primarily as a buffer, keeping unwanted intruders at bay....

But things did not go well.

> The departure of Gérald Robitaille was perhaps the most painful loss. Robitaille claimed that Miller had reneged on a promise to pay him during his lifetime the $10,000 that he had been planning to will to Robitaille. Whether Miller had written Robitaille into his will or not, he perceived Robitaille's quitting as a betrayal, and he was doubly stung when Robitaille wrote a diatribe against him, published as *Le Père Miller* in 1971. It revealed less about Miller's failings than it did about the toadying and exploitation going on around him in those years – in which Robitaille appears to have participated fully.

Robitaille is the author of the bilingual prose poem *Images* (1970). Miller, quite taken with Robitaille's prose, once claimed, "He writes like Jesus Christ the Second."

167. Who created Staff Sergeant Renfrew of the Mounties?

Comedian David Broadfoot has created a whole host of comic characters. Federal politicians from Western Canada inspired the bombastic, Stetson-wearing Member for Kicking Horse Pass in 1954. Sergeant Renfew of the Mounties came from a column "Nicol of the Mounted" written by Vancouver humourist Eric Nicol in 1957. He began as a corporal but was promoted by successive RCMP commissioners to Sergeant and then Staff Sergeant. Also promoted, noted Sid Adilman in *The Toronto Star*, 4 January 1992, was his mascot, Cuddles, to the rank of Corporal. Broadfoot also created the semi-literate, professional hockey player Bobby Clobber, who is always saying "anyway." Clobber was inspired by professional player Gordie Howe.

168. What rock group was once known as the St. James Rhythm Pigs?

The rock group now called the Crash Test Dummies consists of four Winnipeggers who first played together in summer 1986 under the band name St. James Rhythm Pigs. Members of the group were Brad Roberts, Ben Darvill, Ellen Reid, and Dan Roberts.

169. Who are the Crash Test Dummies?

The Crash Test Dummies is a pop group that was founded in Winnipeg in 1989. Singer/composer Brad Roberts leads the group; other members are Mitch Dorge, Ellen Reid, Ben Darvill, and Dan Roberts. The group rose to fame with an elegiac audio and video single called "Superman's Song" on its album *The Ghosts that Haunt Me* (1991).

170. Are any of the Henty novels set in Canada?

G.A. Henty was an English author who specialized in writing adventure novels for young readers. His novels were popular with generations of boys, at least until the 1960s when their popularity flagged. Henty saluted individual heroism and sang the praises of the British Empire. At least two of Henty's novels are set in Canada. *With Wolfe in Canada: The Winning of a Continent* (c. 1880) describes the Battle of the Plains of Abraham from the point of view of an English lad. *Fighting in Canada* (1885) tells the story of the suppression of the Second Riel Rebellion.

171. Did Henrik Ibsen write about Canadian theatre?

Henrik Ibsen, the great Norwegian dramatist, expressed no interest in the plight of an indigenous Canadian theatre. It was John Palmer, the Canadian playwright, who wrote an ironic play in which Ibsen lectures an unresponsive audience on the need for a national theatre in Norway.

Palmer's short play, a curtain-raiser, was first produced by the Factory Theatre Lab in Toronto, 10 Oct 1976. In effect, *Henrik Ibsen on the Necessity of Producing Norwegian Theatre* is a monologue in which the actor, dressed to resemble the aged Ibsen, endorses the need for an indigenous Norwegian theatre. It is expected (or hoped) that a present-day Canadian audience will recognize in Ibsen's concern the equally pressing need for an indigenous Canadian theatre today.

172. Did a Canadian found the Glyndebourne Festival?

No. Yet there is a Canadian connection with the Glyndebourne Festival Opera. England's world-famous music festival was established in 1934 by philanthropist and music lover John Christie who, three years earlier, had married the talented soprano, Audrey Mildmay. Sometimes known as Grace Mildmay, she was born in 1900 in Sussex, not far from Glyndebourne, but was raised in Vancouver. Her father was a vicar in Penticton, British Columbia. As a youngster she admired two Canadian opera singers, Louise Edvina and Edward Johnson. When she was twenty-four, she returned to England and commenced her singing career. She died at Glyndebourne in 1953. For many years Audrey and John Christie presided over the proceedings of the annual opera festival at Glyndebourne, according to Spike Hughes's *Glyndebourne: A History of the Festival Opera* (1965).

173. Did Elvis ever appear in Toronto?

Only during his lifetime. Elvis Presley performed in his trademark all-gold suit for a total of 23,000 fans in two performances held at Maple Leaf Gardens, Toronto, 2 April 1957. "I think Toronto audiences are terrific," said his manager, Col. Tom Parker, who added that the audience for the second show was the largest number of people the performer had played for to date.

174. Did a Canadian found *The Reader's Digest?*

No, but it was co-founded by a person born in Canada. *The Reader's Digest*, often called the best-loved magazine in the world, is one of the most successful publications of all time. It was founded in Pleasantville, New York, in 1922, by the husband-and-wife team of DeWitt Wallace, an American publisher, and Lila Acheson Wallace. Mrs. Wallace was born in Virden, Manitoba; she died in 1984 at the age of 94.

175. Did a Canadian write "Roll Out the Barrel"?

From time to time one hears or reads that it was a Canadian composer who wrote "The Beer Barrel Polka," the frolicking picnic song also known by its first line which goes "Roll Out the Barrel."

Research has established that "The Beer Barrel Polka" has no connection with any Canadian. It comes from Czechoslovakia where it was called "Skoda Lasky" (Lost Love). Jaromir Vejvoda wrote the catchy tune in 1934; Vasek Zeman and Wladimir A. Timm added the Czech words. The tune was retitled and given new English words by Lew Brown in 1939 and introduced into the United States by Will Glahe and his Musette Orchestra. No Canadians need apply.

176. Was Wolf Larsen a Canadian?

Wolf Larsen, the central character of Jack London's novel *The Sea-Wolf* (1904), although English-speaking, has no specified nationality. He is a captain, the "sea-wolf" of the title, and a mean-spirited one at that. But the popular novel offers the reader a character from Canada named Louis, for as one of the crew members narrates: "I have made the acquaintance of another one of the crew – Louis, he is called, a rotund and jovial faced Nova Scotia Irishman, and a very sociable fellow, prone to talk as long as he can find a listener."

177. Did Mae West star in a movie set in Canada?

The Hollywood movie *Klondike Annie* (Paramount, 1936) starred Mae West. It was based on her own stage play *Frisco Kate* and it made use of much of her dialogue. The part she played was that of a madame on the lam who impersonates the evangelist known as Soul-Savin' Annie in the Klondike, Yukon Territory. (The evangelist was probably modelled on Ontario-born Aimee Semple McPherson.) According to Fergus Cashin's *Mae West: A Biography* (1981), censors cut some eight minutes of running time because of its religious satire; still it is considered one of her funniest movies. Such lines as the following survived the censor's scissors: "Between two evils, I always pick the one I never tried before." "Give a man a free hand and he'll try to put it all over you."

178. Who is la p'tite Québécoise?

La p'tite Québécoise (the "little Quebec girl") is the affectionate moniker of the young female vocalist Céline Dion, a native of Charlemagne, Quebec, who rose to fame in Quebec during the 1980s and in the 1990s became an international performing and recording superstar. She released albums in French in Quebec and in France before she decided to tackle the English-speaking world with *Unison* (1990), the first album of her songs in English. Her widest exposure followed her sound-track recording in the 1998 movie *Titanic*.

179. Who created *Ballet Adagio, Pas de Deux,* and *Narcissus?*

These are the titles of short films, inspired by the movement of ballet dancers, created for the National Film Board by the world-famous animator Norman McLaren. The films are short and vivid. *Ballet Adagio* runs 9 minutes 59 seconds, *Pas de Deux* runs 13 minutes 22 seconds, and

Narcissus is all of 21 minutes 47 seconds long. So their entire viewing time totals 44 minutes 28 seconds.

180. Are Canadians predominantly Catholic or Protestant?

According to Statistics Canada, for more than one hundred years, Protestants outnumbered Catholics. In 1971, for the first time in Canadian history, Catholics outnumbered Protestants. They remain the dominant religious group. In 1990, Catholics accounted for 45% of adult Canadians, and mainline Protestant denominations accounted for 30% of the adult population. The third most populous group was composed of those Canadians who answered "no religion." They accounted for 13% of the adult population.

181. Who is behind The Royal Canadian Air Farce?

The popular CBC Radio comedy troop known as the Royal Canadian Air Force was formed in 1973. It consists of four farceurs, Luba Goy, Don Ferguson, Roger Abbott, and John Morgan, and two writers, Rick Olsen and Gord Holtmann; a former member is comic Dave Broadfoot.

182. Who created the record album titled *I'm Your Fan?*

The 1991 record album *I'm Your Fan* was produced by Jennifer Warren and it includes interpretations by popular recording artists of Leonard Cohen's songs. The title itself recalls Cohen's album *I'm Your Man* (1988). It sparked a revival of interest in Cohen's performing career – always a matter of fits and starts as the poet-singer-songwriter eschews the media (except when a new book or album is on offer).

183. Did Sir Richard Francis Burton ever visit Canada?

Sir Richard Francis Burton, English officer, linguist, traveller, adventurer, popularizer of the word "safari," and translator of *The Thousand and One Nights,* made one trip to North America. In April 1860, he boarded the S.S. *Canada* in England and landed at Halifax where he found the people friendly. "He seems not to have lingered in Halifax but immediately went down to New York, where he spent a few days talking to publishers ... and then he went south to Washington." Ultimately he travelled across the American continent and in the West he spent some time among the Mormons. So wrote Edward Rice in *Captain Sir Richard Francis Burton* (New York: Charles Scribner's Sons, 1990).

184. Who appeared most often on *The Ed Sullivan Show?*

Ed Sullivan himself appeared most often on *The Ed Sullivan Show*, in its day the most popular variety show on American television. Sullivan loved the comedy team of Wayne and Shuster and over the life of the show Johnny Wayne and Frank Shuster appeared sixty-seven times, more often than any other single entertainer or group.

185. Did a Canadian inspire Walt Disney's Snow White?

There is a tradition in Iceland and in Manitoba that the appearance of Snow White in Walt Disney's film *Snow White and the Seven Dwarfs* owes a lot to the looks of a young Icelandic woman who spent four years in Arborg and Winnipeg, Manitoba.

Kristin Solvadottir died in Reykjavik, Iceland, in 1981 at the age of sixty-nine. In 1932, when she was twenty years old, she was working as a waitress at the Wevel Café, an Icelandic eatery in Winnipeg. It was frequented by Charles Thorson, a forty-two-year-old artist who fell in love with Kristin and proposed to her. She spurned him and thereafter accompanied her sick mother back to Iceland. It is said that Thorson never forgot her lovely face and gentle manner, even after moving to Los Angeles where he became a character artist in Walt Disney's studio. Apparently he created the visual character, costume, and personality of Snow White for *Snow White and the Seven Dwarfs* (1937), Disney's first animated feature film.

Whether the charming story can be proved or not, it circulated for many years in Reykjavik. When the film classic was re-released in 1993, the story was recalled by Carreen Maloney of *The Winnipeg Free Press* and was carried by *The Globe and Mail* on 17 July 1993. There is a resemblance between Kristin's smile and Snow White's.

186. How many Canadians are unable to speak either English or French?

According to the 1991 census, 378,000 residents indicated that they spoke neither English nor French. That figure includes children up to the age of five. Referring to the population five years of age and over, the figure is somewhat lower: 309,000 residents could speak neither official language when the census was taken. That means one Canadian in ten is unable to speak either official language. That person has a number of characteristics: likely an immigrant, though not necessarily a recent one, a member of an ethnic community (notably Chinese, Italian, or Portuguese), more certainly a woman than a man, and a dweller in a major centre.

187. Who is the Wealthy Barber?

The Wealthy Barber is named Roy in the runaway bestseller, *The Wealthy Barber*. This book of financial-planning advice subtitled "The Common Sense Guide to Successful Family Planning" was written by David Chilton, a Kitchener-based stockbroker. In 1989, he printed, published, and distributed it himself, largely as backup for his talks and seminars. It was immediately popular and the publication rights were soon acquired by a major trade publishing house in Toronto. Financial advice is dispensed in a barber shop in Sarnia, Ontario, and the financially secure barber, Roy, advises his customers that they should invest 10% of their gross income, no more, no less.

188. Who was the last Miss Canada?

The last person to win the Miss Canada contest was Nicole Dunson who completed her reign in October 1992. She was the last Miss Canada because the annual beauty and talent pageant was cancelled after a women's group lobbied that the contest was degrading to women.

189. Who is the first woman to play in the NHL?

Manon Rhéaume, a native of Quebec City, became the first female to play in the National Hockey League. Since childhood she has wanted to play professional hockey. In 1992, when she was twenty, she played with the Tampa Bay Lightning as goalkeeper in an exhibition rather than a league game.

190. Was Jack the Ripper a Canadian?

No one knows the identity of the man (or woman) who in a series of bloody attacks murdered and mutilated prostitutes on the London waterfront at the turn of the century.

The Montreal journalist Don Bell has suggested that Jack the Ripper was none other than the scion of a wealthy Montreal family. The jury is out on that one, as well as on the following question: Did Jack the Ripper keep a record of his thoughts and deeds? A journal purporting to be his was edited by Shirley Harrison and published as *The Diary of Jack the Ripper* (1993). Harrison noted that the Ripper had a son, James Fuller, who in 1911 was working as a mining engineer in British Columbia. "He was engaged to a local girl, and apparently free from the shadow that had clouded his childhood. On April 10th, while working alone in his laboratory, he telephoned his fiancée. That was the last time she spoke to him. James was later found dead in his laboratory. He had apparently mistaken a glass of cyanide for water. The verdict was accidental death."

191. Did John Ashbery set a play in Canada?

John Ashbery, a contemporary American writer who is a member of the so-called New York School of Poets, set his play *The Compromise, or Queen of the Caribou* in Canada. Premiered in New York City by Poets Theatre on 4 April 1955, it was described by Brad Gooch in *City Poet: The Life and Times of Frank O'Hara* (1993) as "a miraculous new three-act play which takes place in the Canadian Northwest and is full of Mounties and Indians." A pastiche of Hollywood Westerns, it is apparently based on the Rin Tin Tin movie *Where the North Begins* (1923). The text appears in *Three Plays* (1978) where the locale is identified as "the Canadian North Woods" in the 1920s. Characters include RCMP Captain Harry Reynolds and his "Indian maidservant" named Mooka, and Sam Dexter, "manager of the Cariboo trading post," and "his Indian henchman" named Lucky Strike.

192. Who discovered Canada, John Cabot or Jacques Cartier?

The country that is now known as Canada was first settled by bands of American Indians and Inuit. The first Europeans to arrive on the East Coast were the Vikings about 1000 A.D., then Basque fisherman who established fishing ports and whale-oil refineries. In 1497, the Italian navigator Giovanni Caboto, who sailed for the English as John Cabot, made a landfall on the island of Newfoundland, Labrador, or Cape Breton Island – the site has never been established. From 1534, the French navigator Jacques Cartier discovered and explored what is now Quebec and the other eastern provinces. In 1535, he first used the word "Canada" to refer to Indian settlements on the north shore of the St. Lawrence River. French Canadians have long regarded French-speaking Cartier as one of their own and the founder of New France. But in terms of chronology, the laurels should go to Caboto/Cabot who made his East Coast landfall thirty-seven years earlier than the jean-come-lately, Cartier.

193. Who is the Urban Peasant?

The Urban Peasant is the sobriquet of James Barber, a bearded, opinionated, culinary expert who hosts his own national television program from Vancouver. He came into prominence in the late 1980s and he promotes fast cuisine and the use of natural ingredients.

194. Who are the Canadian Governors General?

Until the year 1952, the Governors General of Canada were all titled Britishers. Since that year, Canadians citizens have been appointed to the vice-regal position, the highest office in the land. Here are their names and years of office: Vincent Massey (1952-59), Georges Vanier (1959-67), Roland Michener (1967-74), Jules Léger (1974-79), Edward Schreyer (1979-84), Jeanne Sauvé (1984-90), Ramon Hnatyshyn (1990-95), Romeo LeBlanc (1995-99), Adrienne Clarkson (1999-present).

195. Who was the only princess born in Canada?

In the past, explorers and other travellers often described Indian women as "princesses," especially when they were the daughters of hereditary chiefs. Aside from any so-called Indian princesses, the sole royal princess to be born in Canada was Princess Margriet who was born on 19 January 1943 at the Civic Hospital in Ottawa to Princess Juliana, daughter of the Queen of the Netherlands. The Dutch royal family had taken refuge in Canada when their country was invaded by Germany. The Canadian Parliament passed a special law declaring extraterritorial the four-room suite Juliana occupied in order to guarantee that there would be created no question about the infant's nationality. The name Margriet means "daisy." That flower has come to symbolize in the Netherlands all those men, women, and children who had perished in World War II.

196. Do linguistic minorities outnumber Francophones in Canada?

The Quebec Referendum of 1995 drew attention to the ethnic groups who live in Quebec and by extension in the rest of Canada. Demographically, the largest group in the country is composed of people of British background, linguistically referred to as Anglophones; the second-largest group is of people of French background, or Francophones; the third largest-group is of people of other linguistic backgrounds, commonly called allophones. In general terms, based on the Census of 1991, 61% of Canadians speak English, 25% speak French, and the 14% speak other languages as their mother tongue. So allophones do not outnumber the Francophones in Canada.

197. Is a Canadian buried in Arlington National Cemetery?

Yes. His name is Jerry Cronan and he enlisted in the Confederate Army's 10th Louisiana Infantry, Company "E." He was a bachelor, a labourer, and a resident of St. Landry Parish. The Canadian Confederate soldier fought as a Private for the Confederacy against the Union and died on 2 June 1864 of wounds received earlier at Spottsylvania Court House. Some 482 members of that unit fell in battle and lie buried in Arlington National Cemetery. Cronan lies with them, the only Canadian to do so. The eight other Canadians who fought with the unit survived. Their stories are told by Thomas Walter Brooks and Michael Dan Jones in *Lee's Foreign Legion: A History of the 10th Louisiana Infantry* (1995).

198. How many Canadians have dual citizenship?

According to the 1991 Census, 400,000 Canadians enjoy the privileges of dual or multiple citizenship. Few native-born Canadians have dual citizenship, but many naturalized Canadians maintain such status. It became possible for Canadians to hold dual or multiple citizenship since 1977, although in 1994 a parliamentary committee reviewing the matter recommended that Citizenship and Immigration Canada curtail the practice.

199. How many Canadians were born outside Canada?

According to the 1991 Census, some 15% of Canadians were born in other countries and have become or are becoming citizens.

200. Who were the Neutrals?

The Neutrals were the members of an Indian group or nation who occupied land in the Niagara Peninsula and south-central Ontario. The French called them *la nation neutre* because they maintained a state of neutrality with respect to the long-standing enmity between the Iroquois and the Hurons and their ongoing, bloody battles. In this they showed marked success, but between 1649 and 1651 the population was destroyed and today only stones and bones remain to attest to their peace-loving presence. They called themselves the Attawandarons, "the people with the country," in the sense of "the best country." It is often said – on what basis is uncertain – that the sole word of their language to survive to the present is the word for the cataract in their hunting grounds, "niagara."

201. Which Quebec singer had his first big hit at the age of nine?

René Simard, born in 1961 on Ile d'Orleans, Quebec, began his performing and recording career in 1970 at the age of nine. His earliest hit singles were "Ave Maria," "L'Oiseau," and "Un Enfant comme les Autres."

202. Who was the first Prime Minister who did not bear a title?

Arthur Meighen, Prime Minister from July 1920 to December 1921, was the first who was not titled. His eight predecessors were titled; none of his successors have been titled (except for R.B. Bennett who acquired a title following retirement from political life).

203. Was Jack Armstrong the All-Canadian Boy?

No, but there is a Canadian connection.

Jack Armstrong was the All-American Boy. The phrase "All-American Boy" is familiar from the Jack Armstrong series heard on U.S. radio in the 1930s and 1940s. The action-adventure series for young listeners presented a globe-trotting hero with "all-American" ideals, just as Superman expressed "the American way." The series was sponsored by Wheaties "the breakfast of champions."

As it happened, the sponsors of the show took the hero's name from a real-life Jack Armstrong (1908-1982), who was known to one of the sponsors. Jack Armstrong was born in Winnipeg, raised from the age of four in Minneapolis, and enlisted in the U.S. Air Force and after the war was assigned to the Atomic Energy Commission, rising to the rank of Colonel. In later years he worked for the Rocketdyne Division of Rockwell International in Los Angeles, developing the engines later used in the Apollo and Gemini space programs.

204. Who was the youngest Prime Minister?

Joe Clark was the youngest person to assume the office of Prime Minister. He was born on 5 June 1939 and assumed office on 4 June 1979, so at the time he was one day short of his fortieth birthday.

205. Who is the Canadian-born actress who married Vidal Sassoon?

Born in 1945, Beverly Adams starred in *How to Stuff a Wild Bikini* and as "Lovey Kravezit" in the Matthew Helm flicks, retiring from acting following her marriage to hairdresser Vidal Sassoon.

206. Was Oskar Schindler's heroism discovered by a Canadian?

The quintessential "good German" was Oskar Schindler who saved the lives of many Central European Jews in Nazi Germany by employing them in his various "key" enterprises. Hardly any attention was paid to him or his actions until Australian author Thomas Keneally published his book called *Schindler's Ark* in Britain and *Schindler's List* in North America. Under the latter title it was filmed by Stephen Spielberg in 1993. One journalist who interviewed Schindler at length in the late 1940s was Herbert Steinhouse, who in later life worked in Montreal as a CBC producer. His account of Schindler's deeds appeared in *Saturday Night*, April 1994. It should have appeared half a century earlier, but at the time few editors wanted to publish stories about a "good German."

207. Was a Canadian the last surviving soldier of the Boer War?

Trooper George Ives, who died at the age of 111 in Aldergrove, British Columbia, in 1993, was the last surviving soldier of the Boer War. After service with the 1st Imperial Yeomanry in South Africa, he returned to Britain but he then chose to come to Canada. In 1903, he settled in the Barr Colony, today's Lloydminster, farmed, and then dairy farmed in British Columbia. His obituary in *The Daily Telegraph* noted that "he performed chin-ups on a parallel bar until he was well past one hundred."

208. Who are the Aboriginal Peoples?

The Aboriginal Peoples are the descendants of the original inhabitants of Canada. The Canadian Constitution recognizes three groups of Aboriginal Peoples: First Nations (formerly referred to as Indians), Métis people (persons of mixed First Nations and European ancestry), and Inuit (inhabitants of the region that lies north of the 60th parallel and in Northern Quebec and Labrador).

209. How do we refer to native peoples?

Native peoples, that is indigenous peoples, are to be found in most of the countries of the world. They greeted the newcomers and made way for them. They are sometimes described as "first peoples" or members of "first nations." In the 1960s it was popular to refer to them as "members of the Fourth World." (The First World comprised the capitalist countries; the Second World comprised the communist countries; the Third World comprised the non-aligned countries; and the Fourth World, the world's minority or marginalized peoples. The distinction was dropped in 1989, with the collapse of the Soviet Union and communist régimes in Europe and elsewhere.)

In Mexico the native peoples are referred to by the Spanish equivalent of "indigenous people." In Australia they are the "aborigines." In the United States they are known as Native Americans. In Canada they are called the Aboriginal Peoples, being formerly known as the Aboriginals. They are called First Nations with respect to their political presence. The 1996 Report of the Royal Commission on Aboriginal Peoples sought to standardize the language and refer to Canada's Indians and Inuit as "Aboriginal Peoples." Aboriginal leaders use the term First Nations and reserves are now also referred to as such.

210. Who were the greatest living Canadians in 1924?

While no single answer to that question is possible, one acceptable answer is the list of top ten greatest living Canadians that appeared in *The Maple Leaf* in 1924, a magazine published by the Canadian Clubs. Here, in order of priority, are the "greatest" living Canadians – every single one of them a man.

1. Dr. Frederick Banting, co-discoverer of insulin
2. Bliss Carman, poet
3. Sir Arthur Currie, Army general, principal of McGill University
4. E.W. Beatty, president, Canadian Pacific Railway
5. Sir Robert Borden, former Prime Minister
6. W.L. Mackenzie King, current Prime Minister
7. W.S. Fielding, current Minister of Finance
8. C.W. Gordon, author Ralph Connor
9. Sir Gilbert Parker, historical novelist
10. Dr. J.J.R. McLeod, co-discoverer of insulin

According to Russell R. Merifield in *Speaking of Canada: The Centennial History of The Canadian Clubs* (1993), there were a number of runners-up, including the following:

Adam Beck (founder, Ontario Hydro), Charles G.D. Roberts (author), F.G. Scott (Army chaplain), P.C. Larkin (High Commissioner), Arthur Meighen (former Prime Minister), Sir George Foster (former cabinet minister), N.W. Rowell (former member of the War Cabinet), Stephen Leacock (author), Edward Johnson (opera personality), Emma Albani (opera singer).

211. Who was Chénier and why was he brave?

Jean-Olivier Chénier was a physician who died heroically during the Rebellion of Lower Canada at the Battle of Saint-Eustache, 14 December 1837. "Brave like Chénier" was a byword in nineteenth-century French Canada. It was recalled in Quebec in the name of the Chénier Cell of the FLQ at the time of the October Crisis 1970.

212. Who is King of the Royal Mounted?

Sergeant King serves with a detachment of the Mounted Police based in the Yukon near the Alaska border in the novel *King of the Royal Mounted* (1935) written by the American author of Western novels, Zane Grey. It is assumed Grey based his character on RCMP Constable Alfred King who came to prominence when wounded by the Mad Trapper of Rat River in December 1931, as noted by Don Dutton in *The Toronto Star*, 23 September 1974. King Features Syndicate turned Grey's novel into an action comic strip which ran to March 1955; Grey wrote the outlines and his son Romer wrote the continuities, and the drawings were supplied by Allen Dean then Charles Flanders and Jim Gary. Republic Pictures turned out such serials as *King of the Royal Mounted* (1940), *King of the Mounties* (1942), *Dangers of the Canadian Mounties* (1948), *Canadian Mounties vs. Atomic Invaders* (1953), *Perils of the Wilderness* (1956), etc. Grey's related novels include *Northern Treasure* (1937), *The Far North* (1938), *Getting His Man* (1938), *Policing the Far North* (1938), and *The Great Jewel Mystery* (1938), as mentioned in Frank Gruber's *Zane Grey: A Biography* (1970).

213. Who was Robert Ross?

Robert (Robbie) Baldwin Ross (1869-1918) was an intimate friend of the Anglo-Irish playwright Oscar Wilde and appointed his literary executor. In 1950, Ross's ashes were preserved in Wilde's tomb at Père Lachaise Cemetery in Paris. Ross was Wilde's "first boy." They met when Ross was seventeen and Wilde thirty-two. Ross edited a literary reader, *The English Renaissance* (n.d.). The character was given posthumous fame by Timothy Findley in his novel *The Wars* (1977).

214. Who was Private Price?

Private George Lawrence Price, a native of Port William, Ontario, is believed to be the last Canadian soldier to be killed in the Great War. Indeed, it is occasionally maintained that Private Price was the last Allied casualty of the war. He was fatally shot by a sniper three minutes before the Armistice took effect at 11:00 a.m., 11 November 1918. Private Price fell between Havre and the Canal du Centre, just east of Mons, Belgium, and his remains lie buried in the military cemetery at Mons. The tragic matter of last-minute fatalities is discussed by historian Stanley Weintraub in *A Stillness Heard Round the World: The End of the Great War: November 1918* (1985).

215. Who was Manzo Nagano?

Manzo Nagano is the first Japanese person known to have landed and settled in Canada. This took place in 1877. He was a twenty-four-year-old stowaway on a British vessel travelling from Japan. He first set foot on Canadian soil at New Westminster, British Columbia, and thus became Canada's first Japanese immigrant.

216. What did Don and Dana Starkell accomplish?

Don and Dana Starkell paddled from Winnipeg to the mouth of the Amazon at Belém, Brazil. Their trip of 19,063 kilometres took from 1 June 1980 to 5 June 1982. The father and son team published their experiences in *Paddle to the Amazon* (1987). That is not the only superlative achievement associated with a Starkell. In 1984, by himself, Don cycled from Winnipeg to Charlottetown, Prince Edward Island. And then, in 1986, he canoed the 1,280 kilometres from Vancouver to Fairbanks, Alaska.

217. Was Trotsky slain by a Canadian?

The Soviet revolutionary Leon Trotsky was slain in Mexico in 1940 by a French assassin named Jacques Mornard who entered North America from Europe in the late 1930s on a Canadian passport that bore the unlikely name "Jacson." The document had originally belonged to one Tony Babich, a volunteer in the International Brigade from Princeton, British Columbia. It is surmised that the name on the passport was changed from Babich to Jacson by someone, perhaps a Russian, unfamiliar with English spelling. *RCMP Quarterly*, January 1954.

218. What was Nanook's original name?

Nanook of the North is the title of the influential documentary film that focuses on the life of an Inuit hunter in Northern Quebec. Nanook means Bear. Director Robert J. Flaherty chose a real Inuit hunter to play Nanook. The hunter's name was Allakariallak and he lived in Inukjuak, Northern Quebec. Flaherty maintained that the hunter died of hunger in 1922, the year the documentary film was premiered in New York City.

219. In what movie does Gary Cooper play a Canadian soldier who wears a kilt?

Gary Cooper plays Kenneth Dowey, a young Canadian soldier who wears the kilt of the Black Watch regiment, in *Seven Days Leave* (1930). This is an early "all-talking" movie from Paramount. On leave in London during the Great War, Dowey is surprised to learn that a widowed charwoman of Scottish background, who has no children of her own, is claiming him as her son. The char was played to perfection by Beryl Mercer. Reviewers felt that Cooper underplayed the role of the Canadian. The movie was based on the short story and the stage play titled *The Old Lady Shows Her Medals* by J.M. Barrie, included in *The Plays of J.M. Barrie* (1929).

Some of the elements of *Seven Days Leave* figure in the remake, the musical *Seven Days' Leave* (1942), in which Victor Mature plays the army private who will inherit $100,000 if and when he marries an heiress, played by Lucille Ball. First time tragedy, second time farce.

220. Did Henry Fonda ever play a Canadian in the movies?

Yes. The American character actor Henry Fonda played a Canadian corporal stationed in the Libyan desert in the movie *The Immortal Sergeant* (1943). The lead was played by Thomas Mitchell, as noted by David Shipman in *The Great Movie Stars: I, The Golden Years* (1970).

221. Does Charles E. Goren have a Canadian connection?

It seems he does. Charles E. Goren established himself as a master of bridge and made the contact version of the game his own in innumerable columns, articles, and books. According to the *Reuters* obituary (carried by *The Globe and Mail*, 12 April 1991), Goren was "Mr. Bridge." Apparently he started playing bridge when he fell in love with a young woman while a student of law at McGill. He evolved the famous point system (which apparently was further elaborated by a Canadian named William Anderson). Goren died on 3 April 1991 at Encino, California.

222. Is Montreal mentioned in the Bible?

For a number of reasons the City of Montreal goes unmentioned in the King James Version of the Bible. One reason is that the site was founded in 1535 and the Old and New Testaments of the Bible, though translated in 1611, cover events that date from 500 to 1,500 years earlier. However, there are two references that may be relevant. Montreal found its origins in the Ojibwa Indian settlement known as Hochelaga, described by Jacques Cartier in 1535. Over fifty years later, Champlain visited the site and named it Place Royal. Then, in 1642, Paul de Chomedy renamed it Ville-Marie. It was finally called Montreal, after the mountain so named by Cartier.

A word that sounds like "Hochelaga" appears in the Old Testament. The word is "Hachilah," and it may be found in Samuel 23:19 and 16:1, where it refers to a "place of refuge." Was Montreal founded as a "place of refuge"? Traditional historians maintain it was founded to serve as a trading post and religious mission. Michael Bradley, a "rehistorian" who speculates on early history and the Grail legend, has argued that Montreal served as a "refuge" or "refugium" for the Holy Grail and, indeed, was founded to serve this sacred purpose (*Holy Grail Across the Atlantic*, Hounslow Press, 1988; *Grail Knights of North America*, Hounslow Press, 1998).

223. Did Soviet Premier Mikhail Gorbachev ever visit Canada?

No. Mikhail Gorbachev visited Canada, but he was not the Premier of the Soviet Union at the time of his visit. He was then a member of the Politburo (its youngest member) and a minister in the government of Leonid Brezhnev. He headed an agricultural committee that travelled in Canada for ten days, visiting Ottawa, Niagara Falls, and Calgary. The trip took place in May 1983. In Ottawa he spent time with the Russian Ambassador Aleksandr Yakovlev who was then "rusticated" to Ottawa. When Gorbachev came to power, the Ambassador helped him prepare the Russians for Glasnost and Perestroika. So Canada played a small part in the transformation of Russia from a soviet to a capitalist state.

224. Did Enrico Caruso ever sing in Canada?

The great Italian tenor Enrico Caruso was at the height of his career and on a tour of the opera houses and concert halls of North America when it was arranged that he would give four concerts in Canada. He performed in Toronto on 4 May 1908 and 30 September 1920, and in Montreal on 8 May 1908 and 27 September 1920. He received standing ovations and enthusiastic press reports on all occasions.

225. Are there Canadians whose names are preserved in the heavens?

In a manner of speaking there are. The International Astronomical Union is the scientific association that is concerned with the naming of off-earth bodies and features. Over the years it has authorized the naming of celestial bodies and lunar features after individual Canadians distinguished for their achievements in the fields of astronomy and astrophysics.

Asteroids, or minor planets, bear the names of the following scientists: Anne B. Underhill (named in 1960); Toronto (in 1963 to acknowledge the contribution to astronomy of the University of Toronto); H.S. Hogg (1980); C.S. Beals (1981); J.F. Heard (1981); P.M. Millman (1981); J.L. Climenhaga (1982); J.S. and H.H. Plaskett (1982); C.A. Chant (1984); Gerhard Herzberg (1984).

Craters on the Moon recall the work of the following six deceased scientists: C.A. Chant, J.S. Foster, F.S. Hogg, Andrew McKellar, R.M. Petrie, and J.S. Plaskett. Other celestial features, like comets, acquire the names of their discoverers. In 1987, Ian Shelton of the University of Toronto became the first person since Galileo in 1604 to observe the birth of a supernova. The celestial body will hence be known as Supernova Shelton 1987A.

In a sense the names of these Canadians are inscribed in the sky, preserved in the heavens.

Places

226. How old is Canada?

The age of Canada depends on the starting point. The Dominion of Canada was formed in 1867. The Colony of New France was established by Samuel de Champlain in 1608. Basque mariners were regularly fishing the Grand Banks and operating a whale-oil refinery on the Labrador coast before Jacques Cartier arrived in 1497. The Icelanders founded a settlement at L'Anse aux Meadows around A.D. 1000. No one really knows when the indigenous peoples first crossed the Bering Strait and arrived on soil that is now part of Canada; it was probably about 10,000 years ago. So Canada is both old and young as a country. That reverse chronology is based on the historical record. The prehistorical record of geologists and palaeontologists establishes the beginnings of today's Canada with the laying down of the Precambrian shield more than four billion years ago. Astrophysicists reason that the universe itself was formed fifteen billion years ago.

227. What is the newest territory?

Nunavut is the newest Canadian territory. On 1 April 1999, it was created from the eastern section of the Northwest Territories to be the homeland of

Inuit. In Inuktitut it means "Our Land." The new territory consists of near-ly 2 million square kilometres and covers about one-fifth of Canada's total land mass. Its present population is just over 27,000 people, 85 percent Inuit and 15 per cent non-aboriginal. Inuit own 350,000 square kilometres and hold substantial mineral and hunting rights. Nunavut's territorial government will be responsible for education, health, social services, language, culture, housing, justice, etc. Approximately 56 per cent of the population is under 25 years of age. Its people are scattered in 29 communities, most of them vast distances apart. The territorial capital is Iqaluit. Nunavut will elect one member to Parliament and be represented by one appointed senator.

228. How many square kilometres make up Canada?

In round numbers, Canada comprises 10 million square kilometres. A precise measurement is 9,970,610 square kilometres. The physical size of the country varies from estimate to estimate and from year to year as measuring devices increase in accuracy.

229. What is an Indian band?

An Indian band is not a native musical group! An Indian band is a body of Indians recognized by the Indian Act for whose benefit and use land and money have been set aside and held by the government.

The average band size has grown from about 350 in 1960 to about 525 in 1979, when the smallest band was New Westminster, British Columbia, with two members, and the largest, Six Nations of the Grand River, which numbered 9,950.

230. What is an Indian reserve?

An Indian reserve is a tract of land set aside for the use and benefit of an Indian band, the legal title to which is vested in the Crown by right of the Indian Act. In the United States the term used for an Indian reserve is an Indian reservation.

Indians are free to live on or off reserves. The reserve system is characteristic of southern Canada. There are no reserves in the Yukon and Northwest Territories. Newfoundland is the only province with no Indian reserves.

231. Where was Paradise Alley?

There was a Paradise Alley in Dawson City at the height of the Klondike Gold Rush of 1896. Paradise Alley was simply the designation given by prospectors and miners to the red-light district or prostitutes' quarters in a mining camp or community frequented by prospectors. The Paradise Alley in Dawson City consisted of seventy or so log cabins decorated with the names of their occupants and policed and protected by the Mounted Police. Another name for Paradise Alley was Hell's Half Acre.

232. What are "prairie gold" and "black gold"?

These are fanciful descriptions for wheat and oil. The descriptions refer to the looks and values of these resources. "Prairie gold" refers to the appearance of the wheatfields of the West, golden in the sun. "Black gold" refers to the stygian colour of oil, the worth of which is said to be measured in gold.

233. In which city was Canada's first mosque erected?

Canada's first mosque was erected in 1938 in the city of Edmonton. Fifty years later, dozens of mosques were standing in many cities across Canada.

The Islamic population of Canada is increasing. According to the Census of 1871, there were only three Muslims in the entire country. By the Census of 1981, there were more than 100,000 Muslims in Canada.

234. What is a reference to the "back forty"?

When the Canadian prairies were surveyed, the land was divided into sections. A section consisted of 640 acres. Each settler was entitled to a quarter-section, or 160 acres.

The smallest subdivision used in land and timber surveys consisted of one-sixteenth of a section, or forty acres. The "back forty" was the last and smallest subdivision in the district, usually that farthest from water.

235. Who turned Niagara green?

For decades it has been a tradition to use banks of lights to illuminate the twin cataracts at Niagara Falls. For a few hours each night, various shades of colour are projected onto the waterfalls.

It was Dwight Whalen, a researcher and information officer with the National Parks Commission, who made the suggestion that St. Patrick's Day should be observed by the use of green light. The suggestion was acted upon in 17 March 1989. Whalen's latest suggestion is that a blushing pink light should be used to mark St. Valentine's Day on the14th of February.

236. What is the northernmost point of North America?

The northern coast of Ellesmere Island, Northwest Territories, is the northernmost point of North America. Cape Columbia, located on that coast, lies northwest of Alert, the most northern community. Cape Columbia is 480 miles south of the North Pole.

237. What is Canada's most northerly point?

Cape Columbia is accepted as the most northerly extension of Canada at longitude 83°06'N. But this is not strictly so, as was noted by Alan Rayburn in his column "Places Names" in *Canadian Geographic*, February-March 1987. It was determined in 1967 that a small point of land extends farther north than Cape Columbia in the vicinity of Cape Columbia, Northwest Territories. As yet this most northerly point lacks a name.

238. How great is the range of temperature on Ellesmere Island?

The range of temperature on Ellesmere Island in the Northwest Territories is great. L. David Mech, author of "Life in the High Arctic," *National Geographic*, June 1988, observed that the temperature goes from a high in the summer of 70 degrees Fahrenheit, to a low in the winter of minus 70 degrees Fahrenheit. That is, in Celsius, from a high of 19 degrees to a low of minus 19 degrees.

239. What is unique about Triple-Divide Peak?

Rain that falls upon Triple-Divide Peak may ultimately make its way into one of three oceans: the Pacific Ocean (via lakes and rivers), the Atlantic Ocean (by the Gulf of Mexico), and the Arctic Ocean (through Hudson Bay). Triple-Divide Peak, which is located in the Montana part of the park, rises 2442 metres above Waterton-Glacier International Peace Park. It has been called the "crown of the continent."

240. What is the national song of Newfoundland?

Newfoundlanders reserve a special place in their hearts for "Ode to Newfoundland." This is recognized to be the national song or anthem of the Great Island. Sir Cavendish Boyle, Governor of the island in 1901-4, composed the lyrics and arranged to have the verses set to music by a friend, Sir C.H.H. Parry. Parry is best remembered for his memorable setting of Blake's "Jerusalem."

"Ode to Newfoundland" is a stately patriotic song which celebrates the "pine-clad hills" and the spirit of "our fathers." The first verse runs like this:

> When sun rays crown thy pine-clad hills,
>   And Summer spreads her hand,
> When silvern voices tune thy rills,
>   We love thee, smiling land.
>
>   We love thee, we love thee,
>   We love thee, smiling land.

241. Is Canada closer to the United States than the United States is closer to Canada?

This might seem to be a senseless question because, after all, the two countries share a common border. Yet as the Quebec-based geographer William Bunge explained in his book *Nuclear War Atlas*, there are degrees of closeness:

> Are the United States and Canada as near neighbours as possible? In one important sense, yes, they share a common border. How

could they get any closer? Well, if two countries share a very tine common border, like the Soviet Union and Czechoslovakia, they are not as close as if they share a very long border, as do the Soviet Union and China. Also, Canada is much closer to the United States than the United States is to Canada; this is clear from calculating how close the average Canadian is to the United States (around 100 miles) and how close the average American is to Canada (around 300 miles). This has such practical effects as U.S. television being available to almost all Canadians while the reverse is true only in border cities, such as Detroit and Buffalo. Nations can be even closer, as in the case of Palestine-Israel, where the populations intermix throughout the two nations which occupy each other's space.

Therefore the answer to the question posed above is that in the sense of the population of one country influencing the population of another, Canada is thus closer to the United States than the United States is to Canada. This is so because Americans influence Canadians more than Canadians influence Americans. Yet as Bunge went on to note:

Geography has its subtleties like any other science. But the compelling answer is that the United States is much closer to Canada than the other way about because the United States occupies the space above Canada whereas Canada merely occupies its own land surface. The United States is a three-dimensional power and Canada merely a two-dimensional one so the United States has a surfaced boundary which blankets Canada, while Canada only has an old-fashioned line boundary with the United States.

242. Which city has the distinction of including the largest enclosed farm in the world?

The claim is made that Ottawa has within its boundaries the largest enclosed farm in the world. As Gene Bodzin wrote in *Not Just Another Tour Book: A Practical Guide to the Sights and Traditions of Ottawa* (1987), "No other city in the world encloses a farm as large as Ottawa's Central Experimental Farm. No other capital city encloses a farm at all. But this achievement came about totally by accident: as Ottawa grew, it simply spread to the country and swallowed up the farm."

The Central Experimental Farm for government research was established on 466 acres of land well outside the city limits in 1886. By 1950 it was within hailing distance of the city and by 1974 it was surrounded by the fast-growing capital. It now consists of 1,350 acres and is completely surrounded by houses.

243. Where is the world's largest log building?

Château Montebello is a resort hotel built on the north bank of the Ottawa River at Montebello, Quebec. It is often called the world's largest log cabin or building. Ten thousand red cedar logs, transported by the CPR from British Columbia, were used in the construction of the star-shaped building which was opened on 1 July 1930. The architect gave the log building a modified French château style. Originally called the Seignory Club, it is now a resort hotel with a full complement of facilities suited for government and business conferences. On its grounds may be found the historic home of Louis-Joseph Papineau, a leader in the Rebellion of Lower Canada.

244. Which place has the most Ph.D.'s per acre?

It is frequently claimed that the town of Deep River, Ontario, has the most Ph.D.'s per acre of any place in Canada. The community was established as the residential community for neighbouring Chalk River, the site of the National Research Council of Canada's atomic-energy plant. As Joan Finnigan noted in *Finnigan's Guide to the Ottawa Valley: A Cultural & Historical Companion* (1988), "The town consists largely of scientists and related professionals and is frequently cited as a place 'with more Ph.D.'s per acre than anywhere else in Canada.'" For the record it is often noted that Calgary has more university graduates than any other Canadian city.

245. The annual Oktoberfest is hosted by which Ontario cities?

The "twin cities" of Kitchener and Waterloo in Central Ontario host the annual, week-long Oktoberfest. Oktoberfest was first held in 1968 and is billed as Canada's Great Bavarian Festival, bringing "the best that Gemütlichkeit can offer." There is continuous Bavarian and

German-style entertainment at the Festhallen. Children shake hands with Onkel Hans and adults ogle Miss Oktoberfest. There is a Thanksgiving Day Parade. A miniature castle recalls King Ludwig who was responsible for the original Oktoberfest in Bavaria. The Kitchener-Waterloo Oktoberfest annually attracts over 700,000 visitors and celebrants.

246. Where is the world's longest bar?

The world's longest bar, as attested by the editors of the *Guinness Book of Records*, runs part of the length of Lulu's Roadhouse, a bar, restaurant, dining room, and nightclub complex with three stages located off Highway 401 outside Kitchener, Ontario. As for the longest bar in the world, there are actually two bars at Lulu's. One is 340 feet in length; the other is 300 feet. The roadhouse has the capacity to serve up to 3,000 seated and standing patrons.

247. How many newly married couples honeymoon each year at Niagara Falls?

Niagara Falls is one of the world's wonders. Part of its attraction is its claim to be "the honeymoon capital of the world." Each year fifteen million visitors are attracted by the two cataracts, so there are elaborate tourist facilities and attractions at the two cities with the same name in the Province of Ontario and in the State of New York. Casinos are now attracting even larger numbers.

It is estimated that about 25,000 of the visitors are newly married couples. Those who care to identify themselves as honeymooners are offered special gifts and price reductions. The association of Niagara Falls and romance goes back to the middle of the nineteenth century when it became a North American tradition for newly married couples to take the train to honeymoon at Niagara Falls. Indeed, on his visit to the Falls in 1882, Oscar Wilde suggested, "Niagara Falls must be the second major disappointment of North American married life."

248. The largest lake that lies entirely within Canada is shaped like a giant amoeba. What is the name of that lake?

Great Bear Lake in the Northwest Territories is the largest lake that lies entirely within Canada. It is the eighth-largest lake in the world and the fourth largest in North America. It is 320 kilometres long, up to 175 kilometres wide, and 413 metres deep at one point. As the writer James Marsh noted, it is shaped like a giant amoeba with five great arms – Keith, McVicar, McTavish, Dease, and Smith – which meet in a common centre.

249. Which city is farther north, Venice or Halifax?

Most people assume Halifax is a more northern city than Venice in Italy. But the truth is the opposite. The Nova Scotian capital lies south of the Italian seaport.

Halifax's latitude is 44° 39' N, whereas Venice's is 45° 27' N. Therefore the Nova Scotian city is 88' south of the Italian city. As one degree of latitude is the equivalent of 110 kilometres, Halifax lies roughly 100 kilometres south of Venice.

250. How much larger was the Soviet Union than Canada?

Everyone knows that the Soviet Union was the world's largest country. Every Canadian knows that the world's second-largest country is Canada. But few people have any idea of their relative sizes and the fact that the Soviet Union was considerably larger than Canada.

The Soviet Union covered an immense geographical area of 8,649,490 square miles – one-sixth the earth's land area. Canada covers an area of merely 3,849,670 square miles. The difference in size is 4,799,820 square miles. Thus the area covered by the Soviet Union was more than twice the area covered by Canada.

But the Soviet Union – formally the Union of Soviet Socialist Republics – was less a single country than it is a federal union of fifteen republics, the largest being the Russian Soviet Federated Socialist Republic. A number of the republics were independent nations in the past and regained their independent status in 1991 with the collapse of the Soviet Union.

How large was the largest republic, the Russian SFSR? By itself it covered an area of 6,593,391 square miles. So Russia by itself is 2,743,721 square miles larger than Canada.

The world's third-largest country is the United States of America which covers 3,623,420 square miles. Canada and the United States combined cover 7,473,090 square miles – an area larger than Russia but not larger than the Soviet Union. Mexico covers 761,604 square miles. The combined areas of Canada, the United States, and Mexico come to 8,234,694 square miles. Add to that the area of the Republic of South Africa (435,868 square miles) and they are approximately the same size of the gigantic and once-powerful Soviet Union!

251. Where in the country is there the smallest and finest public collection of Canadian art?

Perhaps the smallest and finest public collection of Canadian art is at Riverbrink. The gallery and library overlook the Niagara River at Queenston, Ontario, housing more than one thousand works of art – paintings, drawings, prints, decorative arts – and over five thousand volumes on Canadian history and art – a wealth of unfamiliar works.

Riverbrink was designed and built as a private home by Samuel E. Weir (1898-1981), a prosperous and public-minded lawyer who practised in London, Ontario, before retiring to Queenston. The Samuel E. Weir Collection and Library of Art was established by the terms of his will as a public trust. Riverbrink is open to members of the public who will marvel at the unpretentious display of Krieghoffs, Kanes, and Suzor-Côtés, the Tom Thomsons, A.Y. Jacksons, and Lawren Harrises, and the Augustus John and Sir Jacob Epstein sculptures. Also on display is a Kenneth Forbes portrait of Samuel E. Weir, the benefactor, who lies buried on the grounds of Riverbrink.

252. What would Canada be like had the United States insisted on acting on the slogan "Fifty-four Forty or Fight!"?

The slogan of the Democratic Party of the United States in 1844 was "Fifty-four Forty or Fight!" The martial slogan was originally the rallying cry of U.S. Senator William Allen who demanded that the United States extend the boundary line between Oregon and the Canadian Northwest all the way up to present-day Prince Rupert, British Columbia. However, the Democratic President James K. Polk reached a compromise with Great Britain and established the 49th parallel as the boundary line between the United States and the British colonies of North America.

Had the boundary been fixed at 54 ° 40', to meet the demands of Allen and the Democratic Party, Western Canada would be very much smaller than it is today. Everything south of a line drawn from Prince Rupert on the West Coast of present-day British Columbia all the way to the mouth of James Bay, with the exception of Canada West which huddled the northern shores of the Great Lakes, would be incorporated into the American Union. Victoria, Vancouver, Edmonton, Calgary, Winnipeg, etc., would be American cities, many of them no doubt under new names. The incorporation of such a vast territory would entail the creation of at least half a dozen American States, plus the diminishment – and impoverishment – of Eastern and Central Canada.

253. Is it possible for naturalists to "read" a lake's shoreline in the clouds?

Surprisingly, the answer to this question is yes. Canoeists report that in the wilderness areas of the north, the clouds in the sky on occasion accommodate themselves to the shoreline of lakes. Eric W. Morse described the phenomenon in *Freshwater Saga: Memoirs of a Lifetime of Wilderness Canoeing in Canada* (1987):

> When we tired of thinking about the shape of the shoreline, we would read pictures into the clouds, or simply let the mind wander for hours at a time. Usually, the clouds that built up during the day would give a perfect outline of the shore, because of the warm air rising from the land. Even each small island would have its "cloud-map" overhead, and more than once we would locate a low-lying island by its cloud before we could actually see the island. This cloud-pattern phenomenon is often noticeable when flying over any of the Great Lakes in summer.

The climatic phenomenon, at one time useful to native canoeists and voyageurs, is of passing interest to latter-day, recreational canoeists.

254. Where and when was the first game of soccer played in early Canada?

The earliest recorded game of soccer in what today constitutes Canada was played at a harbour on Baffin Island on 21 August 1586 by sailors aboard the *Sunshine* and the *North Sea*. These were ships in the fleet of the English mariner John Davis who was commanding his second voyage in search of the North West Passage.

The sailors played games against themselves ("some of our company") but also games against Inuit ("one and thirtie of the people of the countrey"). The account of the English-Inuit match preserved by the English historian Richard Hakluyt makes out that Inuit had a lot to learn about the game: "Divers times they did wave us on shore to play with them at the football, and some of our company went on shore to play with them, and our men did cast them downe as soone as they did come to strike the ball."

255. Is Canada's largest city ranked among the world's twenty-five largest cities?

Toronto may be Canada's largest city, but it does not rank among the world's twenty-five largest cities. Toronto's world rank in terms of population is twenty-seventh. In terms of population density, it ranks ninety-fourth. In the *Book of World City Rankings* (1986) by Immanuel Ness and Stephen T. Collins, Toronto's population is given as 2,998,947 and its population density is given as 2,497 persons per square mile. Mexico City is considered by this source to be the world's most populous city.

256. Did Newfoundland ever offer to sell Labrador?

On three occasions Newfoundland offered to sell Labrador to Canada, but the Dominion declined each offer. As Bren Walsh pointed out in *More Than a Poor Majority: The Story of Newfoundland's Confederation with Canada* (1985), "In 1890 the price was reported to be $9 million, in 1923 the bargaining commenced at $30 million, and then dropped to half that figure, and in 1932 it was reportedly offered for about $110 million." In 1949 Newfoundland and Labrador entered Confederation, so without a sale the territory became part of Canada.

257. When did the so-called Battle of Labrador occur?

The Battle of Labrador is the title of a cartoon drawn around 1940 by the American humourist James Thurber as part of his series of cartoons titled "The War Between Men and Women." The pen-and-ink drawing is reproduced in *A Thurber Carnival* (1962). It shows men and women pitilessly pelting each other with snowballs.

258. Where will you find the log cabin – and the replica of the log cabin – built in the Yukon by the author Jack London?

Jack London, the American author and adventurer, spent youthful years in 1897-98 prospecting for gold in the Yukon. The vein he succeeded in working was literary rather than auriferous. The would-be prospector erected a rustic log cabin at Henderson Creek. It was moved to Dawson in 1965 where it occupies land not far from the log cabin once owned by Robert W. Service. Both are prime tourist attractions.

Visitors to London's hometown of Oakland, California, should make their way to Jack London Square. In the midst of the Square they will find a reconstruction of London's log cabin. Inside is the slab of wood into which he carved these words: "Jack London Miner Author January 27 1898."

259. Where is the Malamute Saloon?

Anybody who has ever heard anything about the Klondike Gold Rush has heard about the Malamute saloon. The saloon is the setting of Robert W. Service's popular poem "The Shooting of Dan McGrew." The ballad was included in Service's first collection *The Spell of the Yukon* (1907). It refers to the saloon in its first lines: "A bunch of the boys were whooping it up in the Malamute saloon; / The kid that handles the music-box was hitting a rag-time tune...."

Service spells it "Malamute." In Service's day there was a Malemute Saloon (spelled with an e rather than an a). It was located in Ester, a town near Cripple Creek, about ten miles west of Fairbanks, Alaska. The saloon was reopened in modern times, readings of Service's verses are staged there, and it is a prime tourist attraction – all because of the ballad.

Whichever way it is spelled, the word "malemute" refers to a dog bred by Malemuit Inuit of Western Alaska. At one time Europeans used the word as a contemptuous way of referring to Inuit.

260. What is "lower" about Lower Canada and "upper" about Upper Canada?

When the Province of Quebec was divided along geographical lines, the names Lower Canada and Upper Canada were applied to the two parts of the division. They were used from 1791 to 1841; thereafter Lower Canada was known as Canada East, and Upper Canada was called Canada West. In 1867 they became, respectively, the Province of Quebec and the Province of Ontario.

The designations "lower" and "upper" refer to the lower and upper reaches of the St. Lawrence River. The point of demarcation is the mouth of the Ottawa River: everything east of the Ottawa is lower, everything west is upper.

261. How many Canadians winter in Florida each year?

The State of Florida is a popular winter vacation destination for Canadians both French and English. As the journalist Richard Gwyn explained in *The 49th Paradox* (1985): "On any day in January and February, there are about one million Canadians, or four per cent of the total population, in Florida, and also great numbers – this is one of the prime cultural distinctions between eastern and western Canada – in Hawaii. For all these people, the U.S. has become an essential extension of their native land, for a winter or two or year-round once they retire, except for summer visits to children and grandchildren."

Prime Minister Jean Chrétien once wittily suggested, "Canadians love Canada, but not for fifty-two weeks of the year." Winterers are known as "snowbirds." It has been estimated that some 350,000 French Canadians alone winter in Florida, largely in or around the Atlantic coast resort community called Hollywood. About 50,000 French Canadians have retired permanently to Florida. The Quebec-made movie *La Florida* (1993) pokes fun at the "snowbirds."

262. Are any Canadian newspapers published in Florida?

The number of Canadians who spend the winters in Florida is large enough to warrant the publication of two local newspapers. The weekly papers which appear between December and April are *The Sun-Times of*

Canada from Tampa and *Canadian News* from Auburndale. Since late 1991, winter residents have been able to subscribe to *The Globe and Mail*, same-day delivery, six days a week.

263. Name a federal constituency that has elected four Prime Ministers.

Prince Albert in northern Alberta has elected Sir Wilfrid Laurier, W.L. Mackenzie King, John G. Diefenbaker, and Joe Clark, all of whom at the time were or subsequently served as Prime Ministers of Canada.

264. Where does the singer Rita MacNeil make her home?

Rita MacNeil, the popular Maritime singer and songwriter, makes her home in an old farmhouse at Big Pond. Big Pond is a village on the outskirts of Sydney, Cape Breton Island, Nova Scotia. Her finest songs celebrate the enduring values of that part of the world.

265. Who was the first person to sail the North West Passage?

It was not until 1988 that the North West Passage was sailed. The transit was accomplished by the adventurer Jeff MacInnis, son of the deep-sea explorer Joseph MacInnis, and photographer Mike Beedell. They sailed and hauled their vessel, *Perception*, an 18-foot catamaran, 4,000 kilometres from Inuvik in the Western Arctic to Pond Inlet in the Eastern Arctic. The ordeal took them three summers to accomplish – from July 1986 to August 1988. Theirs was the first attempt to sail the Passage since the disappearance of Sir John Franklin's expedition in 1845. They followed in the wake of the RCMP vessel, *St. Roch*, which made the transit twice under the power of steam. The story of the sailing is told in *Polar Passage: The Historic First Sail through the Northwest Passage* (1989) by Jeff MacInnis with Wade Rowland.

266. How many "north poles" are there?

There are five "north poles," according to the naturalist and author Barry Lopez in his book *Arctic Dreams: Imagination and Desire in a Northern Landscape* (1986). They are as follows: The North Pole, the Geographic

North Pole, the North Magnetic Pole, the North Geomagnetic Pole, and the Pole of Inaccessibility.

267. Was the referendum on Newfoundland's union with Canada rigged?

Newfoundlanders voted twice on whether or not they wanted to confederate with Canada.

In the first referendum, held on 3 June 1948, a total of 155,677 Newfoundlanders voted for Commission Government (14%), Confederation with Canada (41%), or Responsible Government (45%). In the second referendum, held on 22 July of that year, a total of only 149,657 Newfoundlanders voted for Confederation with Canada (52%) or Responsible Government (48%).

Why were 6,020 votes fewer cast in the second referendum than in the first referendum? Was there a conspiracy to suppress ballots? Harold Horwood, no believer in the conspiracy theory, answered these questions in his book *Joey* (1989):

> One or two writers have even published the wild suggestion that the second referendum was fraudulent, and that seven thousand votes for responsible government were destroyed, all as part of the official conspiracy – this fraud being carried out, somehow or other, under the noses of scrutineers from the various responsible government parties, who sat in all the polling booths.

> Such speculations could only have been made by people who knew nothing about the social realities of Newfoundland in 1948. On June 3, when the first referendum was held, nearly everyone was at home. On July 22, when the second referendum was held, almost ten thousand fishermen were at sea, and only a minority of them managed to reach a polling both. Few of the Labrador floaters (as distinct from the stationers) and few of the banking crews, got the chance to vote at all. Had they been able to reach polling booths, the confederate majority would have been increased accordingly.

268. Is Meech the proper spelling of the lake's name?

No. Meech Lake is the official name of a small lake in Gatineau Park. Beside the lake stands the Thomas L. Willson House where, on 30 April 1987, the Meech Lake Constitutional Accord was signed by the prime minister and the provincial premiers. The lake bears the last name of the earliest settler in the area, Asa Meech, a Congregational minister from New England, who settled beside the lake in the mid 1820s.

On the 1870 plan of the region, the lake is identified as L. Charité and, according to Alan Rayburn in "Place Names" in *Canadian Geographic*, April-May 1988, it was named after a French settler François Lacharité or an Irishman who may have been called Lacharity. However, attached to the plan was the name Meach, a spelling confirmed by the Geographic Board of Canada in 1931. The Board upheld this spelling when it was asked by Marion Meech, a descendant of Asa, to change or correct the Meach spelling.

In 1982, the National Capital Commission sent the Commission de toponymie du Québec a copy of Asa Meech's will and other documents and the Commission formally changed the name to Lac Meech. Since 1982 the official name is Lac Meech. English-speakers refer to it by its English name: Meech Lake. The historian Ramsay Cook, in "Alice in Meachland or the Concept of Quebec as 'A Distinct Society,'" a polemical article which appears in Pierre Elliott Trudeau's *With a Bang, Not a Whimper* (1988), distinguishes between "Meach Lake" and "Meech Lake."

269. What is the name of the island in the Niagara River that separates the Horseshoe or Canadian Falls and the American Falls?

Goat Island, situated in the Niagara River at the brink of the Falls, separates the two cataracts.

270. How much of the flow of Niagara Falls is diverted before it goes over the brink?

At least half the flow of the Niagara River is diverted above the Falls for hydroelectric purposes. It is said that 93 million gallons of water a minute would plunge over the brink without diversion. Diversion was introduced in 1893. International treaties call for a minimum of 100,000 cubic feet per second to run over the Falls in daylight hours and half as much at night during the tourist season.

271. Where did Marcel Marceau make his North American début?

Marcel Marceau, the French mime, made his North American début in the 1954 production of Igor Stravinsky's musical composition *A Soldier's Tale*, which featured Alexander Schneider as the wandering violinist. The premiere took place at the Stratford Festival in 1954. Since then Marceau has toured North America on many occasions.

272. Who is known as the Cousteau of the Arctic?

The fame of the French scientist, ecologist, and adventurer Jacques Cousteau has spread around the world. Dr. Joseph MacInnis is world renowned, if not yet famous, for his similar work and concerns connected with the Arctic. Born in Toronto and trained as a physician, MacInnis is a poet as well as a marine scientist who has specialized in underwater survival. He was the first person to dive beneath the North Pole in his Sub-Igloo, now on permanent display at the Living Sea Pavilion in Florida's Disney World. In 1975, he persuaded Prince Charles to dive beneath the waters of Resolute Bay, "holding a big black umbrella aloft and wearing a very English bowler perched rakishly atop his divine helmet. The effect was a sort of princely Mary Poppins," according to journalist Frank Rasky.

273. Who walked upside down at the North Pole?

National Geographic's centennial issue, celebrating one hundred years of exploration, concluded with an amusing stunt photograph. It showed Joseph MacInnis and Gilbert Grosvenor, the magazine's former editor, defying the laws of gravity with buoyancy, literally standing on their heads under the ice at the North Pole. First they inflated their red neoprene rubber diving suits with extra air from a buoyancy compensator chamber. Their weightless bodies could thus be pictured strolling upside down on the ice ceiling transformed into an ice floor, as though the pair were ambling arm-in-arm on a leisurely moon walk.

So wrote Frank Rasky in "Dr. Joe MacInnis: Canada's Ace Aquanaut," *Leisure Ways*, April 1990.

274. How were the prairies originally organized?

In 1869, the Canadian government divided the prairie lands into a series of townships, six miles square, each divided into thirty-six sections. Each section included four, 160-acre quarter-sections. Townships were numbered from the United States border and ran east-west from the first meridian which went through Fort Garry, Manitoba. North-south roads were one mile apart, while east-west roads were two miles apart. A similar pattern was adopted for homesteading on the American plains. In this way the prairies and the plains were turned into a grid.

275. Where in San Francisco is there a memorial to a Canadian Indian?

There is a memorial to the Canadian Indian who is known as the Lily of the Mohawks in the cemetery attached to Mission San Francisco de Asis. The mission is popularly known as Mission Dolores. This mission building, completed in 1791, is the oldest intact standing building in San Francisco.

Among the memorials in the cemetery there is a small marble plinth which bears the inscription: "Prayerful Memory of the Faithful Indians." The plinth holds the small ceramic head of a young Indian woman and the identification "Kateri Tekakwitha (1656-1680)." Tekakwitha died in Caughnawaga after she converted to Christianity.

276. What is the meaning of the word "Ontario"?

The word "Ontario" is composed of two Huron words, ontara (lake) and the ending -io (good, large, or beautiful). The place name was adapted from native use and adopted by the French in the late 16th century. "So arose Ontario, meaning vaguely 'fine lake,'" wrote George R. Stewart in *Names on the Land* (1967).

277. How many of the Great Lakes bear names of native origin?

There are five Great Lakes: Superior, Michigan, Huron, Ontario and Erie. All their names are derived from the native languages of the Indians of the areas in the late 16th century except Superior which was named by the French (Lac Supérieur).

278. What is the meaning of the word "Niagara"?

George R. Stewart answered that question in *Names on the Land* (1967):

> A French priest came to an Indian town called Ongniaahra, 'point of land cut in two,' because it stood near Lake Ontario, where a wide river cut through the land. Farther up this river, the Indians said, was a waterfall; but the priest did not go to look at it, probably thinking all waterfalls were alike. The French remembered the name of that town, and called the river after it, and later the waterfall. But they twisted it on their tongues until it became Ongiara and finally Niagara."

279. Is there an Indian reserve or reservation that crosses the international border?

The Akwesasne Reserve straddles the Canada-United States border. Six thousand Mohawks live in Canada, five thousand in the United States. The closest cities are Cornwall, Ontario, and Massena, New York. It is the only Indian reserve or reservation in North America that straddles an international border. Cigarette and arms smuggling are common. In the 1990s, the reserve was divided over the issue of gambling, as bingo halls and gambling casinos were permitted on the American side but at the time not on the Canadian side of the line.

280. At how many points is it legal to cross the Canada-U.S. border?

There are 96 legal border crossing points, and thousands of points that are not legal. Every year more than 100 million people cross legally. The border is guarded, in Canada, by the Royal Canadian Mounted Police and in the United States by the U.S. Border Patrol.

281. What is the so-called Evergreen Triangle?

The Evergreen Triangle is a reference to the area bounded by Vancouver and Victoria in British Columbia and Seattle in the State of Washington. It brings to mind the fact that this West Coast region of North America, which cuts across the Canada-United States border, has characteristic environmental, social, technical, and developmental features.

282. What is Maritime Union?

Maritime Union is the notion that the three Maritime provinces – Nova Scotia, New Brunswick, Prince Edward Island – should identify common needs, define common goals, and move towards some form of common market and perhaps political integration, along the lines of the European Union. The notion first found expression in 1970 in a study called "Report on Maritime Union." Two decades later the idea was rekindled by then New Brunswick Premier Frank McKenna.

283. Which cities always have "white Christmases"?

Three cities always have "white Christmases" and will presumably continue to have them. These are Quebec City, Winnipeg, and Saskatoon. As long as meteorological records have been kept, these three Canadian cities – and no others – have experienced snow on December 25.

284. What place name went from "waiting" to "hope" to "spear"?

Cape Spear in Newfoundland is the most easterly point of North America. Its name first appeared on a Portuguese map issued in 1505 as Cauo de la spera, which could mean "place of waiting." The small bay near here was a point of rendezvous for the Grand Banks fishery. In the 1540s, French maps identify the point as Cap d'Espoir, or Cape of Hope. According to Alan Rayburn, writing in "Place Names" in *Canadian Geographic*, February-March 1987, the English fishermen and cartographers pronounced and spelled this as "Cape Spear."

285. Does any part of Canada lie south of the northern boundary of California?

Middle Island, the most southerly land feature of Canada, lies in Lake Erie at latitude 41°41'N. It is an unoccupied island due south of Point Pelee Island, Canada's most southerly occupied point. Middle Island lies so far south that it lies south of the northern boundary of the State of California.

286. What did Vitus Bering first note in 1741?

The Danish-born explorer Vitus Bering, during a voyage of discovery on behalf of the Russian government, first noted the existence of Mount St. Elias on 16 July 1741. This mountain, which lies on the western boundary of the Yukon Territory with Alaska, is the fourth highest peak in North America.

287. Is it true that two brothers founded Ontario in 1882?

Surprisingly, yes.

The Canadian-born brothers are George and William B. Chaffey and they were irrigational land developers. In the fall of 1882 their operation, The Ontario Land Company, staked out the townsite between the Santa Ana Mountains and the Santa Ana Canyon. Here the Chaffeys established "the Model Colony of Ontario." They gave the community the name of their native Province of Ontario. The Chaffeys are given recognition as the founders of the City of Ontario, San Bernardino County, Southern California. In 1886, they sold their business interests and left the United States, as they had earlier left Canada, for Australia.

At one time the City of Ontario was celebrated for the "Gravity Mule Car" (the narrow-gauge tram was hauled up the foothills by mule-power, the tram with mule aboard descended by gravity power); for the first successful hydro-electric plant in Western America; for its model irrigation works; and for the factory that produced the famous Hotpoint Iron. Today it has a population of approximately 130,500, and is familiar as the site of the Ontario International Airport which serves the flight needs of much of Southern California.

288. How many Ontarios and Torontos are there?

There is only one Ontario in Canada and it is the name of one of the ten provinces. Yet Ontario is a popular place name in the United States. There are communities called Ontario in the following states: California, Indiana, Ohio, Oregon, New York, Wisconsin, Virginia. (A place called Antero is to be found in Colorado.)

Toronto, the capital of the Province of Ontario, is also a popular place name. There are Torontos in the following states: Iowa, Kansas, Ohio, and South Dakota. Variations of the name are Taranto, Trani, and Trento in Italy and Trona in California. There are also Tran Ninh (Laos) and Tomato (Arkansas). The information comes from columnist and place-name observer William Burrill writing in *Eye*, 17 June 1993.

289. Is there a Canada in California?

Not quite, but there is a community called La Cañada Flintridge in the greater Los Angeles area. The Spanish-Mexican name La Cañada is pronounced "la can-yah'-da." It means "The Glen between the Hills."

A residential community with a population of 21,000, 8.5 square miles in extent, it lies south of the Sierra Madre Mountains and north of the California cities of Glendale and Pasadena. Its history goes back to the Rancho La Cañada land grant of 1843. La Cañada itself was established in 1875. Nearby Flintridge was named after U.S. Senator Frank P. Flint. Incorporation of La Cañada Flintridge took place in 1976. The community prides itself on the quality of its schools.

290. What was the Royal Arctic Theatre?

Plays performed between 1819 and 1879 by officers and members of the crews of vessels wintering in the Canadian Arctic are today referred to under the generic – and somewhat generous – title "Royal Arctic Theatre." Both classical plays (like *The Taming of the Shrew*) and original entertainments (there is one called *King Glumpus*) were performed on board ships of sail, according to theatre historian David Gardner writing in *The Oxford Companion to Canadian Theatre* (1989).

291. Does an episode of *The Avengers* take place in Montreal?

Indeed, it does. "Mission to Montreal" is the title of an episode in the first series of the British TV espionage series released in 1961-62, which starred actor Patrick Macnee as the secret agent known as Mr. John Steed. The episode of *The Avengers* takes place aboard a luxury liner cruising from England to Montreal, and the action concerns the theft by enemy agents of a microfilm of DEW Line secrets.

In later episodes, Mr. Steed was paired with a series of curvaceous sidekicks, including Miss Tara King (played by Canadian-born actress Linda Thorson). Four episodes of *The New Avengers* series in 1971, which enjoyed some Canadian financing, had locales set in this country. For further particulars, see Dave Rogers's study *The Avengers: All 161 Original Episodes – Story, Cast, Pictures* (1983).

292. What is the "braillard de Madeleine"?

The French words mean "the sobber of Madeleine," and they refer to the little Gaspé community of Sainte-Madeleine-de-la-Rivière-Madeleine. The legend goes that in 1814 a missionary arrived to deliver the people of Madeleine from a spirit that was moaning and groaning in the deep forest.

293. What does Gaspésie mean?

Gaspé is derived from the Micmac word *gespeg* which means "lands end." The town of over 17,000 in 1991 is named Gaspé; the entire region which extends into the Atlantic is called Gaspésie.

294. How many Québécois have Acadian roots?

It has been estimated that as many as one million Québécois have Acadian roots.

295. Where is the oldest Marian Shrine in North America?

Notre-Dame du Cap Shrine is the oldest and most important Marian shrine in North America. The church and shrine are located at Notre-Dame du Cap, northeast of Trois-Rivières, Quebec. The Roman Catholic site traces its history back to Jesuit missionaries who arrived here as early as 1634. The parish church, the oldest preserved in its original state in Canada, was dedicated to the Virgin Mary in 1720. Thousands of pilgrims and tourists are attracted to the shrine each year.

296. What is the word for "township" in Quebec?

The word for "township" in Quebec is canton. Adoption of the word used in Switzerland for a territorial division was recommended by the novelist Antoine Guérin-Lajoie, author of *Jean Rivard, le Défricheur* (1858).

The novelist was the first person to use the words Cantons-de-l'est to describe the Eastern Townships, Quebec's resort region south of Montreal. The words are still used but they have been overtaken by the word Estrie which was coined by Monsignor Maurice O'Bready in 1946; the French Academy approved its use as meaning "Kingdom of the East." "Estrie" received official recognition in Quebec in 1981.

297. What was Wolfville's original name?

In 1893, Wolfville, Nova Scotia, became the second officially incorporated town in Canada. It is situated in the Annapolis Valley on the Bay of Fundy. Its original name was Mud Creek. The story goes that in the 1800s this name was changed when the daughter of a local judge was to attend finishing school. She was embarrassed to say she was from Mud Creek, so her father, Judge DeWolf, requested that the name be changed, and it was, so the name now recalls his.

298. Which community is the oldest on the continent north of Mexico?

The oldest community on the continent (north of Mexico) is said to be the parish of Nôtre-Dame which is today part of Quebec City. The Basilique Nôtre-Dame-de-Québec was founded some 350 years ago and has met the needs of parishioners ever since.

299. Which island is known as "forty-two miles of tranquility"?

The chansonnier Félix Leclerc has a song about "quarante-deux milles de choses tranquilles," which translates "forty-two miles of tranquility." He was referring to the circumference of Ile d'Orléans, in the St. Lawrence River near Quebec City, which is classified as an historical district.

300. What is so unusual about the Pont de Québec?

The Pont de Québec is a suspension bridge with a span 549 metres in length between its two main pillars. It crosses the St. Lawrence River and is the world's longest cantilever bridge. During construction its central span collapsed not once but twice – in 1907 and 1916. It was opened to railway traffic in 1917 and to motor traffic in 1929.

The Pierre-Laporte bridge, erected in four years and opened in 1970, is the longest suspension bridge in Canada. It too crosses the St. Lawrence River in the vicinity of Quebec City.

301. What is an MRC in Quebec?

The initials MRC stand for Municipalité régionale de comté, or regional county municipality.

302. What are the Reversing Falls?

The Reversing Falls are rapids and whirlpools located at a crook in the Saint John River in downtown Saint John, New Brunswick, where tide-water arriving from the Bay of Fundy rises above the river emptying into the Bay. The tide rises and falls twice a day, so the phenomenon is apparent from Fallsview Park near low tide and near high tide. The tidal waters are more than fourteen feet higher than the river-water.

303. Which city boasts the Tidal Bore?

The Tidal Bore of the Petitcodiac River is visible twice each day from Bore Park in downtown Moncton, New Brunswick. The waters of the Petitcodiac River roll back upstream in one wave, which can range from inches to two feet in height, due to the tides of the Bay of Fundy.

304. Where is the oldest summer hotel in Canada?

The Shiretown Inn claims to be the oldest summer hotel in Canada. It is located in historic St. Andrews-by-the-Sea, New Brunswick, and was built in 1881. Now part of the Best Western chain, the 26-room inn with dining room and tea room and sidewalk café is open year-round. The first hotel on the site was built here about 1800.

305. Is Quebec larger than Texas?

The Province of Quebec is more than twice the size of the State of Texas. The largest of the provinces, Quebec is seven times the size of the United Kingdom and fifty times the size of Belgium.

306. Did L.M. Montgomery live in Green Gables?

L.M. Montgomery, the author of the "Anne" books, never lived in Green Gables House, Cavendish, Prince Edward Island. It was the pleasant country home of her cousins and their parents, Alexander and Lucy MacNeill, and here, in this comfortable house, the budding author spent many a happy hour. In 1937, Green Gables was restored by Parks Canada.

307. In which province is there an international golf course?

The Province of New Brunswick boasts that it has an international golf course. The club at Four Falls, north of Aroostook, New Brunswick, has its clubhouse and course in Canada and its pro-shop in the adjoining State of Maine in the United States.

308. Which city regards itself as the pewter capital of Canada?

Fredericton, New Brunswick, is often called the pewter capital or the pewtersmith capital of Canada. Many pewtersmiths live and work here, including Ivan (Bill) Crowell, one of the chief craftsmen. It has the New Brunswick Craft School, the only school in the country devoted exclusively to the training of professional artisans.

309. Where is the largest military training area in the Commonwealth?

Canadian Forces Base Gagetown, located in Oromocto, New Brunswick, is the largest military training area in the Commonwealth.

310. Where was coal first mined in North America?

The site of the first coal-mining operation in North America is Minto, New Brunswick.

311. Which province is known for its fiddleheads?

The Province of New Brunswick is renowned for its fiddleheads. The delicious, edible fern is harvested in its marshlands. Tide Head is often called the fiddlehead capital of the world.

312. What folksong festival is held annually at Newcastle?

The Miramichi Folksong Festival is held every August at the town of Newcastle in the Miramichi region of New Brunswick. In 1991, the 34th festival was held here. It included fiddling as well as traditional and contemporary singing by individuals and groups. The festival was founded by the eminent folklorist and native of the region, Louise Manny.

313. What is distinctive about Halifax harbour?

Halifax harbour has been described as a deep sheltered inlet which penetrates nine kilometres inland from the Atlantic coast. It is the largest ice-free port on the east coast of North America and the world's second largest natural harbour. Sydney, Australia, has the world's largest natural harbour.

314. Which two bridges cross the harbour and connect Halifax and Dartmouth?

Halifax and Dartmouth, Nova Scotia, are connected by two bridges. The "old bridge" is the Angus L. MacDonald Bridge, completed in 1955; the "new bridge" is the A. Murray MacKay Bridge, completed in 1979.

315. In which city may be heard the Noon Day Cannon?

The Noon Day Cannon is fired seven days a week from the Citadel in Halifax.

316. Why do the bells toll at Fort Needham Memorial Bell Tower?

The Fort Needham Memorial Bell Tower, a modernist architectural sculpture, was erected in the North End of Halifax, the section most devastated by the Halifax Explosion on 6 December 1917. It was raised to commemorate the victims of the largest single, man-made explosion that occurred before the Atomic Age. Its many bells toll in memory of the 2000 victims of the disaster.

317. Where can you mail a letter from a lighthouse?

Only one of Canada Post's post offices is located in a lighthouse, and that is the post office in the picturesque village of Peggy's Cove, Nova Scotia. It is popular with the community's fifty permanent residents – as well as with droves of tourists who visit the community during the summer months. Its postal code is B0J 2N0.

318. Where is the world's deepest man-made causeway?

The Canso Causeway, which crosses the Strait of Canso and connects Cape Breton Island with mainland Nova Scotia, is the world's deepest man-made causeway. It was officially opened on 13 August 1955. Although a rough-hewn structure, it is known poetically as the Road to the Isles.

319. Why was the Cabot Trail named after John Cabot?

Nova Scotia has many tourist routes which are designated "trails." The scenic Cabot Trail, which hugs the northern tip of Cape Breton Island, bears the name of the famous explorer John Cabot. A plaque at Cape North, just off the Cabot Trail, draws attention to the fact that John Cabot and his son Sebastian Cabot made their historic landfall in 1497 in the vicinity of Cape North.

320. Where are the two oldest permanent settlements in North America?

French mariners established the oldest permanent European settlement in North America on St. Croix Island in the St. Croix River, which separates the State of Maine and the Province of New Brunswick. This was in 1603-1604. The island is now part of the State of Maine and an International Historic Site administered by the National Park Service, U.S. Department of the Interior, in cooperation with the Canadian Government.

St. Croix is considered the first permanent European settlement. The second-oldest such settlement was established not far away at Port Royal, Annapolis Valley, Nova Scotia, in 1604. Each site is officially recognized in its own country.

321. How is the word "Ceilidh" pronounced?

The word "Ceilidh" is commonly encountered on Cape Breton Island. One of the popular tourist routes, for instance, is known as the Ceilidh Trail. The word is Gaelic and has at least three meanings: visiting, sojourning, and pilgrimage. It is pronounced "kay-lee."

322. Where are Gaelic studies taught?

The Gaelic College of Celtic Arts and Crafts is located on a campus of 400 acres at St. Ann's, Cape Breton Island. The College offers full-time summer and part-time winter instruction in traditional Gaelic arts and crafts – from bagpipes, drumming, singing, dancing, and hand-weaving to studies in Gaelic language and literature. It was founded on 26 July 1939.

323. Where is held the International Gathering of the Clans?

Every four years the Scots societies of Nova Scotia unite to sponsor the International Gathering of the Clans. The event is held at The Gaelic College of Celtic Arts and Crafts at St. Ann's, Cape Breton Island. It consists of a week of Highland events, including pipes and drums, dancing and singing and caber-toss. The 54th Gaelic Mod was held in August 1991.

324. What is the sole city on Cape Breton Island?

Sydney is the sole city on Cape Breton Island. After Halifax, it is the second-largest city in Nova Scotia. It was named for Britain's colonial secretary Lord Sydney, as was Sydney, Australia. The Canadian city was developed as a refuge for Loyalists, whereas Australia's was founded as a prison for convicts.

325. Is there a community named after Madame de Maintenon?

Isle Madame on Cape Breton Island, Nova Scotia, was named in honour of Madame de Maintenon, the second wife of Louis XIV of France.

326. Are there government-operated lodges in Nova Scotia?

Three lodges are operated by the Department of Tourism and Culture of the Province of Nova Scotia. These are Liscombe Lodge on the Eastern Shore, near Sherbrooke Village; The Pines Resort at Digby, Annapolis Valley; and Keltic Lodge at Ingonish Beach, Cape Breton Island. All three offer accommodation for the affluent.

327. How many sites are there on Prince Edward Island associated with L.M. Montgomery?

It is hard to say. At times it seems the author Lucy Maud Montgomery is responsible for all the tourism to Prince Edward Island!

Visitors nostalgic about Montgomery's novels often seek out these sites. Here are the ones in Cavendish: Green Gables House; Cavendish

Home; and Gravesite. The Montgomery Birthplace is at nearby New London, and the Anne of Green Gables Museum is close by at Silverbush. The Province of Ontario has signposted the United Church manses she occupied with her minister husband in Leaskdale and Norwood, as well as the park near the house where she spent her declining years in the Swansea district of Toronto.

328. Why is Anne so popular in Japan?

Second to none in popularity in Japan is Anne Shirley, the red-headed heroine of *Anne of Green Gables*, the novel by L.M. Montgomery and the television mini-series starring actress Megan Follows. No one is quite sure why she is so popular, but here are some possible reasons. Japanese girls and women, bound by convention, see Anne as a free spirit, and they find her hair colour exotic. (They call her Akage no An, "Anne of the Red Hair.") The evocatively described island landscape of the books appeals to the Japanese, an island people, who have a pronounced love of nature. The first Anne book was translated by Hanako Muraoka in 1952; the musical has played successfully in Tokyo; Anne dolls and other products are promoted; mini-series based on L.M. Montgomery's novels are frequently telecast; there is an "Anne of Hokkaido" house (it resembles Green Gables) in the Canadian World theme park on the northern island of Hokkaido; and Japanese tourists are sure to include Green Gables at Cavendish, Prince Edward Island, on their itinerary of important sites to visit in North America.

329. If Japanese tourists head for Cavendish, where do Chinese visitors go?

Japanese tourists, familiar with Anne of Green Gables, head for Cavendish, Prince Edward Island. Chinese visitors head for Gravenhurst, Ontario, to visit the Bethune Memorial House, the boyhood home of Norman Bethune, the physician whose devotion to the revolutionaries made him a hero in the eyes of the Chinese Communist Party.

330. Where is the Thumbs Up Church?

During the nineteenth century, soldiers of the British regiments stationed in Fredericton, New Brunswick, referred to Wilmot Church – originally Fredericton Methodist Church, now Wilmot United Church – as the Thumbs Up Church. The reason for this is the large frame church, constructed in 1850, had a 199-foot spire which was extended by a seven-foot, upright-pointing hand with an extended, skyward-pointing finger carved in wood. The spire was removed in 1973 for structural reasons but it is now on display on the landing to the sanctuary. Three other churches in North America are known to have such a symbol, and these are in Nova Scotia, Newfoundland, and Port Gibson, Mississippi.

331. Which church has a William Morris window?

In the 1980s it was determined that one of the windows of Wilmot United Church in Fredericton, New Brunswick, the one with art-nouveau green tracery and four figures, comes from the studio of William Morris. Specifically its two archangels are the work of his chief designer Edward Burne-Jones, a major artist of the pre-Raphaelite school.

332. Where is there a replica of the Silver Dart?

Canada entered the age of aviation on 23 February 1909 when the pilot J.A.D. McCurdy made the first heavier-than-air flight in the British Empire at Baddeck, Cape Breton Island, Nova Scotia. He piloted the Silver Dart, the 33-foot long biplane built by Alexander Graham Bell's Aerial Experiment Association. The original Silver Dart was destroyed in a plane crash some months later.

To mark the 50th anniversary of the event, a re-enactment of the historic flight was held at Baddeck. Local craftspersons constructed replicas. There are now three replicas of the Silver Dart in existence. They are on display in the National Aviation Museum, Rockcliffe, Ottawa; the Royal Air Force Museum, Hendon, England; and at the Birthplace of Canadian Aviation Museum, Baddeck, Nova Scotia.

333. What aviation feature was invented in Canada?

The aileron was invented by the Aerial Experiment Association and incorporated into the wing structure of the Silver Dart which was first flown at Baddeck, Nova Scotia, on 23 February 1909. An aileron is an airfoil which redirects the flow of air across the surface of the wing.

334. Who lived at Clifton?

Clifton is the name of the frame house at Windsor, Nova Scotia, which was built and occupied for five years by Thomas Chandler Haliburton, creator of the literary character Sam Slick. Clifton was built in 1836 and named after Haliburton's wife's family home in Briston, England. While residing here with his family, Haliburton wrote the first of *The Clockmaker* (1836) books. The villa and grounds were acquired by the Province of Nova Scotia as an historic site in 1939.

335. What are the five B's in Alexander Graham Bell's life?

The five B's in the life of Alexander Graham Bell are the initial letters of the following five place names: Brantford, Ontario, where he conceived the notion of the telephone; Boston, Massachusetts, where he built the first telephone; Bras d'Or Lake, which attracted him to Cape Breton Island; Baddeck, Nova Scotia, where he built his summer home and constructed the first hydrofoil; and Beinn Bhreagh (said to be Gaelic for "beautiful hill"), where he built his estate which is still owned by his descendants.

336. What is the Habitation?

The Habitation is the replica of the fur fort established in 1605 by the French under Samuel de Champlain and Sieur de Monts. The fort was erected overlooking the Annapolis Basin, which is fed by the Bay of Fundy, in present-day Nova Scotia. The reconstruction is known as the Port Royal National Historic Site. The community closest to Port Royal is Granville Ferry which is located across the river from the town of Annapolis Royal.

337. How many islands has Mahone Bay?

It is traditional to say that there are 365 islands in Mahone Bay on Nova Scotia's South Shore. One of them, Oak Island, is said to be the site of a pirate's "money pit."

338. Is there treasure on Oak Island?

The truth is that no one knows whether or not any sort of treasure is to be found on Oak Island in Nova Scotia's Mahone Bay. There is said to be a pirate's money pit buried on the island. Excavations to discover it have been intermittently conducted since 1795. It is claimed that more money has been spent here than on any other treasure hunt in the world. During the last two centuries, no treasure of any sort has been excavated. In the 1990s, limited excavation work was being conducted by Triton Alliance Ltd., a Montreal syndicate which sells stock and conducts the profitable tourism operation.

339. Where is North America's first tidal power generating station?

The first tidal power generating station in North America is located on an island near the mouth of the Annapolis River at Annapolis Royal. A turbine propeller is powered by the force of water flowing from the reservoir to the sea, after the lowering tide has receded. Operation commenced in 1982. Its success could lead to the full-scale development of the tidal power of the Bay of Fundy as a source of reliable, renewable electric power.

340. In which state is Roosevelt Campobello International Park?

Roosevelt Campobello Park is a 2,800-acre park on Campobello Island which lies in Passamaquoddy Bay. It is part of the Province of New Brunswick, not the adjoining State of Maine, although the approach by land to the small island is by a bridge across the Narrows from the fishing community of Lubec, Maine. Franklin Delano Roosevelt spent his boyhood summers here. The park was declared open on 13 July 1967.

341. Where is the Dulse Capital of the World?

Grand Manan, the island in the Bay of Fundy, New Brunswick, is known as the Dulse Capital of the World. This edible seaweed, locally called Dark Harbour Dulse, is handpicked at low tide on the west side of the island, landed at Dark Harbour, sun dried, and packaged for export as a condiment and seasoning. It is also nibbled as a snack food.

342. Where will you find the world's largest perogy?

The world's largest perogy is a sculpture that is the centrepiece of Pyrogy Park in the village of Glendon, Alberta. It was erected in August 1991 to mark the centenary of Ukrainian settlement in Canada. The sculpture is 8 metres (26 feet) long and consists of a dumpling, a fork, and a plaque that reads as follows: "European food was first brought to Western Canada in the early 19th century by the working and poor people. It originated as a boiled dumpling and later people added whatever they desired inside."

343. Who is the actress who bought the property on Prince Edward Island once owned by Elmer Harris?

Colleen Dewhurst, the late Montreal-born stage and screen actress, loved to holiday at Bay Fortune on Prince Edward Island. In the 1970s she bought the rambling frame house and cottages on a tract of land owned in the 1930s and 1940s by playwright Elmer Harris (author of *Johnny Belinda*). She summered there with her husband, actor George C. Scott, and their two children. She subsequently sold the property and it is now operated as a popular restaurant named Inn on Fortune Bay, according to Sid Adilman in *The Toronto Star*, 25 August 1991.

344. Where do you eat in Canada?

This question is easy to answer if you have handy a copy of *Where to Eat in Canada*, which is the country's leading national guide book to restaurants, ranging from small eateries to classy dining rooms. The author of the opinionated text is Anne Hardy and the publisher is Oberon Press of Ottawa. Issued annually since 1970, the 1991 edition surveys some 500 eating establishments.

345. Which railway line runs from Whitehorse to Skagway?

The White Pass & Yukon Route, a narrow-gauge railway line, once ran the scenic route of 175 kilometres from Whitehorse, Yukon Territory, to Skagway, Alaska. The line was completed in July 1900 to carry gold prospectors into the Yukon. Today, operated as an excursion train from May to September each year, it takes about 100,000 tourists the 45 kilometres from Skagway to Fraser, British Columbia.

346. Was there ever a Golden Spike?

A couple of ordinary iron spikes were used to mark the completion of the Canadian Pacific Railway in 1885. But a Golden Spike was driven into the rail at Carcross, Yukon Territory, on 29 July 1900 to mark the completion of the narrow-gauge White Pass & Yukon Route.

347. Does Alaska lie north or south of British Columbia?

Both. The bulk of the State of Alaska lies north of the Province of British Columbia, but a small part of the American state, including the town Skagway, lies south of the northern boundary of British Columbia.

348. What is Uncle Sam's Canadian connection?

Uncle Sam, the symbolic American, is usually depicted as a tall, lean, bearded, cagey figure, dressed in the colours of the American flag. The fact that the name originated early in the War of 1812 constitutes its Canadian connection. Until that war, the symbolic American was the Colonial figure, Uncle Jonathan. If the Americans had not fought the British in early Canada, there would be no Uncle Sam today.

The name Uncle Sam recalls the businessman Samuel Wilson (1766-1854), the proprietor of a meatpacking business in Troy, New York. He provisioned the U.S. forces at nearby Greenbush for the Canadian campaign, and was as surprised as anyone to find that his first name had become a byword among the soldiers and then the American people. It took U.S. Congress until 1961 to officially recognize Sam Wilson as the original Uncle Sam. Today the City of Troy makes much of their local hero.

349. Where is the Lester B. Pearson Peace Park?

The Lester B. Pearson Peace Park, a privately owned park open to the public, is found near the town of Tweed, Ontario. It was opened on 1 July 1967 and was named after Lester B. Pearson, Prime Minister and recipient of the Nobel Prize for Peace. The park has slowly fallen into a state of disuse and disrepair. It once boasted an Avenue of the Provinces, with columns for each of the ten provinces; Memorial Gardens; an International Peace Column; a Vietnamese Pavilion; a Mother's Shrine; a Tower of Hope; and a Peace Pagoda Shrine (the sole such structure in the country). Once a year a noted Canadian has received the Man of the Year Award. The park also sponsored an annual contest for poems written on the subject of peace.

350. Are there more moose than people in the Yukon?

No one knows the moose population of the Yukon Territory but the human population in 1991 was 17,925. It is the contention of Max Fraser, author of *The Lost Moose Catalogue* (1979), a compendium of Northern lore, that the moose in the Yukon outnumber the men, women, and children.

351. What is the pronunciation of Bienfait?

The Saskatchewan town of Bienfait bears a French name. It is pronounced, curiously, "Bean Fate."

352. Which province remains on Standard Time all year?

Saskatchewan is the sole province that remains on Standard Time. All the others shift to Daylight Saving Time in the fall and back to Standard Time the following spring.

353. What did Canada Park replace?

Canada Park is a 32,000-hectare public park in Israel, located on a height of land that lies between Jerusalem and Tel Aviv. It was built as a sign of

Canadian-Israeli friendship in 1968, and is approached via John Diefenbaker Parkway which was opened in 1975 by former Prime Minister Diefenbaker. The project, completed in 1984, was sponsored by the Jewish National Fund of Canada.

Razed to create the park were three villages occupied by Palestinians – the villages of Emmaus, Beit Nuba, and Yalu. According to Bob Hepburn, writing in "Wiped off the Map," *The Toronto Star*, 6 October 1991, a group of Christians in Switzerland formed the Association for the Reconstruction of Emmaus as a sign of reconciliation between Arabs and Jews. The village of Emmaus, known in Arabic as Amwas, had many biblical, historical, and cultural associations.

354. Does Elvis have a street in Ottawa named after him?

Elvis Presley – or at least the memory of him – is alive and well in Ottawa. Elvis Lives Lane is the name given a short suburban street by the city council in 1991. In the past the city authorized the naming of other celebrity streets: Paul Anka Drive, Rich Little Drive, and William Shatner Drive. Presley had no connection with Ottawa, but the other celebrities have an Ottawa connection, according to Susan Delacourt writing in *The Globe and Mail*, 16 October 1991.

355. Which province was the last to shift traffic from the left-hand side of the road to the right?

Driving vehicles always on the right-hand side of the road was established by statute in Upper Canada as early as 1812, twenty-three years before driving on the left-hand side was established in England. But other parts of the country followed the British keep-left custom. According to "You Asked Us" in *The Toronto Star*, "British Columbia, New Brunswick, Nova Scotia and Prince Edward Island moved right from the British way between 1922 and 1924." Newfoundland was the last to keep-left, which it did until 1947.

356. Did England prefer Guadeloupe to Canada?

One of the issues of the day in Great Britain between the years 1760 and 1763 was whether the commercial interests of the British Empire were better served by retaining Canada (New France fell in 1759) or the island of Guadeloupe in the West Indies. Over forty pamphlets on the subject were written and distributed. Ultimately it was decided that Canada could be counted upon to supply the products of field and forest, principally furs, whereas the produce of Guadeloupe was limited to the supply of sugar. Britain ceded Guadeloupe to France by the Treaty of 1763 which ended the Seven Years War.

One of the pamphleteers was Benjamin Franklin. His so-called Canada Pamphlet (the title begins *The Interest of Great Britain Considered with Regard to Her Colonies and the Acquisitions of Canada and Guadeloupe* ... (1760) offered arguments in favour of England retaining Guadeloupe! The entire issue is reviewed by the historian William L. Grant in "Canada Versus Guadeloupe, an Episode of the Seven Years War," *American Historical Review*, Volume XVII, October 1911.

357. Could someone swim across the Bering Strait?

The Bering Strait separates Asian Siberia from American Alaska. The strait is about ninety kilometres wide. It is unlikely that anyone would or could swim that distance, especially as the waters are freezing cold throughout the year. It is known, however, that tagged bears have walked from one continent to the other and back again, crossing the Bering Strait by stepping gingerly on ice floes.

358. Who was known as the Baron of Buctouche?

K.C. Irving, the business executive who began his impressive career in 1925 with a gas station in his hometown of Buctouche, New Brunswick, was sometimes called the Baron of Buctouche. Irving's three sons Jim, Arthur, and Jack oversee the Irving interests which touch almost every aspect of the economy of New Brunswick. In the 1980s and 90s, the financial sources ranked the Irving family among the world's ten richest families.

359. How many U.S. cities are larger than Toronto?

Three cities in the United States have populations greater than Toronto's. The cities are New York, Los Angeles, and Chicago.

360. What is known as the Spirit of Haida Gwaii?

The Spirit of Haida Gwaii is the name given by master Haida carver Bill Reid to his massive sculpture which, since 18 November 1991, has graced the courtyard of the Canadian Embassy in Washington, D.C. The sculpture consists of a six-metre-long, black, bronze canoe paddled by its thirteen passengers –including the trickster Raven, the Eagle, and mythological beasts and beings from Haida mythology.

Photographs of the sculpture appear in Robert Bringhurst's *The Black Canoe: Bill Reid and the Spirit of Haida Gwaii* (1991). "Haida Gwaii" means Islands of the People, the traditional Haida name for the Queen Charlotte Islands. Reid regards the work itself as a lifeboat for his people and for man and nature.

361. What is 7,777 kilometres long?

The Trans-Canada Highway, the longest paved roadway in the world, is described as being 7,777 kilometres in length. It was officially opened on 3 September 1962.

362. What is the status of Machais Seal Island?

Machais Seal Island lies off the coast of New Brunswick and Maine. Its sovereignty remains undetermined despite the fact that Canadians have manned a lighthouse on the island since 1832, and a Canadian game warden patrols it in summer. The island, 600 yards long by 300 yards wide, has no permanent residents.

363. Which National Park includes Canada's highest mountain?

Kluane National Park, Yukon Territory, includes Mt. Logan, Canada's highest mountain. The same park has the world's largest expanse of non-polar ice fields.

364. When did cross-border shopping reach its apogee?

Canadians have always engaged in cross-border shopping. Until the late 1980s it was merely one of the perks at the end of a trip to the United States for business or vacation purposes. The passage of the Free Trade Agreement, the imposition of the Goods and Services Tax, the statutes against Sunday shopping, and the recession of the early 1990s so increased the price of goods in this country, both those made in Canada and those imported from the United States and elsewhere, that citizens began to make regular, even weekly trips over the U.S. border to buy not just appliances, but also food, petrol and other staples. Though paying customs duties and other taxes levied on them, shoppers were still saving money. Cross-border shopping reached its apogee during the summer of 1990, when Canadians made a record number of 53.2 million trips with expenditures of $1 billion. The decline the following year was the result of the drop in the value of the Canadian dollar, the country's low inflation rate, more competitive retail pricing, and Ontario's introduction of Sunday shopping.

365. Is there a village where the GST is neither paid nor collected?

The village of Elstow, which lies southeast of Saskatoon, Saskatchewan, came to national attention in 1991 when its mayor, with the backing of the village council, declared Elstow to be a "GST-Free Zone." Although the declaration was legal, it is illegal to avoid or to evade paying the 7% consumption tax. Elstow has a population of 150. Presumably its merchants simply absorb the GST in their prices and costs.

366. Who first completed a solo trek to the North Pole?

Naomi Uemura, a professional explorer, was the first person to complete a solo trek to the North Pole. On foot and by dogsled he travelled from Cape Columbia, Ellesmere Island, to the Pole, covering the 800 kilometres in fifty-seven days. Once he had attained the Pole, he was airlifted back to his base camp. The Japanese explorer was in good shape for the polar ordeal. He practised by climbing Mount Everest and by dogsledding from Greenland to Alaska.

367. Is there a museum on Parliament Hill?

A museum on Parliament Hill? Perhaps the Senate Chamber might be regarded as a museum. Another answer is that a suite of offices in the East Block containing the offices of Sir John A. Macdonald, Sir George-Etienne Cartier, Governor General Lord Dufferin and the original Privy Council Office (restored since 1981) constitute "one of the best little museums in Canada," in the words of Stevie Cameron in *Ottawa Inside Out* (1990).

368. What famous landmark is constantly moving backward?

Niagara Falls. "The rim is being worn down by the millions of gallons of water that rush over it every minute, and the falls recede about two and a half feet a year. At that rate, the falls will meet up with Lake Erie (now about twenty miles away) in forty thousand years or so." So wrote Scot Morris in *The Emperor Who Ate the Bible and More Strange Facts and Useless Information* (1991).

369. Is Lake Superior the world's biggest freshwater lake?

No. Lake Superior is the world's largest freshwater lake, covering some 32,000 square miles, but not its biggest. Lake Baikal in Siberia covers less than 12,000 square miles, but because it is so deep (over one mile in places), it has more volume than any other lake. "Lake Baikal accounts for one fifth of all the volume of all the freshwater lakes in the world," according to Scot Morris in *The Emperor Who Ate the Bible and More Strange Facts and Useless Information* (1991).

370. Do the Badlands resemble the Barren Lands?

Not at all. The Badlands are found in Southern Alberta. They are a desert-like region rich in dinosaur fossils. The Barren Lands, located in the Northwest Territories, are a vast expanse of tundra that sparsely supports vegetation, animal life, and bands of northern Indians.

371. What is the connection between Dharmsala and Canada?

The connection between the city of Dharmsala in Northern India and the Dominion of Canada is the life of a statesman. James Bruce (1811-1863), the 8th Earl of Elgin, served as Governor General of Canada and thereafter as Viceroy and Governor General of India. He died in Dharmsala and he is buried in the cemetery of the Church of Saint John in the Wilderness, where a monument was erected in his honour. Dharmsala, near Simla, is the seat of the government-in-exile of the Dalai Lama of Tibet.

372. What was the best-known streetcorner in Toronto in the late nineteenth century?

The intersection of King Street and Simcoe Street in Toronto acquired an amusing reputation with the construction of St. Andrew's Church in 1876. Across the street from the church stood Government House. The third corner was occupied by Upper Canada College, and the fourth was the location of a popular tavern. The four corners were known locally as Legislation, Education, Damnation, and Salvation. Today only the Presbyterian church remains, so Salvation seems to have won the day!

373. What is unique about the mace of the Northwest Territories?

The mace of the government of the Northwest Territories was specially designed and handmade in 1956 from oak from the 1825 wreck of the H.M.S. Fury, a copper kettle from a Lapland reindeer herder, discs of pure gold, muskox horns from the high Arctic, porcupine quill work, a Narwhal tusk, and much more. No other mace resembles it. The arresting-looking mace is on display in the Legislative Assembly of the Northwest Territories in Yellowknife.

374. Has Lake Ontario ever frozen over in winter?

Only twice in the past 150 years has it been possible to walk across the ice on Lake Ontario from Toronto, Ontario, to Rochester, New York. The lake froze over in the winter of 1875 and again in 1934. Lake Erie regularly freezes over, but during severe winters Lake Ontario remains open.

375. Where is there a fifty-foot statue of Hiawatha?

A fifty-foot statue of Hiawatha is a tourist attraction at Ironwood, Michigan. There is no statue to the Canadian hero Hiawatha in Canada.

376. What is the meaning of Auyuittuq?

The word Auyuittuq in Inuktitut means "the land that never melts." It is a good description of the land on Baffin Island, Northwest Territories, which is now part of Auyuittuq National Park. Much of the parkland is covered by the Penny Ice Cap.

377. What happened at Wrangel Island?

In 1921, British and Canadian flags were raised on Wrangel Island in the Chukchi Sea near Bering Strait when a Canadian expedition claimed the island for the British Empire. "In 1926, a Soviet ice-breaker took the Canadians into custody, and raised the Soviet flag. Soviet sovereignty was fully recognized by 1945." So wrote Martin Gilbert in *Russian History Atlas* (1972).

378. What was the Bowmanville Break?

The Ontario Training School for Boys in Bowmanville, Ontario, was turned into Internment Camp No. 30 for the duration of World War II. German officers of the three services were imprisoned there after April 1941 until April 1945. The peak population of prisoners of war was about 800. One of the prisoners was Rommel's "desert general," General von Ravenstein.

There were a number of escape attempts as well as a three-day riot over the handcuffing of inmates. The Bowmanville Break refers to the abortive attempt to tunnel to freedom. Construction of a tunnel under the wall was never completed. Hans Krug, a Luftwaffe pilot, escaped the internment camp and made it to the United States; he was subsequently arrested in Texas and returned to custody. Another Luftwaffe pilot, Von Werra, who was touted as "the one who got away," had never been a prisoner at Bowmanville. (Leaping from a passenger train that was travelling through the still-neutral United States, he succeeded, by a circuitous route, in returning to Germany only to be killed at Stalingrad.)

379. Who sponsored the "Cities of Canada" exhibit?

The travelling art exhibit "Cities of Canada" consisted of paintings of twenty-six Canadian cities. The paintings were commissioned from twenty-three artist members of the Royal Canadian Academy by the Seagram Corporation. The exhibit, assisted by the Vickers and Benson advertising agency, opened in Montreal in 1954. Over the years it travelled some 30,000 miles and appeared in fifteen countries in Europe and Central and South America, as noted by Michael R. Marrus in *Mr. Sam: The Life and Times of Samuel Bronfman* (1991).

380. What is the Route of the Totems?

Nineteen totem poles were erected on Vancouver Island along Highway 19, from Victoria to Prince Hardy and on to Prince Rupert, British Columbia. They were commissioned by the province's Centennial committee. Eleven native carvers and their assistants were employed to carve the poles which were about 3.5 metres in height and 1 metre in diameter at the base, and each was to be dominated by the figure of an upright Bear. There are nineteen related poles in all.

In the same vein, the city of Duncan, British Columbia, calls itself the City of Totems. Within the city there are eighty-two totem poles. Thirty-nine of these were erected by the City of Totems building program from its inception to 1998.

381. Does Rick Hansen's image appear on a totem pole?

As unlikely as it might seem, the dedication of wheelchair athlete Rick Hansen, who wheeled around the world for his 1985-87 Marathon of Hope, inspired Salish artist Corky Baines to add Hansen's image to the totem pole he carved for the City of Duncan, British Columbia, according to Pat Kramer, "Notable Totems," *Beautiful British Columbia*, Winter 1996.

382. Is there a monument in Vancouver to the victims of the Montreal Massacre?

The massacre of fourteen women students at the École Polytechnique in Montreal took place on 6 December 1989. Chris McDowell, at the time a student at Capilano College in Vancouver, reasoned that the name of the murderer (Marc Lepine) would be remembered but the names of his victims would be forgotten. She resolved to raise a memorial that featured their names. Eight years later the Women's Monument Project was unveiled in Vancouver's Thornton Park. The monument consists of fourteen pink granite benches arranged in a circle. Designed by artist Beth Alber in competition, each bench is about the length and breadth of a woman's body, and each is scarred with an indentation to suggest a tear or perhaps a vulva. Each bench bears the name of one of the fourteen women, all young engineering students: Geneviève Bergeron, Hélène Colgan, Nathalie Croteau, Barbara Daigneault, Anne-Marie Edward, Maud Haviernick, Barbara Klucznik, Maryse Laganière, Maryse Leclair, Anne-Marie Lemay, Sonia Pelletier, Michèle Richard, Annie St-Arneault, and Annie Turcotte. Controversy swirled around the words of the inscription which appears in seven languages – it is dedicated to "all women who have been murdered by men," as noted by Chris Dafoe, "Graven Memories," *The Globe and Mail,* 6 December 1997.

383. Did a Canadian accompany Scott on his Antarctic Expedition?

Yes. Sir Charles Seymour Wright (1887-1975), a Toronto-born physicist who worked at the Cavendish Laboratory, served as the glaciologist with the British Antarctic Expedition (1910-13) under Captain Robert F. Scott. Wright was navigator of the sledge team that in November 1912 found the tent containing the bodies of Scott and his companions who died upon their return from the South Pole.

384. What is Niagara's Freedom Trail?

Niagara's Freedom Trail consists of three plaques erected by the Niagara Parks Commission which stretch along the Niagara Parkway in the Niagara Peninsula. The first plaque, near Beatrice Street, is titled "The

Crossing," and it tells how ferry traffic on the river aided slaves fleeing the United States. Another plaque at the Mildred Mahoney Silver Jubilee Dollhouse Gallery marks a house which sheltered travellers who followed the Underground Railroad. The plaque at the Niagara Parks Marina describes Little Africa, a black community established west of Fort Erie and East of Stevensville in the 1840s. There is another Freedom Trail in the Windsor-Chatham area.

385. Where is more maple syrup produced, Quebec or the United States?

The Province of Quebec produces more maple syrup each year than do all the states of the United States of America.

386. How many countries extend north of the Arctic Circle?

Seven countries extend north of the Arctic Circle. They are Canada, Finland, Iceland, Norway, Russia, Sweden, and the United States. These countries are called the Circumpolar Nations.

387. What is the northernmost mainland point of North America?

Boothia Peninsula of the Northwest Territories is the northernmost mainland point of North America. It is almost an island.

388. What is the second-longest river in North America?

The Mackenzie River is the second-longest river in North America. The first-longest is the Mississippi River.

389. Which province borders on all the Great Lakes?

No province borders on all the Great Lakes. The Province of Ontario borders on four of the five Great Lakes (and comes close to bordering on the fifth, Lake Michigan).

390. Which is the world's smallest ocean?

The world's smallest ocean is the Arctic Ocean. At 3.6 million square miles, it is much smaller than the second-smallest ocean, the Indian Ocean, which is 28.3 million square miles.

391. Where is "Iceberg Alley"?

"Iceberg Alley" is a popular reference to the eastern coast of Labrador where the current brings cold weather – and icebergs – down from Greenland.

392. How many Canadians live in a "miniaturized town"?

The geographer George J. Demko wrote about visualizing the population of the world living in a "miniaturized town" in his book *Why in the World: Adventures in Geography* (1992).

"If the world were miniaturized to a town of 1,000 people, there would be 564 Asians, 210 Europeans, 86 Africans, 80 South Americans, and 60 North Americans; and that 700 of the 1,000 people would be illiterate and 500 would be hungry."

Adding to Demko's calculations, the number of Canadians in this "miniaturized town" would be in the neighbourhood of 2.5! They would all be literate, about .5 of them in French.

393. When was the North East Passage first navigated?

Canadians know about the navigation of the Northwest Passage, but few know about the navigation of the North East Passage round the top of Russia. It was first navigated in 1932.

394. Where is New Canada?

New Canada is a railroad station and a district in the Union of South Africa. It lies near the National Exhibition Centre, southwest of Johannesburg, between that city and Soweto.

395. What are the time zones in Canada?

There are six time zones in Canada, at the usual one-hour intervals, except for Newfoundland Time which is thirty minutes ahead of Atlantic Time. Newfoundland Time is not used in Labrador, only on the island of Newfoundland. Except for Saskatchewan, which is always on Standard Time, all areas of Canada observe Daylight Saving Time, moving clocks ahead by one hour for the summer. Currently the DST period is from the first Sunday in April to the last Sunday in October, the same as in the United States.

There was once a Yukon Time zone, but this was abolished in the early 1970s, when the Yukon Territory changed to Pacific Time. The whole province of Newfoundland tried advancing two hours instead of one hour ahead for the DST period about 1990. This was found to be confusing for most folk and was done only once.

396. Where was the movie *Black Robe* filmed?

The reconstructed native village of l'Anse-à-la-Croix was the principal shooting locale for the film *Black Robe*. The village, built to recall an Algonkian settlement in 1634, may be found outside Saint-Félix-d'Otis, south of the Saguenay River, Northern Quebec. The village lies southeast of the city of Chicoutimi. The 1991 film, directed by Bruce Beresford, is based on Brian Moore's novel *Black Robe* (1985) which examines devotion and doubt among the Jesuit Fathers in seventeenth-century New France.

397. What is the attraction of Tadoussac?

Tadoussac is a picturesque Quebec village on the north shore of the Saguenay River where it meets the St. Lawrence River. The village has many points of interest, but the principal tourist attraction is whale-watching. Excursion vessels take tourists from Tadoussac and other local port communities into the St. Lawrence where whales – belugas, minkes, and finbacks – may be viewed cavorting in the waves.

398. What Quebec place name means "nipple"?

It is said that the name of the village of Tadoussac at the mouth of the Saguenay River and the St. Lawrence is derived from the Montagnais Indian word *tatoushak* which means "nipple." If so, the designation is appropriate as the rocky and wooded hills to the west of the village are breast-shaped.

399. What stands on the first summit of Cape Trinity?

On the first summit of Cape Trinity, which overlooks the fjords of the Saguenay River in northern Quebec, stands an impressive blue-and-white statue of the Blessed Virgin Mary. The eight-metre-high wooden statue was erected as a private act of devotion and thanksgiving in 1880-81. It is known as Notre-Dame du Saguenay (Our Lady of the Saguenay).

400. Which cities are found in the Kingdom of the Saguenay?

There is an impressive ring to the words "the Kingdom of the Saguenay" (le Royaume du Saguenay). Whether in English or in French, the words refer to the rugged and once-remote region along the banks of the Saguenay River in Northern Quebec. There are three cities in the so-called Kingdom: Chicoutimi, Jonquière, and La Baie. Early explorers were told fabulous tales by the Indians about "the Kingdom of the Saguenay" with its rich deposits of gold.

401. Where is the Musée Louis-Hémon?

The Musée Louis-Hémon – the Louis Hémon Museum – may be found outside the town of Péribonka in the Lac Saint-Jean region of northern Quebec. The museum overlooks Lake St. Jean and honours the memory of Louis Hémon, the French teacher and traveller who lived in the district for some months in 1912 while gathering material for his posthumously published classic novel *Maria Chapdelaine* (1913). On the museum's grounds are three buildings erected in period styles: the Pavilion d'Accueil or reception area erected in 1976; the Maison Samuel-Bédard, the farmer's house in which Hémon boarded, a traditional building erected in 1904; and the grand Pavilion Principal erected in 1986.

402. What is unique about the bridge at Jonquière?

The bridge that spans the Saguenay River at Jonquière is made entirely of aluminium. It is called Pont d'aluminium (Aluminium Bridge). At 164 tons, it weighs one-third less than the weight of a comparable steel bridge. The Alcan aluminium works is located at nearby Shipshaw.

403. Where is there a snowmobile museum?

Snowmobiles were first developed and built by Bombardier at Valcourt in Quebec's Eastern Townships. But you have to travel to the town of Desbiens on the Saguenay River in Northern Quebec to see the Musée de la motoneige (the Museum of the Snowmobile). The private collection is open to the public and includes prototypes, unusual models, and home-made machines.

404. What was the original name of Murray Bay?

The site of this Quebec resort town on the north shore of the St. Lawrence River was named La Malbaie (Bad Bay) by Samuel de Champlain in 1608. In later years it was known as Murray Bay, after James Murray, Governor of Canada, yet the original name La Malbaie persists to this day. The town is the administrative centre of the Charlevoix region and boasts the oldest golf course in Canada, the Murray Bay Golf Course.

405. What are the Montérégiennes?

These are the six hills that occupy the centre of the St. Lawrence Lowland. The hills lie southeast of Montreal and are visible from the Quebec-Vermont border. The six hills or mountains are Mont Saint-Bruno, Mont Saint-Hilaire, Mont Rougemont, Mont Saint-Grégoire, Mont Yamaska, and Mont Rigaud.

406. Where is the world's longest pedestrian suspension bridge?

The 169-metre long suspended footbridge over the gorge at Coaticook in Quebec's Eastern Townships is recognized as the world's longest such bridge by the *Guinness Book of Records*. It crosses the 50 metre (164 foot) gorge created by the Coaticook River. The bridge is the showpiece of the Parc de la Gorge de Coaticook.

407. Where is there the house built by the Brownies?

The house built by the Brownies is called Château Brownies. It is located on 125 Elgin St., Granby, Eastern Townships, Quebec, and it was erected by the illustrator and children's author Palmer Cox. He was the creator of the gnomish Brownies, mischievous, Smurf like cartoon figures that were popular in the 1910s.

408. Which city is known as the Queen City of the Eastern Townships?

The Queen City of the Eastern Townships refers to Sherbrooke, the largest city in that region of Quebec.

409. What is on display at the Musée J.-Armand-Bombardier?

Snowmobiles are featured at the Musée J.-Armand-Bombardier located at 1001 J.-Armand Bombardier Avenue, Valcourt, Quebec. The museum focuses on Bombardier's work as inventor and manufacturer of the ever-popular snowmobile.

410. Where are there round barns?

Some barns that are still standing in Quebec's Eastern Townships were built in the late nineteenth century in a shape that is round rather than square or rectilinear. As the tourist guide *Estrie: Eastern Townships* (1994) notes, "According to legend, the distinctive shape of round barns comes either from an attempt to protect them against strong winds or to keep the devil from hiding in corners." The best-preserved round barns may be seen in Barnston, Mansonville, and West Brome. At Mystic, there is a barn that is twelve-sided.

411. Where is the world's largest panorama?

The world's largest panorama is the Cyclorama of Jerusalem, an educational and tourist attraction to be found next to the Basilica at Ste-Anne-de-Beaupré, the Catholic shrine near Quebec City. In its own circular, Moorish-looking building, the monumental canvas, which is 14 metres high and 110 metres in circumference, depicts the city of Jerusalem at the time of Christ. The canvas was created in Munich by muralist Paul Philippoteaux with the help of five assistants. The Cyclorama of Jerusalem has been on permanent exhibit here since 1895. Spectators are given the illusion that they are actually present at the time of the Crucifixion.

412. Are the Iles-de-la-Madeleine closer to Nova Scotia than Quebec?

The Iles-de-la-Madeleine consist of an archipelago of a dozen or so islands in the Gulf of the St. Lawrence. Some are connected by sand dunes. They form a half moon, stretching across a distance of 65 kilometres in a southwest-northeasterly direction. The islands are located 215 kilometres from Quebec's Gaspé peninsula, 105 kilometres from the shore of Prince Edward Island, and 95 kilometres from Nova Scotia's Cape Breton Island. So they are closer to Nova Scotia than to Quebec. They are occasionally called "the Maggies" by the English.

413. Where is the Graveyard of the Gulf?

Grosse-Ile has been called the Graveyard of the Gulf. This Quebec island in the Gulf of the St. Lawrence served as Canada's main quarantine station from 1832 to 1837. Tens of thousands of immigrants stopped at Grosse-Ile and many never left, having been buried there. It was marked by Parks Canada as a National Historic Site.

414. What is the Kamouraska Roof?

The Kamouraska Roof is a regional architectural style characteristic of Quebec's Bas-Saint Laurent area and particularly the village of Kamouraska. Both the roof and the eaves are arched, the eaves extending beyond the roof to keep rain away from the walls of the building. In the words of a Quebec guide book, "The rounded shape of the eaves recalls the bottom of a ship's hull. It appears that this technique was borrowed from naval carpentry, well known in this region of seamen and ship-builders." The style was popular in the late seventeenth century.

415. Where will you find Ponik?

Ponik is the name of a sea serpent that is said to inhabit the depths of Lac Pohénégamook, Quebec. The eel-like creature has been reported by inhabitants of Saint-Eleuthère and Estcourt, villages on the shore of the lake.

416. How did Saint-Louis-du-Ha! Ha! acquire its name?

No one really knows how Saint-Louis-du-Ha! Ha! acquired its odd name. Located in Quebec's Bas-Saint-Laurent region, it had a population of 1,500 in 1990. The name may have come from the early settlers' exclamation upon seeing Lac Témiscouata around the year 1874. It is also said that "Ha! Ha!" means "something unexpected" in the language of the Hexcucwaska Indians of the region.

417. Where is Canada's second-largest port?

Sept-Iles on the St. Lawrence River in Quebec is Canada's second-largest port in terms of tonnage handled. The deep-water port is accessible year round to ocean-going vessels from all parts of the world.

418. Who is the poet of Natashquan?

The Quebec chansonnier and poet Gilles Vigneault celebrates the affecting beauty of the village of Natashquan on the North Shore of the St. Lawrence River. It is Vigneault's birthplace and continuing inspiration.

419. What community in the Gaspé was named after a rock resembling a crouching cat?

In the Gaspé region of Quebec, the community of Cap-Chat, with a population 3,200, was named because of a rock resembling a crouching cat.

420. Who coined the geographical term Les Laurentides?

The toponym or geographical term Les Laurentides was coined by the historian François-Xavier Garneau in 1845 to refer to the region of mountains that run parallel to the St. Lawrence River, generally north of the island of Montreal. The English term is the Laurentians or Laurentian Mountains. The resort region includes the St. Lawrence Lowland and the Canadian Shield.

421. Where is the Jackrabbit museum?

Musée du Ski des Laurentides Jackrabbit is a tourist attraction in the town of Piedmont in the Laurentians of Quebec. The museum occupies the cottage where cross-country ski pioneer Herman (Jackrabbit) Johanssen lived from 1959 to his death at the age of 111 in 1987. The museum includes the Laurentian Ski Hall of Fame.

422. What is the Musée de Séraphin?

Séraphin's Village is a pioneer village outside the Laurentian town of Sainte-Adèle, Quebec. It bears the name of Séraphin Poudrier, the old habitant whose sin is miserliness in the novel *Un Homme et Son Péché* (1933) written by Claude-Henri Grignon, a native of Sainte-Adèle. Popular radio and television series were based on the novel, so the character of Séraphin is familiar to generations of Québécois.

423. Where does Santa Claus spend his summers?

Outside Val-David in Quebec's Laurentian Mountains is Le Village-du-Père-Noël, a tourist attraction with appeal to children. Here is were Père-Noël or Santa Claus spends his summers. He may be seen performing various tasks during the tourist season. There is, additionally, a Santa's Village outside Bracebridge, Ontario.

424. Where is North America's oldest grocery store?

The distinction of being the oldest grocery store in North America is claimed by Épicerie Moison located at 699 rue Saint-Jean, Quebec City. It was opened in 1871 and has been continually operated on the same site since then. In the words of the Quebec guide book, "It has kept the character of the good old days and the scent of spices combined with the sound of French music creates a very special atmosphere."

425. What is the Chemin du Roy?

The Chemin du Roy is the name of the route that connected settlements along the north shore of the St. Lawrence River from Quebec City to Montreal. It was opened in 1734 and was the first road in Canada suitable for vehicular traffic. It was the route taken by the representatives of the Kings of France when they journeyed from Quebec to Montreal and back again during the Ancien Régime. Today the 150-kilometre chemin is part of Route 138 and is prized for its scenic and historical character. It was the route taken by French President Charles de Gaulle when he travelled from Quebec City to Montreal in 1967.

426. Where is North America's first French-language Catholic university?

Université Laval is the first French-language Catholic university to be established in North America. It was founded in 1852 in Quebec City. Its Cité Universitaire is located not in Quebec City itself but in the neighbouring region of Sainte-Foy.

427. Where was Félix Leclerc born?

The Quebec chansonnier Félix Leclerc was born at La Tuque, near Trois-Rivière, and he celebrated the town and its inhabitants in his popular poems and songs. La Tuque was named after *la tuque*, a woollen bonnet. In later years Leclerc made his permanent home on the Ile d'Orléans.

428. Where would you hear the playing of bagpipes at twelve noon six days a week?

Outside Ogilvy's department store, located at Sainte-Catherine St. W. in Montreal, a musician played the bagpipes. The playing was meant to recall the store's Scottish origins way back in 1866. It is uncertain whether the custom continues to this day.

429. Where did Irving Berlin write "Always" and "Blue Skies"?

Among Irving Berlin's best-loved songs are "Always" and "Blue Skies." Tradition has it that the Tin Pan Alley composer wrote them at the Berlin family's summer home on St. Lawrence Park Island in the Thousand Islands. The family home was named "Always."

430. Where is Last Duel Park?

Last Duel Park is a public park in Perth, Ontario, where, the evening of 13 June 1833, the last known public duel was fought on Canadian soil. Two townsfolk fought. John Wilson challenged Robert Lyon over remarks made about the schoolteacher Elizabeth Hughes that were reported by a third party to a fourth party. Lyon was killed and Wilson was charged with his murder.

431. What is the new name of Frobisher Bay?

In 1987, residents of the town of Frobisher Bay on Baffin Island, the largest community in the Northwest Territories, voted to change the town's name to Iqaluit. The name Frobisher Bay was retained for the bay itself. In Inuktitut, the meaning of Iqaluit is "the place of fish." In the media it is frequently misspelled "Iqualuit," which has the unfortunate meaning in Inuktitut of "unwiped buttocks," according to Gordon McBride of the Baffin Emergency Response Committee, Iqaluit, "Letters to the Editor," *The Globe and Mail*, 24 November 1994.

432. Are there reindeer at the North Pole?

No reindeer are found in the vicinity of the North Pole or the South Pole, it is too cold for them. However, they do inhabit the northern areas of Canada, Alaska, Siberia and Scandinavia.

433. How thick is the ice at the North Pole?

The thickness of the ice at the North Pole varies. It has been measured to a depth of 1.6 kilometres.

434. Where is there a foreign suburb with Canadian names?

A suburb in Harare, Zimbabwe, has streets named after Canadian cities, provinces, and territories, according to Maureen Murray writing in *The Toronto Star*, 28 December 1994. "It's a mystery how an enclave – anchored by a roadway called Canada Dr. and intersected by Winnipeg Rd., Toronto Rd., Montreal Rd., Vancouver Rd., and Yukon Rd. (there is an Alberta Rd. nearby) – came to be located in this southern African capital."

The subdivision was surveyed in 1951. No one knows why the district of Harare, Zimbabwe (before 1980 known as Salisbury, Rhodesia) was given these names. One suggestion is that the names are the legacy of gratitude for Canadian pilots who attended the RAF training centre nearby during World War II.

435. Is there a village named Sheshatshit?

There is a village named Sheshatshit on the Quebec-Labrador peninsula occupied by the native Innu. They call it Nitassinan, "Our Homeland." It is currently threatened by mining and forestry activity as well as low-flying, low-level NATO fighter-jet training.

436. Where does Northern Ontario begin?

The Province of Ontario is composed of Northern Ontario and Southern Ontario for the purposes of comparison and contrast. The economy of the southern part is highly agricultural and industrial, the economy of the northern part is principally resource-based. The dividing point has long been a subject of contention, as there are subsidies earmarked for communities and companies in the north that are not available to those in the south. In the 1960s, the Conservative administration under William Davis defined the dividing point as the city of Barrie which was considered northern. Other administrations have accepted North Bay as the first northern city. As one northern politician said, "The brains begin at Barrie." He did not specify whether they are located north or south of that city.

437. Where is Las Cañadas?

Las Cañadas is the name of a rain forest in Mexico. The forest is found in the province of San Cristóbal de las Casas.

438. Are some of the states in the United States younger than some of the Canadian provinces?

Yes. Alberta and Saskatchewan joined the Dominion of Canada in 1905; Newfoundland followed in 1949. Five of the states are younger than Alberta and Saskatchewan, two younger than Newfoundland. Oklahoma joined the Union in 1907, Arizona and New Mexico in 1912. Alaska and Hawaii became states in 1959, ten years after Newfoundland joined Canada.

439. Is the Niagara Peninsula a peninsula?

The landmass that lies between Lake Ontario and Lake Erie has two designations. In Canada it is called the Niagara Peninsula. In the United States it is known as the Niagara Frontier. Neither designation is correct. It is neither a peninsula nor a frontier. In geographical terms it might best be described as an isthmus, a neck of land connecting two larger bodies of land.

440. What is Cascadia?

Cascadia is the name of the geographical area that comprises the Province of British Columbia and the States of Washington and Oregon. According to broadcaster Bill Casselman, "It encompasses roughly the watershed of the Cascade Range, a part of the Rocky Mountains cordillera that runs right up into southern British Columbia. The name may have been suggested by Cascadia State Park in Oregon." The coinage also suggests a state of mind: a bucolic region separated from the rest of the North American continent.

441. Is Hudson Bay a bay or a sea?

Hudson Bay, named after the explorer Henry Hudson, is basically an inland sea. As Ken MacQueen wrote in "Toponomy" in *The Toronto Star*, 14 December 1996, "Together, Hudson Bay, James Bay, Foxe Basin, Hudson Strait and Ungava Bay constitute the world's largest inland sea to be confined within the borders of a single country."

442. What is the Canada Sea?

Canada Sea (or Mer du Canada) is the unofficial name given the waters of Hudson Bay and James Bay, along with the adjacent Foxe Basin, Hudson Strait, and Ungava Bay. According to *Maclean's*, 23 September 1996, two attempts have been made to give this designation to these waters. W.F. Maclean introduced a private member's bill to the House of Commons in 1903. The idea was revived in November 1994 by a Dartmouth couple, Harvey Adams and Barbara Schmeisser, as a gesture toward Canadian unity and a desire to assert national supremacy over the body of water.

443. When did John Cabot make his landfall at Newfoundland?

John Cabot, or Giovanni Caboto, sailed for the merchants of Bristol and made his landfall on the coast of Newfoundland in 1497. It took the navigator six weeks to cross the Atlantic in his caravel the *Matthew*. Five hundred years later a replica of the original vessel was built. In the summer of 1997, the *Matthew II* was sailed across the Atlantic and the vessel made a seventeen-port tour of "the new founde lande."

444. Is the population of any American state greater than the total population of Canada?

California is the most populous of the American states. In 2000 its population was estimated to be 32,000,000. In comparison, Canada's total population is estimated to be 30,000,000. The most populous U.S. state after California is New York, with a population of 20,000,000. Therefore California is the sole U.S. state with a population greater than Canada's.

There may be more Californians than Canadians, but they have less room to roam. The U.S. state covers 412,602 square kilometres, whereas Canada covers 9,976,139 square kilometres. Canadians are neither cramped nor confined!

445. Is Canada the best country in the world in which to live?

Canada has the distinction of being "the best country in the world in which to live," according to the Human Development Report 1992 released by the United Nations. Subsequent annual rankings have confirmed this distinction. Canada was ranked higher than its principal competitors, Japan and the United States. The high ranking is based on quality of life measured in terms of national income, life expectancy, and educational attainment. The findings of the UN report first appeared in *The Globe and Mail*, 17 April 1992.

Things

446. What are "snow worms"?

There are no such things as "snow worms" – worm-like lifeforms that live in the northern environment of ice and snow. From time to time scientists have encountered some minute forms of life – larvae, etc. – embedded in fields of ice and snow, but such forms of life are non-native to ice and snow and were introduced accidentally to the domain. They thrive there for but a short period of time.

Yet rumours persist that "snow worms" thrive in northern fields of ice and snow. Charles Fort, the American collector of oddities, discussed this notion in *The Book of the Damned* (1919). "I accept that there are 'snow worms' upon this earth – whatever their origin may be," he stated. "There is a description of yellow worms and black worms that have been found together on glaciers in Alaska. Almost positively there were no other forms of insect-life upon these glaciers, and there was no vegetation to support insect-life, except microscopic organisms. Nevertheless the description of this probably polymorphic species fits a description of larvae said to have fallen in Switzerland, and less definitely fits another description."

447. Who talks about "Canada Grays," "Canada Peaker," and "Canadian Way"?

A logger talks about them. These are slang terms that are used by workers employed in the forest industry.

According to L.G. Sorden and Jacque [sic] Vallier in *Lumberjack Lingo* (1986), "Canada Grays" are warm woollen socks; "Canada Peaker" is a system of arranging logs on a load in the form of a triangle; "Canadian Way" is the practice of cutting logs into lengths instead of hauling entire log trunks to the landing.

448. Is a "Quebec choker" a strangler from Chicoutimi?

Not quite! A "Quebec choker" is a slang term for a peavey, and a peavey is the proper term for a spiked cant hook used by a logger. A logger uses an ordinary cant hook to move a log on land, but a log in the water requires a cant hook with a spike which is called a peavey or sometimes a Quebec choker.

449. What are mackinaws?

Mackinaws may be overcoats or boats.

A mackinaw is a winter overcoat traditionally worn by a lumberjack. It is a short, double-breasted, woollen, plaid coat. The mackinaw is not to be confused with the mackintosh, the raincoat made of rubber cloth. It recalls the name of the nineteenth-century Scottish inventor Charles Mackintosh, whereas the mackinaw bears the name of the eighteenth-century trading post on Mackinac Island in Lake Huron at the entrance to the Straits of Mackinac.

The flat-bottomed boat used to haul lumber and supplies on the Great Lakes is called the mackinaw boat. Its name recalls Mackinaw or the Michilimackinac area of Upper Michigan and Northern Ontario.

450. What are other names for the Lumberjack Bird or the Camp Robber?

The Canada Blue Jay, the Canadian Jay, and the Whiskey Jack are other names for the Lumberjack Bird or the Camp Robber. The latter terms are identified as "lumberjack lingo" by L.G. Sorden and Jacque [sic] Vallier in their book *Lumberjack Lingo* (1986).

451. What dish is named after Pierre Sévigny?

Pierre Sévigny served as the Associate Minister of National Defence under Prime Minister Diefenbaker. The public links Sévigny with the Munsinger Affair, a political sex scandal which came to light in the 1960s. His name is also recalled in connection with another "dish," this one being pâté de fois gras Sévigny, also known as pâté de fois gras Canadien. According to Susan Cartwright and Alan Edmonds, authors of *The Prime Ministers' Cook Book* (1976), "The recipe found its way into many Ottawa kitchens, including the one at Sussex Drive." The authors include the recipe for the pâté, which is highly spiced, includes cognac, and should be served four or five days after preparation.

452. What was Pierre Elliott Trudeau's favourite snack food?

According to Susan Cartwright and Alan Edmonds, authors of *The Prime Ministers' Cook Book* (1976), Pierre Elliott Trudeau, while Prime Minister, most enjoyed nibbling on chocolate chip cookies. He also had a special liking for bread and drippings – a French-Canadian specialty called *graisse du rôti* (grease of the roast). "Just as the French peasant talent for dignifying poorer cuts of meat and offal with sauces has become the measure of today's haute cuisine, so French Canadians have elevated bread and dripping to the status of a gourmet's delight."

453. Is beer heavily taxed?

Yes. "Unfortunately for consumers, Canada also ranks very high with respect to taxes on a case of beer. In Canada commodity and sales taxes alone make up 52% of the average retail price of beer, ranking Canada third highest among free-world countries. By comparison taxes in United States average 16% and rank 19th out of 21 countries surveyed." The information is reprinted from the brochure *The*

Brewing Industry in Canada in 1988 issued by the Brewers Association of Canada.

454. Is Canada among the top ten in terms of world's beer-producing countries?

Canada does not rank among the top-ten of the world's beer-producing countries. It ranked eleventh on the list for the year 1987. The top three were the United States, West Germany, and the United Kingdom. Canada fell between Spain and Czechoslovakia. However, the Canadian brewing industry ranks as the world's fourth-largest exporter of beer.

455. Which provinces or territories have no breweries?

There are breweries in operation in all ten provinces, but there are none in the two territories. In 1988, there were 63 plants in operation, as well as innumerable microbreweries and brewpubs. The brewing and marketing of beer contributed $10 billion to the Canadian economy that year.

456. What are microbreweries and brewpubs?

The Brewers Association of Canada recognizes breweries, microbreweries, and brewpubs. Breweries (like Carling O'Keefe) operate nationally. Microbreweries (like Brick) service a region of the country. A brewpub is a public house licensed to brew its own brand of beer for sale on its own premises.

457. What were the eighteen beautiful Park Cars?

The Canadian Pacific Railway acquired 173 new pieces of rolling stock for its passenger service in 1954. These were light-weight, stainless-steel cars – day coaches, sleepers, and dining cars. Eighteen of the day coaches were of the Vista-Dome type and were reserved for use on *The Canadian,* then at its height of fame as "the best, long-distance train in the world." The interiors of these cars were specially decorated with murals designed and drawn by leading Canadian artists.

These were the so-called Park Cars because each took its name and its artistic motif from a Canadian park. Ian Thom, who researched the history of this unique adventure in national iconography in *Murals from a Great Canadian Train* (1986), noted that there was room in each car for a mural the length of the car (with provision for windows) and a picturesque map at the end of the car. The murals were painted on canvas and mounted on the walls.

Each artist was commissioned to paint in his or her characteristic style. A.Y. Jackson depicted Kokanee Provincial Park and A.J. Casson did the same for Algonquin Provincial Park. Other artists painted other subjects. A note of controversy was sounded by Charles Comfort whose preliminary sketches for Banff National Park included a miniature recreation of Manet's *Le Déjeuner sur l'herbe* (which depicts two clothed males picnicking with one naked female) set in a stylized Bow Valley, but that depiction was deemed inappropriate by the CPR's advisers and rejected. (Comfort completed a larger version of this curious work in 1968.)

The Park Cars were in use until 1984. The cars were scrapped but the murals were preserved. Reproductions of all of them appear in *Murals from a Great Canadian Train* – much reduced in size, of course!

458. Was the CPR really the first transcontinental railway?

No. The Canadian Pacific Railway's transcontinental line was completed on 7 November 1885. This marked a considerable achievement for the newly formed CPR, as well as for the fledgling Dominion of Canada, a country hardly two decades old. The CPR was the first transcontinental railway line on Canadian land, but it was not the first on the North American continent.

Priority must be accorded to two American railroad companies, Union Pacific and Central Pacific, which laid track which met on 10 May 1869 at a site known as Promontory Point. Thus the American transcontinental railroad was completed sixteen years before the completion of the Canadian transcontinental railway.

459. What was the original name of the Genies?

The Genies are the awards for excellence in Canadian filmmaking. As such they have been called the Canadian Oscars. Each year the Academy of Canadian Cinema awards a range of Genies in various categories. Such awards go back to the Canadian Film Awards which were first presented on 27 April 1949 at Ottawa's Little Elgin Theatre. Early recipients were presented not with Oscar-like statuettes but with original oil paintings and soapstone sculptures. Some of the paintings were the works of members of the Group of Seven and so today are extremely valuable works of art in their own right.

The current award is an Oscar-like statuette designed by the noted sculptor Sorel Etrog. In fact, the statuette bore the name of the sculptor: The Etrog was the name of the award from 1968 to 1979. With the creation of the Academy of Canadian Cinema, the old Etrog was given a new bilingual name: The Genie. The first Genies were presented in a number of categories on 20 March 1980. They continue to be awarded in Genie ceremonies every year.

460. What happened to the Governor General's Awards for Film and Radio?

In 1947, J. Roby Kidd of the Canadian Institute for Adult Education decided it would be a good idea for the Governor General to institute an annual series of awards (modelled on the Governor General's Awards for Canadian Literature first dispensed in 1937) to honour excellence in film production and radio programming.

Rideau Hall made it known that the Governor General was willing to go half way. He would grant viceregal honours to two annual awards – one for film and one for radio – but not to the panoply of "industry" or "craft" awards envisioned by the CAAE. So the search was joined for an alternative name for the awards. Officials in Ottawa objected to such titles as the Canadian Awards, the Dominion Awards, the Confederation Awards, the W.L. Mackenzie King Awards, the Maple Leaf Awards, and the North Star Awards.

No one had any objection to naming the prizes the Canadian Film Awards and the Canadian Radio Awards, so these were pressed into service. The CAAE sponsored the first annual CFAs at Ottawa's Little Elgin Theatre on 27 April 1949. In time the Canadian Film Awards became the Etrogs and then the Genies; the Canadian Radio Awards became the Actra Awards. Thus the Governor General does not honour filmmaking and broadcasting as such. The full story is told by Maria Topalovich in *A Pictorial History of the Canadian Film Awards* (1984).

461. Where is the world's largest natural phallic symbol?

The world's largest natural phallic symbol rises off the eastern shore of Lake Superior. A feature of the suitably named natural promontory called Cape Gargantua. In these words it was wryly described by the historian and canoeist, Eric W. Morse, in *Freshwater Saga: Memoirs of a Lifetime of Wilderness Canoeing in Canada* (1987):

> One name, though, puzzled us. As we approached Cape Gargantua, we expected to see a towering shoreline, but though not flat, it was not particularly impressive. There was no question that we were in the right place. Perhaps, we thought, the name came from massive hills further inland, for the map was dotted with Gargantua-names, and there was even a Grandgousier Hill. Suddenly I broke into laughter, as the reason for the name struck me. There, stretching into the lake, was a perfect profile of a certain human appendage, two miles long. Those voyageurs had a good sense of humour. The allocators of geographical names had solemnly picked up the theme, perhaps not knowing its reason, for the shape of the point's profile cannot be guessed from the blunt coastline on the map.

462. Who designed the Canadarm?

Credit for the design of the Canadarm, the robotic arm built by Spar Aerospace Ltd. of Toronto and deployed by NASA's U.S. Space Shuttles, has been accorded to Frank Thurston of the National Research Council of Canada, who as early as 1969 established a program to develop the "appendage."

463. Which hockey club has won the Stanley Cup more often than any other?

The Montreal Canadiens hockey club has won the Stanley Cup more often than any other hockey club. In the ninety-two years from 1893 to 1984, the Montreal Canadiens claimed the cup a record twenty-two times.

464. Who invented the electric light bulb?

Everyone knows that Thomas A. Edison invented the electric light bulb in 1878, which he patented on 1 November 1879. But the discovery is not that straight-forward.

A Canadian patent for an "Electric Light" was granted to two Torontonians in 1874. The invention of Henry Woodward, a medical student and subsequently a physician, and Matthew Evans, a hotel-keeper, consisted of a block of carbon enclosed in a glass "lamp." In the words of correspondent Ernest Wooton, writing in *The Globe and Mail*, 13 October 1979, "The carbon gave off light when an electric current passed through it ... in a state of incandescence."

The rumour is that Edison, recognizing the importance of the Woodward-Evans invention, purchased their important patent from them. While this cannot be demonstrated, what can be shown is that Edison's American patent called for "an improvement in electric lamps and the method of manufacturing the phrase," which acknowledges an earlier invention of the incandescent lamp.

465. Who were the Symphony Six?

The Symphony Six were six musicians, all members of the Toronto Symphony Orchestra, who were refused admission to the United States on the ground that they constituted a "security risk." This occurred in 1951 when U.S. Senator Joe McCarthy and other professional anti-Communists were intensifying the Cold War. The TSO had been invited to perform in New York, and it did so – minus its six members. The following year the TSO management decided not to renew the musical contracts of these performers – Dick Keetbass, William Kuinka, Abe Mannheim, John Moskalyk, Russ Ross, and Steven Staryk. The cowardice of the TSO blackened its reputation for decades.

466. How many channels are Toronto television viewers able to regularly receive?

Toronto television viewers are regularly able to receive more channels than are viewers anywhere else on the continent and probably anywhere else in the world. The television critic Morris Wolfe, in his study *Jolts:*

The TV Wasteland and the Canadian Oasis (1986), noted that on the set in his Toronto home in 1985 he could regularly watch 36 channels. As two channels were duplicated, his set received 34 different channels.

Reception could be divided into publicly owned stations, privately owned stations, cable-originated services, and subscription (pay-TV) services. There were four publicly owned stations: CBC English Network, CBC French Network, TVO (Ontario's educational service), and PBS (the American Public Broadcasting Service). The privately owned stations, 14 in number, presented their versions of American network programming (ABC, CBS, NBC) and the Canadian CTV Network. Cable-originated services, totalling 8, included public-access shows in various languages, the parliamentary channel, and printouts for the stock market and weather. Then there were ten subscription channels, largely music, movies, news, and sports. Duplication of specific programs was endemic, and of the 36 channels only four were Canadian and even they presented American programs at least half the time. Had Wolfe acquired a "dish" for satellite reception, he could have more than doubled the number of channels and probably tripled the duplication.

Since this stocktaking in 1986, dozens of so-called specialty channels have been added through enhanced cable and satellite reception. It is not uncommon to have ninety-six channels and more available through receivers attuned to satellite signals. Even with so many channels, it is unfortunately true that quite often "there is nothing worth watching on television."

467. Whose face and voice were first seen and heard on Canadian English-language television?

Canadians who owned television sets before the CBC-TV began its transmissions were able to pick up programs from American border stations. CFBT in Montreal began telecasting in French on 6 September 1952, and CBLT in Toronto in English two days later. On English-language television, the first face to be seen was that of Percy Saltzman, the bespectacled weatherman, and the first voice to be heard was the baritone of Gil Christie.

468. Who was Newfoundland's last Prime Minister?

The last Prime Minister of Newfoundland was F.C. Alderdice (1872-1936), an Irish-born businessman and politician. He headed his administration from 1932 to 1934. It was succeeded not by another administration but by the Commission Government which lasted from 1934 to 1949. During this period the status of Newfoundland reverted from a self-governing dominion headed by a prime minister to an administered Crown colony headed by a British Governor. The period of dependency ended with a bang when Newfoundlanders voted to confederate with the Dominion of Canada. On 1 April 1949 they entered Confederation with J.R. (Joey) Smallwood as Newfoundland's first Premier.

469. Who is the author of these literary works: *Faire surface, La Vie avant l'homme, Marquée au corps, La Femme comestible, L'oeuf de Barbe-Bleue, Les Danseuses et autres nouvelles, La servante écarlate,* and *Meurtre dans la nuit?*

These are the titles of the French translations published in Montreal or Paris or both of works of fiction by the popular and prolific author Margaret Atwood. *Faire surface* was published in 1978, *La Vie avant l'homme* in 1981, *Marquée au corps* in1983, *La Femme comestible* in 1984, *L'oeuf de Barbe-Bleue* in 1985, *Les Danseuses et autres nouvelles* in1986, *La servante écarlate* in 1986, and *Meurtre dans la nuit* in1987.

470. What is the connection between the Canadian Embassy in Moscow and the Costakis Collection of Russian modernist and avant-garde art?

Modernist and avant-garde art flourished in Russia between the years 1908 and 1922. Then it fell out of favour under the yoke of Stalin.

George Costakis, its greatest collector, was born in Moscow of Greek parents. In 1946, quietly and unassumingly, he began to collect the art that was in such disfavour. There was some harassment, but in the main the authorities turned a blind eye. In 1977, after donating an immense number of paintings and sculptures to the Tetriakov Gallery in Moscow, he and his family were permitted to leave the Soviet Union with 1,200 selected works. These formed the basis of the Costakis Collection which has been widely exhibited in the West. It is rich in the works of Malevich, Tatlin, Lissitzky, and other great artists.

The important question remains how a minor administrative clerk at the Canadian Embassy in Moscow was able to acquire the capital and the political elbow-room to amass so much valuable if undervalued art? In the article "Russia's Lost Revolution in Art" in *The New York Times Magazine*, 11 October 1981, art critic Hilton Kramer asked this question, but he had no ready answer for it. It is unlikely that the Canadian government assisted Costakis, for the collector had no good words for the Canadian Ambassador R.A.D. Ford who, it seems, did not assist Costakis. However it was managed, Kramer wrote, "George Costakis remains one of the most distinctive figures in the entire annals of modern art collecting."

471. What was the so-called Crepitation Contest?

Cognoscenti and aficionados of such matters value very highly a single 78 r.p.m. record called, memorably, "The Crepitation Contest." It was recorded in the early 1950s, but for reasons of content was never commercially released. Its Canadian connection was discussed by the opera singer and parodist Anna Russell in *I'm Not Making This Up, You Know* (1985):

> Syd Brown had made it for a CBC stag night at the time we had our own program in Toronto. It was entitled "The Crepitation Contest," and to put it delicately, it was a wind-breaking competition set up in the form of a boxing match between the British contender, Lord Windershmere, and the Australian contender (whose name I had suggested, incidentally), Paul Boomer. It was exceedingly vulgar but very funny. Someone (certainly not Syd) pirated it and made a fortune. I even saw it in Texas, done up in a very fancy album.

472. What did the artist William Kurelek propose to install at the top of the CN Tower?

The CN Tower, the world's tallest free-standing structure, was completed in 1976. One year before it was finished, the artist William Kurelek proposed to install a prayer on a plaque at the summit of the Tower "where no one but God would see it." Kurelek, who held strong religious convictions, approached the Tower's chief designer, Malachai Grant, and made the following proposal. He would prepare a plaque with a prayer on it at his own expense and even pay for its installation at the top of the Tower. The text would read: "O Supreme Builder of the Universe help us not to make the mistake of the builders of the first tower which you confounded." To Kurelek's dismay, Grant rejected the proposal as inappropriate for a public structure.

473. Have any Canadians won Pulitzer Prizes?

Pulitzer Prizes are awarded each year to American citizens to acknowledge the previous year's outstanding achievements in a variety of fields. From time to time the award is made to a Canadian or to someone who subsequently becomes a Canadian.

One of the first year's Pulitzer Prizes was awarded to Captain Mansell Richard James, D.F.C., of Watford, Ontario. The award made on 28 May 1919 was a posthumous one. James had flown a *Sopwith Camel* from Atlantic City, New Jersey, to Boston, Massachusetts, in record time for a long-distance flight. Alas, it was the last flight he completed. The next day, flying from Tyringham, Massachusetts, back to Atlantic City, he disappeared, and no trace of his aircraft was ever found.

A Special 1937 Pulitzer Prize was awarded to John Imrie, managing editor of *The Edmonton Journal*, for leading a crusade against the Alberta Press Bill – An Act to Ensure the Publication of Accurate News and Information – passed by the provincial legislature at the behest of the Social Credit government. On 4 March 1938, the Act was declared *ultra vires* by the Supreme Court of Canada. For the first time the Pulitzer committee recommended that an award be made outside the United States.

The correspondent Jeff Sallot received a 1971 Pulitzer Prize for investigative reporting connected with the Kent State Massacre. Settling in Canada, he joined *The Toronto Star* and then *The Globe and Mail.*

American-born, Canadian-based, Carol Shields was awarded both the Pulitzer Prize and the Governor General's Award for her novel *The Stone Diaries* (1993), the first time that this has happened.

474. Are many UFOs reportedly seen in Canadian skies?

Reports of UFOs or Unidentified Flying Objects are a global phenomenon. The late J. Allen Hynek said that on a per capita basis more Canadians report sightings of UFOs than do natives of any other country. The statement was made in the 1960s, and Hynek was the man to make it. He was an astronomer who became convinced of the reality of the phenomenon. It was Hynek who coined the phrase "close encounters of the third kind" to refer to actual contact between humans and aliens.

Reasons for the prevalence of Canadian UFO reports include the immense size of the Canadian skies, the clarity of the northern air for unobstructed viewing, and the proximity to the United States where UFOs have been in the public eye and print since the first modern reports of "flying saucers" in 1947.

475. Have any Canadians been abducted by aliens?

Widespread interest in the claims of otherwise unremarkable people that they were the victims of abductions by alien beings followed the appearance of books in the 1980s by Budd Hopkins and Whitley Streiber. The most-watched episode of CBC-TV's *Man Alive* dealt with the subject of alien abductions. Philip J. Klass, a debunker of such claims, once noted that aliens apparently prefer American bodies to non-American bodies because the majority of abduction reports come from American citizens and hardly any from Canadian citizens or the citizens of other foreign countries.

At least four Canadians have reported being abducted. A.H. Matthews, a farmer from Lac Beauport, Quebec, maintained he was taken aboard a space ship, the *X-12*, and transported to Venus and back. Oscar Magosci, a Toronto-based technician, published four booklets about meeting the "Cosmic Guardians" on his "odyssey in UFOs." The two male abductees enjoyed their experiences.

Pain and suffering were the lot of the two women abductees. Dorothy Wallis, a housewife who lives in the Niagara Peninsula, sustained emotional trauma and physical scarring. Betty Stewart Dagenais, a native of Bond Head, Ontario, recalled being abducted on five separate occasions. Emotional trauma was the result. It is claimed that the abductee was left with an "implant" in her left ear.

It is likely that innumerable Canadian men and women feel that they have suffered alien abduction, but there is no proof that such abductions occur or even that benevolent or malevolent alien beings exist.

476. What is the Canadian equivalent of Country and Western music?

Canadians, like Americans, have taken Country and Western music to heart. Its Mecca may be the Grand Ole Oprey in Nashville, Tennessee, but in their heart of hearts, Canadians also nourish a special affection for the Country and Eastern music that originates in the Maritime provinces. Some leading Country and Eastern composers and performers are John Allan Cameron, Rita MacNeil, Don Messer, and Anne Murray, whose songs celebrate the simple pains and pleasures of unrequited love.

477. What are the most important videos by Canadian popular performers?

This question was asked – and answered – by music promoter John Martin in *Shakin' All Over: The Rock'N'Roll Years in Canada* (1989) edited by Peter Goddard and Philip Kamin. Here is his list of "The Most Important 16 Videos in Canadian Pop" (with the star's name in parentheses):

"Try" (Blue Rodeo), "I Am a Hotel" (Leonard Cohen), "Peace Train" (Janis Joplin), "Crying" (k.d. lang), "Closer to the Heart" (Rush), "High School Confidential" (Carole Pope & Rough Trade), "Blinding Light Show" (Triumph), "This Note's for You" (Neil Young), "Don't Forget Me" (Glass Tiger), "Rocket Launcher" (Bruce Cockburn), "Strange Animal" (Gowan), "I'm an Adult Now" (Pursuit of Happiness), "China Girl" (Payola$), "Closer Together" (The Box), "My Secret Place" (Joni Mitchell), "Heart's on Fire" (Barney Bentall).

478. What are some of the most important albums recorded by Canadian popular performers?

The record archivist Alan Guettel made public his list of a good number of the most important albums recorded by Canadian popular performers. These album titles (with performers' names in parentheses) are selected from those Guettel contributed to *Shakin' All Over: The Rock'N'Roll Years in Canada* (1989) edited by Peter Goddard and Philip Kamin. Here it is:

"Anka's 21 Greatest Hits" (Paul Anka), "Great Speckled Bird" (Ian and Sylvia), "The Hawk" (Ronnie Hawkins), "Lightfoot" (Gordon Lightfoot), "Clouds" (Joni Mitchell), "Rust Never sleeps" (Neil Young), "Blood, Sweat and Tears" (David Clayton Thomas of Blood, Sweat and Tears), "Classics" (Mandala), "Honey Wheat and Laughter" (Anne Murray), "Waiting for a Miracle" (Bruce Cockburn), "Sweeping the Spotlight Away" (Murray McLauchlan), "Wheatfield Soul" (The Guess Who), "Northern Lights, Southern Cross" (The Band), "Downchild So Far" (Downchild Blues Band), "Rough Trade Live" (Carole Pope & Rough Trade), "Japan Tour Live" (Bachman-Turner Overdrive), "Aujourd'hui" (Michel Pagliaro), "Kate and Anna McGarrigle" (Kate and Anna McGarrigle), "All the World's a Stage" (Rush), "Live after Dark" (Streetheart), "Get Lucky" (Loverboy), "You Want It – You Got It" (Bryan Adams), "I'm Your Man" (Leonard Cohen).

479. Which building has the world's largest, fully retractable roof?

The world's largest, fully retractable roof covers Toronto's SkyDome. The all-weather, all-purpose stadium was officially opened on 3 June 1989. The roof covers a 10-acre field (the size of a 32-house subdivision) some 300 feet above the middle of the field (the height of a 30-storey building). The roof, which weighs 19 million pounds and measures 680 feet at its widest point, opens to reveal 100% of the field and 91% of the stadium's interior. It consists of four panels, three of which are moveable and one fixed. They are manually operated and take twenty minutes to open or close – to the joy of SkyDome fans. Maximum seating is 63,000 spectators.

480. What was the longest telegram of protest ever sent?

The longest telegram of protest ever sent was half a mile long. It consisted of a brief resolution followed by the names of 177,000 Canadians. According to an item in *The Vancouver Province*, 5 November 1971, the telegram took Western Union four days to send. It was addressed to the U.S. President at the White House in Washington, D.C., and it was sponsored by Greenpeace. It protested the continued U.S. testing of atomic devices on the Aleutian island of Amchitka.

481. What is the current name of the Huron and Erie Savings and Loan Society?

The Huron and Erie Savings and Loan Society was founded in 1864 in London, Ontario. The growth of "the old Huron and Erie" was steady but unspectacular until 1959 when it became the first trust company to sponsor a mutual fund.

Today, as Canada Trust, it offers a range of financial services. Its corporate name is Canada Trustco Mortgage Company, and in the late 1980s it had assets of $24 billion and some 10,300 employees. Acquired by the Toronto Dominion Bank, it is the country's largest trust company and seventh largest financial institution.

482. Who opened the first McDonald's in Moscow?

George Cohon, who owns and operates the McDonald's fast-food franchise in Canada, officially opened the first McDonald's restaurant in the Soviet Union. On 7 February 1990, the first Big Mac was served under the Golden Arches in Moscow's Pushkin Square. Cohon, a Chicago-born, Toronto-based lawyer, was responsible for the McDonald's chain expanding into the Communist world.

483. Who are the so-called Language Police or Tongue Troopers?

French was proclaimed the official language of Quebec and the sole language of the province's Courts and Legislature with the passage of Bill 101 in 1977. It has come to be known as the Charter of the French Language. When the Supreme Court of Canada declared many of its provisions to be unconstitutional, it was replaced in part by Bill 178, which offered the ingenious and infamous "inside-outside" regulation. By this rule English-only signs may be displayed inside an establishment but only French signs may be displayed outside an establishment.

To police these measures and to investigate complaints of violations of its "language laws," the Quebec government established the Office de la langue française with its Commission de protection de la langue française. Agents of the latter group are known derisively in English as the Language Police or the Tongue Troopers.

484. Which items appear on Peter Gzowski's list of the ten best things in the world?

Peter Gzowski, the popular host of CBC Radio's *Morningside*, included a list of the ten best things in the world in his memoir *The Private Voice: A Journal of Reflections* (1988). Here is his list:

Home-made strawberry ice cream; Sable Island; Roger Angell writing about baseball in *The New Yorker*; Gas barbecues; Handknit socks; September; Shirtwaist dresses; Evelyn Hart; Newly talcumed babies; "Somewhere Over the Rainbow."

485. Which three feature films have soundtracks with contributions by the pianist Glenn Gould?

Three feature films make use of performances of the works of Bach by the pianist Glenn Gould who contributed musical advice and musical bridges to make the editing easier. The films are the following: *Slaughterhouse-Five* based on Kurt Vonnegut's novel; *The Terminal Man* which starred Sir Laurence Oliver; and *The Wars* based on Timothy Findley's novel and directed by Robin Philips.

486. What Canadian book was extravagantly praised by Edith Sitwell?

The English poet and author Edith Sitwell wrote a review in which she praised Northrop Frye's *Fearful Symmetry* (1957) in the following words: "It is a book of great wisdom and every page opens fresh doors on the universe of reality and that universe of the transfusion of reality which is called art."

487. Who is the author of the *Lemon-Aid New Car Guide* and *Lemon-Aid Used Car Guide*?

The Lemon-Aid New Car Guide and *The Lemon-Aid Used Car Guide* are the titles of annual paperbacks that rate, the best and worst new and used cars and minivans. As well, they offer car buyers tips on sales traps and "lemons" to avoid.

The best-selling guides were launched in 1975. By 1990, over 150,000 copies of the used car guide alone had been sold. The guide is the work of Phil Edmonston, founder of the Automobile Protection Association guides. A journalist by training and a car enthusiast by avocation, Edmonston was elected a Member of the Quebec National Assembly in 1990.

488. What slap caused a flap in diplomatic circles?

Sondra Gotlieb caused a flap in diplomatic circles when she slapped another woman's face in public. The sound of one hand slapping was heard if not around the world then at least across Canada.

The woman who did the slapping, in public and in anger, was Sondra Gotlieb, spouse of Allan Gotlieb, Canada's Ambassador to the United States. The woman on the receiving end of the slap was her veteran social secretary, Connie Connor, who was delivering bad news – there were five, last-minute cancellations that required changes in the seating arrangements for the reception and dinner party organized by the Gotliebs at the official Canadian residence in Washington, D.C.

Among the 225 guests were Prime Minister Brian and Mila Mulroney and U.S. Vice-President (later President) George and Barbara Bush. There were apologies and red faces (not just Connor's) all around. The incident, which took place on 19 March 1986, effectively ended Canada's campaign of "dinner diplomacy" in Washington.

489. Is there is a connection between Earl Grey Tea and the Dominion of Canada?

There is a connection, albeit a slight one, between Earl Grey Tea and the Dominion of Canada. The English tea is quite popular in Canada, as it is throughout the world, so even a minor relationship is of interest, as it sheds light on two otherwise unrelated aspects of life: a beverage and a statesman.

Earl Grey tea is the world's best selling tea. "Until recently, Earl Grey was not a very popular tea, but the basic formula was changed to conform to current tastes," wrote Jennifer Harvey Long in *Tastings: The Best from Ketchup to Caviar* (1986). "Thus it is now the best-selling tea not only in the United States but also throughout the world. It is generally made by blending Darjeeling, Ceylon, and China black teas, and flavoured with oil of bergamot, a Turkish pear-shaped orange. It is named after Earl Grey, who was Prime Minister of Britain in 1830. The recipe is supposed to have been given to an emissary of Earl Grey's by a grateful Mandarin."

Charles Grey (1764-1845), 2nd Earl Grey, was the Whig leader who presided over the passage of the Reform Act of 1832. It was his grandson, Albert Henry George Grey (1851-1917), 4th Earl Grey, who served as the imperial-minded Governor General of Canada (1904-11). Although the statesman presided over innumerable music and drama festivals, and even allowed the football trophy to be named the Grey Cup, it remains a moot point to this day whether or not Governor General Earl Grey served Earl Grey tea while serving as Governor General.

490. Why is the hockey club called the Maple Leafs and not the Maple Leaves?

No one knows the answer to this question. The plural form of the noun "leaf" is, as every schoolchild should know, "leaves," not "leafs." Yet the Toronto hockey club and team are known as the Toronto Maple Leafs. The choice of the leaf emblem as the insignia of the team followed the use of the emblem on the chest of sweaters worn by members of the 1924 Canadian Olympic team. The name of the hockey team dates from February 1927, when a group of sportsmen acquired the St. Patrick's, a Toronto hockey club with many Irish members and followers and renamed them the Toronto Maple Leafs. For almost half a century, they reigned as the country's dominant sports team.

491. What are *télé-romans?*

Télé-romans, or "television novels," are daytime television series that are popular among Francophones in Quebec. They are a cut or two above the level of American soap operas in sophistication.

492. Why is *Voice of Fire* the best-known work of art in the National Gallery of Canada?

The National Gallery of Canada announced in March 1990 its acquisition of a painting called *Voice of Fire* by the abstract expressionist painter Barnett

Newman. Newman's minimalist canvas is approximately eighteen feet high and consists of a colour field of three panels (blue on the peripheries, red in the centre). This minimalist work attracted expressionistic interest.

The purchase met with public hostility for a number of reasons: its price ($1.78 million), Newman's nationality (American), Newman's strong presence in the Gallery's permanent collection (three canvases and two watercolours before the major acquisition), and the Gallery's spotty representation of major Canadian artists (no works by Louis de Niverville, Doris MacCarthy or Charles Pachter, for instance).

Related issues ranged from the silly (anyone with a paint-roller and two cans of paint could do as well) to the serious (anyone who criticizes the traditional "arm's-length" relationship between the Government and a Crown corporation should be ridiculed). Defenders of the acquisition pointed out that Newman influenced Canadian artists through his teaching at the Emma Lake school in the 1950s and the fact that "Voice of Fire" was initially exhibited at the American Pavilion at Expo 67.

Critics of the acquisition felt that the painting was overpriced, that the sale was ill-advised at a time of budget constraints, that the art it represented (abstract expressionism) was passé, that the Gallery's purchasing priorities were haywire, and that *Voice of Fire* was irrelevant to the Canadian experience.

One effect of the public's outcry was to focus attention on this canvas, with the result that *Voice of Fire* became the best-known modern work of art in the permanent collection of the National Gallery of Canada.

493. What are *the fifth estate* and *W5*?

These are the names of two popular weekly public affairs shows shown on Canadian television networks. *The fifth estate* (for no ascertainable reason the title always appears in lower-case letters) is a CBC-TV production, and *W5* emanates from the CTV Network. The *fifth estate* is a traditional French reference to the press; *W5* refers to the journalist's questions: who, what, when, where, and why.

494. What was the name of the Queen's favourite mount?

Queen Elizabeth II's favourite mount was Burmese. The jet black mare was presented to Her Majesty by the Royal Canadian Mounted Police in

1969. Photographs of Her Majesty and Burmese were widely reproduced throughout the Commonwealth. Burmese was used for the Trooping the Colour ceremony which each year marked Her Majesty's birthday. It was an international news story when, at the age of twenty-eight, Burmese was officially retired from ceremonial duties in 1986. Burmese died in July 1990.

495. Is the Prime Minister's official office located in the Central Block on Parliament Hill?

No. The Prime Minister's Office and the Privy Council Office are both located in the Langevin Block, an old office building on Wellington Street which faces Parliament Hill.

496. What was the so-called Trojan Lamb?

The Trojan Lamb, a parade float, made its appearance in the streets of Montreal on 25 June 1990, part of the festivities sponsored by Quebec's Société Saint-Jean Baptiste. The society's float consisted of a three-story high, papier-mache construction in the shape of a lamb so designed as to represent the Trojan Horse of Greek mythology. The lamb was led by school children representative of all ethnic groups.

The lamb is the traditional image of this ultra-nationalistic society. The Trojan Lamb rejected the traditional image of a meek little boy with a docile lamb, implying, instead, that in the future it would be ultra-nationalism that would inform the values of Quebec society – an especially meaningful message, following so soon after the rejection of the Meech Lake accord.

497. What is *Newsworld?*

CBC Newsworld is the name of the all-news, English-language, satellite cable television network, a joint offering of the Canadian Broadcasting Corporation and the private cable sector. Cablecasting commenced at 6:30 a.m., Monday, 31 July 1989. It telecasts twenty-four hours a day in English from Toronto with much regional programming.

498. What is RDI?

RDI stands for *Réseau de l'Information*, Radio-Canada's equivalent of *CBC Newsworld*. It is a twenty-four-hour cable news channel in French from Montreal, inaugurated 1 January 1995.

499. What is the title of the Quebec feature film that was retitled in advertisements by the editors of some American newspapers?

How to Make Love to a Negro without Getting Tired is the title of the English version of the feature film made in Quebec in 1989 that ran into difficulties with American newspaper editors. Rather than run the full, attention-getting title, they abbreviated it in the advertisements in their papers to the following: *How to Make Love without Getting Tired*.

It is actually a charming study of sexual stereotypes and racial politics based on the French-language book by Dany Laferrière, a Haitian émigré writer from Montreal.

500. What happened to the nymph on the cover of the Canadian edition of "Weird Tales"?

The drawing of a semi-naked nymph, blonde and lissome, appeared on the cover *Weird Tales*, September 1939, a pulp magazine devoted to fantasy fiction. A fetching cover illustration, the prancing nymph illustrates the story "The Blue Woman" written by John Scott Douglas. There are differences between the American edition and the Canadian edition of this magazine with respect to editorial matter and design and illustration. The same cover art appears on the Canadian edition, but Forrest J. Ackerman, the collector of fantasy memorabilia, noted that the Canadian censor had been at work, airbrushing not only the nymph's nipples but also her breasts. On the Canadian cover, the female nymph was turned into a male nymph (at least from the waist up)!

501. In what Hollywood movie did Errol Flynn play a Mountie?

The Australian-born Hollywood actor Errol Flynn was cast as a Mountie in the 1943 movie *Northern Pursuit*. His task was to capture Nazi spies who, having landed in the Canadian Arctic, are making their way to the United States where they had orders to undermine the U.S. war effort. According to critic Jim Bawden, the best actor in the film was Canadian-born actor Gene Lockhart who played a Nazi spy at a Hudson Bay outpost.

502. In what Hollywood movie did Dick Powell play a Mountie?

Dick Powell, the suave character actor, played a rugged Mountie named Mike Flannigan in the 1949 Hollywood film *Mrs. Mike*. It tells the story of a Boston girl, played by Evelyn Keyes, who marries the Mountie and succumbs to the attractions of the northern lifestyle.

503. In what Hollywood movie did Montgomery Clift play a Catholic Priest in Quebec?

The 1953 Hollywood film in question was called *I Confess*. In this psychological thriller directed by Alfred Hitchcock, who set it in Quebec City, Montgomery Clift plays a priest with a bad conscience because he has heard a confession of murder from a criminal. It ends with a chase sequence that goes through the cavernous Chateau Frontenac.

The ambience of Hitchcock's dark thriller is recalled in *The Confession* (1995), a pretentious feature film that marked the movie début of Quebec theatre director Robert LePage. The later film includes sequences that recreate the making of *I Confess* and show an actor impersonating Hitchcock. It tries for no reason to counterpoint events in the 1950s with those in the 1990s. The "remake" gives the original version a bad name.

504. Who named the Loonie?

In 1987, the Royal Canadian Mint made an announcement that it would issue a new, one-dollar coin which featured the image of a loon. The announcement inspired Charles Cook, a retired Toronto school principle. He decided to name the new coin. As he subsequently told Lew Gloin, "Words," *The Toronto Star*, 6 September 1987, "I have attained etymological nirvana. I lay claim to having introduced a word, albeit slang, into the language."

To this end, Cook wrote a letter to the editor of *The Globe and Mail,* published on 21 January 1987, which suggested that the new coin be called the "looney."

"My letter, unless preceded by another, should provide lexicographers with a verifiable first reference point," Cook told Gloin.

"Repeated references to looney (spelling variances allowed for) in subsequent articles in national newspapers plus its increased use by the public seem to indicate that it will find a place in Canadian dictionaries."

Cook was right. Despite the fact that he spelled it "looney" (as in Looney Tunes) and that it is now spelled "loonie," he named it. No one has yet named its successor, the two-dollar coin, feebly known as the "twoonie."

505. What was the connection between the Devil and the Prairie scene on the back of the old one-dollar bill?

A stretch of lonely Prairie with storm clouds was the scene depicted on the reverse side of the one-dollar bill which was in circulation since the 1960s and withdrawn in the 1980s with the appearance of the Loonie. The scene was based on a photograph of Gronlid, Saskatchewan, whose residents maintained that the road and the railway end there. In fact, it is locally said at Gronlid that "this is where the Devil says good night." This piece of folklore was noted by Paul Wilson in his column "Street Beat" in *The Hamilton Spectator*, 27 February 1990.

506. Are penguins and a dinosaur depicted on the reverse side of the two-dollar coin?

The short answer is no. The long answer is maybe. The reverse side of the twoonie (or two-dollar piece) is dominated by a giant polar bear. Turn the polar bear upside down. Place your hand over the body of the bear. The inverted legs resemble four penguins. As for the dinosaur, turn the polar bear on its nose so that the final S of Dollar and the final A of Canada are at the bottom. Cover those letters and the bear's head with your finger and examine the bear's rump. That looks like a left-looking Tyrannosaurus rex; the bear's two legs look like the dinosaur's stubby arms. Needless to say, these images are unintentional and a testimonial to the ingenuity of the public rather than the work of the designer of the twoonie.

507. Is a beaver depicted on the twenty-five cent piece?

Yes and no. A caribou with mighty antlers is depicted on the reverse side of the Canadian quarter. However, if you turn the caribou's head upside-down and trace the outline of the jaw and neck, you will find that the area so defined resembles that of a fat beaver, facing right. The image is an accidental illusion.

508. What is the most valuable Canadian coin?

The 1911 silver dollar is valued at more than $1 million. That is because only two of these coins were issued, the federal government having decided to cancel its production. According to Mark Kearney and Randy Ray in *The Great Canadian Trivia Book 2* (1998), "The 1911 silver dollar depicts King George V and is 92.5 per cent silver. It weighs 23.3 grams and is 36 millimetres in diameter." Both coins are in mint condition. One of them is displayed at the Bank of Canada Currency Museum in Ottawa. The other was purchased by an American collector/dealer Jay Perrino in 1998 for more than $1 million from a Calgary coin dealer.

509. Whose face appears on Canadian Tire "money"?

In the late 1950s, the Canadian Tire company began to issue paper vouchers to be honoured at their stores and outlets against purchases. In 1962, to appear on the vouchers, artist Bernie Freedman drew the face of a wily old Scott, bewhiskered and tam o'shanter-wearing, who was soon dubbed Sandy McTire. He is the embodiment of frugality. Over the years Canadian Tire has issued $50 million dollars worth of its "paper money," and Sandy McTire smiles on all of them.

510. Whose photographs are the basis of images on the $1 Canadian bill?

The one-dollar Canadian bill featured two photographs. On the front of the bill appears the portrait of Queen Elizabeth II; on the back, a panoramic view of logs floating on the Ottawa River below Parliament Hill. The studio portrait was taken by Karsh of Ottawa; the panorama by his brother Malak, a specialist in landscape photography. Some 3.5 billion one-dollar bills were issued over a period of thirteen years, until it was replaced by the Loonie in 1987.

511. Who designed the distinctive Maple Leaf on the Maple Leaf Flag?

The actual design of the Maple Leaf was the work of the Ottawa-based designer Jacques Saint Cyr who at the time was a member of the Canadian Government Exhibition Commission. He determined the technical requirements for the new flag in November 1964, according to Patrick Reid, "Letters to the Editor," *The Globe and Mail,* 6 August 1990.

512. Who is credited with the design of the Maple Leaf Flag?

The National Flag of Canada is popularly known as the Maple Leaf Flag. Although the work of a committee, the basic design was proposed in 1965 by George F.G. Stanley, who had been, in his day, a professor, historian, army colonel, and Lieutenant-Governor of Nova Scotia. A bust in the designer's honour (executed by sculptor Elizabeth Holbrook) was unveiled at the new civic offices in Stoney Creek, Ontario, on 22 June 1991.

513. Are there some "lost" Canadian manuscripts or books?

One can only take a run at referring to lost or misplaced Canadian manuscripts or books.

Anthropologist A. Irving Halliwell made a contribution to the "Case Study Series on the Northern Ojibwa" titled "The Berens River Fairwind's Drum Dance," but it went unpublished during his lifetime because the manuscript was lost about 1963 in transit to the United States. A version of the book-length study was compiled, edited, and completed by fellow ethnographer Jennifer S.H. Brown of the University of Winnipeg as part of the series "Case History in Cultural Anthropology" and published as *The Ojibwa of Berens River, Manitoba: Ethnography into History* (Fort Worth: Harcourt Brace Jovanovich College Publishers, 1992).

In 1882, Oscar Wilde delivered addresses in numerous halls throughout Ontario, Quebec, New Brunswick, and Nova Scotia. "The Decorative Arts" was the title of one of his addresses. The MS has been lost, but it was brilliantly reconstructed (using fragments quoted in sixty local newspapers of the day) by the literary scholar Kevin O'Brien. It appears in the appendix to his study *Oscar Wilde in Canada* (1982).

The naturalist Grey Owl liked to boast that he could "talk" to beavers and that they would answer him. He certainly had a way with beavers. He even claimed that he was compiling a "Beaver Dictionary" that included lists of sounds and their meanings that beavers recognized. No such manuscript was found among his papers after his death in Prince Albert, Saskatchewan, in 1938.

Another lost MS is one that was stolen: the correspondence of Morley Callaghan. In the early 1990s, a sheaf of Callaghan's letters from famous people was stolen from the safe in the office of a Toronto rare book dealer and has never turned up.

Then there is the top-secret, 423-page secret history of the undercover operations during World War II conducted by Sir William Stephenson. *An Account of Secret Activities in the Western Hemisphere, 1940-1945* (British Security Co-ordinator, Rockefeller Centre). It was written by Stephenson and bears his 1945 foreword. "Only ten copies of which are said to exist," noted John Picton, who examined one of them in "Spymaster 'Intrepid' Caught in Middle of a War of Words," *The Toronto Star*, 8 October 1989.

514. Is there a "lost" portrait of Oscar Wilde?

Yes, there is a "lost" portrait of Oscar Wilde. It was sketched by an artist known as Miss Lily Burton, a daughter of the Senior Justice of the Court of Appeal for Ontario, the Hon. George William Burton. As Kevin O'Brien noted in *Oscar Wilde in Canada* (1982), "She was an 'apostle' of Aestheticism and, when she heard that Oscar Wilde was coming to Toronto in May 1882, she begged for an invitation to meet him." They met and Wilde was charmed, later describing her as "very pretty and sweet." Apparently she sketched him from life. Alas, the drawing is a "lost" portrait of Oscar Wilde. Perhaps it has survived the vicissitudes of years and will one day reappear.

515. Whose three books were published in the same year by New York publisher Alfred A. Knopf?

The distinguished publisher Alfred A. Knopf, to draw attention to the writing of Margaret Laurence, accepted three of her books for publication or republication in the United States. These were *The Prophet's Camel Bell* (a book of literary essays), *The Tomorrow Tamer* (a collection of stories), and *The Stone Angel* (a novel). As Laurence later wrote in her memoirs, "This was truly a breakthrough.... This had rarely, if ever, been done, but it helped draw attention to my writing." They appeared in the fall of 1965.

516. What important novel, while still in manuscript form, was first called "Hagar" and then "Old Lady Shipley"?

Margaret Laurence used these as the working titles for the novel she retitled, immediately prior to publication, *The Stone Angel* (1964). The final and most fitting title is based on a reference in the novel's first line to a stone statue that has the shape of an angel that stands in the cemetery in the author's birthplace, Neepawa, Manitoba.

517. Did a game of lacrosse end in a massacre?

Yes. "The most famous game of lacrosse involved two native teams, who offered to help the British celebrate the King's birthday on June 4th, 1768, near the fortress gates of Fort Michilimackinac, at the northern end of Lake Michigan. It had been less than three years since the final collapse of New France, when the British had captured Montreal. To the Ojibways, former allies of the French, the English were still the enemy. Although forewarned that they were up to no good, the British commander, Major Etherington, allowed the game to proceed."

William Humber in "The Spirit of the Black Bear" in *The Idler*, No. 24, July-August 1989, continued: "The game inched closer to the garrison, and at one point the ball was tossed through the garrison's open gates. Players rushing to regain possession threw down their sticks and grabbed guns, tomahawks, and knives that had been concealed by native women standing near the gate. There was a terrible massacre. Only a few inside the fort were spared and later ransomed back to the British. Not one French trader or half-breed inside the fort was molested."

Never before or since has a game of lacrosse been so bloody.

518. Did Bovril originate in Montreal?

It is sometimes said that Bovril originated in Montreal, but that is not so. Yet the food product does have a connection with that city.

John Lawson Johnston, a Scots provisioner, secured the contract to supply the British Army with a beef extract. He began producing what he called Johnston's Fluid Beef in England in 1871.

The story goes that a Montreal nutritionist invented the product in the 1880s. But the only connection with Montreal is that in 1879, when his original factory near London burned down, Johnston moved to Montreal and built a plant which produced the extract using cattle raised in Canada. Johnston's Fluid Beef was dispensed as a hot drink from the "Ice Palaces" at the Montreal winter carnivals from 1881 to 1884. Johnston returned to England in 1884 and produced it from London. It slowly caught on as a medicinal and recreational drink.

The name Bovril dates from sales at the South Kensington Exhibition of 1887, where it was dispensed in imitation "Ice Palaces" made of glass. Bo comes from the Latin *bos* for ox, and vril comes from Vril, an "electric fluid" described by Lord Bulwer-Lytton's novel *The Coming Race*. Newly named, its popularity was unprecedented. It was dispensed at pubs, it provisioned the troops in the Boer War, and it became a favourite of mountain-climbers and other adventurous travellers.

As Richard Bennett explained in *The Story of Bovril* (issued by Bovril Limited in 1953), cattle was in short supply in England. The extract requires ten pounds of prime beef to produce one pound of the extract. An early Bovril label shows one ox saying to another, "Alas, my poor brother."

519. What is the so-called Eskimo Diet?

No one had ever heard of "the Eskimo Diet" until two British physicians, Reg Saynor and Frank Ryan, published their diet book: *The Eskimo Diet: How to Prevent a Heart Attack* (London: Ebury Press, 1990). The authors, noting the low incidence of heart attacks among the world's Inuit population and observing their widespread consumption of fish oil, recommended "the revolutionary effect of fish oil in helping to prevent a blood clot forming within the coronary arteries."

520. Should everyone vote during the same period of time in a federal election?

It is not uncommon for the press to declare on election night that a federal government has been elected even before the polls have closed and the ballots counted in British Columbia. Therefore it is possible that knowledge of voting patterns in Atlantic and Eastern Canada influences the voting in the Pacific province.

To deal with this concern in the early 1980s, the federal government considered adopting a measure that would ensure that members of the electorate, regardless of where they resided in the country, would vote during the same period of time. This was merely a matter of adjusting voting hours in different time zones. The proposed hours for casting a ballot, expressed in regional standard times, were as follows:

Newfoundland: 12:00 noon to 10:00 p.m.
Atlantic: 11:30 a.m. to 9:30 p.m.
Eastern: 10:30 a.m. to 8:30 p.m.
Central: 9:30 a.m. to 7:30 p.m.
Mountain: 8:30 a.m. to 6:30 p.m.
Pacific: 7:30 a.m. to 5:30 p.m.

The measure was not adopted.

521. What are Northerners?

The Northerners are – or were – works of fiction set in the frontier days of Alaska, the Yukon, the Barrens, Hudson Bay, and other locales in the Far North. According to Bill Prozini and Martin H. Greenberg, editors of the anthology titled *The Northerners* (1990), these stories appeared in pulp magazines and later in book form and were widely read in the United States and Canada during the period from the Klondike Gold Rush of 1898 to the end of the Depression in 1939. The best-known writers of Northerners were Jack London, Rex Beach, James Oliver Curwood, and Robert W. Service. The stories they wrote evoked the Spirit of The North and described the clash between good and evil in terms of everyday lives of prospectors, hunters, trappers, traders, North American Indians, Inuit, and Mounties. These stories are not widely read today except in historical anthologies of popular writing like *The Northerners*.

522. What film explores the backgrounds of eight women who are stranded in the Quebec countryside?

In the Company of Strangers (1991), directed by Gloria Demers and Cynthia Scott, is the semi-dramatic, semi-documentary film that explores the backgrounds and examines the relationships of eight women who are stranded in the Quebec countryside after their bus breaks down. The women are strangers to each other; except for the young female bus driver, the women are old. They take shelter in an abandoned farmhouse and tell their stories until help arrives. The women were not actresses. One woman is Mary Meigs, the artist and memoirist. The film is regarded as a feminist classic.

523. Who wrote the song "Nous Vivons Ensemble / We've Got to Stay Together"?

Gordon Lightfoot composed the patriotic, bilingual song "Nous Vivons Ensemble / We've Got to Stay Together" in 1971 in the wake of the October Crisis. He sang it for the first time at a concert in Quebec City. It may be heard on his album *Summer Side of Life*.

524. What has been called "the most important single political document in twentieth-century Canadian history"?

Military historian and biographer C.P. Stacey described W.L. Mackenzie King's voluminous and detailed political and personal diary in this way: "It is the most important single political document in twentieth-century Canadian history." The diary, kept from 1893 to within three days of his death in 1950, was the late Prime Minister's legacy. Portions of it have been published. Portions that deal in detail with his interest in spiritualism await publication.

525. What happened to Kaiser Bill's bust?

The bust of Kaiser Bill was pitched into the lake in Victoria Park, Berlin, Ontario.

It happened the night of 22 August 1914 when militia members, smarting at criticism that local men were slow to enlist for combat in the

Great War, met at the David Street entrance to the park where on a prominent pedestal stood the bust of old German Kaiser Wilhelm II. The militia men knocked the bust off its pedestal, dragged it to the shore of the park's little lake, and rolled it over the brink.

The bust was quietly recovered from its water repose and installed at the town's Concordia Club. On 15 February 1916, soldiers from the 118th Battalion broke into the club and took Old Bill on a parade up King Street. Thereafter Old Bill disappeared. Rumours about the whereabouts of Old Bill have circulated, including the one that the metal was melted and moulded into serviette rings. This story, among others, is told by Richard O'Brien in "Hunting for Kaiser Bill's Bust," *Kitchener Marketplace*, 10 June 1987.

526. What was predictive about the portrait of Mackenzie King's mother?

A large portrait in oil of Isabel Grace Mackenzie, beloved mother of the late Prime Minister Mackenzie King, adorns the wall of King's study in Laurier House, King's Ottawa home, now a national museum. The painting has been called "the predictive portrait."

It was prepared by the well-known artist J.W.L. Foster in 1905, and it depicts Mrs. Mackenzie as a stern lady in white, seated, with a book in her lap. King maintained that the book is identifiable as Morley's *Life of Gladstone* and that it lies open at the chapter titled "Prime Minister." King always maintained that this was a sign that Mrs. Mackenzie's son would one day attain the office of prime minister. King became Prime Minister in 1921, sixteen years after the portrait was painted.

527. Which church in Montreal is known as "the parish church of French Canada"?

That distinction belongs to Notre-Dame Basilica, Place d'Armes, Montreal. The beautiful basilica "has seen the great funerals of George-Etienne Cartier and Pierre Laporte and heard the great speeches of Henri Bourassa and Archbishop Charbonneau," according to Ron Graham in *God's Dominion: A Sceptic's Quest* (1990). No doubt he would add to those names that of Pierre Elliott Trudeau in 2000.

528. What towers are named Temperance and Perseverance?

The twin towers of the Notre-Dame Basilica in Montreal, erected in 1824-29, have names. The east tower is known as Temperance and the west tower is known as Perseverance. The east tower encloses a ten-bell carillon, the west tower le Gros Bourdon, a bell that weighs 11,240 kg.

529. Are the electronic media superior to the medium of print for the purpose of learning?

This question intrigued Marshall McLuhan and Edmund S. Carpenter of the University of Toronto. They organized a study at the CBC studios in Toronto in Spring 1954 which divided 100 students into four equal groups. Each group was exposed to the same lecture. The first group watched the lecture on television, the second saw it in a television studio, the third listened to it over the radio, and the fourth read it in printed form. When comprehension and retention of the contents of the lecture were tested, it was found that television fared best and print fared worst. Results of subsequent studies conducted by educators were less clear-cut.

530. How did Marshall McLuhan read a book?

Marshall McLuhan, the communications theorist, was an omnivorous reader. But he treated books as if they were useful tools. "To determine whether a book was worth reading, he usually looked at page 69 of the work, plus the adjacent page and the table of contents. If the author gave no promise of insight or worthwhile information on page 69, McLuhan reasoned, the book was probably not worth reading. If he decided the book did merit his attention, he started by reading only the left-hand pages. He claimed he didn't miss much with this method, since there were so many redundancies in most books." So explained Philip Marchand in *Marshall McLuhan: The Medium and the Messenger* (1989).

531. What does the acronym CPR represent?

CPR is the acronym for Canadian Pacific Railway or Cardio-Pulminary Respiration.

532. What plaque appears in every major CNR train station?

This question is answered by railway enthusiast Robert F. Legget in his book *Railways of Canada* (rev. ed., 1987):

> It is small wonder that in every major railway station throughout Canada that is used by CNR trains there will be found today a bronze plaque bearing these words: In Memory of / Sir Henry Thornton K.B.E. / Chairman and President / Canadian National Railways / 1922-1932 / Died March 15th 1933 / This table erected by the Employees / of Canadian National Railways.

The plaque honours Sir Henry Thornton as a railway executive. It might well acknowledge his leadership in the field of public radio broadcasting. Through his initiative, radios were introduced to the dining cars of transcontinental trains in the era before the creation of national broadcasting systems.

533. What are the CRTC's categories for FM radio program content?

The Canadian Radio-television and Telecommunications Commission (CRTC) is the government agency that regulates national radio and television broadcasting. In its Public Notice on FM policy, 17 December 1990, it established the following "content categories":

> Category 1. Spoken Word: News; Spoken Word – Other.
> Category 2. Music – General: Pop, Rock, and Dance; Country and Country-oriented; Folk-oriented; Jazz oriented.
> Category 3. Concert Music: Folk; Jazz; Non-classic religious.
> Category 4. Musical Production: Musical Themes, Bridges, and Stingers; Technical Tests; Musical Station Identification; Musical Identification of Announcers, Programs; Musical Promotion of Announcers, Programs.
> Category 5. Advertising: Commercial Announcement; Sponsor Identification; Promotion with Sponsor Mention.

534. Are there mistakes engraved on the Stanley Cup?

As surprising as it seems, there are mistakes engraved on the Stanley Cup. According to Wayne Gretzky, writing in *Gretzky: An Autobiography* (1990), "The 1963 Maple Leafs are spelled 'Leaes,' and Peter Pocklington put his dad's name on it and the NHL didn't allow it, so if you look closely you'll see all these x's through the name."

535. Who is the largest employer in Canada?

The Public Service of Canada is the country's largest single employer. At its height in the early 1980s, before the substantial reductions of the 1980s and 1990s, approximately 212,000 Canadians worked for the Government of Canada. Perhaps an equal number of Canadians are employed by the ten provincial governments.

One-third of the federal employees live in the Ottawa area. Public servants are recruited through the Public Service Commission (PSC) which staffs some seventy departments and agencies. There are six categories of employment.

536. Is the Public Service increasing or decreasing in size?

The workforce of the Public Service Commission has been decreasing. In 1978, the number of public servants was 137,359. In 1988, the number was 121,135. Since then the size of the public service has been steadily reduced by successive federal administrations.

537. What are the Public Service Commission's categories of employment?

The PSC's six broad occupational categories are as follows:

1. Management. Incumbents are engaged in policy formulation, program development and delivery, the design and operation of management systems, personnel and financial administration and public affairs.
2. Scientific and Professional. These groups range from Actual Science to Veterinary Medicine.
3. Administrative and Foreign Service. Characteristic groups are

Administrative Services, Commerce, Foreign Service, Information Services, Welfare Programs, etc.

4. Technical. The groups include Air traffic Control and Technical Inspection.

5. Administrative Support. Here the range is Clerical and Regulatory to Secretarial, Stenographic, and Typing.

6. Operational. Included are Correctional Services, Lightkeepers, Ship Repair, etc.

In addition there are categories of occupational groups within the Management Category of the Public Service Commission. Senior personnel working under the Deputy Minister comprise either the Executive Group (EX) or the Senior Management Group (SM). There are five levels of EXs, but there is only one level of SM.

Finally, the workforce of the Public Service Commission is grouped horizontally by six categories and vertically by level. For instance, employment in Forestry (FO) begins at entry level, FO-1, and proceeds to FO-4, which is head of a management section.

538. What does Employment Equity in the Public Service mean?

The Public Service Commission is committed to Employment Equity so that all Canadians have the opportunity to be considered for positions in the Public service. Special programs include Access Program for Disabled Persons, Visible Minority Employment Program, Northern Careers Program, National Indigenous Development Program, and The Non-Traditional Occupations Program for Women.

539. Where in Canada is Burns's walking stick on display?

As surprising as it might seem, the walking stick of the great Scottish bard Robert Burns may be viewed at the Gaelic College of Celtic Arts and Crafts, St. Ann's, Cape Breton Island, Nova Scotia. In 1788, Burns accidentally left it behind in a friend's house in Tarbolton, Scotland. It passed from one family to another until 1942 when it came into the possession of Fred Turley of Marion Bridge, Nova Scotia, who eventually donated it to the Gaelic College. The gnarled, well-honoured, well-polished cudgel resides in a display case with a complete account of its provenance.

540. Where can one view "the boat who wouldn't float"?

The Boat Who Wouldn't Float is the title of a semi-fictional narrative written by Farley Mowat and published in 1968. It is the humorous account of the life and times of Mowat's schooner, *The Happy Adventure*. By happy chance, the vessel, complete with compass and flag, has been restored and is dry-docked on a bluff overlooking a craft shop at Margaree Harbour, Cape Breton Island, Nova Scotia. It was formally dedicated 8 July 1990. For decades Mowat maintained a summer home in the vicinity.

541. Which universities are the oldest publicly owned universities in North America?

The University of New Brunswick, in Fredericton, New Brunswick, and the University of Georgia, in Atlanta, Georgia, are the oldest publicly owned universities in North America. Both were founded in the year 1785, and they are now twinned. The Old Arts Building on the Fredericton campus is the oldest university building still in use in the country.

542. Where is the newest Anglican Cathedral?

Christ Church Cathedral was erected in eight years in the Gothic Revival style in Fredericton, New Brunswick, and consecrated on 31 August 1853. The edifice was the first entirely new Cathedral foundation on British soil constructed since the Norman Conquest and the first built in the Anglican Communication following the Reformation. It is the sole true Cathedral Church in Canada, as it does not function as a parish Church, but as the "Mother Church" of the entire Diocese of Fredericton.

543. Which painting is the centrepiece of the Beaverbrook Art Gallery?

Santiago El Grande is the centrepiece of the Beaverbrook Art Gallery in Fredericton, New Brunswick. The grandiose canvas, which features a rearing horse and a crucifixion, was painted by the Spanish surrealist artist

Salvador Dali in 1957. It was acquired for the gallery by the Sir James Dunn Foundation and it occupies the place of honour in the gallery.

544. Are there Canadian tartans?

The City of Fredericton acquired its official Scottish dress tartan in 1961. As well, Cape Breton Island and Nova Scotia have official tartans. The island's tartan is black, grey, green, and gold. The colours of the province's tartan, registered in 1956, are blue with white, green, red, and gold.

545. What is the name of the oldest bookstore in Canada?

The Book Room is the oldest bookstore in Canada. Founded in Halifax, Nova Scotia, in 1839, it has made books available to readers since then. Today it is the largest non-chain bookstore in Eastern Canada.

546. Where is the oldest and smallest legislative building in Canada?

Province House in Halifax, the seat of the Nova Scotia legislature, is the oldest legislative building in the country. It was erected in 1811-18. It is also the country's smallest legislative building.

547. Who built the wireless station at Table Head?

The Italian inventor Guglielmo Marconi established the first radio communications between Canada and the British Isles. He built a wireless station at Table Head, Glace Bay, Cape Breton Island, Nova Scotia. In 1902, he transmitted the first complete one-way radio message across the Atlantic Ocean; they were received at Clifden, Ireland. Duplex (or two-way) service followed. Twenty-four hour commercial service commenced in 1907. Marconi Towers, the last of his stations, closed in 1945.

Today, three of Marconi's station sites as well as the Marconi National Historic Site at Table Head may be visited. Orientation information is available in three languages – English, French, and Italian.

548. Why does no one sing the "Canadian Boat-Song"?

The moving words of "Canadian Boat-Song" (from the Gaelic), first published in 1829, are recalled today on Cape Breton Island, yet no traditional singer performs them, and they have yet to be recorded. The reason for this is, it seems, no composer or singer has yet set the words to music. The words appeared anonymously as a poem and have been ascribed to the novelist John Galt; they are more likely the work of David Macbeth Moir, a Scottish versifier. The poem is the lament of a Highland settler from the Hebrides exiled in Upper Canada. The refrain runs: "Fair these broad meads – these hoary woods are grand; / But we are exiles from our fathers' land."

549. What are *hebdos?*

In French, *hebdos* is the short form of the word *hebdomadaires* which means "weekly." Hebdos are weekly tabloids published in Quebec. They are sold in supermarkets and feature scandalous accounts of crime and suggestive stories about *vedettes* or media stars. Among the leading tabloids are *Echoes Vedettes, Allo Vedettes, Allo Police,* and *Photo Police.*

550. Which ship is "Canada's *Mayflower*"?

The sailing ship *Hector* has been called "Canada's *Mayflower*." It transported the first of the Scottish Highlanders to Canada. Some two hundred settlers, the beginning of the tide, set out from Loch Brom in Northern Scotland and landed at Pictou, Nova Scotia, on 15 September 1773. The original Hector, a 110-foot vessel of 200 tons, was both heavier and longer than the *Mayflower* which earlier brought the Pilgrims to Plymouth Rock. In 1991, a modern replica of the *Hecto*r was built at Pictou harbour as a tourist attraction.

551. Whatever happened to Simpsons?

In 1987, Simpsons Ltd., the chain of quality department stores, was acquired by The Hudson's Bay Co. which, in turn, was acquired by the Thomson Organization. By August 1991, all the Simpsons stores were either closed down, sold to Sears Canada Inc., or renamed Bay stores. Thus a Canadian institution, established in 1872, became the victim of the "store wars," corporate concentration, the recession of the early 1990s, and the Free Trade Agreement.

552. Why wasn't Moosehead Beer sold in Ontario?

Moosehead Beer, the potent Maritime brew, is popular in Atlantic Canada and in a number of American states, but it was not always sold in Ontario and in many of the other provinces. For a long time Moosehead was the victim of the policy of provincial protectionism which raised interprovincial trade barriers and encouraged the practice of provincial preferences. Provincial legislation had long required brewers to locate their breweries in provinces where their product was sold. The same was true for wineries. Thus "free trade" was not practised domestically, only internationally, until the 1990s when Moosehead was finally made available in Ontario and many of the other provinces.

553. What books are indispensable to Alberto Manguel?

Alberto Manguel, a leading essayist and commentator on literature, was born in Buenos Aires but has lived in Canada since 1980. In a personal essay about his favourite books, published in *The Globe and Mail*, 27 July 1991, he noted: "When some time ago, I dreamt that I was going to die, the books I took with me on that final journey were only those without which I cannot conceive the world." He then listed the books, which are Jorge Luis Borges's *A Personal Anthology* (1968), Richard Outram's *Selected Poems* (1984), G.K. Chesterton's *The Man Who Was Thursday* (1908), and Lewis Carroll's *Alice's Adventures in Wonderland* (1865) and *Through the Looking Glass* (1872). The least-known of these authors is Richard Outram, a Toronto-based poet of accomplished, somewhat concentrated and conservative verse.

554. What became of Massey-Ferguson Ltd.?

Was there a name more respected than that of the farm-implement manufacturing company, Massey-Ferguson Ltd.? Founded in Toronto in

1847, once known as Massey-Harris, the firm's bright, orange-painted tractors, combines, and harvesters were a familiar sight on the Prairies and, indeed, around the world. Following World War II, the firm moved into auto engines, parts, and industrial equipment, became a conglomerate, fell victim to corporate concentration, and eventually changed its name to Varity Corp. In 1991 it ceased to be a Canadian company altogether, incorporating itself in the State of Delaware and shifting its corporate offices south from Toronto, Ontario, to Buffalo, New York. It finally collapsed in 1995.

555. Who won the War of 1812?

The War of 1812, which lasted two years, was a series of battles fought on land and sea. The United States declared war on Britain and attacked Britain's colonies in what is now Canada. There were gains and losses on both sides before hostilities ceased with the signing of the Treaty of Ghent which brought about the return of the prewar status quo. The British did not yield territory; the Americans did not gain territory. While the outcome could be called a stalemate or a draw, the comedian Don Harron maintains that Canada won: "18 to 12." What colonial Canadians won was a sense of purpose and a wary regard for American expansionism.

556. Which country had the world's largest telescope?

Canadians could boast about building and operating the world's largest and most powerful telescope – but only for a few months in the summer of 1917. According to Terence Dickinson, writing in *The Toronto Star* on 28 July 1991, the 72-inch reflector telescope, erected at the Dominion Astrophysical Observatory near Victoria, British Columbia, was the world's largest telescope in its day.

But its days were numbered. "Later that year the 100-inch telescope at Mount Wilson Observatory near Pasadena, California, was completed, but the 72-inch remained the second-largest telescope on Earth for decades." Since those halcyon years for astronomers, Canadian governments have decreased rather than increased funding for primary research, especially in the field of astronomy.

557. What is the movie *Beautiful Dreamers* all about?

Beautiful Dreamers, released in 1989, is a feature-length motion picture which tells the unusual story of the visit made by a poet in 1880 to London, Ontario, at the invitation of a younger friend who is a medical doctor and the director of the asylum for the insane. The American poet is Walt Whitman (played by Rip Torn) and the friend is Dr. Richard Maurice Bucke (Colm Feore). The film, written and directed by John Kent Harrison, tracks a literary affinity that blossoms into a personal friendship and contrasts new and traditional lifestyles and values. Despite the unlikely storyline, the film is sprightly and appealing.

558. What are visa students?

Visa students are foreign nationals who have received visas from the Canadian government to allow them to study at Canadian educational institutions. Unless they come on scholarships, visa students are assessed enrolment fees to attend primary and secondary schools, which are otherwise free to nationals, and pay increased tuition fees to attend colleges and universities.

559. What is distinctive about the Blyth Festival?

The Blyth Festival is a summer theatre which is devoted exclusively to Canadian productions, ranging from original dramas and adaptations to musicals. It was begun in 1974 in the community hall, which serves as the festival theatre, in the small town of Blyth, near Georgian Bay, Ontario.

560. What is the *Curse of the Viking Grave?*

Curse of the Viking Grave is the title of an adventure novel for young readers written by Farley Mowat and first published in 1974. It continues the action of the same author's earlier novel, *Lost in the Barrens* (1965). It is set in the 1930s and tells how two teenage boys, one Indian and one white, prevent the pillage of an ancient grave site. Both novels have been turned into made-for-TV movies.

561. Why should December the Eleventh be a day of national celebration?

The British North America act was signed on 11 December 1866. It brought the Dominion of Canada into existence on 1 July 1867. Thus, December the Eleventh is the country's original Independence Day and should be marked as a day of national celebration.

562. What was the first non-sport trading card?

Collectors of trading cards maintain that a lithograph of the Marquis of Lorne, the Governor General, was the first trading card that was not a sports card. It was issued in 1879 to promote a brand of cigarette. According to Gary Belsky, writing in *Money*, May 1991, a copy of the Lorne card in good condition will fetch up to $5,000.

563. What distinguishes Canadian gum cards?

Canadian gum cards are trading cards issued by chewing gum companies in Canada. According to the collector John Bell, the years between 1933 and 1942 were the golden age of gum cards in the United States and Canada.

Canadian cards were generally variations of American cards. Bell explained, "These Canadian gum card cousins take three basic forms: firstly, U.S.-produced cards distributed in Canada, but stamped – presumably as a result of import regulations – 'Printed in USA'; secondly, Canadian reissues of U.S. cards; and, finally, Canadian sets based on U.S. issues, but consisting of original cards."

Producers of Canadian gum cards include Canadian Chewing Gum Co.; Gum Inc.; Hamilton Chewing Gum Co.; O-Pee-Chee Co. Ltd.; and World Wide Gum Co. In addition, a series of candy cards was released by Willard Chocolates. As Bell noted, Canadian cards should command high prices from collectors, given their rarity, but as it happens few American (and even fewer Canadian) collectors pay particular attention to them.

564. Did the Stratford Festival lose money in its first season?

The Stratford Shakespearian Festival, as it was originally known, opened the evening of 13 July 1953. The original season was extended from four to six weeks and had 97 per cent attendance. Its first-season deficit (a sign of things to come) was $2,258.

565. What is the licence number of the Prime Minister of Canada's official automobile?

Since 1973, when vanity licence plates were first issued, the official automobile of the Prime Minister bears the Ontario licence plate designation CAN 001.

566. Has the Public Service ever held a general strike?

The Public Service Alliance of Canada, the union for all the workers in the employment of the federal government, declared a general strike on 8 September 1991. Some 65,000 PSAC public servants struck and picketed to protest the government's civil-service wage freeze. The government legislated its employees back to work. The courts determined that the government had negotiated in bad faith.

567. How many words do Inuit have for "snow"?

The usual answer to this question is that there are twenty-three words for "snow" in Inuktitut, the language of the people who used to be called the Eskimo but who are now identified as Inuit. The standard reason for this is that Inuit distinguish many different kinds of snow (sleet, slush, etc.) and find them so varied that there is no concept of snow itself. In 1911 the ethnologist Franz Boas talked about three types of snow (falling, drifting, lying). Thirty years later the philosopher Benjamin Lee Whorf suggested that there were seven words for types of snow. Since then the number has increased; sometimes twenty-three is mentioned. The truth is that Inuktitut is an agglutinative language, somewhat like Latin and German, with many lengthy compounds, so it does not have separate "words" in that sense that English or French do. The issue is discussed in detail by the linguist Geoffrey; K. Pullum in *The Great Eskimo Vocabulary Hoax and Other Irreverent Essays on the Study of Language* (1991). It has been said that Inuit have twenty-three words for "snow" but not one word for "camel."

568. What is "beaver fever"?

What is sometimes called "beaver fever" is a form of stomach flu or food poisoning known scientifically as giardiasis. It is similar to salmonella and other gastro-enteric illnesses. According to Carol Alaimo, writing in *The St. Catharines Star*, 23 April 1991, the bug that causes it was found in feces from a certain beaver pond. The disease travels an oral-fecal route and is spread by poor hygiene.

569. What was the name of the first, Canadian-built paddle-wheeler on Lake Ontario?

The first, Canadian-built paddle-wheeler to navigate Lake Ontario was the *Frontenac*. The steam-powered, 700-ton vessel was built by Kingston merchants and launched at the Bay of Quinte in 1816. The 1991 Commemorative Dollar issued by the Canadian Mint featured the *Frontenac's* image.

570. Is Yuk Yuk's a laughing matter?

Yuk Yuk's is the name of a chain of comedy clubs which feature food and drink and entertainment supplied by comedy performers. The chain was started by Mark Breslin, a comedy writer, in a church basement in Toronto in 1976. It expanded to nineteen clubs across the country and then shrank to nine clubs in 1991.

571. Is the French language doomed in Quebec?

The notion that the French language has a diminished role to play in the future in the Province of Quebec is based on the projections and models of demographers and sociologists, notably the Laval sociologist Léon Dion who has argued, on the vaguest of grounds, that unless the National Assembly passes tough measures (like restrictive language laws), the use of

French in business, among immigrants, and finally by the Québécois people themselves will decline and ultimately disappear. Although little more than a notion, the doomsday scenario fuels separatist sentiment and the secessionist movement. There is no present-day evidence to show that the use of French is threatened in Quebec, any more than there is evidence that its use is under siege in France. It is unlikely that French will ever regain its status as the international language of diplomacy.

572. How did George Longley cause the deaths of thousands?

George Longley, a railway conductor, contracted smallpox in Chicago. He was admitted into a hospital in Montreal where he was not quarantined. The highly contagious disease spread like wildfire and turned into an epidemic. Over three thousand people died in 1885. The tragic incident in medical history is the subject of Michael Bliss's study *Plague: A Story of Smallpox in Montreal* (1991).

573. What are Mr. Christie's Book Awards?

Mr. Christie's Book Awards are annual literary awards. Each year since 1989, two awards have been offered to the authors/illustrators of the best books in English and French written by Canadian authors for readers twelve years and younger. There is a cash prize and a certificate. The title of the award honours the founder of Christie's Biscuits, the company that established the prizes.

574. What is the distinction of CKAC in Montreal?

The French-language radio station CKAC in Montreal went on the air on 27 September 1922. It was the first French-language radio station in all of North America.

575. What are "Pink Liberals"?

The unofficial term "Pink Liberals" refers to members of the Liberal Party of Canada who encourage reform and favour the mixed (socialist-capitalist) economy. The unofficial term in widespread use for their counterparts in the Conservative Party of Canada is "Red Tories," Conservatives who encourage reform and favour the mixed economy. The term "Pink Liberals" was given national exposure at the Liberal Party's policy convention at Aylmer, Quebec, 22-25 November 1991, despite the fact that the party, in Opposition, remained cool to what they endorsed.

576. When is the National Day of Remembrance and Action on Violence Against Women?

In 1991, Parliament designated December the Sixth to be the National Day of Remembrance and Action on Violence Against Women. The day recalls the Montreal Massacre when fourteen women students were murdered at the École Polytechnique.

577. What is the aquatic equivalent of the Ski-Doo?

The Bombardier company, which introduced the Ski-Doo as a vehicle for snow, also produces its equivalent for water, the Sea-Doo. The Ski-Doo was immediately popular. The Sea-Doo is less popular with vacationers because of its noise.

578. What is the purpose of the Calmeadow Foundation?

The Calmeadow Foundation is a private, non-profit organization which develops ways to help the self-employed poor gain access to credit in order to start, sustain, or build their businesses. It is concerned with "micro-enterprise," not only in the Developing World (Bangladesh, Brazil, Bolivia, etc.) but also in Canada (through the First Peoples' Fund). Calmeadow does not itself fund or grant; instead, it encourages the formation of "borrowers' circles" for peer-group lending to the local working poor of sums as small as $150 or as large as $3,000.

Calmeadow was established by the Toronto entrepreneur Martin P. Connell in 1983 and named after the family home Meadowlands in the Caledon Hills area north of Toronto. To date, Calmeadow support for credit programs has helped not fewer than 50,000 people.

579. Was there a "panic broadcast" during World War II?

A fictitious "news flash" was broadcast over radio station CFRB in Toronto on 11 April 1943. Evening listeners to a musical program heard the following announcement: "We interrupt this program to bring you a special bulletin. Japanese troops have landed in force on the coast of British Columbia! For further details, keep tuned to this station!" The voices were those of Art MacGregor and Frank Deauville, members of the then-popular radio comedy team of Woodhouse and Hawkins. The "news flash" was pure invention, not a hoax, as it was followed by a comedy routine about recruitment written to spark volunteers for the Reserve Army.

CFRB, alarmed by phone calls from anxious listeners, carried subsequent announcements that the "news flash" was part of a comedy routine: "A statement made in the dramatic portion of the Maher Shoe Stores' broadcast tonight, dealing with an imaginary situation to help recruiting for the Reserve Army, had caused some concern to a few listeners who believe it to be true. To those listeners may we assure you there is no cause for alarm. It was purely fictional."

Such was Canada's "panic broadcast" during World War II. It recalled Orson Welles's *The War of the Worlds* broadcast of 1938.

580. When was Toronto's last Dark Day?

In meteorology, a Dark Day is a period of darkness in the daytime that is caused by the obscuring of the sun. The effects of nighttime darkness in daytime are arresting and of sociological and psychological interest.

Toronto's last Dark Day occurred on 24 September 1950, from approximately 12:00 noon to 6:00 p.m., when the sky above the city was obscured by a cloud of smoke the colour of saffron. The following day *The Toronto Star* described the sight in these moving words: "It was beautiful with a strange and dreary beauty and filled with ominous portent for some of the scores of people from across Ontario who called police and weather stations for an explanation of the phenomenon."

The meteorological explanation for this particular phenomenon was the formation of an immense cloud some forty hours earlier over Northern Alberta. Smoke from up to forty separate fires burning through acres of scrub timber collected. Heavy winds drove the heavy cloud over much of Southern Ontario. The unnatural darkness caused lights to be turned on in most cities in Southern Ontario as well as in Detroit, Cleveland, Pittsburgh, and New York. Rumours abounded that an atomic bomb had been exploded, that flying saucers were seen in the skies, and that it signalled "the end of the world."

581. How popular is junk mail?

Junk mail is the popular term for unsolicited advertising material. It takes the form of unaddressed leaflets, pamphlets, brochures, etc., that are delivered by Canada Post, newspaper carriers, and other door-to-door distribution services. It is more popular with advertisers than it is with householders. According to Martin Mittelstaldt, writing in *The Globe and Mail*, 16 January 1992, 13 billion pieces of junk mail were distributed in 1992. That is 500 pieces for each Canadian. No doubt there are more pieces per citizen today.

582. What is Tafelmusik?

The German word Tafelmusik means "banquet music." Tafelmusik is the name of the Canadian orchestra that specializes in the music of the baroque period. The ensemble, which now includes the Tafelmusik Chamber Choir, was founded in Toronto in 1979 by oboist Kenneth Solway and bassoonist Susan Graves. The musicians play "period" instruments, giving the compositions of Mozart and other seventeenth and eighteenth-century composers a distinctive fast tempo and sprightly sound. Tafelmusik has led in the "reconstruction" of the baroque sound.

583. What are the three phases of the James Bay Project?

The James Bay Project is the overall plan to develop the hydroelectric-power generating potential of the rivers in Northern Quebec that flow into James Bay. As promoted by Quebec Premier Robert Bourassa in the 1980s and 1990s, and as undertaken by Hydro-Québec, the plan had three phases: the La Grande River complex, the Great Whale complex, and the Nottaway, Broadback, and Rupert project. The flowing waters of mighty rivers over an area about the size of France were dammed, diverted, even reversed to generate hydroelectric power to meet anticipated needs in Quebec and the State of New York. There is much Native opposition to past, present, and future phases of development on the basis of destruction of ecology and environment and way of life.

584. What is the Grand Canal Project?

The Grand Canal Project seems to be the dream of a science-fiction writer (of the pre-ecological awareness period): extend a dike across the mouth of James Bay so that it turns from a salt-water sea into a sweet-water sea; then construct a "grand canal" from its southern tip to Southern Quebec and Northcentral New York State; then sell the resource. Quebec Premier Robert Bourassa promoted the multi-billion-dollar scheme to direct northern waters to southern markets in his book *Power from the North* (1982). It may well be that when the James Bay Project is completed, plans to work on the Grand Canal Project will be revived.

585. Did Dick Francis set one of his novels in Canada?

Dick Francis, the English jockey turned novelist, set his twenty-ninth mystery novel in Canada. The murder mystery is called *The Edge* (1988). The action takes place aboard a CNR train (during "The Great Transcontinental Mystery Race Train") and in various cities (and raceways) along the way.

586. What are the Prix Gémeaux?

Les Prix Gémeaux are Quebec's television awards. They are made by the Quebec division of the Academy of Canadian Cinema and Television in various categories, like English Canada's Gemini Awards. The awards ceremony is televised in late December.

587. When did Kellogg's introduce bilingual packaging?

It comes as a surprise to realize that Kellogg's introduced bilingual packaging of the food products it sells in Canada in 1907. That was one year after the founding of the American company and seven years before the breakfast-food company (then known as the Kellogg's Toasted Corn Flakes Company) opened its Canadian branch office in Toronto. Its founder, W.K. Kellogg, felt that the best way to sell the cereal in Canada, including Quebec, was to offer it for sale in bilingual cartons. In 1992 it was selling 26 products in Canada.

588. Are there references to Canada in the writings of William Shakespeare?

There are three references to the New World in the writings of the 16-century poet and dramatist William Shakespeare. It is possible that all or some of them relate directly or indirectly to present-day Canada.

The earliest reference comes from *The Comedy of Errors* (c. 1591). One character asks another the following rhetorical questions: "Where America, the Indies?"

If the North Pole is considered to be partly in Canada, the following dialogue refers to the northernmost part of this country: "By the north pole, I do challenge thee." "I will not fight with a pole, like a northern man: I'll slash; I'll do it by the sword. I bepray you, let me borrow my arms again." The dialogue, with atrocious pun, comes from *Love's Labour's Lost* (c. 1594).

It is possible that the Bard had in mind the North-West Passage when he has the Dane make the following admission: "I am but mad north-north-west. When the wind is southerly, I know a hawk from a handsaw." The speech is heard in *Hamlet* (c. 1601).

It is apparent from these references that Shakespeare knew about the exploration and settlement of the New World, but that he regarded such activity as peripheral to his main dramatic interests. In so thinking he no doubt expressed the concerns of the London audiences of his plays in Elizabethan England.

589. Who is the Trickster?

Anthropologists have noted the presence of the Trickster in the myths and legends of the world. The Trickster of traditional lore possesses all the ambivalence of man; for instance, the Raven is part conniver and part benefactor, bringing fire which both warms and burns. To make dramatic and literary use of the figure, the Committee to Re-Establish the Trickster was founded in Toronto in Summer 1986 by a group of native writers that included playwright Tomson Highway, activist Lenore Keeshig-Tobias, and poet Daniel David Moses.

590. What is Clearly Canadian?

Clearly Canadian is the brand name of a popular soft drink. The carbonated, sweetened mineral water, available in a range of six fruit flavours, bottled in a distinctive blue-tinted bottle with a label showing the Rocky Mountains, was introduced to health-conscious American and Canadian consumers by the Clearly Canadian Beverage Corporation of Vancouver in 1990.

591. What are CanCon and MAPL?

CanCon is short for the CRTC's Canadian Content rating system; MAPL stands for Musician, Artist, Production, and Lyrics. The CRTC is the Canadian Radio-television and Telecommunications Commission which requires that the electronic media include various amounts of Canadian content.

A record album is considered Canadian when it scores two out of four in the MAPL categories. The ruling came under scrutiny in January 1992 when the CRTC decided that Bryan Adams's new album *Waking Up the Neighbours* failed to qualify because the lyrics were not by Adams alone but by Adams and his British producer and lyricist.

592. When will Southern Ontario next experience a total eclipse?

The next total solar eclipse will occur over Southern Ontario on 8 April 2024. "Darkness at midday will sweep over Toronto, Hamilton, Niagara, London, Kingston and many other heavily populated parts of the province," wrote the astronomer Terence Dickinson in *The Toronto Star*, 9 February 1992. A partial solar eclipse occurred over the same region on 10 May 1994.

593. Is there a World's Fair held every year at Rockton, Ontario?

The Rockton World's Fair is an annual autumn tradition that is held in the village of Rockton, near Hamilton, Ontario. The "fall fair" was first held on 20 October 1853. So popular did it become that it was dubbed "The World's Fair at Rockton" in 1878. The evolution of the fair was traced by the columnist Brian Henley in *The Hamilton Spectator*, 12 October 1991.

594. Is the country imperial or metric?

The system of measurement in Canada was imperial until it "went metric" in 1970. After more than two decades the system is a muddle or a medley of systems. Indeed, the Consumers Association of Canada once referred to measurement in Canada as "an imperial system measured in metric units."

595. What is the origin of the National Research Council's Official Time Signal?

The National Research Council's Official Time Signal is heard each day on the CBC Radio Network at 1:00 p.m. The announcer's words "The beginning of the long dash" announce the precise time in local time.

Timekeeping began in Canada with the astronomical pendulum; this action was replaced by the quartz oscillator and then the atomic resonator. Here is what Malcolm M. Thomson wrote in *The Beginning of the Long Dash: A History of Timekeeping in Canada* (1978):

> Today, Canada's time service is based on the most sophisticated equipment to be found in any laboratory. The long beam cesium standard was designed and built at the National Research Laboratory, and is one of three operating in national laboratories. As a group these laboratory instruments stand out in a large population of commercially designed cesium 'clocks.' Time is made available to the Canadian public by every available means of communication, radio, TV, telephone; by seconds pulses, bilingual voice announcements, and by special code. Perhaps the best-known outlet is the CBC's one o'clock signal at "the beginning of the long dash," and almost as well known internationally is the short-wave broadcast CHU.

596. Which provincial legislature does not print the text of its proceedings?

The legislature of Prince Edward Island is the sole provincial legislature that does not print the text of its proceedings. Nevertheless its proceedings are recorded and transcribed and made available on request. Only what transpires during Question Period is actually printed.

597. How many languages are spoken in the Legislature of the Northwest Territories?

Eight languages are officially recognized by the Legislature of the Northwest Territories. In addition to English and French, six native languages are recognized and spoken. The proceedings are published in only one language, English.

598. Do all the provinces and territories include slogans on their automobile licence plates?

No. Saskatchewan alone of the provinces produces automobile licence plates that lack a slogan or phrase of some sort. (Instead it features the image of three sheaves of wheat.) Here are the slogans (as of April 1992):

Alberta: Wild Rose Country
British Columbia: Beautiful British Columbia
Manitoba: Friendly Manitoba
Ontario: Yours to Discover / Keep It Beautiful
Newfoundland: Newfoundland and Labrador
New Brunswick: Nouveau-Brunswick / New Brunswick
Nova Scotia: Canada's Ocean Playground
Prince Edward Island: Canada
Quebec: Je me souviens
Saskatchewan: –
Yukon Territory: Friendly Yukon
Northwest Territories: Explore Canada's Arctic

599. Are all the automobile licence plates produced in Canada rectangular in shape?

No. Eleven of the provincial and territorial governments produce automobile licence plates that are identical in shape and size. The interesting "hold-out" is the Northwest Territories, which issues a shaped plate. Although the same overall size as the other plates, the shape of the Northwest Territories plate is the distinctive one of a mature bear facing right.

600. Why are they laughing in Montreal?

Laughter is not a laughing matter in Montreal. The city hosts the world's biggest annual comedy festival called "Festival Juste Pour Rire/Just for Laughs" (launched in 1983); a National School of Humour (established in 1987); and an International Museum of Humour (opened in 1992). Montreal is also the home of the monthly satirical magazine *Croc* (*Fang*) and the birthplace of the Rhinoceros Party of Canada, the group that fields candidates in federal elections and ridicules the election promises and platforms of the mainline parties. Comedian Gilbert Rozon refers to Montreal as "the Cannes of comedy."

601. Did J.M. Barrie write a play about Montreal's Black Watch Regiment?

Not quite. The playwright J.M. Barrie (best known as the author of *Peter Pan*) wrote a play, which was popular on the West End, about a returned soldier: Private Kenneth Dowey, 5th Battalion, Black Watch, Canadian Expeditionary Force. The play was called *The Old Lady Shows Her Medals*. It was filmed by Hollywood as *Seven Days Leave* (1930) and it starred Gary Cooper as Private Dowey.

602. Was the inventor of the Schick electric razor a Canadian?

Yes and no. The famous Schick electric razor bears the name of Jacob Schick, its inventor and manufacturer. Born in Iowa, a former Lieutenant-Colonel in the U.S. Army, Schick conceived the need for a "dry shaver" – a brushless electric razor. He did so between the years 1910 and 1914, when he was employed as a prospector for various mining companies in the interior of British Columbia where he found it too cold to shave with brush and lather. Not until the year 1929 did Schick perfect the razor's design and establish Schick Dry Razor Inc. and open manufacturing plants at Stamford, Connecticut, and Montreal, Quebec. The electric razor, first marketed in 1931, was widely successful. In 1935, Schick established residency in Montreal and forsook his American citizenship, becoming a naturalized Canadian without further ado. The move generated controversy. He and his family maintained the move was made for reasons of health; American authorities argued the measure was taken to evade U.S. income and inheritance taxes. Whatever the reason, the inventor of the Schick electric razor died two years later in a New York City hospital, a Canadian citizen. He was buried in Montreal's Mount Royal Cemetery, 7 July 1937.

603. Why does the Minister of Finance wear a new pair of shoes before presenting the annual budget in the House of Commons?

No one is certain when the custom began. It is often said the tradition originated with Walter Harris when he became Minister of Finance in the 1954. The practice was drawn to national attention by Mitchell Sharp in 1966. Since then it has been an extra-Parliamentary practice for the Minister of Finance to wear a pair of brand-new shoes for budget presentation in the House of Commons. John Crosbie wore mukluks in 1979. Michael Wilson pointedly donned a pair of old shoes when he presented his austerity budget in 1991. Don Mazankowski sported a new necktie when he presented the budget in February 1992. When he delivered the speech on 22 February 1994, Paul Martin Jr. wore a newly bought pair of work boots, perhaps to suggest a "back to work" budget. Pierre Elliott Trudeau wore sandals in the House of Commons, but he never served as Minister of Finance, only Attorney General.

604. Can a SIN be read?

The only information that the Social Insurance Number (SIN) will yield is the region that issued the number. If the number begins with the number 1, the person received the card while living in the Atlantic provinces; 2, Quebec; 4 and 5, Ontario; 6, Prairie provinces and the Northwest Territories; 7, British Columbia and the Yukon Territory. The remaining numbers merely record the sequence of card issue.

605. Was a Canadian involved in the world's first telethon?

The world's first telethon to raise money for charity was conceived, staged, hosted, and named by broadcaster Hugh Trueman. History's first telethon was called "Uncle Bill's Annual Appeal on Behalf of The Evening Times-Globe Empty Stocking Fund," Uncle Bill being Trueman's on-air name at the time. The telethon was carried by Radio Station CHSJ in Saint John, New Brunswick, just before Christmas 1936. As Trueman later noted, tele refers to telephone, not television; thon comes from marathon, as it was a marathon broadcast. One extra telephone line was supplied by the New Brunswick Telephone Co. "Television was still twelve years in the future. First year's goal was $50 (Depression!) but we raised over $400. Fifty-five years later (1991), total figure pledged: $108,500.57" – from a fact sheet issued by *Hugh Trueman Marketing*, September 1992.

606. What were the main achievements of the Constitution Act, 1982?

The Constitution Act, 1982, achieved three things: it patriated the Canadian Constitution from the British Parliament; it entrenched the Charter of Rights and Freedoms; and it gave constitutional recognition to the native peoples.

607. What were the principal proposals of the Charlottetown Agreement, 1992?

The Charlottetown Agreement, 1992, proposed, among other things, to recognize inherent aboriginal rights to self-government; to recognize Quebec's "distinct society"; to reorganize the Senate to make it elective and equal; and to transfer federal powers in such fields as culture and labour market to the provinces. It never became law.

608. What was the Citizens' Forum on Canada's Future?

Public servant Keith Spicer headed the Citizens' Forum on Canada's Future. The Forum held public hearings from September 1990 to June 1991. Its report stated that the citizenry, especially in English Canada, favoured unity but not at the price of provincial hegemony. The press said it encouraged "grassroots Canadians" to debate the future of the country in the wake of the collapse of the Meech Lake Accord in 1990. The report documented wide-spread dissatisfaction with the initiatives of the Mulroney administration.

609. What was the Canada Clause?

The so-called Canada Clause was a provision of the Charlottetown Agreement of 1992. It defined Canada as a parliamentary (but not monarchical) democracy; it identified three orders of government (aboriginal, federal, provincial); it termed Quebec a "distinct society" within Canada; it called upon Canadians – not governments – to respect official-language minority communities, ethnic and gender equality, and individual and collective human rights. The Canada Clause was intended as Section 2 of the Constitution Act, 1867.

610. What did "opting out" refer to in the Charlottetown Accord?

The so-called "opting out" formula was a provision of the Charlottetown Accord of 1992 which would allow any provincial government to "opt out" of any national shared-cost program in areas of exclusive provincial jurisdiction and receive full compensation provided its own program met national objectives.

611. What does CCDO mean to a jobhunter?

It could meant a lot. CCDO stands for the Canadian Classification and Dictionary of Occupations, a system whereby the Canada Employment Centres assign a unique, seven-digit code to each occupation. For instance, 2114-122 is a weather forecaster. Each job profile includes the code number, title, description of the nature and purpose of the occupation, and a list of the normal duties. It is one way for a jobhunter to learn the required educational levels, environmental conditions, aptitudes and other work-related factors.

612. How many farms are there in Canada?

According to Statistics Canada in 1981, there were 280,043 farms in Canada. The number of farms is decreasing as this figure represents a decline of 24% since 1971.

613. What are the GDP and the GNP?

These are two measurements of production. The GDP measures Gross Domestic Product; the GNP, Gross National Product. GDP measures value of production originating within Canada, regardless of the ownership of the means of production. The GNP is the GDP plus the interest, profits, and dividends received by Canadians from investments abroad. While the GDP is a better indicator of the productive performance of a country, the GNP is a better indicator of the welfare of the population in monetary terms.

614. What is "fax" in French?

The word fax is short for facsimile. The French term is *télécopieur*.

615. Where is the largest mosque in the Western Hemisphere?

The largest Moslem mosque in the Western Hemisphere is located in Maple, a small Ontario community north of Toronto. The Bai'tul Islam mosque occupies 20,000 square feet and can accommodate 2,000 worshippers of the Pakistani-based Ahmadiyya Movement. It was opened on 17 October 1992 at the cost of $4.5 million and erected by the region's Ahmadi Moslems.

616. What is "Man Seeing"?

"Man Seeing," the symbol of the National Film Board of Canada, is a little stick figure of a man (or woman), with arms raised and hands clasped to suggest celebration. The head becomes the iris of a human eye. Its colours are green and blue. The symbol was designed by the NFB's graphic designer George Beaupré and adopted in 1970; a version animated by Ishu Patel was introduced in 1986.

617. What are some of the most embarrassing events in Canadian history?

1. Sir Martin Frobisher returns from Baffin Island to England in 1578 with gold. It turns out to be pyrite, "fool's gold."
2. Maurice Duplessis, as Quebec Premier and leader of the Union Nationale Party, speaking at the dedication of the bridge at Trois-Rivières, declares that it will stand as long as the Union Nationale Party. The bridge collapses three years later.
3. Cost overruns on Montreal's Olympic Stadium, erected in 1976, make it the most expensive structure of its kind in the world. The oval-shaped structure is dubbed "the Big Owe." Parts of it began to crumble in 1992.
4. Ontario Cabinet Minister Shelley Martel takes a lie detector test in 1992 to prove that she was lying when she said in public that she had seen an Ontario dentist's confidential medical file.

618. What is the Second Price Tag?

The "first" price tag is the purchase price of an appliance. The "second" price tag is an imaginative way of referring to the cost of the energy it takes to run the appliance. Over the years the "second" price can exceed that of the "first" price. The designation, used in consumer publications by the Ontario Ministry of Energy in 1992, is a rating from the government's *Energuide*.

619. When did "universality" end?

The principle of "universality," whereby social benefits would be available to all regardless of means, etc., was introduced into Canada's social welfare system in 1945 with the establishment of family allowance payments. The principle was then extended to old-age pensions. The principle, eroded in 1973 with the taxation of the latter, was delivered a grievous blow in 1978 with the introduction of the child-tax credit. With the cutbacks of the late 1980s, Canada's welfare system was no longer "universal."

620. What was the Canadian Peace Research Institute?

The Canadian Peace Research Institute was an organization dedicated to undertake social research and the publication of data with respect to issues of war and peace. In a way it was a think tank committed to peace rather than one dedicated to "strategic studies" (a euphemism for war studies). The CPRI was established on 2 November 1961 under the directorship of James S. Thomson, Moderator of the United Church of Canada. It was the brainchild of the Canadian nuclear physicist Norman Z. Alcock who recommended its formation in March 1961 in the booklet *The Bridge of Reason.* Among CPRI directors were Brock Chisholm, Pierre Elliot Trudeau, Hugh L. Keenleyside, and Kenneth E. Boulding.

621. What are Quebec's "language laws"?

Over the years the Quebec government has passed legislation to preserve and promote the French language in the province. Here are some of the so-called "language laws."

Bill 63, introduced by the Union Nationale Government on 23 October 1969, conferred official status on French and English. It was replaced by Bill 22 which was passed by the Liberal government in July 1974. Called Quebec's Official Language Act, it made French the language of civic administration and services and of the workplace. Bill 101, called the French-language Charter, was passed by the Parti Québécois on 26 August 1977. It made French the official language of the state and courts and made education in French compulsory for immigrants. In 1980 and in 1984, the Supreme Court struck down some of its provisions. Bill 178, passed by the Liberal Party in December 1988, required outside commercial signs to be in French only but allowed bilingual signs inside stores. The government invoked the "notwithstanding" clause in the Canadian Constitution to override its unconstitutional provisions.

The sign laws were subsequently modified on the "inside-outside" basis. Source: "Legislative Linguistics: A History," *The Globe and Mail,* 2 April 1993.

622. Who was called the "last living link" with insulin?

Theodore Ryder was five years old and at death's door when he was given an insulin injection by Dr. Frederick Banting at the Toronto General Hospital in 1922. It had an immediate effect – the so-called "resurrection" effect – and Ryder returned to good health, his diabetes kept in check. He died from heart failure at the age of seventy-six on 8 March 1993 in Connecticut, the longest-lived of Dr. Banting's original patients.

623. What is Duncan Macpherson's best-known cartoon?

Fans of the cartoons of Duncan Macpherson, the editorial cartoonist whose work appeared from 1958 to 1993 in *The Toronto Star*, will generally single out as his best-known cartoon the black-and-white drawing of Prime Minister John G. Diefenbaker, dressed and coiffured as Marie Antoinette, cancelling the Avro Arrow, with the caption, "Then let them eat cake." The superbly drawn caricature appeared in the *Star* shortly after the Arrow's cancellation 20 February 1959.

624. What is Dian Cohen's Major Canadian Turnaround Project?

Financial columnist and commentator Dian Cohen, writing in her book *No Small Change: Succeeding in Canada's New Economy* (1993), favours a Major Canadian Turnaround Project that "could trampoline the whole country into the new economy." What we have is a "relatively low-growth, high-cost, industrially organized country undergoing a painful transition to a new economy – an information-based, global economy...." The government should establish an "electronic highway" to boost communications and computer-related development. It would involve establishing a competition-free national consortium to supply essential communication and computer information free of charge to encourage innovation, productivity, and creativity. Too bad the initiative was ignored.

625. What was Ontario House?

Ontario House was the financial, commercial, cultural, and political office of the Ontario government in England and opened in 1869 on Charles II Street in London. It was closed in 1934 by the cost-paring Hepburn administration but reopened in 1944 by the Drew administration to assist in immigration. In 1987 it relocated to 21 Knightsbridge. It was closed by the cost-conscious Rae administration in July 1993, after 124 years of service.

626. What are some great Canadian success stories?

"Great Canadian Success Stories" is the title of a report issued by the Natural Sciences and Engineering Research Council of Canada in 1991. The NSERC report draws attention to the work of twelve university researchers who are described as "leaders in Canadian science" and whose work is said to "exemplify the spirit of the Canadian university research community." Names of the scientists, university affiliations, and capsule comments on their achievements follow:

Ron Clowes, geophysicist, University of British Columbia; head of the Lithoprobe project which maps the Canadian land mass to the depth of 80 kilometres.

Raymond Lemieux, chemist, University of Alberta; developer of testing techniques in carbohydrate chemistry, notably the study of new medical products for use in preventing organ rejection in transplants.

Bill Costerton, researcher, University of Calgary; developer of the biofilm concept which increases knowledge of the actions of bacteria.

Lorne Babiuk, virologist, University of Saskatchewan; developer of a vaccine for the treatment of scours, a common disease among livestock.

Patricia Shewen, researcher, University of Guelph; developer of a vaccine to treat cattle for shipping fever.

Frank Tompa, computer scientist, University of Waterloo; director of the collaborative project to produce the electronic version of the Oxford English Dictionary.

Ronald Melzack, psychologist, McGill University and Montreal General Hospital's Pain Clinic; developer of the "gate" theory of pain and its relief.

Gilles Fontaine, astrophysicist, Université de Montréal; theorist of the evolution of pulsating white dwarf stars which allows the measurement of the lifespan of a star in a single observation.

Wagdi Habashi, engineer, Concordia University; developer of air-flow equations in engines through the use of the supercomputer.

Pierre-Claude Aïtcin, engineer, University of Sherbrooke; researcher of high-strength concrete.

James Tranquilla, engineer, University of New Brunswick; designer of antennae to refine navigation and survey techniques.

Kelvin Ogilvie, chemist, Acadia University; synthesizer of RNA molecules and developer of the AIDS drug Ganciclovir.

627. Does Canada have a distinctive potato?

The country grows two distinctive potatoes. Both potatoes are hybrids produced in the 1980s by Gary Johnston, a horticulturalist with the University of Guelph, working with Agriculture Canada and the Ontario Ministry of Agriculture. The two hybrids are Red Gold and Yukon Gold. Red Gold is an all-Canadian, all-purpose potato, moist, with red skin and yellow flesh. Yukon Gold is a blend of Norglean from North Dakota for size and shape and Yena de Huevo (egg yoke) from South America for texture and colour. Yukon Gold is very popular. For more details see Marion Kane's "Which Spud's for You?" *The Toronto Star*, 13 October 1993.

628. Is the dollar bill still legal tender?

The dollar bill was displaced but not replaced by the Loonie in 1987. The dollar bill is still legal tender in Canada, but it is hard to find one in the 2000s.

629. What is a shinplaster?

"Shinplaster" is the colloquial term for 25 cent bank-notes issued by the Canadian government from 1870 to 1923 as a temporary measure to foil the effects of American silver coinage circulating in Canada. When it was formed in 1935, the Bank of Canada recalled the paper "quarters."

630. Who registered the trademark "Canada First"?

The trademark "Canada First" was registered in 1897 by the Aylmer Canning and Evaporating Co. located in Aylmer, Quebec. The words on the labels of the company's canned foods distinguished Canadian products from canned foods imported from the United States.

631. What is "the monkey-in-the-hat stamp"?

Stamp collectors especially value the 32 cent commemorative postage stamp issued by Canada Post on 16 November 1984. It honours Trefflé Berthiaume and marks the 100th anniversary of *La Presse*, the daily newspaper that he founded in Montreal. The image on the stamp, based on a photograph of Berthiaume wearing his familiar bowler hat, was designed by Pierre-Yves Pelletier. When the stamp is turned upside-down, a small monkey seems to be visible in the hat – no doubt accidentally!

632. Can a Cadillac run on railway tracks?

The automobile used by Norman Crump when he was President of the Canadian Pacific Railway was a gleaming black Cadillac built in 1946. Crump drove in it to inspect railway tracks. It weighed seven tonnes and its solid steel wheels were like those of a rail car. It had a turntable underneath so it could turn around on the track for the return journey, according to Marge George writing in *The Toronto Star* about Ontario's Smiths Falls Railway Museum where the Crump Cadillac is on display.

633. How many Royal museums are there in Canada?

There are four: Royal Ontario Museum in Toronto, Royal British Columbia. Museum in Victoria, Royal Tyrrell Museum in Drumheller, Alberta, and Royal Saskatchewan Museum in Regina.

634. What was Conslidated Press?

Consolidated Press was the country's largest magazine publishing company in the 1940s and 1950s. Its own five-story building was located at 73 Richmond Street, Toronto, with its printing presses on nearby Duchess Street. Among the mass-market periodicals that it published were *Canadian Home Journal* (established 1904) and *Saturday Night* (1887), plus a raft of profitable trade magazines for the food, tobacco, automobile, jewellery, engineering, and manufacturing industries. In 1952 it was acquired by capitalist Jack Kent Cooke and publisher Roy Thomson who already owned *Liberty* which was then renamed *New Liberty*. Over the years Cooke disposed of each publication in turn.

635. What was "Babies for Export"?

"Babies for Export" was the title of a controversial article commissioned and published in *New Liberty* on 27 December 1947. Based on a report prepared for the IODE by Charlotte Whitton, later Mayor of Ottawa, it stated that a "black market" existed for Alberta-born babies because of loopholes in the provincial adoption laws. It was commissioned by Jack Kent Cooke and written by Harold Dingman. The Attorney-General of Alberta, failing to suppress the article, sued both publisher and journalist under an old statute concerned with conspiracy. Alberta lost, *New Liberty* gained subscribers, and the law was amended.

636. What are minority governments?

A minority government is an administration that in order to govern requires the consent of elected members of another party because it lacks a majority in its own right. There have been six minority Canadian governments in the postwar period: 1957 and 1962 under John G. Diefenbaker, 1963 and 1965 under Lester B. Pearson, 1972 under Pierre Elliott Trudeau, and 1979 under Joe Clark. Canada has had minority administrations for nineteen of the years between 1918 and 1993. Politicians deplore minority government status, but the public is often the beneficiary in these situations.

637. When was the first federal election held?

The first federal election was held in Canada in 1867. Unlike today's elections, which are held on a single day, this one ran from August 7 to September 20.

638. When did Native Canadians gain the right to vote?

Not until the general election of 1960 was the franchise extended to Native Canadians (Inuit and Indians).

639. What is a Bloquiste?

A Bloquiste is a member of the Bloc Québécois, a political party committed to Quebec separatism. It was formed following the collapse of the Charlottetown Accord by disgruntled federal Conservative cabinet minister Lucien Bouchard. He led a group of Quebec members of the House of Commons to break away from the federal Conservative Party. In the General Election of 25 October 1993, the Bloc Québécois won more than fifty seats and became Her Majesty's Loyal Opposition. A Bloquiste is a member of a federal party; a Péquiste is a member of the Parti Québécois, a provincial party founded by René Lévesque which first formed the government in Quebec in 1976.

640. What is the collective term for beavers?

A bevy of beavers? A dam of beavers? Neither of these is the proper collective for beavers, according to James Lipton, author of *An Exaltation of Larks* (1968, 1991). He claims that the proper term is a malocclusion of beavers. The term is appropriate (though more apparent to dentists than to the rest of us) as a "malocclusion" is basically an overbite: beavers have prominent front teeth.

641. What is Beavertail?

A beavertail is a snack food, not the tail of a beaver. Popular in the Ottawa area in the winter, the beavertail is a deep-fried slab of dough sprinkled with melted sugar and cinnamon, sometimes smeared with jam or chocolate.

642. Do any Canadian newspapers have nicknames?

The Times of London is known around the world as "The Thunderer." Some Canadian newspapers have nicknames that have a pejorative sting. The most familiar ones are the following: "The Sub-Standard" (for *The Kingston Whig-Standard)*, "The Racket & Crimes" (for *The Orillia Packet and Times*), and "The Mop & Pail" or "The Grope and Flail" (for *The Globe and Mail*). *The National Post* is "The National Pest." *The Toronto Star* is sometimes called "The Toronto Scum." *The Economist and Sun* of Markham, Ontario, is inevitably "The Communist and Slum."

643. What is the difference between a Genie and a Gemini?

Both are performing arts awards. A Genie is one of the annual awards for Canadian cinema. A Gemini is one of the annual awards for Canadian television.

644. What is the *Historical Atlas of Canada?*

The *Historical Atlas of Canada* is an impressive set of three atlases published by the University of Toronto Press in English and in French. Each volume combines graphs, charts, paintings, with cartography and original scholarship produced under the direction of Geoffrey Matthews, Byron Moldofsky, and Louis Gentilcore. The volumes appeared out of chronological order: *Volume I: From the Beginning to 1800* (1987), *Volume II: The Land Transformed* (1993), and *Volume III: Addressing the Twentieth Century* (1990). The set represents the high-water mark of cartographic publishing in Canada.

645. Does Canada have a Department of External Affairs?

It did. Sir Wilfrid Laurier created the first Department of External Affairs in 1909. Before that time Britain handled Canada's international concerns. In December 1993, Prime Minister Jean Chrétien renamed "External" the Department of Foreign Affairs, or the Foreign Affairs Department (Ministère des affaires étrangères).

646. Where in Canada is the Apollo 7 Lunar Module on display?

NASA's Apollo 7 Lunar Command and Service Module made 163 orbits of Earth between 11 and 21 October 1968. The first of NASA's manned Apollo missions, the spacecraft is on permanent display at the National Museum of Science and Technology in Ottawa.

647. What is Canada's Robot?

Canada's Robot is the country's contribution to NASA's Space Station Freedom which may some day orbit some 200 miles above Earth. According to Anthony R. Curtis in *Space Almanac* (2nd ed., 1992), "Canada's contribution to the space station effort will be a roving service robot to act as hands and arms of the station. The computerized machine will have sight, touch and reasoning powers and be able to unload cargo, repair satellites, service spacecraft visiting the station, and maybe even fly away from the station's normal orbit path to retrieve and service satellites. Canadian astronauts would go to the station three months a year for experiments."

648. Where is Canada's Spaceport?

Canada's Spaceport, operated by the Canadian Space Agency, is located at the Churchill Rocket Research Range at Churchill, Manitoba. NASA has launched small sounding rockets – Nike-Orion and Black Brant – from Churchill, according to Anthony R. Curtis in *Space Almanac* (2nd ed., 1992).

649. What World War II invention looks like the Iroquois long house?

The Quonset hut looks like the traditional Iroquois long house. The first Quonset hut was a portable, temporary shelter built in 1941 at Quonset Point Naval Air Station, Rhode Island, U.S.A. It was semi-cylindrical in shape and constructed of corrugated metal that could be prefabricated and shipped to bases anywhere in the world and quickly assembled. The British equivalent was called the Nissen hut.

650. Is the drink spelled "whisky" or "whiskey"?

The word for the drink distilled in Scotland and Ireland (and elsewhere) is spelled with an "e" in England, Ireland, and the United States, but without an "e" in Scotland and Canada.

651. What disease afflicted Alexander Graham Bell, Paul Anka, and Walter Pidgeon?

As youths, inventor Alexander Graham Bell, singer Paul Anka, and actor Walter Pidgeon all suffered from tuberculosis.

652. Which company introduced Living Needs Benefits?

Living Needs Benefits is a new option in life insurance that allows ill and dying policyholders to draw cash benefits while still living to pay for surgery or other medical expenses. The option originated with the Canadian Division of the Prudential Insurance Co. in 1990. The option has particular appeal to AIDS victims.

653. What are the titles of Canada's Ten Best Films?

An international poll conducted by Toronto's Festival of Festivals among film critics, historians, filmmakers, and members of the Canadian film industry established its list of "Canada's Ten Best Films." Here in order of priority are the films, directors, and years of release:

1. *Mon Oncle Antoine*, Claude Jutra (1971).
2. *Jesus of Montreal*, Denys Arcand (1988).
3. *Goin' Down the Road*, Don Shebib (1970).
4. *Decline of the American Empire*, Denys Arcand (1986).
5. *Les Bon Debarras*, Francis Mankiewicz (1980).
6. *Les Ordres*, Michel Brault (1974).
7. *The Apprenticeship of Duddy Kravitz*, Ted Kotcheff (1974).
8. *The Grey Fox*, Phillip Borsos (1982).
9. *I've Heard the Mermaids Singing*, Patricia Rozema (1987).
10. *The Adjuster*, Atom Agoyan (1991).

The list appears in *The Writers Guild of Canada Newsletter*, Autumn 1993. A similar list was prepared in 1984; films in common to both lists are Nos. 1, 3, 5, 6, 7, and 8. Since that year there have been no "official" lists.

654. What was the "Examination Unit"?

The so-called Examination Unit was a signals intelligence organization established in Ottawa during World War II to break codes and cyphers gathered by Canadian wireless intercept stations. It was established in 1940 by the maverick U.S. intelligence agent, Herbert Yardley. The organization continues its work and today is called the Communications Security Establishment. The story of the Examination Unit is told by John Bryden in *Best-Kept Secret: Canadian Secret Intelligence in the Second World War* (1993).

655. What is Benjamin Britten's *Canadian Carnival?*

Canadian Carnival is the title of a musical composition that was written by the English composer Benjamin Britten in 1939 during the course of his trip to Canada and the United States. Peter Evans in *The Music of Benjamin Britten* (1979) described the work, Opus 19, as "little more than a sophisticated pot-pourri of folky song and dance, arranged inside a quasi-programmatic frame."

656. Are there songs characteristic of the provinces?

CBC Radio's *Gabereau* show devoted an hour's program on 23 March 1994 to the songs of the provinces. Guest hosts Bill Richardson and Marg Meikel selected the following traditional and modern songs as closely tied to their provinces:

"Ode to Newfoundland" sung by the Carl Tapscott Singers; "Lester the Lobster" by Stevedore Steve and "The Island Hymn" for Prince Edward Island; "The Nova Scotia Songs" as sung by Catherine McKinnon; "Gens du Pays" by Gilles Vigneault; "Land of the Silver Birch" by Sandra Beech for Ontario; "Prairie Town" by Randy Bachman for Manitoba; "Spring on the Prairies" by Connie Kalor for

Saskatchewan; "Springtime in Alberta" by Ian Tyson; "Land of Gold" by Jim Vautour for the Yukon; "Inland Passage" by Shari Ulrich for the Northwest Coast.

On a later program, for Prince Edward Island, they offered "Fair Island of the Sea" (a.k.a. "The Island Hymn," 1908) written by L.M. Montgomery.

657. What is Farquhar's luck?

"Farquhar's luck" is a catchphrase in the Maritimes. It refers to James Augustus Farquhar, the son of a Nova Scotia sailor, who became a wealthy sealing captain. "Farquhar is a wealthy man who has earned every penny of his fortune himself ... everything he has touched since then has turned to gold," wrote Richard Brown in *Voyage of the Iceberg* (1983), referring to Farquhar who was living in retirement in Monte Carlo in the 1910s.

658. What is the Canadian Internet Network?

Canadian Internet Network was established to provide global networking capabilities to Canada's education and research communities. It was founded by the National Research Council in 1989. Its short title is CA*net.

659. How many "points" has the Maple Leaf emblem?

The Maple Leaf emblem that appears on the national flag of Canada is a stylized leaf that has eleven tips, or points, as they are called in heraldry.

A real-life maple leaf has 32 points, as Air Canada discovered in 1993 when it altered its logo, eschewing the traditional, bright red, eleven-point leaf in favour of the new, brownish, natural-looking leaf with 32 points. Interestingly, the national airline then found that its trade-mark application on the natural-looking leaf was declined on the basis that one cannot secure such coverage for something produced by nature.

660. What is the taste of Kanata?

Historians and others know that kanata, the Algonkian word for "huts" or "settlements," is the basis of the name of the country, Canada. It is to be distinguished from Kanata, the brand name of a liqueur: "An Original Liqueur Based on Fine Aged Canadian Rye Whiskies" distilled by Melchers Inc. of Montreal. It has a sweet, syrup-like taste. In fact, it tastes like Drambuie, the Scottish liqueur distilled from Scotch rather than from Rye.

661. What is the name of the first periodical published in today's Canada?

The first periodical – journal or magazine – published in today's Canada was issued in Halifax in 1789. The journal's full title appeared as follows: *The Nova-Scotia Magazine and Comprehensive Review of Literature, Politics and News: Being a Collection of the Most Valuable Articles Which Appear in the Periodical Publications of Great-Britain, Ireland and America; with Various Pieces in Verse and Prose Never Before Published.* The journal was edited by John Howe and today issues are extremely rare. The contents of *The Nova-Scotia Magazine,* etc., were described by Fraser Sutherland in his study of periodicals called *The Monthly Epic: A History of Canadian Magazines* (1989).

662. What beast will not be seen alive at the Royal Tyrrell Museum of Palaeontology?

No one will see a live dinosaur at the Royal Tyrrell Museum of Palaeontology. Visitors will view bones and fossils and life-size reconstructions and reproductions of some two hundred dinosaurs. All these are on display in the museum which was built and opened in Drumheller, Alberta, in 1987. This is the largest display of dinosaur remains under one roof to be found anywhere in the world. But since dinosaurs have been extinct for more than 80 million years, they are not to be seen, in the flesh so to speak, as they would be seen if they were alive and well today in a zoo or botanical garden.

663. Who is Rocky Balbolder?

Rocky Balbolder is the name given the mascot of the Arctic Winter Games. The man-like figure is based on the inukshuk, the man-shaped cairn erected by Inuit to serve as guideposts.

664. What is the shape of the Church of Fatima?

The Church of Fatima outside the municipality of Fatima on Ile du Cap aux Meules, one of the Iles-de-la-Madeleine in the Gulf of the St. Lawrence, has the shape of a shell. A tourist guide for the islands describes it as "a beautiful example of modern religious architecture. The simplicity of its interior decor adds to the pleasant and comfortable atmosphere of this church."

665. Can a party decide against becoming the Official Opposition?

The Official Opposition is the political party with the second greatest number of seats in the House of Commons. A political party may decline to form the Official Opposition. This happened in 1921, when the Liberals finished first, the Progressives second, and the Conservatives third. The Progressives were a new Western-based protest party, and they decided not to become the official opposition, so that status went to the Tories. This was the first time since Confederation that a party other than the Grits or the Tories finished second. In the 1990s, the Bloc Québécois, the Conservative Party, and the Reform Party were hesitant to act as the Official Opposition, but Reform's successor, Canadian Alliance, has no hesitation doing so.

666. What are the Heritage Minutes?

The Heritage Minutes is a series of sixty-second telefilm dramatizations of interesting or important events in Canada's past, usually connected with an outstanding personality played by a well-known actor or actress. Produced in French and English and launched in 1991, the series has been seen on network television and in movie theatre chains. It is also available in video cassette form for classroom use with accompanying educational materials. The series was sponsored by The CRB Foundation of Montreal (the initials stand for the name of the businessman Charles

R. Bronfman) and overseen by TV personality Patrick Watson as part of a long-term educational program intended to stimulate greater interest among Canadians in the country's heritage. Marshal Boulton wrote the book based on the series called *Just a Minute: Glimpses of Our Great Canadian Heritage* (1994).

Here is a list of the first fifty Heritage Minutes (with explanations):

Peacemaker (Dekanahwideh), Vikings (settlement), Naming of Canada (Jacques Cartier), Jean Nicollet (exploration), Governor Frontenac (defence of Quebec), Laura Secord (War of 1812), Etienne Parent (tolerance), Victoria (responsible government), Orphans (Irish adoptees), Underground Railroad (Afro American slaves), Casavant (musical organs), Saguenay Fire (fire of 1870), Jeannie Trout (woman doctor), Les Voltigeurs de Québec (rehearsal of national anthem), Sir Sandford Fleming (standard time), Nitro (CPR construction), J.B. Tyrrell (dinosaurs), Louis Riel (Métis struggle), Rural Teacher (Robert Harris's painting), Soddie (prairie settlers), Midwife (rural medicine), Basketball (James Naismith), Steele of the Mounties (Klondike), Marconi (transatlantic communication), Nellie McClung (women's suffrage), Valour Road (Winnipeg's Victoria Cross winners), Halifax Explosion (heroism in 1917), Joseph-Armand Bombardier (snowmobile), Emily Murphy (women's rights), Superman (cartoonist Joe Shuster), La Bolduc (singer Mary Travers), Inukshuk (Inuit landmarks), Wilder Penfield (neurosurgery), Agnes McPhail (penal reform), Emily Carr (artist), Peacekeepers (Pearson's conception), Le Réseau (microwave network), Maurice Ruddick (Afro-Canadian collier), Jacques Plante (goalie mask), Marshall McLuhan (communications theory), John Matheson (flag design).

667. What is the origin of the name Proud to be Canadian?

Proud to be Canadian is the name of a grass-roots group of concerned Canadian citizens with the mandate to make young Canadians more aware of their feelings about Canada. It was started in May 1991 by Sheila Craig Casgrain who developed a t-shirt with the legend "Proud to be Canadian" for an office picnic.

668. What is the setting of the world's first werewolf film?

Transylvania is a reasonable answer, with a nod to the classic cinematic version of Bram Stoker's novel *Dracula* starring Bela Lugosi as the king of the vampires. Predating this is the movie shot in 1913 by the Canadian director Henry McCrae. He based it on the short story "The Werewolves" written by Henri Beaugrand (1855-1929) which was set in New France in 1706. It told of a brand of cannibalistic Iroquois who camped at the mouth of the Richelieu River, south of Montreal. The Indians not only drank the blood and ate the flesh of their victims, but turned into *loups-garous* (werewolves) during the process of their horrible feast, according to horror buffs Don Hutchison and Peter Halasz.

669. What sometimes-controversial decision was handed down by the Judicial Committee of the British Privy Council on 1 March 1927?

On 1 March 1927 the Judicial Committee of the British Privy Council handed down a twenty-one page ruling on the boundaries of Labrador. The ruling read in part: "The true construction of the Statutes, Orders in Council and Proclamations referred to in the Order of Reference, the boundary construed, was to give the Government of Newfoundland not mere rights of inspection and regulation exercisable upon a line of shore, but territory which became as much a part of the Colony as the island of Newfoundland itself, and which was capable of being defined by metes and bounds...."

The Judicial Committee was ruling on the request made five years earlier to answer the following question: "What is the location and definition of the boundary between Canada and Newfoundland in the Labrador peninsula under the statutes, Orders-in-Council and proclamations?" The decision surprised everyone, delighting the Newfoundland government but irritating the government of Quebec which has continued to maintain that Labrador is or should be part of that province.

670. What are some Canadian icons?

Here, at random, are some icons or symbols that are familiar to almost all Canadians:

The Canadian Broadcasting Corporation, The National Film Board of Canada, The Royal Canadian Air Farce, The Grey Cup, The Maple Leaf, The Beaver, The Montreal Canadiens, The Royal Canadian Mounted Police, The Snowbirds, The Stanley Cup, Governor General of Canada, National Hockey League, The Royal Family.

Canadians should take pride in the following icons if only because they are known abroad and regarded as being of signal significance: the Pugwash Conferences and the Antigonish Movement.

671. How can a Canadian check his or her own credit record?

Write a letter to Equifax and include your full name, home address, date of birth, social insurance number, phone number, and the name of your employer. Sign the letter and mail it to: Equifax, 60 Bloor Street West, Suite 1200, Toronto, Ontario, M4W 3C1. Then Equifax will call you and you can review the information over the phone.

672. What form does the postal code take?

The postal code has the form A9A 9A9. In cities, a postal code specifies the address down to one side of a city block, or even more precisely in the case of high-rise buildings or large-volume mail receivers. To avoid confusion with similar letters and digits, the letters D, F, I, O, Q, and V are never used. All letters must be capitalized and a blank space (never a dash or period) must separate the first three characters from the last ones. The postal code should appear on its own line in an address. Canada Post Corporation sells copies of its Postal Code Directory. The first letter of the postal code identifies the province:

A, Newfoundland; B, Nova Scotia; C, Prince Edward Island, E, New Brunswick; G, Eastern Quebec; H, Metro Montreal; J, Western Quebec; K, Eastern Ontario; L, South Central Ontario; M, Metro Toronto; N, Southwestern Ontario; P, Northern Ontario; R, Manitoba; S, Saskatchewan; T, Alberta; V, British Columbia; X, Yukon Territory; Y, Northwest Territories.

673. What are the most common, non-official mother tongues in regions of the country?

The most common, non-official mother tongues differ by regions. In the Atlantic region, the mother tongue is Micmac; in Central Canada, Italian; on the Prairies, German; in British Columbia, Chinese; in the Northwest Territories, Inuktitut; and in the Yukon Territory, Dene. Details are taken from Dianne Rinehart's "Spectrum," *The Hamilton Spectator*, 2 July 1994.

674. What is "All Our Yesterdays"?

"All Our Yesterdays" is the title of a series of weekly columns devoted to Montreal's past contributed by freelance writer and antiquary Edgar Andrew Collard. The columns have appeared on the editorial page of *The Montreal Gazette* without a break since 14 August 1944. They were usually illustrated with black-and-white sketches by cartoonist John Collins. On 13 August 1994, Collard contributed his 2,600th column, titled "All His Yesterdays." It dealt with the genesis of the column and the origin of its title, Shakespeare's *Macbeth:* "All our yesterdays have lighted fools / The way to dusty death...."

675. How many Canadians have criminal records?

For the year ending 1993, the number of people in Canada with criminal records was 2,568,912. That includes young offenders convicted of a criminal offence, according to Gay Abbate, "How Our Prison System Works," *The Globe and Mail*, 24 August 1994. The figure is astonishingly high when it is borne in mind that Canada's population of 27 million consists of a goodly number of babies and children.

676. What is the size of the prison population?

In round numbers, the number of adults in prison in Canada on any given day in 1993 was 31,700. This figure includes all adults in both provincial and federal correctional facilities under sentence, remand, or lockup, according to Gay Abbate, "How Our Prison System Works," *The Globe and Mail,* 24 August 1994. At any one time, the average number of persons on probation, parole, and statutory release numbers about 112,080.

677. What is the cost of maintaining a prisoner?

In 1993, the cost of incarcerating an offender in a federal institution was $47,760 annually. Maximum security costs the most, followed by medium security, and then minimum security. It costs more to incarcerate women prisoners.

678. Are prisoners paid for their work in prison?

Yes. "They earn anywhere from $5.25 to $6.90 a day depending on the job they do. Those willing to work but who cannot for a variety of reasons, including medical problems, receive a daily base rate of $1.60," according to Gay Abbate, "How Our Prison System Works," *The Globe and Mail,* 24 August 1994.

679. What is CANCOPY?

CANCOPY is the Canadian Copyright Licensing Agency. Founded in August 1988, the national, non-profit organization represents Canada's leading writers and publishing groups. It ensures collective copyright management of reprographic use of published material.

680. What is MuchMusic?

MuchMusic is the name of a popular music cable network created by TV mogul Moses Znaimer. Launched on 31 August 1984, it was a success from the first, and it combines rock videos with lively commentary. Ten years later it was being seen in 5.6 million households in Canada and millions more in the U.S., the U.K. and countries in Latin America, according to Antonia Zerbisias, *StarWeek,* 20 August 1994. MuchMusic has consistently promoted new performers from Canada and Quebec.

681. What is the Cosmodôme?

The country's first space museum is called the Cosmodôme and it is located in Laval, Quebec. Dedicated to space sciences, technology, and communications, the complex includes a Science Centre (opened in December 1994) and includes the Canada Space Camp (opened in August 1994) where youngsters may learn more about the science and wonder of space and space exploration.

682. What is mouth-watering about the Maison J.A. Vachon?

The Maison J.A. Vachon is a museum located in the town of Sainte-Marie in the Beauce-Appalaches region of Quebec. The museum is housed in the family residence of J.A. Vachon whose name in Quebec is synonymous with *petits gâteaux*, chocolate-covered marshmallow cookies. On display is the first stove used by Rose-Anna and Arcade Vachon. Elsewhere in Sainte-Marie is the Vachon bakery.

683. What are settler's bridges and depression bridges?

Covered bridges built of wood in the Province of Quebec are often divided into two classes, those that were built by the original settlers to span bridges, those that were erected during the Great Depression of the 1930s as make-work projects.

684. What is unusual about Mary Queen of the World Cathedral?

This Montreal cathedral is a scaled-down replica of St. Peter's Basilica in Rome, complete with the gilded neo-baroque baldachin that overlooks the altar.

685. What is symbolic about the Sun Life Building?

Montreal's Sun Life Building, erected in 1918 and subsequently enlarged, long held the distinction of being the largest building in the British Empire. "At one point," runs an official guide book, "it represented the power of the Anglo-Saxon establishment in Montreal." In 1980, the Sun Life insurance company decided to move its headquarters from Montreal to Toronto to protest restrictive legislation in Quebec. The joke that went the rounds was that the building that had served as the office of a life insurance company would henceforth serve as the office of an unemployment insurance company. The move was anticipated by novelist Wiliam Weintraub in his futuristic novel *The Underdogs* (1979).

686. What was Windsor Station?

Windsor Station, at the corner of Peel and de la Gauchetière in Montreal, was designed as a train station by Bruce Price in 1889 and is a fine example of Richardson's Romanesque Revival style. At one time it was the hub of Canada's railway system.

687. Where is the so-called Sailors' Church?

Notre-Dame-de-Bonsecours Chapel in Montreal occupies a site first consecrated in 1657. Hanging from the ceiling are models of ships dedicated to the Blessed Virgin Mary by sailor parishioners.

688. In which city is there a Film St.?

Film St. is the official name of a street that runs off the main street in Belleville, Ontario. It leads to a small plant that during the early years of this century acted as Canada's premier film studio. The best-known silent film produced was *Carry on Sergeant* released in 1928 just as sound was being introduced. A plaque describes the site as "Hollywood North."

689. What is the fate of the Diefenbunker?

Canada's most famous fallout shelter, built by Prime Minister John G. Diefenbaker in the 1950s, in the village of Carp in West Carlton Township outside Ottawa, was dubbed by the press the Diefenbunker. It consisted of a vast underground bunker with suites for the vice-regal and prime-ministerial families, a war room, meeting rooms, communications headquarters, storage areas, etc. It is now known as CFB Carp. In November 1994 there was the suggestion that it would become a museum to attract tourists to the area, but the Armed Forces decided to seal off the underground areas but continue to operate its surface facilities. It has intermittently been opened for visitors.

690. Is there a Donkey Sanctuary in Canada?

The Donkey Sanctuary of Canada is a 100-acre refuge located on farmland south of Guelph, Ontario. It offers refuge to abused and neglected donkeys. In 1989, Sandra and David Pady, former Torontonians, offered their sheep-grazing land as a donkey refuge. They established the sanctuary as a non-profit charitable organization, according to A. Finaly, "Donkey Heaven," *The Canadian Vegetarian Magazine*, November-December 1994.

691. Where did Houdini first learn about strait-jackets?

Harry Houdini, the great magician, could escape from all manner of handcuffs, fetters, manacles, and strait-jackets. In 1908, he explained that he encountered his first strait-jacket during a visit in 1895-96 to "a large insane asylum" in Saint John, New Brunswick. Then and there he resolved he would devise ways and means to free himself from its restraint, and he did, as Ruth Brandon reports in *The Life and Many Deaths of Harry Houdini* (1993).

692. Where is the manuscript of "A Visit from St. Nicholas"?

The seasonally popular narrative poem "A Visit from St. Nicholas," which begins "'Twas the night before Christmas and all through the house ..." was written by the American poet Clement Moore in 1822. As Margaret Ness noted in "Fredericton Linked to Christmas Story," *The Toronto Star*, 17 December 1994, "Moore sent a copy to his godfather, the Rev. Jonathan Odell of Fredericton, New Brunswick's first provincial secretary. Moore didn't publish the poem until 1837, but it's certain that long before that it was being recited in Fredericton. The hand-written copy sent to Odell is now in the Odell Papers in the New Brunswick Museum in Saint John."

693. Is the swastika a Canadian symbol?

The swastika became the symbol of the Nazi Party of Germany in 1919 and thereafter the world's most hated symbol. Yet the swastika (or twisted cross) is an ancient symbol known to the Hindu people of Ancient India as a good luck sign. A sign of devolution, the Hindu symbol has its arms so arranged as to rotate in a clockwise fashion, whereas the Nazi symbol rotates counter-clockwise. In modern times the revival of the symbol is associated with the archaeologist Heinrich Schliemann who unearthed such signs in Hissarlik in Turkey and gave the sign its present name, which is Hindu for "twisted cross."

The symbol is not without its Canadian associations. It was used by a girls' ice-hockey team in Alberta in 1916, two years before it was adopted by the National Socialist German Worker's Party (the Nazi Party). There is also the tradition that the small mining community named Swastika, now part of Kirkland Lake, Ontario, may have been known to Adolf Hitler at the time the leader chose the symbol. The interesting if inconclusive story is told by Malcolm Quinn in *The Swastika: Constructing the Symbol* (1994).

694. What is the Bradford Triangle?

The triangle-shaped district in Ontario north of Toronto bounded by the towns of Bradford, Uxbridge, and Aurora is sometimes called the Bradford Triangle. The area is rumoured to be buzzed by UFOs. In the spring of 1994, a one-day conference on the subject of unexplained aerial phenomena and psychic mysteries that was organized by UFO abductee Joyce Halfin drew attention to the description.

695. Is there a "beaver dictionary"?

Is there a dictionary for the sounds and words used by the beaver population of Canada? In the 1930s, naturalist and conservationist Grey Owl maintained, with a wink, that he had compiled a "beaver dictionary." Apparently it consisted of forty-nine words and expressions that beavers understood. John G. Diefenbaker, who admired Grey Owl as a brilliant raconteur and fabulous impostor, would joke about Grey Owl's conversations with the beavers at Prince Albert National Park.

696. Who coined the term "cineplex"?

Veteran film exhibitor Nat Taylor, one of the founders of Toronto's Cineplex Odeon Corporation, coined the word "cineplex" to refer to a movie theatre with multiple screens under a single roof. According to columnist Sid Adilman, "Eye on Entertainment," *The Toronto Star*, 1 April 1995, Taylor created the term and then pioneered "multiplexing" existing movie theatres. He opened the world's first dual-screen theatre (Elgin and Little Elgin) in Ottawa in 1957. He followed that with the world's first triplex in Burnaby, British Columbia, and then with four theatres at Mississauga's Square One. Taylor told Adilman, "I invented the name 'cineplex.' I was driving home from the golf club one day with my wife and one of my friends. We were thinking about all kinds of names and I came up with 'cineplex.' It means 'cinema complex.'"

697. What have Canadians contributed to the Internet?

Tens of thousands of Canadians use the Internet as a communications device and database. At least two Canadians have made signal contributions to Internet use.

Peter Deutch and other scientists at McGill University developed the popular Archie system. First deployed in 1991 to track the anonymous FTP archive sites that are maintained around the world, Archie quickly grew to become a general server. In January 1992, Deutch formed Bunyip Systems Incorporated in Montreal to create and market a range of network-based tools and information services.

HYTELNET was created in late 1990 by Peter Scott of the University of Saskatchewan's Library Systems Department. The program (HYpertext browser for TELNET-accessible) provides a front end to accessing the Internet. It is particularly favoured by librarians and others who search distant library holdings.

698. What are the outstanding Canadian mystery novels?

Here is a list of the outstanding mystery novels – "classic chillers" written by Canadians. The list, compiled by journalist James Adams with the help of writer David Skene-Melvin and bookdealer J.D. Singh, originally appeared in "Masters of Mystery," *The Globe and Mail*, 22 April 1995.

1. *Geoffrey Hempstead* (1890) by Thomas Stearns Jarvis
2. *The Gnome Mine Mystery* (1936) by Pearl B. Foley writing as Paul DeMar
3. *The Beast Within* (1955) by Margaret Millar
4. *The Weird World of Wes Beattie* (1963) by John N. Harris
5. *The Sin Sniper* (1970) by Hugh Garner
6. *A Reason to Kill* (1978) by Eve Zaremba
7. *Needles* (1979) by William Deverell
8. *The Suicide Murders* (1980) by Howard Engel
9. *The Night the Gods Smiled* (1983) by Eric Wright
10. *The Suspect* (1985) by L.R. Wright
11. *The Red Fox* (1985) by Anthony Hyde
12. *Swann: A Mystery* (1986) by Carol Shields
13. *Harry's Fragments* (1988) by George Bowering
14. *A Stone of the Heart* (1988) by John Brady
15. *Death on 30 Best* (1989) by Maynard Collins
16. *Hot Shots* (1990) by Laurence Gough
17. *The Return of Lieutenant Boruvka* (1990) by Josef Skvorecky
18. *Sniper's Moon* (1990) by Carsten Stroud
19. *Deadly Appearances* (1990) by Gail Bowen
20. *Gypsy Sins* (1993) by J.L. Reynolds

699. What is the Arthur Ellis Award?

The Arthur Ellis Award is a series of annual awards made to the authors of the best Canadian crime writing, fictional and actual. The awards are sponsored by the Crime Writers of Canada, founded in Toronto in 1981.

700. What was *SwiftCurrent?*

SwiftCurrent was the name of "the world's first on-line electronic literary magazine." Its launch in September 1984 with UNIX-based software was arranged by two poets with computer expertise, Frank Davey of Toronto, Ontario, and Fred Wah of Swift Current, Saskatchewan. Contemporary writers of prose and poetry from across Canada were able to send and receive each others' work on-line for purposes of communication and critiquing. Davey and Wah compiled *SwiftCurrent: The SwiftCurrent Anthology* (1986).

701. Did a Canadian create Bugs Bunny?

The popular cartoon character Bugs Bunny was not created by a Canadian, but it is frequently said that a Canadian Charles Thorson drew the raucous rabbit. "There have been almost as many cartoonists claiming the distinction of having created Bugs Bunny as there were ancient Greek cities vying for the honour of having been Homer's birthplace," according to Maurice Horn in *The World Encyclopaedia of Cartoons* (1990). Many studio animators, working under producer Leon Schlesinger at Warner Brothers, drew the smart-alec hare who first appeared on the screen in 1938.

702. Who is the subject of the first book of Canadian literary criticism?

"Not one in a hundred students of Canadian literature would recognize Tate's name, but few Canadian writers have received more scholarly attention. Franz Boas's largest book, *Tsimshian Mythology* (1916), is nothing less and little more than a comparative study of the writings of George Hunt. It is also, I believe, the first substantial study of the work of any Canadian writer, regardless of language."

So wrote Robert Bringhurst in his essay "That Also Is You: Some Classics of Native Canadian Literature," included by W.H. New in *Native Writers and Canadian Identity* (1990), about George Hunt (1854-1933), the half-Tlingit, half-Scots translator who lived among the Kwakiutl near Fort Rupert, British Columbia. He supplied the ethnologist Franz Boas with linguistic transcriptions and interlinear translations of traditional tales and songs and poems of the West Coast people.

703. Is there a Canadian version of Monopoly?

Monopoly, the ever-popular board game, was devised by Charles Darrow of Atlantic City, New Jersey, in 1935. The game popularized Atlantic City's street names: Boardwalk, etc. Over the decades, local versions appeared under license. The Hungarian version was known as Capitalist. There was a Canadian version and even one for Toronto. But it was not until the year 2000 that Hasbro released the authorized Canadian version. It features such familiar names as Bay St., Portage & Main, and Robson St. The card Luxury Tax is called the Goods and Services Tax card. The card Go to Jail/Allez en Prison features the image of a Mountie.

The counters are in the shapes of a moose, a hockey player, a bear, etc.

704. Where was the first baseball game played?

A game that resembles modern baseball was first played in Beachville, near Woodstock, Ontario, 4 June 1838. This game had four "byes" or bases as well as a home "bye," and was according to *The Toronto Star*, 9 July 1991, "the first recorded match between two teams organized specifically to play the game, the first to have nine innings (though seven later became the norm), runs for scoring, three outs an inning, tagging and force outs." The two teams were the Beachville and the Zorra, from Zorra and North Oxford townships. It was played one year before Abner Doubleday played what the Americans consider the first baseball game in Cooperstown, New York.

705. What is Babe Ruth's Canadian connection?

The Bambino, the Slugger, hit his first professional home run in Toronto, helping the Providence Grays defeat the hometown Maple Leafs with a 9-0 no-hitter at Hanlan's Point Stadium, 5 September 1914. It was the Bambino's only minor-league home run. He went on to hit 714 major-league homers, dying in 1948 at the age of 54. A plaque, unveiled by his daughter Dorothy Ruth Pirone, was unveiled at the site in September 1986.

706. Who was the first person to benefit from insulin?

Leonard Thompson was the first person in the world to benefit from the insulin treatment for diabetes. The thirteen-year-old youngster was facing imminent death when Dr. Frederick Banting persuaded his parents to agree to an experimental treatment that might prolong his life. The afternoon of 11 January 1922 at the Toronto General Hospital, Leonard was injected with 15 c.c. of the extract devised by Dr. Banting that is now known as insulin. There was an observable improvement that has been dubbed "the resurrection effect." Leonard's condition improved dramatically, and through repeated injections, his health was stabilized. Leonard defied all the odds and was alive and well some thirty years after the experimental treatment.

707. What is *Frank?*

Frank is a national news and satire magazine, the Canadian *Oz*. Begun in Halifax in 1987, it is now published biweekly in Ottawa, Halifax, and Toronto. In 1993, it boasted a newsstand and subscription circulation of 18,000 copies. Michael Coren, sometime columnist, wrote, "It makes Canada's equestrian class uneasy in the saddle. After all, Canada's establishment elite knows as much about us, isn't it time we found out something about them?"

708. What is CanCon?

CanCon is a journalist abbreviation of Canadian Content Regulations. These were first applied in 1970 to the music broadcast industry in Canada by the Canadian Radio-Television Commission in its attempt to advance the Canadianization of radio and television broadcasting. Essentially the regulations require that thirty percent of the weekly playlist of each radio or television station has to be devoted to Canadian music. The Canadian Association of Broadcasters opposed the imposition of CanCon regulations from the first for commercial and artistic reasons.

Stan Klees, editor of RPM Chart Weekly, created the acronym MAPL. It stands for the four determining conditions: Music, Artist, Production, Lyrics. To be deemed Canadian, a composition must meet two of these conditions.

Quebec French-language stations are required by the CRTC to play sixty-five percent French-language songs, according to Chris Cobb in "How CanCon Regulations Work," *The Ottawa Citizen*, 8 July 1995.

709. How many people Shared the Flame?

Some 6,500 Canadians "shared the flame." The lucky Canadians were chosen, largely by lottery from 6.6 million submissions, to be torchbearers of the Olympic flame. They carried the symbolic flame, which was lit on Mount Olympus in Greece and flown to Signal Hill, Nova Scotia, 17 November 1987, in the Olympic Torch Relay. They held it high, running, ski-dooing, skiing, sailing, and flying across all provinces and territories right into McMahon Stadium, Calgary, Alberta, site of the XV

Olympic Winter Games, 13 February 1988. The route covered 18,000 kilometres and took 88 days to complete. Each torchbearer wore a distinctive red and white track suit with a white toque. The imaginative undertaking was sponsored by Petro-Canada. *Share the Flame: The Official Retrospective Book of the Olympic Torch Relay* appeared and was published for distribution before the completion of the games.

710. What is the difference between a "snowbird" and a "snowback"?

A snowbird is a popular reference to a Canadian who winters in the United States, especially in the southern states. The term reflects the fact that many birds fly south of the border for the winter and return in the spring.

A snowback is a popular reference to a Canadian who, after legally entering the United States, remains illegally and works there. The term recalls wetback, a description for a Mexican who crosses the Rio Grande and illegally lives and works in the United States.

711. Did Pauline Johnson write a parody of her famous poem "The Song My Paddle Sings"?

Pauline Johnson grew tired of reciting her famous poem "The Song My Paddle Sings," so after a visit to Fort MacLeod, Alberta, she wrote a parody which she called "His Majesty the West Wind." It was found in her manuscripts by Sheila Johnston of the Grand Theatre in London, Ontario, who is completing her study of the poet called *Buckskin and Broadcloth*. The parody was quoted by Val Ross in "The Perils of Pauline" in *The Globe and Mail,* 2 September 1995.

Once in a fit of mental aberration
I wrote some stanzas to the Western wind,
A very stupid, maudlin invocation
That into ears of audiences I've dinned.

A song about a sail, canoe and paddle,
Recited I, in sailor's flannels dressed,
And when they heard it people would skidaddle
Particularly those who had been West.

For they, alas, had knowledge, I was striving,
    To write of something I had never known,
That I had ne'er experienced the driving
    Of Western winds across the Prairie blown.

I never thought when grinding out those stanzas,
    I'd live to swallow pecks of Prairie dust,
That I'd deny my old extravaganzas,
    And wish His Majesty distinctly – cussed.

712. Were the Pugwash Conferences awarded a Nobel Prize?

More or less. The Pugwash Conferences on Science and World Affairs date back to the days of the Cold War when an anti-war manifesto was drafted by Bertrand Russell and signed by Albert Einstein and ten other scientists. It urged scientists and statesmen from both sides of the Iron Curtain to meet regularly to discuss the need for nuclear disarmament. In 1955, the Canadian-born, Cleveland-based industrialist Cyrus Eaton hosted the first conference at his summer home in Pugwash, Nova Scotia. The Nobel Prize Committee, on 13 October 1995, awarded its Peace Prize to British physicist Joseph Rotblat, current president of the Pugwash Movement, the last surviving member of the Pugwash Eleven.

713. Who first reported the sinking of the *Titanic?*

Harry Stranger, marine reporter for *The Montreal Gazette*, first reported to the world the news that the "unsinkable" *Titanic* was sinking. "The story, which is part of this newspaper's history, is that the Allan Steamship liner *Virginian* picked up the *Titanic*'s distress signals and called George Hannah, traffic manager of the Allan Steamship line in Montreal for permission to alter course and go to the *Titanic*'s assistance. Mr. Hannah immediately called Harry Stranger at *The Gazette*. *The Gazette* shared the news with *The New York Times*, which is generally credited with breaking it because *New York Times* managing editor, Carl Van Anda, took a calculated risk and assumed the ship had gone down before the fact was confirmed." So wrote Alan Hustak, reporter, *The Gazette*, "Letters to the Editor," 18 November 1995. He concluded, "A Canadian reporter for *The Gazette*, Harry Stranger, broke the story."

714. What are the Superhero Stamps?

The Superhero Stamps are a packet of 45 cent commemorative stamps issued in October 1995 by Canada Post to honour Canadian comic-book superheroes. The brightly coloured series depicted five superheroes in characteristic poses: Superman, Nelvana of the Northern Lights, Johnny Canuck, Captain Canuck, and Fleur-de-Lys.

Superman was co-created by Canadian-born artist Joe Shuster and American-born writer Jerry Siegel. (The suggestion was made that Clark Kent would have been more appropriate for a stamp, as Superman is only fifty percent Canadian, if that.) Superman made his debut in *Action Comics*, No. 1, June 1938.

Nelvana of the Northern Lights was created by artist Adrian Dingle, and she first appeared in the inaugural issue of *Triumph-Adventure-Comics*, August 1941. Johnny Canuck, "Canada's answer to Nazi oppression," was the brainchild of Leo Bachle (as Les Barker) and first appeared in *Dime Comics*, No. 1, February 1942. Captain Canuck was a Johnny-come-lately, the inspiration of Richard Comely and Ron Leishman, first appearing in *Captain Canuck*, No. 1, July 1975. Fleur-de-Lys was conceived by writer Mark Shainblum and artist Gabriel Morrisette and made her debut in the first issue of *New Triumph Featuring Northguard* in 1984.

715. Which province had grade thirteen?

High school students attended school for three or four years in all the provinces except one. Ontario is the provincial exception. Here students were enrolled in high school for a total of five years. The fifth year was known as grade thirteen and it was sometimes regarded as the equivalent of "university admittance" or "first-year university." In 1982, the Ontario Department of Education moved away from the notion of years of enrolment (largely because groups of students were unable to advance year by year) and accepted, instead, the concept of credits, establishing the Ontario Academic Credits (OACs) system. In 1995, as a cost-saving measure, the Ontario government announced that grade thirteen would be abolished – yet the credit system remains in place.

716. Who painted *The Blasted Pine?*

Peter Gzowski, host of CBC Radio's Morningside, created a stir on 1 October 1995 when he referred on the air to the painting called *The Blasted Pine*. Listeners immediately pointed out that members of the Group of Seven and other artists painted canvases called *Jack Pine* and *White Pine*, etc., but there is no painting called *The Blasted Pine*. Gzowski then recalled that *The Blasted Pine* (1957, expanded 1967) was the title of an anthology of satiric and disrespectful verse by Canadians edited by F.R. Scott and A.J.M. Smith. The editors had long wanted to compile a prose anthology to place alongside the poetry anthology; they would call it *The Ruddy Maple*, but it never appeared.

717. Are there Canadian tabloids?

No. But the so-called supermarket tabloids – sensational weekly papers – are readily available at checkout counters in supermarkets and on news-stands across Canada. These are American publications, although three of these leading tabloids – *Globe, National Examiner, Sun* – are owned by a Canadian publisher, Michael Rosenbloom, who publishes them from Rouses Point, New York. There used to be a thriving Canadian tabloid industry in Montreal that included *Hush, Flash*, and *Midnight*. The latter became today's *Globe*. Information about these and other tabs appears as "Tabloid Turns Housewife into Zombie!" by Michael H. Randall in *The Fringes of Reason: A Whole Earth Catalog* (1989) edited by Ted Schultz.

718. What is *Canada Calling?*

Canada Calling is the name of a live radio broadcast of news of interest to Canadians that is heard daily throughout Florida and the Phoenix area of Arizona. In 1995 it was carried by 30 stations between November 1 and April 30. It is prepared by veteran broadcaster Prior Smith from a studio north of Peterborough, Ontario. The news service, launched in 1952 by broadcaster Dave Price, is continued by Smith, who described the unique service in "Canada Calling Snowbirds," *LeisureWays*, November-December 1995.

719. Are they Roughriders or Rough Riders?

They are both. The Saskatchewan Roughriders were members of the Western Interprovincial Football League; the Ottawa Rough Riders were in the Interprovincial Rugby Football Union, also known as the Big Four. When the Rough Riders and the Roughriders met on the gridiron for the first time in 1951, the Rough Riders beat the Roughriders 21-14. As the writer of the "You Asked Us" column in *The Toronto Star*, 15 September 1992, concluded: "Good thing this is not a radio script." The Canadian Football League established its interlocking season games only in 1961, by which time the names of the two teams, although confusing to sportscasters, were so well entrenched that neither team would consider changing theirs.

720. Was Brigham Young ever in Canada?

Although not much is known about their activities, Joseph Smith and Brigham Young undertook foreign missionary work for Mormonism in Upper Canada, present-day Ontario. As well, Young's son-in-law, Charles Ora Card, led polygamy-practising members of the Church of Jesus Christ of Latter Day Saints on a trek in 1887 from Utah into the Northwest Territories, present-day Alberta, and settled in the Cardston area. The community was named after Card who became the town's first mayor. In 1901, it became the site of the first Mormon Temple which, when enlarged from 1913 to 1923, assumed the shape of a white Maltese Cross.

721. Did Eva Peron receive cancer treatment in Canada?

It was rumoured that Eva Peron, wife of Argentine dictator Juan Peron, travelled incognito to London, Ontario, where she visited the Cobalt 60 Bomb Therapy Unit at the Ontario Cancer Foundation's London clinic in Victoria Hospital. The clandestine visit and covert treatment are said to have occurred in late October 1951. Dr. Ivan Smith, the clinic's director, always denied the rumour.

The source of the rumour is often said to be a misunderstanding based on two news stories which appeared side-by-side on the front page of *The London Free Press*, 27 October 1951: "New Cancer Weapon Hailed" and a story that mentioned Peron's battle with "her illness." That too is rumour, as the issue of the newspaper in question has no such stories.

At the time a news story published by *The London Free Press* reported the rumour that Juan Peron "frantically attempted to secure the world's first Cobalt 60 Bomb Therapy Unit before it ever reached the London Cancer Clinic in Victoria Hospital." That is one variant. The other is that when the bribery failed Eva herself travelled to London. This is highly unlikely; any treatment was ineffective. Eva Peron died of uterine cancer in Buenos Aires on 26 June 1952. Further details are included by Mark Kearney and Randy Ray in *The Great Canadian Trivia Book 2* (1998).

722. Who sculpted the Eternal Flame at Yad Vashem?

The Eternal Flame at the Yad Vashem holocaust memorial in Jerusalem was designed and created by Kosso Eloul, a Canadian sculptor of Polish-Jewish background who resided in Israel for a number of years in the 1950s. Thereafter he made Toronto his home until his death in 1995. Moishe Shafdie, the Israeli-Canadian architect, has been commissioned to redesign the entire Yad Vashem complex.

723. Where was "O Canada!" written?

The English words of the national anthem "O Canada!" were written by R. Stanley Weir during the summer of 1908. At the time he held the position of Recorder of Montreal. The actual writing took place at his summer home at Reid Bay, south of Cedarville, Stanstead County, on the shore of Lake Memphremagog, Quebec. This information comes from Jacques Boisvert of Magog who noted that "the English version of our national anthem was written less than one mile from the U.S. border."

724. Did Canada ban a Salman Rushdie novel?

Canada has the distinction of being the sole Western democracy to ban Salman Rushdie's controversial novel *The Satanic Verses* (1988). It was denounced as blasphemous by religious leaders in Iran, and a *fatwa* was placed on Rushdie's life. In February 1989, acting on protests from Iranian-Canadians, Canada Customs banned the book. Protests from civil libertarians and coverage from the news media around the world made the Mulroney administration government look ridiculous. Canada Customs lifted the ban within forty-eight hours. The incident showed that the government and its agencies had no consistent policy with respect to censorship and that its officers were unable to distinguish between literature and libel. It is especially ironic that the incident occurred during "Freedom to Read Week."

725. Does Canada have think tanks?

Given the lack of national definition and faltering sense of social purpose among politicians and public figures in this country, it would seem Canada lacks any think tanks. But there are a number of organizations, independent of government but beholden to business or special-interest groups, that dispense research and analysis on public policy and adminis-tration. In the United States, the models are the Brookings Institution in Washington, the RAND Institute of California, and Herman Kahn's Hudson Institute. Murray Campbell's "Wonks" in *The Globe and Mail*, 2 December 1995, describes a number of their Canadian counterparts, notably the following: Institute for Research on Public Policy, C.D. Howe Institute, Fraser Institute, Canadian Centre for Policy Alternatives, Canadian Policy Research Networks Inc., Canada West Foundation, Mackenzie Institute, Pearson-Shoyama Institute, Business Council on National Issues, Conference Board of Canada, Public Policy Forum, Caledon Institute of Social Policy, Canadian Council on Social Development, Canadian Tax Foundation, and the North-South Institute.

726. What famous camera was named after which now-forgotten cartoon character?

The handy box camera for still photography was developed by George Eastman in 1888. Two years later he launched the model he called the Brownie, and for convenience and ease-of-use it held the market until replaced by the Instamatic in the 1960s. Eastman named the camera after the industrious little elves created by Quebec cartoonist Palmer Cox.

727. Did a Canadian reporter photograph both Kennedy assassinations?

The story persists that a Canadian photographer, who found himself in Dallas on the fatal day, 22 November 1963, when U.S. President

Kennedy was assassinated, took a photograph that clearly shows two assassins in the window of the Texas School Book Depository.

According to Peter Spohn, "Canadian Was Accidental Witness to History," *The Toronto Star*, 22 November 1998, the photographer was Toronto trade reporter Norman Similas. Now a resident of Richmond Hill, Ontario, Similas is the only known Canadian to have witnessed the assassination.

Seconds after the shooting, Similas turned his camera onto the Depository, though he "was not sure that's where the shots came from." He took six pictures. He sped back to his hotel room and phoned an editor at *The Toronto Star* and confirmed the newswire story. Spohn continued, "The Dallas airport was sealed off, so Similas caught a bus to St. Louis, then a flight to Toronto – via Chicago – to get home. Word was spreading fast that Similas had film of the assassination, and that earned him a motorcycle escort to downtown Chicago, where the film was developed. In Toronto, Similas showed his negatives of the depository to a man claiming to be a *Toronto Telegram* reporter camped outside his Willowdale home."

Similas recalled, "He held my negative up to the light, and said, 'Jesus, there's two guys in the window.'" The window was the one from which Lee Harvey Oswald, the "lone gunman," fired his high-powered rifle. The negative that showed the two figures handling a gun-shaped object was taken "immediately after" the shooting, Similas said. According to Spohn, "He let the reporter leave with six negatives, all of which were subsequently 'lost.' 'I think the one showing two figures was one of the most important negatives taken in this century,'" Similas said. The RCMP interviewed the reporter who later denied he saw the two figures.

So who knows?

728. What was the Saxby Gale?

The Saxby Gale is "a fascinating weather story," according to climatologist David Phillips. In November 1868, Lieutenant S.M. Saxby of the Royal Navy sent a letter to several British newspapers in which he predicted that an unusual alignment of the Sun and Moon would cause an intense storm and exceptional tides almost one year later at 7:00 a.m., 5 October 1869. True enough, a storm of hurricane proportions struck the Bay of Fundy, and at Saint John, heavy waves pounded ships against the wharves. Buildings were unroofed or blown down, cattle drowned, and almost every community around the Bay of Fundy was flooded.

According to Phillips, the alignment of the sun and moon explained the unusually high tides, but did not account for the storm. "Saxby was indefinite as to the place where the storm would occur. He just said somewhere in the world. That it occurred in New Brunswick makes it a Canadian legend."

729. Is the Mayor of a city referred to as "Your Honour"?

No. In the United States it is customary to refer to a city's Mayor as "Your Honour." In Canada the correct form of address is "Your Worship."

730. Which Canadian community has a Lord Mayor?

Strange as it might seem, the sole Lord Mayor in Canada is the Mayor of the Town of Niagara-on-the-Lake, Ontario. Custom hallows this convention which likely stems from the time the community was the capital of Upper Canada.

731. Who invented the game of crokinole?

No one knows who invented the once-popular board game known as crokinole, if any single person may be said to have invented it, but what is known is that the world's earliest crokinole board was carved from wood by a carpenter, Echardt Whettlaufer of Waterloo County, and dated 1875. It is displayed in Joseph Schneider Haus in Kitchener, Ontario. So Whettlaufer has a strong claim to being the inventor of the game. He certainly produced the first known board.

732. What is *Frank Harrington's Kristmiss Book?*

Frank Harrington's Kristmiss Book is a literary curiosity, the alleged diary of a pioneer farmer.

Frank Harrington is said to be the pseudonym of a farmer who settled in the Queen's Bush (the Ontario counties of Huron, Bruce, and

Grey) where he farmed 100 acres of land. For forty years he kept a diary, making one entry annually on Christmas Day from 1860 to his death in 1900. The terse diary entries, complete with misspellings, document the joys and especially the sorrows of the pioneer life. The last entry says it all, "God help us all."

The so-called diary first appeared in print in the *Family Herald* magazine, 19 December 1963, then in the 1971 issue of the *Year Book of the Bruce County Historical Society*. H. Gordon Green, who edited the *Family Herald* at the time, said that "Frank Harrington" was a pseudonym; it may even be the pen name of Green himself. The standard edition, titled *Frank Harrington's Kristmiss Book* (1993), was edited by Nelson Ball with photographs by the historical photographer R.R. Sallows.

733. What is C-PAC?

C-PAC (pronounced see-pack) stands for Cable Parliamentary Channel. Established in 1993 by a consortium of cable providers to supersede the coverage supplied by CBC-TV, it offers viewers of cable television live, no-cost, unedited, and comment-free coverage of the proceedings of the House of Commons and of a number of its committees and hearings.

734. When was the $2.00 coin introduced?

The two-dollar coin replaced the two-dollar bill on 19 February 1996. It had yet to receive its nickname. Jad Hemeon writing in *The Globe and Mail*, 16 February 1996, listed some of the front-runners for the naming of the coin adorned with a portrait of Queen Elizabeth II and a bear on an icefloe: Toonie, Doozie, Doubloon, etc. One wit called it Flaubert (after the nineteenth-century French novelist) based on puns: on an icefloe there is a bear.

It is a "toonie," to agree with a "loonie," the nickname of the $1 coin. According to *Copy Talk*, June 1996, the editors of The Canadian Press news service came to the conclusion that "toonie" was preferable to "twoonie" because the latter was unwieldy. As of that month no name for the $2 coin was well-established, though certainly "toonie" was the forerunner.

735. What are HEW, MUSH, and POGG?

Political scientists use the acronym HEW to refer to Health, Education, and Welfare, which are jurisdictions of provincial rather than federal responsibility. At the same time they use the acronym MUSH to refer to the four main program areas that are funded by the federal government: Municipalities, Universities, Social Security, and Health. POGG refers to Peace, Order, and Good Government, which are guaranteed by the BNA Act, 1867, and the Constitution Act, 1982.

736. What are the government's "sharing and caring" programs?

The so-called sharing and caring programs are those program areas funded by the federal government that directly affect people. They include welfare, unemployment, and foreign aid.

737. What is Newfoundland's time zone?

Newfoundland lies on the divide of the time zones of Greenland and the North Atlantic, so it opted for its own unnamed time zone which is thirty minutes later than Greenland's and thirty minutes earlier than that used by the other maritime provinces. This convention goes back to 1884 when the time zones were first determined. Newfoundland time is Greenwich Mean Time (GMT) -330; when Daylight Saving Time is in force, it is GMT -230. Therefore Newfoundland is a half-hour "ahead" of Eastern Canada. One section of Labrador near the Strait of Belle Isle is also on Newfoundland time; the rest of Labrador runs on Atlantic time.

738. What is *Margaret's Museum?*

Margaret's Museum is the title of a 1995 feature film set in the mining community of Glace Bay, Cape Breton Island, Nova Scotia. It is based on Antigonish-based writer Sheldon Currie's short story called "The Glace Bay Miner's Museum" about Margaret MacNeil, a woman whose husband and brother die in a mine cave-in in the 1940s. The eight-page story appeared in the anthology *The Cape Breton Book of the Night* (1979) where it caught the attention of Montreal screenwriter Gerald Wexler.

Wexler wrote a treatment and then a screenplay and the movie was directed by Mort Ransen, with Helena Bonham Carter playing Margaret. There was also a CBC Radio drama written by Dartmouth playwright Wendy Lill, who also wrote a stage version. Currie himself wrote the novel-length version called *Glace Bay Miner's Museum* published in 1995. There actually is a miner's museum at Glace Bay, but it is nothing like the one in the movie.

739. Who first electrified a musical instrument?

Where would contemporary musicians be without electrical amplification? Nowhere! Reginald Aubrey Fessenden, the inventor of voice radio, also invented the first electrified musical instrument. This was his violin, the same one he played on the first announced radio broadcast "to all the ships at sea" heard on Christmas Eve 1906. His wife sang a carol to his accompaniment. When Les Paul inaugurated the electric guitar, he chose the song "The World Is Waiting for the Sunrise" composed by two Canadians in 1919.

740. Why do the Chinese in Canada refer to July 1st as "the Day of Shame"?

Older Chinese refer to July 1st, Canada Day, as "the Day of Shame" because on that date in 1923 the Canadian government passed the Chinese Exclusions Act. It kept Chinese women out of Canada, according to John Bemrose, "Breaking the Silence of Chinatown," *Maclean's*, 1 April 1996.

741. Does a Canadian work rank as one of the Seven Wonders of the Modern World?

Yes. The American Society of Civil Engineers produced a list of the Seven Wonders of the Modern World. By definition the Seven Wonders are products of the twentieth century. The list appeared in April 1996 and consists of the following structures:

1. Itaipu Dam (Parana River, Brazil-Paraguay border).
2. CN Tower, Toronto (Canada).

3. Panama Canal (Panama).
4. Golden Gate Bridge, San Francisco (U.S.A.).
5. Channel Tunnel, English Channel (England-France).
6. Netherlands North Sea Protection Work (The Netherlands).
7. Empire State Building, New York City (U.S.A.).

742. Who wrote *Footprints?*

Footprints is an inspirational poem that was written in 1964 by Margaret Fishback Powers, an itinerant evangelist based in Coquitlam, British Columbia. She lost the manuscript during a cross-country move from Toronto to Vancouver in 1980; in 1983, she was surprised to discover that her text was appearing on posters, coffee mugs, T-shirts, etc. It had been copied from the syndicated "Dear Abbey" advice column; the column appeared in many North American newspapers, including *The Toronto Sun*, 1 December 1981, where the by-line read "Author Unknown." According to Jerry Horton writing in *Quill & Quire*, December 1994, Powers claimed ownership and struck a royalty deal with the greeting-card company Hallmark. In 1993 she published *Footprints: The True Story behind the Poem that Inspired Millions* (1993).

The prose poem describes a conversation between a man who was once deeply troubled and God who is all-merciful. The man accuses God of having abandoned him in his time of need. But God points out that although there was only one set of footprints in the sand in the trying times, they were made by God because God was carrying the man.

The Powers claim of authorship and ownership did not go uncontested. In the 1990s, Mary Stevenson of Chester, Pennsylvania, maintained that in 1939, when she was a fourteen-year-old girl, she had written "Footprints." She produced a manuscript to back her claim but for reasons said to involve her health she failed to pursue it through the courts.

743. What is "low-bridging"?

Low-bridging is a political concept introduced by strategist and Senator Keith Davey when he advised the Liberal Party of Canada to downplay its leader, Pierre Elliott Trudeau, and run against the record of the leader of the Conservative Party in the general election of 1974. The concept worked. According to Hugh Winsor writing in *The Globe and Mail*, 27

April 1996, the phrase could "be traced back to the era when unemployed people travelled across the country by riding on boxcars. They had to keep their heads down when approaching a low bridge."

744. What is the oldest program on CBC Radio?

The oldest program on CBC Radio is the broadcast of the Metropolitan Opera in New York. The live, Saturday-afternoon broadcasts from the stage of the Metropolitan Opera company in New York City have been heard across Canada through the services of the Canadian Radio Broadcasting Commission, the precursor of the Canadian Broadcasting Corporation. The first broadcast was in 1931. Texaco sponsored them from 1940, and to this day they are heard in season with the same sponsorship, "Texaco: Star of the Open Road." The Met broadcasts are the sole sponsored programs heard on CBC Radio. The original host was musicologist Milton Cross. Canadian-born David Allen is the present host.

745. Is there a hockey player who has a museum named in his honour?

The life and hockey career of the late Maurice Richard are celebrated in Montreal at the museum called Rocket Richard's Universe. Despite the fact that Richard retired from the Montreal Canadiens and from hockey in 1960, he remained the country's best-known player. The museum was opened on 19 April 1996. Admission is free. It is a small museum; it accommodates no more than forty visitors at one time.

746. Is Riel's statue controversial in Winnipeg?

It is.
Louis Riel was the founder of the Province of Manitoba who was hanged for treason in 1885. The tribune of the Métis people remains a controversial figure to this day. He led two uprisings against the Crown; both failed, but since then he has been identified with great lost causes and the triumph of minority rights, a kind of prairie Bonnie Prince Charlie.
The contemporary controversy concerns the statues that were erected on the grounds of the Winnipeg legislature to honour the man and his mission. The first statue, sculpted in stone in 1970 by Marcien Lemay,

depicting a nude male figure writhing in agony. The expressionistic work of art created controversy from the day of its unveiling. In July 1995 it was removed to St. Boniface and replaced by a new statue that depicts the Métis leader as a tall and handsome statesman. This representative work of craft was sculpted in bronze by Miguel Joyal and unveiled in May 1996. Much controversy surrounded the shift from the modernist symbol to the representational likeness of the man.

A semi-naked statue of Riel was removed from the grounds of the Saskatchewan legislature in 1991, according to correspondent David Roberts, "Winnipeg," *The Globe and Mail*, 13 May 1996.

747. Does the image of a Tyrannosaurus rex appear on the two-dollar coin?

The head and jaws of Tyrannosaurus rex appear on the reverse side of the two-dollar coin, the toonie. To see it, cover the head and front leg of the bear with your finger, then turn the coin ninety degrees clockwise. The bear's rear haunches look like the dinosaur's head and its rear legs form its deadly jaws.

Here are two more images from the same coin-purse:

There is an anteater (or a fish) to be found on the one-dollar coin (If you cover the head of the loon).

There is a head of a cow on the five-cent coin when the rear end of the beaver is observed upside-down.

"Most intriguing is the side with the Queen's head on the $2 coin. When this image is observed upside down the impression is that the head of the Queen is supported by a boot. As in 'Canada gives the monarchy the boot,' perhaps." So wrote Brian O'Dowd, a Toronto reader, "Letters to the Editor," *The Globe and Mail*, 20 May 1996.

748. Is the Burning Schoolhouse a Canadian invention?

The Burning Schoolhouse is a piece of fireworks popular with school-age youngsters in Canada but barely known outside the country. It consists of a roman candle set in a cardboard red-brick schoolhouse. When ignited, the candle – the "chimney" of the schoolhouse – bursts into red illumination and then into flame, as smoke pours out the schoolhouse windows and it burns to the ground. It was devised and manufactured in the

1930s by Hands Fireworks Inc., founded in 1873 and based in Milton, Ontario. It is used on the 24th of May.

749. When are fireworks popular in Canada?

Fireworks are identified with Victoria Day (May 24th), Canada Day (July 1st), and Saint-Jean Baptiste Day (June 24th). According to John Saunders, "A Blast from the Past," *The Globe and Mail,* 20 May 1996, in British Columbia and Nova Scotia, the big fireworks day is Halloween. In Newfoundland and parts of the Far North, it is New Year's Eve.

750. When is National Aboriginal Day?

Governor General Roméo LeBlanc, on 13 June 1996, proclaimed that henceforth June 21 would be known as National Aboriginal Day. The Royal Proclamation read that "the Aboriginal peoples of Canada have made and continue to make valuable contributions to Canadian society and it is considered appropriate that there be, in each year, a day to mark and celebrate these contributions and to recognize the different cultures of the Aboriginal peoples of Canada."

The Aboriginal peoples consist of the First Nations, Inuit, and Métis. The day of the year is appropriate, as June 21 marks the Spring Equinox, the longest day of the year, and as such is especially significant to all the world's traditional people.

Recognition of the Aboriginal Peoples of Canada was first prompted in 1982 by the National Indian Brotherhood (now the Assembly of First Nations).

751. What is screech?

Screech is the generic name of a flavoured Jamaican rum bottled in St. John's, Newfoundland. It has been aged for two years and at 40 proof is strong firewater. The word may be derived from the Scottish screigh (for whisky) or from the "screech" of someone drinking it. According to Walter Stefaniuk, writing in "You Asked Us," *The Toronto Star*, 30 May 1996, the word first appeared in print in 1944 when there were American personnel in Newfoundland.

752. What's "pogey"?

To be "in the pogey" is to be in jail, presumably temporarily, for an offence like vagrancy, drunkenness, etc.

To be "on the pogey" is to be on the receiving end of welfare payments. The latter definition is common in Western Canada.

753. Who wrote *52 Kinds of Tea Biscuits?*

That is the actual title of a booklet of recipes written by Kate Aitken who was a popular radio personality and "ideal housewife" in the 1940s and 1950s. She wrote a number of specialized recipe books, and *52 Kinds of Tea Biscuits* was one of them.

754. Who created Broadway's "bedroom farce"?

For half a century the mainstay of the Broadway and the West End stage was the "bedroom farce," a light comedy of bad manners that had to do with suggested infidelity or "bed-hopping." Dramatist Merrill Denison maintained that the genre was inaugurated with the play *Parlor, Bedroom, and Bath* which was produced at the Republic Theatre in New York City in 1917. The play was the work of Charles William Bell (1876-1938), Hamilton-born playwright and lawyer. Earlier Bell wrote *Her First Divorce* (1913) which was followed by *Elsie, Thy Neighbor's Wife*, and *Paradise Alley*. Bell wrote the book for the musical *A Dangerous Maid* for which George Gershwin wrote the music and Ira Gershwin the lyrics. Unlike the sex farces, it was not a great success. It opened poorly in Atlantic City in April 1921 and it closed there in May of that year. Although the genre held the stage until the 1960s, Bell is mainly remembered today as the author of a book of legal reminiscences *Who Said Murder?* (1935). The movie *Parlor, Bedroom & Bath* (1931) starred Buster Keaton and was directed by Claude Autant-Laura.

755. How did the Bell family influence theatre and film?

The family of Alexander Graham Bell, the inventor of the telephone, has inspired theatre and film. George Bernard Shaw, in the preface to his play

Pygmalion (1912), referred to "the illustrious Alexander Melville Bell." Indeed, in his day, Melville Bell (1819-1905) was celebrated in Britain and America as a teacher of phonetics. He was at one time more famous than his son, Alexander Graham Bell. Shaw modelled his didactic Professor Higgins on Professor Bell. Dr. Joseph Bell, one of Alexander's cousins, was a professor at the University of Edinburgh; one of his students was Arthur Conan Doyle, who was so impressed with Joseph's powers of analysis that when he wrote *A Study in Scarlet* (1887), he modelled Sherlock Holmes on Joseph. Actor Don Ameche played the part of the telephone-inventor in the movie *The Story of Alexander Graham Bell* (1939).

756. What happened to Dominion Day?

Dominion Day became Canada Day, to the irritation of many citizens.

The bill "to make the first day of July a Public Holiday by the name of Dominion Day" was introduced in the House of Commons in 1879 and subsequently passed. It marked the anniversary of the founding of the Dominion of Canada, 1 July 1867.

Dominion Day was celebrated for 115 years, until a private member's bill, passed by the House of Commons on 9 July 1982, amended the Holidays Act, renaming it Canada Day.

As columnist Michael Valpy noted in "It's Dominion Day to a T," *The Globe and Mail*, 4 June 1996, the arguments in favour of the change were spurious. The word "Dominion" is not a vestige of the colonialism of the British Empire but a uniquely Canadian concept; there is the French equivalent *domaine*; and it is part and parcel of the history of the country, whether multicultural or not. Backing up its interest for 1 July 1996, *The Globe and Mail* offered t-shirts for sale. They feature an illustration of Sir John A. Macdonald hugging a moose and the words in English and French: "Give Us Back Our Dominion Day ... Canada's True National Holiday."

757. Did Pierre Berton write a pornographic novel?

Not quite, but the prolific author and popular historian did write a novel which some people consider risqué. *Masquerade: 15 Variations on a Theme of Sexual Fantasy* was submitted under the pseudonym Lisa Kroniuk and published by McClelland & Stewart, Berton's regular publishing house, in 1985. At a press conference the identity of the author was made known.

758. Who created Mr. Magoo?

The creator of the nearsighted Mr. Magoo, a humorous character who starred in a series of animated cartoons in the late 1940s and early 1950s, was created by Stephen Bosustow for the company he founded, United Productions of America (UPA). A former Disney employee, Bosustow was born in Vancouver.

759. Who produced *Bambi Meets Godzilla?*

The cartoon cult classic *Bambi Meets Godzilla* (1969) was shot in black and white, is all of 120 seconds long, and most of those seconds are devoted to screen credits. The animated short film shows what happens when the tiny deer Bambi, quietly grazing, is stepped on by the immense foot of the giant lizard Godzilla. (The plot synopsis on Amazon.com runs like this: "Godzilla squashes Bambi. The End.") It was written and directed by Vancouver filmmaker Marv Newland. Some accounts say that it was animated by Gary Larson, the well-known cartoonist, who hailed from British Columbia.

760. Did a Canadian invent the Wonderbra?

In 1964, a Quebec designer, Louise Poirier, designed the Wonderbra for the Quebec lingerie company Canadelle. According to broadcaster Bill Casselman, Poirier's coined the word. "A Canadian word for our very own contribution to mammary density. Instead of elevating and separating the breasts, the Wonderbra pushes them up and squeezes them together.... Playtex bought Canadelle; now Playtex is owned by Sara Lee, the folks who make frozen cheesecake."

761. What was unique about the Three-penny Beaver?

Three-penny beaver was the first postage stamp issued in early Canada. It appeared in 1851. It is said to be the first stamp in the world that did not depict a ruling monarch. Instead it featured a plump beaver, Canada's unofficial emblem.

762. What are the names of some acclaimed classical Canadian musical scores?

Ken Winters, music critic, writing in "In Search of the Great White Score," *The Globe and Mail*, 12 October 1996, named seven favourite, all-Canadian compositions. Here they are:

1. *Blanche comme la neige* (White as Snow), an arrangement of the Quebec folk song by Sir Ernest Macmillan, for unaccompanied male choir in 1928, then for mixed choir in 1958.
2. *Divertimento No. 1.* This is a concertino for flute and strings composed by John Weinzweig in 1946.
3. *North Country*, for string orchestra, was composed by Harry Somers in 1948. "It is the first work I ever heard that I felt could have been composed only by a Canadian."
4. *String Quartet No. 2*, known as *Waves*, composed by R. Murray Schafer in 1976.
5. *String Quartet*, composed by John Beckwith in 1977.
6. *Tales of the Netsilik*, composed by Raymond Luedeke, in 1989. It is based on a narrative of Inuit folk tales.
7. *Epitaph for Moonlight*, a choral composition, "by now has attained the status of a Canadian icon." It was composed for a youth choir by R. Murray Schafer.

763. Did Cartier-Bresson ever visit Canada?

Yes. The extraordinary French photographer Henri Cartier-Bresson took photographs in Cuba, Mexico, and Canada in 1958-60. He returned to Canada for photographic purposes in 1965. The Canada that caught the iris of his camera was Quebec, principally Montreal. Black-and-white photographs of Montreal street scenes are reproduced in various of his publications. In 1960, the National Film Board released *Le Canada*, a documentary film on Cartier-Bresson's work. It has an alternate title: *Le Québec par Cartier-Bresson/ Le Quebec as Seen by Cartier Bresson*. The film was directed by Guy Glover and produced by the National Film Board of Canada in 1969.

764. Who is the Girl in the Photograph?

Associated Press news photographer Nick Ut took a photograph of a young girl screaming with pain as she runs naked down a road near Saigon, her back and arms burning with napalm. The sight brought home to civilians around the world the horrors of the U.S.-ordered air strike on the village of Trang Bang in South Vietnam, 8 June 1972. Ut won the Pulitzer Prize for the photograph. The nine-year-old girl, Phan Thi Kim Phuc, survived the attack that burned all the clothes off her body and left her upper body permanently scarred. In 1984 she was used for propaganda purposes by the North Vietnamese government. Two years later, returning from a trip to Cuba, she defected at Gander International Airport, and since then has lived in Toronto, where she is happily married and the mother of a healthy girl. She has become a symbol of the civilian casualties of war: as noted in the Associated Press news story, "War Survivor," *The Toronto Star*, 12 November 1996. Phan Thi Kim Phuc is "the Girl in the Photograph."

765. Is the so called American Girl really a Canadian girl?

"American Girl in Italy 1951" is the title of a famous photograph that was taken by the American photographer Ruth Orkin on a streetcorner in Florence, Italy, on 21 August 1951. It captures the disregard of a young American girl as she walks past a group of leering Italian males. Over the years the photograph attracted attention and the young woman became something of a feminist icon. The young woman, Ninalee Craig, was an American student of art studying in Florence. She subsequently married a businessman and they settled in Toronto. The full story is told by Susan Walker in *The Toronto Star*, 3 June 1995.

766. What is Pier 21?

Pier 21 has been described as Canada's Ellis Island, that is, its gateway for immigrants. Between 1928 and 1971, Pier 21 of Halifax Harbour welcomed 1.5 million immigrants, 100,000 of them displaced persons and refugees. It also greeted 50,000 war brides with their 22,000 children. Some 368,000 Canadian troops passed through Pier 21, and 3,000 British evacuee children also came there. In the 1990s plans were underway to commemorate the site, now no longer used.

767. Who built the first electronic game?

The world's first electronic game was devised, developed, and built by Josef Kates, an engineer with the University of Toronto. Kates had come to Canada as a refugee from Vienna and studied electrical engineering at McGill University. The notion of the "electronic game" was not yet current, but the "electronic brain" was very much on people's minds. He called his invention "Bertie the Brain," and it was sophisticated enough to play tic-tac-toe with visitors who paused in front of the exhibit at the Canadian National Exhibition in 1951. "Bertie" could have served as the basis for an electronics and computer industry in Canada, had there been bankers and capitalists interested in developing its potential. Instead the modern computer and electronic games were developed and manufactured elsewhere.

768. Who sailed the *Matthew?*

Matthew is the name of the sailing vessel that took John Cabot on his historic voyage of discovery from Bristol, England, to the landfall on the East Coast of North America, the site likely being Bonavista, Newfoundland, 24 May 1497. Such was the discovery of the Great Island and hence of Canada. Upon his return to England, Cabot became known as the Great Admiral.

A replica of the *Matthew* was built in England for the government of Newfoundland. It recreated the historic voyage and landfall at Bonavista on 24 May 1997, the 500th anniversary of the historic voyage.

769. What are lunkers?

Accumulations of ice, sludge, and snow that build up in the wheel wells of automobiles are called "lunkers." No dictionary defines the word that way, but newspaperman Bill Bean, in his column "You Can Call that Icy Fender Crud a Lunker" in *The Kitchener-Waterloo Record*, 8 February 1997, quotes the use of the word by a colleague, Ken Willett. It is possible the term is an instance of local usage common half a century ago in Ontario's Waterloo County. Bean concluded: "Tell your friends, and know that when you next kick that icy stuff off your car, it has a name. It's a lunker."

770. Is Shredded Wheat a Canadian Invention?

The process of producing a cold breakfast cereal that was shredded rather than flaked was developed by two Americans, Henry Perky and his friend, William Ford, who founded, in 1893, the Cereal Machine Company of Denver, Colorado. Perky wanted to sell the machinery, but instead found himself selling its product from wagons on the street. He soon moved to eastern Massachusetts where he produced Shredded Wheat in various plants. In 1901, he moved to Niagara Falls, New York, and opened a plant on Buffalo Avenue.

The property bordered on the Niagara River, but the advertising art of the day often depicted it standing on the brink of the Horseshoe or Canadian Falls, thus perhaps giving rise to the notion that the popular breakfast cereal was "shredded" in Canada within earshot of the waterfall. That plant was eventually closed in 1952, but a second plant nearby in Niagara Falls, New York, continued to make Shredded Wheat until 1995. It now produces Triscuits. A Canadian branch of the company was established around 1908 in Niagara Falls, Ontario. The plant did not stand near the Falls, and today it is the only remaining Niagara Falls plant producing the original Shredded Wheat product; U.S. production, since the company's purchase by Post (Kraft/General Foods), now continues in Napierville, Illinois.

771. Who first mixed the Bloody Caesar?

Walter Chell first mixed the Bloody Caesar, adding Clamato juice and various spices to a shot of vodka. Chell saw his innovation as a variation on the Bloody Mary (tomato juice, vodka, spices).

Chell was a professional bartender and consultant on liquor to various hotel chains. When he developed the Bloody Caesar in 1969, he was working for the Westin Hotel in Vancouver in 1969. Chell was born in Montenegro, raised it Italy, and trained in Switzerland. He spent much of his professional life in Canada. He died in Toronto.

Other accounts of Chell's life state that he introduced the popular cocktail in 1969 in Calgary, where he was manager of Marco's Restaurant, at the opening of the Calgary-Westin Hotel. The cocktail consists of 1 oz. of vodka, 4 oz. of tomato-clam juice, salt and pepper, Worcester sauce, a dash of oregano, and one celery stick.

772. Was the raid on Harper's Ferry planned in Canada?

The American abolitionist John Brown and eleven white and thirty-five coloured associates met in Chatham, Kent County, Ontario, and drafted the "Provisional Constitution and Ordinance for the People of the United States." In nearby Ingersoll, he declared, "The negro must be free!" Later that year, on 16 October 1859, he led the famous but abortive raid on Harper's Ferry, West Virginia. He and his cause of abolition are recalled in the spiritual which begins "John Brown's body lies a-mould'ring in the grave. / His soul goes marching on! / Glory, glory hallelujah! / His soul goes marching on!"

773. Who founded the FLQ?

The Front de Libération du Québec (FLQ) was an underground terrorist organization whose members were committed to the liberation of the people of Quebec from English Canadian capitalists and the founding of an independent Quebec. It was committed to revolution and to terror. It was founded in Montreal in February 1963 by three men: George Schoeters, Gabriel Hudon, and Raymond Villeneuve. "Schoeters was the most important of the original triumvirate, because he was the only one who could be called a trained, professional revolutionary," noted John Gellner in *Bayonets in the Streets: Urban Guerrillas at Home and Abroad* (1974). Schoeters was a former member of the Belgian resistance who had visited Algeria and Cuba before immigrating to Quebec in 1957. Imprisoned in June 1963, he was paroled in 1967 and expelled back to his native Belgium.

774. Does Canada have patron saints?

The Roman Catholic Church recognizes four Patrons Saints for Canada and Canadians. Since 1624, St. Joseph has been honoured as the Patron Saint of Canada, and St. Anne the Patron Saint of the province and diocese that make up today's Quebec. Since 1838, The Virgin Mary, as Our Lady of the Assumption, has been declared to be the Patron Saint of the Acadians. Since 1908, St. John the Baptist (Saint-Jean-Baptiste) has been said to be the Patron Saint of the French Canadian people, both those who reside in and those who live outside Quebec.

775. What are some special days in the Canadian calendar?

Here are fourteen "special days," some of them are holidays by statute, others are days honoured by custom:

New Year's Day (January 1), Good Friday (2 days before Easter Sunday), Easter Sunday (date varies, late March to late April), Mother's Day (2nd Sunday in May), Victoria Day (24th of May or the Monday after the 17th of May), Father's Day (3rd Sunday in June), St. Jean Baptiste in Quebec (June 24), Canada Day (July 1), Civic Holiday (1st Monday in August), Labour Day (1st Monday in September), Thanksgiving Day (2nd Monday in October), Remembrance Day (November 11), Christmas Day (December 25), Boxing Day (December 26).

776. When was Confederation Bridge opened?

Confederation Bridge is a 12.9 kilometre long automobile bridge over Northumberland Strait that links Prince Edward Island and New Brunswick. It was opened on 1 June 1997. It connects Jourimain Island, New Brunswick, and Borden-Carleton, Prince Edward Island. It is the world's longest continuous, multi-span bridge. During winter, when the Strait freezes, it will be the world's longest bridge over ice-covered water. At the inaugural ceremony, the provincial premiers met at the midpoint and shook hands. Prince Edward Island. Premier Pat Binns declared, "It represents the co-operative spirit of Confederation." New Brunswick Premier Frank McKenna added, "In New Brunswick we feel very touched emotionally that Prince Edward Island. has chosen to break its solitude." Confederation Bridge is a joint venture between the Federal government and private enterprise; the bridge authority is Strait Crossing Development Inc. of Calgary. The bridge replaces the century-old ferry service between the mainland and the island. It took forty-five minutes for the ferry ride; the automobile journey takes twelve minutes. The bridge's S-shape prevents it from having a hypnotic effect on drivers.

777. Who owns Ripley's Believe It or Not?

Surprisingly, the American entertainment icon has been owned by two Canadian venture capitalists. Robert L. Ripley, sportswriter and cartoonist, created the popular syndicated newspaper cartoon feature "Believe It or Not!" on 19 December 1918 for *The New York Globe*. From New York City the BION people operated "odditoriums" in United States and Canada. In 1971 Ripley International Ltd. was bought by Toronto businessman Alex Rigby and operated from Toronto. In 1984 it was acquired from Rigby by Vancouver businessman Jimmy Pattison. Thereupon the BION headquarters was moved to Florida.

778. What is Tent 28?

Tent 28 is the designation of the Variety Club of Ontario. The first in Canada, it was founded 11 July 1945 with showman J.J. Fitzgibbons as Chief Barker. It is now the second-largest club in the world. Variety International was established in Pittsburgh, Pennsylvania, in 1927. It is the principal charity of the entertainment industry.

779. Did Brian Moore write Harlequin Romances?

No. The distinguished novelist Brian Moore did not write Harlequin Romances, but in 1951, while still a Montreal newspaperman, he wrote a number of suspense novels that were published by Harlequin Books. They are *Wreath for a Redhead* and *The Executioners*.

Information is not plentiful, but it seems Moore wrote other novels for Harlequin. Their titles are sometimes given as *This Gun for Gloria*, *French for Murder* (as by Bernard Mara), *Intention to Kill*, and *Murder in Majorca* (Michael Bryan). It seems in 1952 Pyramid Books published yet another Moore pot-boiler, titled *Sailor's Leave*.

780. What was Hitler's Victory Jig?

Hitler's Victory Jig was a little dance or jig that the German dictator Adolf Hitler performed as he stepped down from the railway carriage at the train station in Compiègne, France, June 1940, after he and his generals had accepted the French surrender. For the newsreel cameramen he performed what one journalist has described as "a little leap of astonishment at himself." Once seen, it is never forgotten. Under the circumstances, it is more a *danse macabre* than a dance of celebration.

It is a curious fact that Allied newsreels are the only newsreels to record the jig. It never appeared on Axis movie screens. It has been claimed that there was no jig, that enterprising newsreel editors in the West "looped" the film footage to create the illusion that Hitler's straightforward step was a forward-backward-forward movement. On public occasions NFB Commissioner John Grierson took credit for the creation of the jig, maintaining it was accomplished for propaganda purposes at the Ottawa headquarters of the National Film Board of Canada. In the 1990s, Grierson's claim was disputed by Board employees of the day who maintain that even this simple looping was beyond their technical capacity at the time. Sources: Tom Burnam in *More Misinformation* (1980) and Laurence Stalling's article in *Esquire*, October 1958.

781. Did the NFB fake Nazi atrocity pictures?

The National Film Board of Canada was established by Film Commissioner John Grierson in 1939 to aid the Allied effort in the Second World War. Among its early efforts, the NFB produced and released propaganda newsreel footage that depicted the Nazis performing atrocities. It has been alleged that the atrocity footage was faked.

Nicholas J. Cull, author of *Selling War: The British Propaganda Campaign against American "Neutrality" in World War II* (1995), stated in "Second World War," *The Globe and Mail*, 3 June 1995, that there is strong evidence that British Intelligence used the NFB, the RCMP, Camp X, and Station M (a specialist operation for faking Nazi documents) for its propaganda practices, probably including "atrocity pictures," based on examination of Public Record Office documents.

782. Who called himself the Canadian Hick Poet?

To recall the Canadian Hick Poet, I can do no better than to reproduce the author George Woodcock's words from a letter dated 9 February 1978.

> Paul Potts – he remains in some ways as vague in memory as his explanations of his Canadian antecedents were. So far as I can recollect, he came originally from Brandon, but he did write an autobiography, *Dante Called You Beatrice*, and you will find Paul's version of the relevant details there. He also published his

broadsheets of really dreadful poems which at the end of the thirties he used to hawk near the speakers' corner in Hyde Park. In the forties he did arouse a flurry of interest and was patronized by Tambimuttu, who published his work in *Poetry London* (I never touched it for *Now*) and who even published a volume of his poems whose title I have forgotten. He moved in places like the Wheatsheaf and the Fitzroy and the York Minster and Pedro's Club, called himself a revolutionary socialist, and wrote often for the ILP organ, the *New Leaders*. He was very paranoiac, and my relationship with him was rather like my relationship with Irving Layton, protestations of extreme brotherly love alternating with vituperation, all on his part of course. He was very close to Orwell, who endured him more patiently than most other people. You should look at the biography, though, which will give you some approximate facts. He called himself, in the 1950s, THE CANADIAN HICK POET, but dropped the title later when he got a little respectable and took to wearing tweeds. He went to Israel and wrote a book on it. And so on, and so forth.

783. What was *Gilmour's Albums?*

Gilmour's Albums was the name of a popular CBC Radio and Stereo program. It featured newspaperman and broadcaster Clyde Gilmour playing and describing some of the favourite recordings in his personal collection. Fans of the weekly program heard Gilmour discourse on all manner of subjects and all manner of records. First heard on 2 October 1956, ill health forced Gilmour to sign off on 14 June 1997. It was CBC Radio's longest-lasting program.

784. What is the Talking Stick?

The so-called Talking Stick is a reference to the ornamental mace which represents the Speaker's authority in the Legislative Assembly of the Northwest Territories. This particular mace, authorized for use on 14 January 2000, replaces the earlier narwhal-tusk mace which became the property of the Nunavut Assembly established in 1999.

It is called the Talking Stick because of the sound it makes when shaken. Its "foot" consists of a silver receptacle for thirty-three pebbles, selected from the same number of communities across the Territories. Another unusual feature is the inscription engraved on the silver band that encircles the mace's head. It reads "One Land, Many Voices." The words appear in the Territories' ten official languages: Chipewyan, Cree, Dogrib, Gwich'in, North Slavey, South Slavey, Inuvialuktun, Inuinnaqtun, English, and French.

785. When did the auto workers in Canada form their own union?

Canadian auto workers have always enjoyed the benefits of their own union, but according to its constitution, their union was not a national association but a chapter of the United Autoworkers of America (UAW).

It became its own national organization known as the Canadian Auto Workers (CAW) on 4 September 1985 under the nationalistic leadership of its aggressive president, Bob White.

786. What are some landmarks in Canadian industrial design?

Canada Post Corporation unveiled a series of postage stamps to honour achievements in Canadian industrial design. The 45-cent stamps were called Icons of Canadian Industrial Design and were released on 23 July 1997. Canadian industrial designers are among the most competent in the world, but that does not mean there is a school of Canadian industrial design or a recognizable national style. Utilitarian might be the best word to describe the design concepts that animate Canadian designers. The appearance of the stamps marked the fiftieth anniversary of the Association of Canadian Industrial Designers (ACID).

Here is a list of the twenty-six objects depicted on the stamps and their connecting tabs along with relevant years and names of designers:

G.E. Domed Kettle (1940): Fred Moffatt
Bombardier Ski-Doo Snowmobile (1996): Martin Aubé,
    Germain Cadotte, Denys Lapointe, Jérome Foy
Steamer Lounge Chair (1978): Thomas Lamb
Resentel Attaché (1985): Michel Dallaire
Squirrel Point of Sale Terminal (1991): Henry Eng
Aura Chair (1988): Niels Bendtsen
Nylon Chair (1950): Jacques Guillon

Westinghouse Iron 1B22 (1948): Thomas W. Penrose
Plus 4 Garden Tools (1992): Todd Wood
Stethos Electronic Stethoscope (1995): Michel Swift, Garry Savage, Serge Nadeau
Omnicolumn (1993): Jules Bélanger, Michel Soutière, Mario Lehoux
Occasional Chair (1958): Stefan Siwinski
Contempra Phone (1969): John Tyson
Ballet Table (1990): Douglas Ball, Leon Goldik
Bauer Hockey Helmet (1997): Daniel Chartrand
Ball-B-Q Bar B-Q (1970): William Wiggins
Radius Table (1957): Al Faux
Magline Magnesium Snowshoes (1949): Douglas A. Tetu
Contour Chair (1950): Julien Hébert
Vista 350 Phone (1994): Cliff Read
Gazelle Chair (1986): Jonathan Crinion, Randy Johnson
Laser Sailboat (1971): Bruce Kirby, Ian Bruce, Hans Fogh
Actar 911 CPR Training Mannequin: Dianne Croteau, Richard Brault, Jonathan Vinden
E26 Street Letter Box (1987): Bruce Fletcher, Denis Berthiaume, Ross Slade
Newtsuit Diving System (1980): Phil Nuytten
Laberge Speed Skates (1977): Raymond Laberge

787. What upstaged the official roll-out of the first Avro Arrow?

The official roll-out of the first Avro Arrow took place at Malton, Ontario, 4 October 1957. The sleek Arrow, powered by the powerful Orenda engine, was an advanced, delta-wing interceptor jet plane. It was all-Canadian in design and construction. The day of the launching was propitious, not for the appearance of the Arrow, but for the fact that the Soviet Union launched its unmanned Sputnik spacecraft into orbit, thus inaugurating the Space Age and the Space Race. No one realized they would be upstaged that day, as Palmiro Campagna pointed out in *Storms of Controversy: The Secret Avro Arrow Files Revealed* (2nd ed., 1997).

788. Did one of the Avro Arrows escape the scrap-heap?

The Diefenbaker administration cancelled production of the Avro Arrow, the advanced, interceptor jet aircraft that was designed and manufactured by A.V. Roe Canada at Malton, Ontario, 20 February 1959. The decision was a difficult one to make and so divisive in effect that the administration required that all five prototypes be scrapped, as if disguising physical evidence of its decision. However justified the decision to cancel the project was, this act seemed vindictive.

The rumour endures that while four of the Arrows were blowtorched into scrap metal, one of the prototypes escaped destruction. "No government records have yet been found acknowledging that the destruction of all aircraft was completed," noted Palmiro Campagna in *Storms of Controversy: The Secret Avro Arrow Files Revealed* (2nd ed., 1997). "Was it spirited away?" After reviewing the evidence, Campagna concluded, "If one did escape, it would have to have been done so with the knowledge of the Arrow Termination Co-ordination team. Even the pieces and engine on display at the Aviation Museum in Ottawa were released by this group. If it really is in hiding, logical places to look would be Canadian military bases rather than farmers' fields."

789. Was the discoverer of the Comstock lode a Canadian?

History records the claims of many discoverers of the Comstock lode, silver deposits in the Sierra Nevadas of Western United States. It is probable that the Grosch Brothers of Philadelphia came upon the lode first and then others worked it. One thing is certain: the lode bears the name of Henry Tompkins Paige Comstock (1820-1870), the farmer-turned-prospector who claimed he discovered it. Comstock was born in Trenton, in today's Ontario, of American parents, but raised in Connecticut. He was blessed with a baronial bearing and despite the fact that his claim was no better or no worse than any other of the claimants, public opinion and hence history have sided with him in his claim that he discovered the lode.

790. What are the top twenty Canadian children's books?

Quill & Quire, the journal of the book trade, asked this question, and in the October 1997 issue, it supplied the answer. A group of specialists in the field offered these titles, in order of popularity, as the all-time greatest Canadian books for children and young adults.

1. *Anne of Green Gables* by L.M. Montgomery.
2. *Hold Fast* by Kevin Major.
3. *Owls in the Family* by Farley Mowat.
4. *Angel Square* by Brian Doyle.
5. *Alligator Pie* by Dennis Lee.
6. *The Story of Canada* by Janet Lunn, Christopher Moore, and Alan Daniel.
7. *The Sky is Falling* by Kit Pearson.
8. *The Hockey Sweater* by Roch Carrier.
9. *The Root Cellar* by Janet Lunn.
10. *The Paper Bag Princess* by Robert Munsch.
11. *Jacob Two-Two Meets the Hooded Fang* by Mordecai Richler.
12. *The Maestro* by Tim Wynne-Jones.
13. *A Darker Magic* by Michael Bedard.
14. *A Prairie Boy's Winter* by William Kurelek.
15. *Josepha* by Jim McGugan.
16. *Two by Two* by Barbara Reid.
17. *The Cremation of Sam McGee* by Robert Service.
18. *Zoom at Sea* by Tim Wynne-Jones.
19. *The Keeper of the Isis Light* by Monica Hughes.
20. *From Anna* by Jean Little.

The popular editions of some of these classics are illustrated by noted artists. All the titles appear in English language, including story originally published in French (*The Hockey Sweater*).

791. What is poutine and who developed it?

Poutine is a fast-food item particularly prized by non-food lovers in Quebec. It consists of thick French fries topped with fresh cheese curds and bathed in hot beef gravy. According to Th Thanh Ha, writing in *The Globe and Mail*, 9 October 1997, poutine was developed in the kitchen of the Café Ideal (now Lutin Qui Rit), Warwick, Quebec, in September or October 1957, by its proprietor Fernand Lachance. He served one of his customers, a truck driver named Eddie Lainesse, a combination of French fries and cheese curd with salt and vinegar. "You'll get a bloody poutine," Lachance said, using French slang for a "mess." Thus was born the delicacy and the name.

Quebec's poutine has nothing in common with the traditional Acadian poutine, a type of meat pudding, though from time to time

Quebec commentators, upset that their cuisine should be identified with such ingredients, argue that the dish originated in New Brunswick, not in *la belle province.*

792. What are the names of the services of CBC Radio?

Downsizing, reorganizing, and repositioning for the market, the Canadian Broadcasting Corporation in August 1997 renamed its two services: CBC Radio One (AM) and CBC Radio Two (FM/Stereo).

793. What is *Due South?*

Due South is a popular light crime show that is seen one hour each week on CBS in the United States and on the CTV Network in Canada. The pilot was premiered 23 April 1994. It stars actor Paul Gross as Constable Benton Fraser, a straight-as-an-arrow Royal Canadian Mounted Police officer assigned to the Canadian Consulate in Chicago. There he assists street-wise Detective Ray Vecchio, played by Dave Marciano. There are frequent spoofs of national stereotypes and media conventions. Fraser is assisted by his deaf, lip-reading pet wolf named Diefenbaker.

794. Who originated the IGA concept?

The IGA concept is the form of merchandising adopted by the Independent Grocers Association, which is an association of independently owned small grocery outlets across North America that purchase supplies from a central warehouse. The concept was developed and introduced by Frank Grimes, a Guelph-born Quaker who was then living in Chicago, according to Diane Frances writing in *Controlling Interest: Who Owns Canada?* (1986).

795. Who created Scrooge McDuck?

The cartoon character Scrooge McDuck was created by the Disney Studios in Los Angeles as the uncle of the mischievous young ducks named Huey, Dewey, and Louie. The first drawings of the rich-as-Croesus but tight-as-a-drum Scrooge McDuck were made by Carl Barks, an

Oregon-born cartoonist who also drew Donald Duck. Barks contributed cartoons to Bob Edwards's publication *The Calgary Eye-Opener* in late 1920s and early 1930s.

796. Did Eric Ambler set a novel in Canada?

It is too bad that Eric Ambler, the master of the spy novel, did not set a novel in whole or in part in Canada. He would have added glamour and excitement to the setting. Standard Ambler settings are in Western Europe – Geneva, Belgium, France, Milan. At least these are the locales of his novel *The Intercom Conspiracy* (1969). The settings may not be Canadian, but the villain of the novel, a fellow named Carter, is identified as a Canadian who is based in Brussels.

797. What was hockey's famous "gondola"?

"Why, it looks just like the gondola of an airship!" exclaimed C.M. Passmore, advertising executive with the MacLaren agency, the agency that oversaw the commercial sponsorship of the radio program *Hockey Night in Canada* in the 1930s and 1940s. Passmore was commenting on the appearance of the newly built broadcast booth. The booth, or gondola, was used most notably by Foster Hewitt in his play-by-play radio coverage of hockey games played in Toronto's Maple Leaf Gardens. The gondola hung from the rafters above the ice and was accessible only by catwalk. It was erected about 1933 and demolished by club-owner Harold Ballard in the 1970s. Only in this country is the word gondola used to identify a broadcast booth which commands a view of an arena or a stadium.

798. Who named the ionosphere?

The ionosphere is a layer of atmosphere that extends from 100 kilometres above the surface of the Earth to 1000 kilometres. It is rich in ions. The layer or sphere was so named by the Scottish physicist and radar specialist Sir Robert Watson-Watt (1892-1973), who was a postwar Ontario resident concerned with the practical applications of his wartime research, one application of which was the radar detector used by traffic authorities.

799. Did Frank Lloyd Wright design any Canadian buildings?

The great American architect Frank Lloyd Wright influenced architectural design the world over. Banff Park Pavilion, commissioned by the federal government and completed in Alberta's Banff National Park in 1913, was sited on a meadow close to the Bow River. "It was intended to be used as a shelter for picnics and dancers," according to Pamela Young, "Finding Wright's Legacy in Canada Takes Creative Search," *The Globe and Mail*, 7 November 1998. "Working with his former employee, Ottawa-based architect Francis Sullivan, Wright took the model for his ground-hugging, emphatically horizontal Prairie Houses and extended it to stretch-limo proportions." Built of rustic stone and timber, it proved to be a "white elephant." It housed military supplies during the Great War and then reverted to picnic use until being torn down in 1938. There is a movement to reconstruct it using Wright's original plans now in storage at Taliesin West in Arizona.

Statuary based on moulds made from original statues designed by Wright and modelled by sculptor Alfonso Ianelli for Chicago's Midway Gardens (1913-1920s) stand in a condominium building at 33 Jakes Avenue, Toronto. Cast in granite-based aggregate, the replicas show three "robed maidens, with squared-off features reminiscent of Mayan art, and outfits that made them look like futuristic geishas."

Wright also designed many interiors of private residences for wealthy clients. One of his commissions is identified as Dining Room for Remodelling of the C. Thaxter Shaw House, Montreal, 1906. Wright gave his characteristic touch – horizontal planes, geometric shapes, etc. – to dining-room tables and chairs, plant stands, etc. The design itself is on display at the Victoria and Albert Museum in London, England.

It is stated on some authority that the modern American architect Frank Lloyd Wright designed the Gray Lodge that overlooks Lac Témiscouata at Notre-Dame-du-Lac on Quebec's South Shore. The grand hunting lodge was built for William D. Bishop in 1905 at the time when Notre-Dame-du-Lac was still known as Le Détour. The lodge is now known as l'Auberge Marie-Blanc and receives guests.

800. What is the Trans Canada Trail?

The Trans Canada Trail was opened on 9 September 2000. It is a hiking trail that stretches west from St. John's, Newfoundland, to Victoria,

British Columbia, and north to Tuktoyaktuk, Northwest Territories. The continent-wide system of walkways, scenic country lines, historic water routes, and abandoned railway lines runs through large cities and national parks, small villages, and vast wilderness areas. It is designated for recreational use by walkers, cyclists, equestrians, and cross-country skiers. The trail is 15,000 kilometres long. About 20 per cent of the trail already existed in the form of existing trails and waterways.

Ideas

801. Who wrote the "Iroquois Prayer"?

The "Iroquois Prayer" is the text of an inspirational poem which has been widely sold as an Indian souvenir. Reproduced in script form on imitation birchbark scrolls, it is available in native crafts shops. According to the text, the author is one White Cloud, who is presumably an Iroquois Indian of the past. Researchers have, so far, failed to establish the identity of the author. Yet the text's style and sentiment suggest that it was composed in English, not in the Iroquois tongue, by a Christian, and that it dates not from antiquity but perhaps from the late 1950s.

Here is the text as it appears on the tablet which marks the Taber Hill site of an ancient Iroquois ossuary in Scarborough, Ontario. The site was dedicated on 21 October 1961. The text includes the lines: "Credit White Cloud" and "Approved by Iroquois Council 2-2-60."

Iroquois Prayer

O Great Spirit, whose voice I hear in the winds, and whose
    breath gives life to all the world, Hear me.
I am a man before you, one of your many children. I am small
    and weak. I need your strength and wisdom.

Let me walk in beauty and make my eyes ever behold the red
and purple sunsets.
Make my hands respect the things you have made, my ears sharp
to hear your voice.
Make me wise so that I may know the things you have taught my
people, the lessons you have hidden in every leaf and rock.
I seek strength, O Creator, not to be superior to my brothers, but
to be able to fight my greatest enemy, myself.
Make me ever ready to come to you with clean hands and
straight eye, so that when my life fades as the setting sunset,
my spirit may come to you without shame.

802. Did Sir Arthur Sullivan write a national hymn for Canada?

Sir Arthur Sullivan is best known as the composer of the operetta-writing team of Gilbert and Sullivan. (Gilbert wrote the lyrics.) As a guest of Governor General Lord Lorne at Government House (Rideau Hall) in Ottawa, Sir Arthur composed a national hymn for Canada based on the words of Lord Lorne. That was in February 1880. He completed it upon his return to England. The hymn begins "God bless our wide Dominion, Our fathers' chosen land." It was published anonymously in Montreal and London, but never adopted as a national anthem or national hymn. While in Government House, Sir Arthur revised the music of the popular operetta *The Pirates of Penzance*.

803. Where is North America's sole museum of religion?

One would think, given the important role played by religion in the history of the world, that people would be interested in it! Yet there is only one museum devoted to religion in all of Canada and the United States. It is located in the community of Nicolet, which lies across the St. Lawrence River from Trois-Rivières, Quebec. This is the sole museum in North America that is devoted to religion.

The Musée des Religions was founded by former seminarians as a gesture to interfaith understanding. In the foyer are representations of five of the world's major religions: Hinduism, Buddhism, Judaism, Christianity, and Islam. Permanent and rotating exhibits are usually based on themes common to all five religions, according to Mary Ann Simpkins writing in "Travel Extra," *The Globe and Mail*, 27 November 1997.

804. What is the Toronto Blessing?

The so-called Toronto Blessing is a dramatic outpouring of religious feeling, first noted among evangelical Christians who attended the Vineyard Christian Fellowship Church, near Toronto's Pearson International Airport, 20 January 1994. "The physical or external expression of this experience includes tears, shaking, heavy breathing accompanied by arm waving and glossolalia, better known as speaking in tongues," wrote Xan Phillips in "Rolling in the Aisles," *Fortean Times*, No. 77, Fall 1995. "Internally or spiritually, the manifestation is equally intense, stimulating what is described as a 'hunger' for Jesus, God and scripture, an accelerated growth in spiritual gifts (prophecy and healing), and an enhanced ability to resolve personal difficulties. The 'hit' is followed by feelings of elation, renewal and belonging." According to Tom Harpur, writing in *The Toronto Star*, 20 November 1994, word of the Toronto Blessing of the Holy Spirit spread like wildfire and attracted over 250,000 visitors in its first year to the Toronto church. The church is part of the Vineyard Christian Fellowship, an association of evangelical Christian churches in the United States, the United Kingdom, and other countries.

805. How many "bomb shelters" were built by the Canadian government during the Cold War?

Emergency Preparedness Canada designed and built and maintained at least seven bunkers or "bomb shelters" to withstand atomic blasts between 1959 and 1966. There was the so-called Diefenbunker at Carp and the Richardson Transmitter Facility at nearby Perth, Ontario. Six other official shelters were constructed: CF Military Camp, Nanaimo, British Columbia; CFB Penhold, Red Deer, Alta; CFB Shilo, Manitoba; CFB Borden, Ontario; CFB Valcartier, Quebec; and CF Station Debert, Nova Scotia. These bunkers were all below ground; above ground structures proliferated at this time as well. All such structures were decommissioned and closed in 1993-94. They were tremendously costly to construct and maintain; they proved to be architectural "follies" and fostered the illusion that nuclear blasts were "sustainable." Further details are included by Mark Kearney and Randy Ray in *The Great Canadian Trivia Book 2* (1998).

806. Is there an official dessert served at formal dinners at Rideau Hall?

Yes. It is called Maple Moose. It is the familiar French mousse topped off with maple syrup. As well as served, it is bottled and presented to official guests as gifts or souvenirs.

807. What is meant by the Montreal Protocol?

The Montreal Protocol is an agreement reached in Montreal in September 1987 to consider a possible agreement to limit the production and use of chlorofluorocarbons (CFCs). Subsequent agreements signed in London and Copenhagen strengthened the original provisions and extended them to additional member states. At its core is the fact that continued use of CFCs in refrigerators and other appliances have a debilitating effect on the ozone layer when released into the atmosphere. The ozone layer protects animal, plant, and human life on earth from direct exposure to ultraviolet radiation. The subject is discussed by Carl Sagan in *Billions and Billions: Thoughts on Life and Death at the Brink of the Millennium* (1997).

808. What is the Canadian Home Video Classification System?

The Canadian Home Video Classification System is a national rating system for the classification of home videos distributed in Canada. It is a national system based on averaging the ratings of the provincial classification boards. There are seven of these boards, one for each province, with the Maritime provinces being served by a single board. The system was introduced 1 May 1995.

The classification symbols are G, PG, 14A, 18A, R and E.

G: Suitable for viewing by all ages.

PG: Parental Guidance advised.

14A: No rental or purchase by those under 14. May contain violence, coarse language, and/or sexually suggestive scenes.

18A: Suitable for people 18 years of age and older. It will likely contain explicit violence, frequent coarse language, sexual activity, and/or horror.

R: Restricted to 18 years and older. "Contains frequent sexual activity, brutality/graphic violence, intense horror, and/or other disturbing content."

E: Material not subject to classification (e.g., travel, nature, documentaries, sports, instructional, arts and culture).

National and provincial ratings are often displayed side-by-side. In addition, there is the Motion Picture Association of America (MPAA) rating system which is not recognized in Canada but is familiar to home video viewers.

809. Did a Canadian draft the United Nations Declarations of Human Rights?

Credit for writing the first draft of the Universal Declaration of Human Rights, endorsed by the United Nations on 10 December 1948, goes to John Peters Humphrey, a New Brunswick-born lawyer and professor of law at McGill University, and first director of the UN's Human Rights Division. In later years Humphrey went on to establish the Canadian Foundation for Human Rights and the Canadian section of Amnesty International. The fiftieth anniversary of the UN's adoption of the declaration was marked by Canada Post issuing a 45 cent stamp that carries a likeness of Humphrey superimposed on the typewritten document.

810. Who are the Albans?

Archaeologists and historians of early Canada may never have heard of the Albans, but this should be no impediment. The term, which means "white," was popularized by author and adventurer Farley Mowat to refer to a race of people from what is now Scotland who crossed the Atlantic and inhabited parts of Labrador and Newfoundland some three hundred years before the Vikings arrived about the year 1000.

According to Mowat's speculation, the Albans were farmers, stonemasons, and sailors, who travelled in boats built with wooden frames and covered with walrus skins. The Albans fled the Vikings as they advanced into the British Isles, sailed for present-day Canada, settled, and are known in history as the forebears of the Jakatars of Newfoundland, a group of people who inhabit the St. George's Bay area. Mowat's speculation, found in his book *The Farfarers* (1998), is a contribution to theories pertaining to the pre-Columbian occupation of the New World; in fact, to its pre-Viking habitation.

811. What are some widely produced Canadian plays?

No musical comedies are included in the list of Canadian plays that follows. So *Anne of Green Gables* is absent! Named here are widely produced theatrical plays written by Canadians.

The list is derived from the article "Are We There Yet?" from *The Globe and Mail*, 26 September 1998. It was contributed by theatre specialist Ray Conlogue who surveyed the last thirty years of Canadian playwriting. He tried to balance regional loyalties and measure theatrical or dramatic influence, and he tended to favour younger playwrights. (He misses, for instance, John Coulter's Riel Trilogy.) Here are the titles and authors in alphabetical order:

> *Les Belles Soeurs* by Michel Tremblay, *Billy Bishop Goes to War* by John Gray and Eric Peterson, *Blood Relations* by Sharon Pollock, *Crackwalker* by Judith Thompson, *The Donnellys* trilogy by James Reaney, *The Ecstasy of Rita Joe* by George Ryga, *Farther West* by David Murrell, *Goodnight Desdemona (Good Morning Juliet)* by Anne-Marie MacDonald, *Leaving Home* by David French, *I'll Be Back before Midnight* by Peter Colley, *The Melville Boys* by Norm Foster, *Of the Fields Lately* by David French, *Seven Stories* by Morris Panych, *Ten Lost Years* based on the book by Barry Broadfoot, *Unidentified Human Remains and the True Nature of Love* by Brad Fraser, *Zastrozzi* by George F. Walker.

Television programs have been based on a number of these plays but only one or two have been turned into motion pictures.

812. How do you address royalty and vice-royalty?

According to protocol, the Queen is addressed as "Her Majesty" and her Consort is addressed as "His Royal Highness."

The Governor General and her spouse are addressed as "Her Excellency" and "His Excellency." "His Honour" and "Her Honour" are reserved for Lieutenant-Governors and their spouses.

813. Is Velcro a Canadian invention?

Velcro – the hook-like fabric fastener – was invented in Switzerland, but world rights to the invention were acquired by J. Donald (Ben) Webster, a wealthy Toronto-based venture capitalist who did much to make the fabric fastener part of everyday life.

814. What is the Boxcar Service?

The Boxcar Service is a reference to the first religious service sponsored by Trinity Methodist Church in 1882 in North Bay, Ontario. There being no Methodist church building, the inaugural service was held in a railway boxcar on a siding adjacent to the CPR station. The side-door was slid open and worshippers brought their own lawn chairs as pews. The service was recreated by the pastor of Trinity (United Church of Canada, North Bay Presbytery) on its 100th anniversary, 14 June 1982.

815. What is the Crucified Woman?

Crucified Woman is one of two names of a realistic statue; the other name is the Female Christ. The bronze figure which stands seven feet tall was erected on the grounds of Emmanuel College, University of Toronto. A young nude woman is depicted as if nailed to a cross. The figure was executed by the sculptor Almuth Lutkenhaus in 1975 and installed in 1986. The sculptor wished to express the suffering that women face because of their sex within the context of spiritual suffering.

816. What was *Out of the Night*?

Out of the Night was the title of a radio drama series that ran on CFRB Toronto from 1939 to 1942. Donald Lamont Jack, an authority on that radio station, called it "the best suspense series ever done anywhere, without exception."

817. What was *Canadian High News?*

Canadian High News was a weekly high school newspaper filled with youth news, sports, fashion, gossip, and advertising aimed at the teenage market. Launched from Coles Book Store in Toronto in 1940, it went national and quickly became "the world's largest student newspaper." Among its editors were Robert McMichael (who went on to establish the McMichael Canadian Art Collection) and Lloyd Hodgkinson (later a publisher of *Maclean's*). Contributors included Robert Fulford, Arnold Edinborough, Frank Rasky, and Keith Davey. It ceased publication in the 1950s.

818. What is the Emergency Telephone Number?

The Emergency Telephone Number is the 911. Simply dial 911 and you will be connected with an operator equipped to offer multiple responses for fire, police, or ambulance services. The three-digit number – instead of the standard seven-digit number – was instituted as part of the regular telephone system service in Britain in 1937, in North America in 1968, and in Canada (in London, Ontario) in 1974.

819. When did Canada establish a Department of Immigration?

It was not until 1952 that the federal government established a Department of Immigration. Between Confederation in 1967 and 1952, the responsibility for the setting of immigration policies and quotas was passed from department to department, based on need. Thus the Department of Agriculture or the Department of the Interior had the power to admit the immigrants it felt the country needed.

820. What is the meaning of I.O.D.E.?

The initials I.O.D.E. stand for the International Order, Daughters of the Empire. It is a women's volunteer group, the Canadian counterpart of the

American Daughters of the Revolution. The I.O.D.E. was founded in 1900 and is concerned with citizenship, education, and service.

821. What was the Quebexodus?

The so-called Quebexodus was the exodus of Quebeckers from the Province of Quebec to other Canadian provinces, mainly Ontario and British Columbia. The migrants were mainly Anglophone, many of them Jewish Montrealers, who felt that the victory of the Parti Québécois in 1976 would be followed by "French first" policies and procedures that would devalue their contribution and discriminate against them. Statistics Canada has no estimate of the number of political migrants, but it is hardly less than 300,000.

822. How does the Canadian Postal Code differ from the postal codes of Britain and the United States?

The Postal Code of Rideau Hall in Ottawa is K1A 0A1. The code system used in Canada is harder to remember than the British or American systems. There are two reasons for this. According to psychologists, people recall digits better than letters, and beginnings and endings better than middles.

Both the British system and the Canadian systems are alphanumeric, combining both letters and digits, so these codes are inherently more difficult to remember than the American Zip Code. The British system, unlike the Canadian one, arranges the easy-to-remember digits in the middle, the harder-to-remember letters at the beginnings and endings. Therefore the British code is easier to commit to memory than the Canadian system which alternates letters with numbers in a difficult-to-remember pattern. So the Canadian Postal Code is the most difficult to use of the three systems.

The information is based on "Openers," *University of Toronto Alumni Magazine*, Autumn 1987.

823. Could an American citizen become Prime Minister of Canada?

A Canadian citizen could be either natural-born or naturalized; hence it is theoretically possible for a naturalized Canadian to hold "dual citizenship" and be recognized as a citizen of both the United States and Canada. While only a natural-born American may serve as an American President, it seems that a dual American-Canadian citizen could serve as the Prime Minister of Canada.

824. When is Top Secret not Top Secret?

Top Secret is not Top Secret when it is Secret or Confidential or Restricted. These are categories of classifications for documents of the RCMP's Security Service, according to the *Report of the Royal Commission on Security* (1969). It is presumed that the same designations apply to the documents used by the Canadian Security and Intelligence Service (CSIS).

825. What was Operation Featherbed?

Operation Featherbed was the code name for the Top Secret file allegedly kept by the RCMP's Security Service detailing the private activities of Canadian political figures.

826. Have notable riots occurred in Canada?

Notable riots have occurred in Canada. Here are four:

> The Winnipeg General Strike paralysed much of that city from May 15 to May 25, 1919.
> Vancouver's Bloody Sunday occurred on 26 July 1938, when the unemployed organized a "sit-in" which the RCMP dispersed with more than thirty protestors injured.
> Canadian troops confined to quarters rioted in Halifax on VE Day, 8 May 1945.
> The suspension of Rocket Richard of the Montreal Canadiens by National Hockey League president Clarence Campbell for striking another player led to the riot of Montreal hockey fans on St. Patrick's Day in 1955.

827. Who are some prominent Canadian suicides?

A list of thirty-five prominent Canadians known to have committed suicide appeared in *999 Questions about Canada* (1989). Here are some more names of well-known Canadians, many of whom took their own lives because they feared enfeeblement through complications of AIDS, Alzheimer's, cancer, or other terminal conditions: Singer Pauline Julien, author Margaret Laurence, writer L.M. Montgomery, explorer Lawrence E.G. Oates, and symphony orchestra conductor Georg Tintner.

828. What is the Sasquatch?

The Sasquatch is a hairy wild man or animal said to inhabit remote forested places like the interior of British Columbia.

From April 1979 on, comic-book readers knew Sasquatch to be a member of the six-person team of superheroes called "Alpha Flight" co-written by editor Roger Stern and Canadian-born artist John Byrne and published by Marvel Comics. Sasquatch was a wild avenger; in "real life" he was a Walter Lanskowski, Professor of Physics at McGill University.

The other Alpha Flight members were: the leader, Maple Leaf Flag-clad Vindicator (James Hudson), skier Northstar (Jean-Paul Beaubien), Laval teacher Aurora (Jeanne-Marie Beaubien), air-floating Super Shaman (Dr. Michael Twoyoungmen), and shape-changing Snowbird (RCMP Corporal Anne McKenzie).

Working together Alpha Flight members saved Canada from unimaginable menace and pure evil.

829. Have Canadians been officially involved in SETI?

The Search for Extra-Terrestrial Intelligence (SETI) has inspired amateur radio-astronomers in Canada, but also astrophysicists at the National Research Council in Ottawa. Alan H. Bridle and Paul A. Feldman undertook "Qui Appelle?" (Who Calls?) frequency searches of seventy stars in 1974-76, and Jacques P. Vallée and Martine Simard-Normandin in 1982 undertook a galactic-centre search. Such searches are not gambles so much as theoretical attempts to understand the nature of the universe and communication strategies.

830. What was the October Crash?

The so-called October Crash was a stock-market crash that occurred on 20 October 1987. The Toronto Stock Exchange and the Wall Street Exchange in New York opened to two-third demand. In other words, investors sold and stock prices fell in market value by one-third. In Canada alone, close to $150 billion in holdings was lost.

831. Is there lost treasure in Canada?

Fortunes have been lost and found in Canada for centuries, and yours will be made, should you locate one of the lost treasures or mines described by Rosemarie D. Perrin in *Explorers Ltd.: Guide to Lost Treasure in the United States and Canada* (1977). On the East Coast, the treasures that lie in wait are mainly identified with pirates and sunken ships. On the West Coast, there are fabled mines and mother lodes to find.

Alberta has the Lost Lemon Mine.

British Columbia has Polson Mine, Fairview Gold Mine, Bulldog Kelly Treasure, Leechtown Tunnel Treasure, Lost Foster Mine, Indian Point Treasure, and Vancouver Island Gold Mine.

Nova Scotia has the H.M.S. *Tillbury, Le Chameau,* Granby, Oak Island Treasure, H.M.S. *Barabdoes,* and *L'Americaine.*

Ontario boasts Atlantic, Kent, Young, Zion, Northerner, *Griffon,* Glenora, and Le Blanc Henri.

832. Who is the Canadian photographer who photographs nuclear reactors?

Nuclear reactors are off-limits to civilians and if they are photographed the images are seldom made available to the public. The Montreal photographer Robert del Tredici set himself the task of photographing the phenomenon of radiation. It began with *The People of Three-Mile Island* (1980), his collection of photographs of people who had suffered from the disaster at a nuclear power plant near Harrisburg, Pennsylvania, in 1979. Then he spent six years travelling with a Leica and tape recorder through Russia, Japan, Europe, and North America taking photographs. "He amassed some 30,000 negatives of the whole nuclear cycle, from uranium mining to high-tech factories to the human side effects of radiation," as noted by Geoffrey James, "Pictures from an Explosive World," *Maclean's,* 11 January 1988. When he was denied access to nuclear facilities, he took aerial photographs. *At Work in the Fields of the Bomb* (1987) is his selection of these photographs, a documentary excursion that is as chilling as it is compelling because radioactivity – the subject of the inquiry – remains invisible.

833. Who is the art photographer who works with giant transparencies?

The art of Vancouver artist Jeff Wall is innovative and individual in a number of ways. One extreme is the "grab" shots taken on Vancouver streets; another extreme is the elaborate "tableaux" that he constructs with props and professional models so arranged as to allude to familiar compositions by traditional painters. The resulting photographs, whether "grab" or "tableaux," are blown up (to "wall" size) and exhibited as backlit transparencies. His light-boxes are works that are distinctive, eye-catching, and ironic commentaries on both reality and art.

834. What are some odd things that have happened in Toronto?

An editor at *Toronto Life* phoned me one day and asked me if I could think of any "funky" things that had happened in "staid" Toronto. My reply was to ask for his definition of "funky" and "staid." It turned out he wanted "unlikely" events and experiences. I mentioned one or two and that seemed to satisfy him. After I hung up I thought of some more unusual occurrences so I began to keep a record of them. Here they are:

Benjamin Britain and Peter Peers first made love in a Toronto hotel.

James Earle Ray hid out in the city after the assassination of Martin Luther King.

Vladimir Nabokov visited the city; his stay at the Royal York inspired a scene in his novel *Lolita*, and he sought out butterflies in Queen's Park.

Erich Segal wrote parts of the best-selling romantic novel *Love Story*, including the hockey scene, in the apartment of essayist Meryl Shain. So "being in Toronto means you never have to say you're sorry."

Hugh Kenner, the critic and scholar of literary modernism, wrote his first book (on Ezra Pound) on the campus of the University of Toronto.

Geoffrey Ashe, student of Arthurian legend, decided to dedicate the rest of his life to the study of mythology at the old Toronto Reference Library at St. George and College St.

Wyndham Lewis lived in Toronto during the Second World War and painted his portraits of poet Douglas LePan and media maven Marshall McLuhan here.

Ernest Hemingway and William Faulkner lived briefly in Toronto, Hemingway on two occasions, Faulkner on one.

There would have been no *The Elephant Man*, neither play nor movie, but for the chance reference made to the incident in English medical and social history by Royal Ontario Museum anthropologist Edmund Carpenter during the course of a conversation with visiting author Ashley Montague while strolling on Avenue Road just north of the ROM.

835. Does Canada have urban legends?

Urban legends are those unlikely stories you hear that happened to someone else. The stories turn on improbable-but-possible incidents. According to their best-known collector Jan Harold Brunvand, an urban legend is modern story-telling at its best. These incredible-but-true tales enjoy wide "distribution" but are often "localized."

There are a few urban legends that have a distinct Canadian cast to them, though like jokes they travel far and wide and shed any distinguishing characteristics in mid-flight. I have traced the Vanishing Hitchhiker back to the Kitchener area in 1926. (This fellow picks up a hitchhiker who directs him to a location, then disappears when he reaches it.) That may not be the earliest record of the legend but it is certainly early. The Wife on the Flight legend dates from the 1970s and seems to have originated in the Toronto area. (The promotion department of a major airline found that the free flights it offered to the wives of executives were claimed by the secretaries of executives.)

The Economical Engine is a piece of urban lore that has received widespread distribution. It was especially popular with motorists in the 1940s and 1950s before technological breakthroughs revolutionized the automotive industry. In 1937, a Winnipeg mechanic Nelson Pogue announced that he had developed a fuel-efficient carburetor that consumed one-tenth the regular amount of gasoline. The prototype of the Economical Engine performed magnificently, making the trip from Winnipeg to Vancouver and back again on hardly more than a couple of tanks of gasoline. The problem was the invention went nowhere. The urban legend has it that Pogue was approached by "big interests" in the gas and oil industry but refused to "sell out." Then there were threats followed by a fire in his garage and everything was destroyed. Nelson Pogue devised the Pogue Carburetor, which may or may not have functioned as an "economical engine." But his announcement may well have generated something more enduring: the urban legend of the Economical Engine. If it is a legend!

836. Did T.S. Eliot write *Murder in the Cathedral* in Canada?

T.S. Eliot's verse play *Murder in the Cathedral*, which tells the story of the assassination of St. Thomas à Becket, was published in 1935.

It was written, in part at least, at an estate near Mount Orford in Quebec's Eastern Townships where Eliot and his wife Vivian spent some summers. It was here that he wrote some of his poems and worked on this poetic drama. He even referred to "Quebec Country" in the notes to the original edition of *The Waste Land* (1922), later altering it to read "Quebec Province."

837. Who is the American novelist who sets his novels in Canada?

Howard Norman was born in 1941 and grew up in Grand Rapids, Michigan, graduated from the University of Western Michigan in Kalamazoo, and lives in a hamlet in Vermont. He sets all his novels in Canada. Although he has cousins who live in the Toronto area and has travelled widely throughout the country and lived for periods of time in Toronto and in Advocate, Nova Scotia, in the house of American playwright Sam Shepherd, for no explicable reason his imagination is sparked by Canadian locales and characters, as Judy Stoffman noted in "U.S. Writer Follows All-Canadian Muse," *The Toronto Star*, 24 October 1998. *The Northern Lights* (1987) is a coming-of-age novel set in northern Manitoba. *The Bird Artist* (1994) takes place in Witless Bay, Newfoundland, in the early part of the century. *The Museum Guard* (1998) is set in Halifax in 1938. He told *The Globe and Mail*, 24 October 1998: "I'm utterly dedicated to and obsessed with Canada. I will continue to only write about Canada."

838. Was the Cunard Shipping Line financed by pirate's gold?

It is a family legend that the discovery of pirate's gold launched the world-famous Cunard Shipping Line. What is known is that as a youth Sir Samuel Cunard (1787-1865) joined his father in the timber business and expanded into whaling, lumber, coal, iron, and shipping.

By the 1830s they had acquired a large personal fortune, which was more than enough to capitalize their steamship company, which in 1840 undertook to convey mail across the Atlantic Ocean, first by sail and later by steam, from Liverpool to Halifax and Boston.

Within thirty years, Cunard Steamship Company Limited dominated Atlantic passenger trade and travel. In the twentieth century the company built and operated such famous liners as the *Lusitania* and *Queen Elizabeth II.*

It is a Maritime tradition that the basis of the family's fortune was the treasure trove of Edward Teach, better known as Blackbeard, supposedly uncovered by young Samuel in the 1820s. Yet there is no mention of this fact or fancy in Robert E. Lee's Blackbeard the *Pirate: A Reappraisal of His Life and Times* (1974).

So the legend remains a legend.

839. Is the title Right Honourable a distinction reserved for prime ministers?

In the past the title Right Honourable was a designation that was reserved for prime ministers and certain senior members of the Cabinet. Prime Minister Brian Mulroney arranged in 1992 to extend the designation to include individual men and women involved in public life though not in government to acknowledge their outstanding contributions to Canadian society. To give one instance: Conrad Black, the publisher, is properly the Right Honourable Conrad Black.

840. Is there a Canadian style of spelling?

A movement to "Americanize" the spelling of English words in the United States followed the American Revolution of 1776. Thus the "our" endings were shortened to "or," etc. English spelling styles persisted in Canada following the creation of the country in 1867; it took the passage of some years – until 1890 – for Prime Minister Sir John A. Macdonald to formalize the spelling style for the civil service. He imposed "our" endings on forty or so words ("honour" instead of "honor"), and "center" became "centre," etc. Official styles persisted despite the fact that the press and business in the country generally followed the American style. With the Centennial in 1967, "centre" was adopted over "center"; in the mid-1990s, in a surprising move that corresponded to a general typographic make-over, *The Globe and Mail* "Canadianized" its spelling style. In November 1998, Canadian Press (the syndicated news service) adopted as its style manual the newly published *Canadian Oxford Dictionary* (with its 2,000 distinct words and phrases) and opted for the "our" ending, this bringing the press and business in line with Sir John A. Macdonald's wishes.

841. What are some Canadianisms?

According to the *Canadian Oxford Dictionary* (1998), edited by Katherine Barber, some Canadianisms are the following:

> Adult accompaniment (for movies), all-candidates meeting, beer parlour, bloody Caesar, cottage roll (pickled pork), soup dish, hydro (electric power), junior kindergarten, lobster supper, loonie, minor league, pencil crayon, PA day, screech, separate school, smoked meat, town line, transition house, trousseau tea, tube skate, tuque, winter road, etc.

Some Canadian trade names are Jolly Jumper, Freshie, ASA, Javex, and Varsol.

842. What holiday do Americans mark on the day we mark Remembrance Day?

November 11th is Remembrance Day in Canada and Veterans' Day in the United States. Remembrance Day is a time to honour the Canadian War Dead, and Veterans' Day is the time to recall the sacrifices of the American veterans.

843. What are "winning conditions"?

The words "winning conditions" (*conditions gagnantes*) are associated with former Quebec Premier Lucien Bouchard. He popularized the words following the failure of the second Quebec referendum held in 1995 and used them during the provincial election campaign of November 1998. He maintained that only if there were "winning conditions" would he call a third referendum on Quebec's sovereignty. Yet to be defined is the nature of a "win."

844. What is the Ottawa Process?

The so-called Ottawa Process was the culmination of an international effort to control land mines. A comprehensive treaty to ban the use, production, transfer, and stockpiling of land mines was signed by over 120 nations in Ottawa in December 1997. For his initiative, which goes back to the Ottawa Conference of October 1996, Lloyd Axworthy, Minister of Foreign Affairs, was nominated for the 1997 Nobel Prize for Peace. Yet the major land-mine producing countries (including the United States, Russia, and China) are not signatories to the treaty.

845. What are the five national social standards of Medicare?

The five national social standards of Medicare, listed in the Canada Health Act, are accessibility, universality, portability, comprehensiveness, and public administration.

846. Whatever is the Social Union?

Social Union became a political catchphrase when Quebec Premier Lucien Bouchard referred to the notion in a campaign speech, Longueuil, Quebec, 15 November 1998. It seemed to be an alternative to separatism that Quebec and the other provinces could accept and that the federal government would not reject. Social Union calls for fiscal re-arrangements rather than revisions of the Constitution to guarantee a co-operative way to develop social programs and policies.

   According to Graham Fraser, "Primer," *The Globe and Mail*, 14 December 1998, the idea of the Social Union goes back to the ill-fated Charlottetown Accord.

The Social Union is an agreement signed by ten provincial premiers in Saskatoon on 10 August 1998 which would require the federal government to introduce no new shared-spending programs without the approval of the majority of the provinces and any revisions of past programs would be made in light of this agreement.

Provisions for the Social Union spring from Quebec's discontent with present federal-provincial programs, provincial demands for more power, and the federal Throne Speech of 1996 which offered no new shared-spending programs.

847. What are ROC and MOC?

The acronym ROC, popular following the Meech Lake Accord of 1987, refers to the Rest of Canada, that is, Canada without Quebec. In 1998, during the Quebec provincial election, which saw Lucien Bouchard's sovereigntist forces defeat Jean Charest's federalist challenge, the acronym MOC was first heard. It means the Majority of Canadians, including the federalists both outside and inside Quebec.

848. Is there a bird that is emblematic of Canada?

The animal that is emblematic of Canada is the beaver. The leaf that is Canada's emblem is the maple leaf. There is no bird emblem, although in 1927 three nationalistic poets (Bliss Carman, Charles G.D. Roberts, and G.F. Clarke) proposed the white-throated warbler as a suitable emblem (the main reason being its cry, which sounds like "sweet sweet Canada Canada Canada"). The naturalist Jack Miner recommended the Canada goose (because of its splendid appearance and the fact that it mates for life). The editors of the *Canada Year Book 1999* (1998) discovered there is no such bird as the "white-throated warbler." But there is a white-throated sparrow which has the characteristic cry "sweet sweet Canada Canada Canada." The white-throated sparrow would make an ideal bird emblem for Canada.

849. Does the American flag fly over the Centre Block on Parliament Hill on the two-dollar bill?

This is an urban legend that circulated in the United States in 1997, perhaps earlier.

How many Americans have ever seen a two-dollar Canadian bill? How many Americans would find a two-dollar bill trustworthy, considering that such bills (known as "shin-plasters") are shunned by most Americans? For that matter, how many Canadians have seen a two-dollar bill since they were replaced by the two-dollar coin which was introduced in 1985?

An examination of the two-dollar bill displays no signs that the Maple Leaf Flag has been replaced by the Stars and Stripes.

850. Who is the most prolific Canadian author?

The names W.E. (Dan) Ross, George Woodcock, and Robin Skelton appear on the title pages of innumerable books. Ross is a romance writer from New Brunswick; literary critic Woodcock and poet and essayist Skelton hailed from the West Coast. All three authors were immensely prolific, Ross the most. He wrote more than 300 paperback neo-gothic romance novels (many of them under pseudonyms) of little lasting interest.

The accomplishments of these authors should be seen in light of the prolixity of the mystery writer John Creasey, of whom Julian Symons has written in *Bloody Murder* (2nd ed., 1985), "One can safely say that John Creasey produced more books than any other twentieth-century writer." Over 600 appeared during his lifetime, and others written by him have been issued since his death. He used over twenty pseudonyms.

Isaac Asimov published his 400th book in 1988, four years before his death. It is generally said that he published "under 500 books" and that they are so diverse (from science fiction to popular science) that they appear in all the categories of the librarian's Dewey decimal system excepting only volumes of verse.

Continuing importance or enduring interest are certainly relevant here. Asimov's work, especially his novels and stories in the science-fiction vein, will long endure. Next to Carl Sagan, he was the twentieth century's most important popularizer of science.

Let me add a word about my own production in the third person. It has been stated that John Robert Colombo is Canada's most prolific author, being the writer, compiler, and translator of over 150 books between 1957 and 2000. It must be said that many of these books are compilations (original anthologies of poetry, prose, or memoir) and that about one third of them were originally published by Colombo & Company, the imprint Colombo established (in the manner of Mark Twain and Charles Dickens) as an outlet for his own writing.

851. Is the ratio of French to English in Canada changing?

Yes, the ratio of speakers of French to speakers of English is changing and increasing in the latter's favour. In New France in 1666, everyone spoke French. In Canada in 1941, French speakers amounted to 29.2% of the population. By 1991, the figure was down to 24.1%.

852. When was the term "First Nations" first used?

The term "First Nations" is used to refer to the traditional and tribal governments of the aboriginal peoples of Canada. The term was first used in modern times in 1980 with the Declaration of the First Nations. It symbolically recognizes the indigenous peoples as equals in their right to self-determination and self-government alongside the English and French or "founding nations" as they are called. Today the term "First Nations" includes the Indian, Inuit, and Métis peoples. Three centuries ago the French explorers of the continent described the bands they met as "nations."

853. What was the infamous "head tax"?

To stem the tide of immigration from China, the federal government imposed a "head tax" of $50 (the equivalent of $800 in A.D. 2000) on each immigrant in 1885. By 1895 the Chinese presence accounted for ten percent of the population of British Columbia. That year the tax was increased to $500. In 1923, all Asiatic immigration was banned, and in 1931 the federal government denied even resident Chinese the right to apply for citizenship.

China was an ally in the Second World War with the result that there was a shift in immigration policy. In 1947 citizenship was offered to resident Chinese. Thereafter restrictions against Asiatics were revoked. In the 1960s Canadian immigration policy was formulated to be non-racist.

854. When were the Maritime cod fisheries closed?

East Coast cod was regarded as a staple in the Maritime economy and an inexhaustible part of nature's abundance. On July 2, 1992, federal fisheries minister and native Newfoundlander John Crosbie announced the closing of the northern cod fishery at a news conference in St. John's, Nfld. There was to be a two-year moratorium because the cod had been fished to "commercial extinction." The moratorium was then extended. It is estimated that 31,000 jobs were lost.

855. What is the most significant date in Canadian history in the twentieth century?

This is a contentious question with many possible answers. Dates that reflect wars, insurrections, economic depressions, treaties, constitutions, anniversaries, inventions, deaths, etc., are all eligible. But it may be argued that modern Canadian history was most affected by what happened on 6 Dec. 1905.

What happened on that date will be described in no Canadian history text, but it will be found enshrined in history texts that study the association of church and state in modern France. On that date the French Parliament formally abrogated the Concordat of 1801, which had granted the Roman Catholic Church influence on secular affairs in the Republic of France. The new law disestablished the Church, seized its assets, expelled a number of its religious orders, and declared that henceforth the Republic of France would be a secular state. The passage of the secularizing law is identified with the leadership of the socialist anti-clerical Aristide Briand.

How did the passage of this law affect Canada? Its effects on the affairs of the Province of Quebec were marked. Quebec society still had a large number of priests in its population. Well into the middle of the twentieth century, the clergy continued to play an important role in the society of Quebec, influencing laws and behaviour. The French Republic was branded secular and hence "fallen." Members of religious orders like the Jesuits, expelled from France, re-established themselves in Quebec and re-defined their mission as the "re-missionizing" of North America and the redemption of the Republic of France. One result was that French Canadians were reluctant to enlist in the Armed Forces for the defence of France in two World Wars.

What brought about the passage of the law of 6 Dec. 1905 was popular reaction to the Dreyfus Affair – a scandal that exposed corruption within the military and further divided the nationalist and right-wing side of French society from the socialist, anti-clerical republican side. But Quebec had to wait some years for its own equivalent of the Dreyfus Affair – the Asbestos Strike, the Padlock Law, and the Roncarelli Case. It was not until the Quiet Revolution which commenced the year following the death of Premier Maurice Duplessis in 1959 that the government of Quebec began to displace the Roman Catholic Church.

856. Did Ufa produce a film about Canada?

No, the great German film cartel Ufa did not produce a film about Canada, but along with such classic films as *Metropolis* and *The Blue Angel*, it produced the lesser-known *Krischer Wind aus Kanada* (Fresh Wind from Canada). Directed by Heinz Kenter and Erich Holder and released in 1936, the drama is not really about Canada but it does feature a Canadian businessman who capitalizes a German business. In the words of film historian Klaus Kreimeir in *The Ufa Story: A History of Germany's Greatest Film Company, 1918-1945* (1996), it tells the story of how "a North American capitalist puts a Berlin fashion salon on a sound financial footing and marries the owner's daughter."

857. Does Wicca have a Canadian connection?

Yes, it does. Witchcraft may be as old as the hills, but the modern movement known as Wicca is quite recent, having been largely created by the British witch Gerald Gardner in the late 1930s, using some of the spells composed by Aleister Crowley. In *Crafting the Art of Magic* (1991), the sociologist Aiden A. Kelly suggested that Gardner was inspired by Woodcraft, a lodge movement started in the United States by Canadian-born naturalist and author Ernest Thompson Seton, who combined his version of the Boy Scout movement with American Indian spirituality.

858. What is the Canadian Internet Licensing Board?

The Canadian Internet Licensing Board is a clever hoax.

People who surf the Internet are an imaginative and independent lot who place a high value on freedom of expression. They do not take lightly to infringements on their inherent rights. They will approve of advertising on the medium, but not attempts at regulation or censorship. Hence the very notion that the Canadian government had established a board to license internet sites based in the country was repugnant to surfers, the majority of whom are Americans and would be unaffected by the legislation anyway. There were protests and "flaming." The fact that the supposed board was a clever hoax never seemed to have occurred to them. One day they read:

> The Canadian Internet Licensing Board (CILB) is a special operating agency authorized to process and issue English Language Canadian Web Site Licences under Canada's new Information Highway Act. Under this Act, Canadian Web Sites are invited to apply for a licence to operate by March 31, 1999. Applications will be reviewed and licences will be issued by the CILB on a first-come, first-served basis to Canadian Web sites that meet the Information Highway Act's Canadian Web Site Guidelines. French Language Canadian Web Site Licences will be issued by the Régie de l'Internet du Canada. In case you're wondering, it's a joke, eh! Revised May 29, 1998. Copyright 1997-98 Hip Hype Inc.

859. What are the ten top Canadian news events of the twentieth century?

Close to 170 editors and broadcasters with Canadian Press and Broadcast News produced a list of the ten top Canadian news events of the twentieth century. The list mixes military, political and sports moments that defined Canada in the past century. The event had to be a major news story the day it occurred or a continuing news event over a period of time; in either case, the event had to be of major significance in the country's development or history. Here, from *The Globe and Mail*, 8 November 1999, is the list in order of importance:

1. D-Day, 6 June 1944.
2. Patriation of the Constitution / Charter of Rights and Freedoms, 17 April 1982.
3. The October Crisis, 5 October 1970.
4. The Battle of Vimy Ridge, 9 April 1917.

5. Women get the vote, 24 May 1918.
6. The Canada-U.S. Free Trade Agreement, 1 January 1989.
7. The 1995 Quebec referendum, 30 October 1995.
8. Paul Henderson's winning goal in the Canada-Soviet Union hockey series, 28 September 1972.
9. Creation of medicare in Saskatchewan, 1 July 1962.
10. Canadian military raid on Dieppe, 19 August 1942.

Cultural events of considerable moment are conspicuously absent from the list. Some events that could be included are the appearance of the Refus global manifesto, the founding of the Stratford Shakespearian Festival, the creation of the Canada Council, the success of Expo 67, etc.

860. What is Adbusters?

Adbusters Media Foundation describes itself in this way: "We are a global network of artists, writers, students, educators and entrepreneurs who want to launch a new social activist movement of the information age. Our goal is to galvanize resistance against those who would destroy the environment, pollute our minds and diminish our lives."

Adbusters was founded by group of social activists in Vancouver in 1989. The group established the Adbusters Media Foundation; it publishes *Adbusters* magazine, a reader-supported publication with a circulation of 60,000 copies a month; and runs Advocacy Advertising Agency which specializes in "spoof advertisements."

861. Was the Book-of-the-Month Club founded by a Canadian?

The Book-of-the-Month Club was founded by Harry Scherman (1887-1969) who was born in Montreal and raised from the age of two in Philadelphia. He became an advertising copy writer and then a merchandiser and marketer in New York City, producing booklets in the Little Leather Library in 1916 as premiums and then as items for sale through the Woolworth's chain.

Scherman conceived the idea of the Book-of-the-Month with publishing executive Robert K. Haas. In April 1926 they sent 4,570 club subscribers, called "members," their first "selection." By year's end the subscriber list had grown to 46,539 members. Even during the Depression, people bought mail-order books at regular prices with the enticement of premiums. The success of the book merchandising operation launched competitors (like the Literary Guild). Shares in BOMC were first publicly traded in 1947.

Scherman had two special touches. First touch was the "committee of selection" established to ensure a balance between cultural and commercial concerns. (Its original members were Henry Canby, Dorothy Canfield Fisher, Heywood Broun, Christopher Morley, and William Allen White.) The second touch was the principle of "negative-option" billing, whereby a subscriber automatically receives next month's "main selection" (with invoice) unless the subscriber returns a special notice by a given date.

Scherman wrote books on economics, inflation, and democracy, spoke widely on public issues, and engaged in numerous philanthropies, including serving as director of the MacDowell Colony, a writer's retreat.

Canadians subscribed to BOMC from its earliest years. The company established a branch operation in Montreal and in 1976 began to offer Canadian members a limited selection of Canadian titles. Mordecai Richler joined the "committee of selection." The Canadian operation was reduced in scale in the 1980s and ended in 1999.

862. Did Raymond Chandler set the action of one of his novels in Canada?

Yes and no. Raymond Chandler (1888-1954), the creator of Philip Marlowe, chose Vancouver as the locale for an original screenplay which he wrote in the early 1950s for Universal Pictures. It was never produced so Chandler rewrote the screenplay as a novel about the private detective Philip Marlowe and reset the locale in Los Angeles.

All this is explained by Jerry Speir in his study *Raymond Chandler* (1981):

> Wanting a border town for the locale, he chose Vancouver and replaced Marlowe with a Canadian police officer named Killaine. The screenplay was tentatively called *Playback*. Health problems ... interfered with the writing, as did Chandler's general dislike of screenwriting. He was never very pleased with the finished product and neither was the studio. Citing financial difficulties and

the expense of filming in Vancouver, the studio shelved the project and forgot it. *Playback* did finally see the light of day in 1958 as Chandler's last, and generally least-regarded, novel. It was rewritten, of course, with California as background and Marlowe as detective hero."

Chandler's novel *Playback* appeared in print in 1958, four years after his death, but it is regarded as undistinguished. It concerns the disappearance of a young woman who is on the run from a crime she did not commit. No references to Vancouver remain in the novel. Thirty years later the original screenplay, which has Vancouver as its locale, was published: *Raymond Chandler's Unknown Thriller: The Screenplay of "Playback"* (Mysterious Press, 1985). It is surprising that no Canadian film producer has ever expressed interest in the property, especially now that Hollywood studios are using Vancouver for so much location shooting.

863. What are some Canadian advertising classics of the twentieth century?

Try to identify the Canadian advertising classics of the twentieth century.

That was the task assigned to four advertising personalities by the editors of *The Financial Post* on 31 December 1999. To this end, Chris Staples, Graham Watt, Geoffrey Roche, and Patrick Allossery each chose ten mainly national campaigns. Here are the campaigns that were repeatedly mentioned, plus some individual favourites.

1. Canadian Pacific Railway Co.: Posters. These brilliantly drawn posters were issued in the 1920s and 1930s to promote the Rocky Mountains as "the Canadian Alps."

2. Esso: Murray Westgate. Agency: MacLaren Advertising, Toronto. Announcer Westgate, in the overalls of a gas station attendant, met your automobile's needs with Imperial products on TV's *Hockey Night in Canada.*

3. A&W: Let's All Go. Agency: The Woodall Workshop, Vancouver. Originally launched in the late 1950s and revived in the 1990s, the memorable jingle and the lively "A&W Root Bear" remain favourites.

4. Canadian National: Corporate Logo. The streamlined "CN" logo that is still in use was designed by typographer Alan Fleming in the early 1960s.

5. Cadbury's Caramilk: Mona Lisa. Agency: Scali McCabe Sloves, Toronto. This classic TV commercial, executed by Gary Prouk in 1973, shows the Mona Lisa smiling as she takes a bite of a Caramilk bar. The series seemed to reveal the "secret" of how the caramilk ends up in the chocolate bar.

6. Canadian Tire: Bike Story. Agency: Doner Schur Peppler, Toronto. Directed by Bill Irish. A boy, pining over a Canadian Tire Catalogue, is given the bicycle of his dreams.

7. Christie Brown & Co.: Mr. Christie, You Make Good Cookies. Agency: McCann-Erickson, Toronto. Launched in 1974, this campaign made cookies as wondrous as childhood.

8. Ontario Milk Marketing Board: Wear a Moustache. Agency: Ogilvy & Mather, Toronto. Launched in 1974, this campaign featured young people wearing a "milk moustache." Adapted for use in the United States with celebrities like David Copperfield.

9. IKEA: Conveyor Belt. Agency: McCann-Erickson, Vancouver. Created by Dick Hadden, this television commercial shows a slightly goofy Swedish spokesperson standing in front of a conveyor belt explaining the features of IKEA furniture, again and again.

10. Buckley's Mixture: It Tastes Awful. And It Works. Agency: Ambrose Carr DeForest & Linton, Toronto. This old slogan for the foul-tasting but powerfully effective cough medicine has been used for decades but was revived in 1985.

11. Molson Canadian: I Am Canadian. Agency: MacLaren McCann, Toronto. The success of this brash, patriotic campaign surprised everyone in 1994.

12. Archdiocese of Toronto & the Knights of Columbus: Dare to Be a Priest like Me. Agency: Martin Keene and Associates, Toronto. This odd-man-out campaign for the Roman Catholic Priesthood generated considerable controversy in 1983.

Information on other inspired advertising campaigns is included in *Colombo's Canadian Quotations* (1974) and its successor volumes.

864. Did a Canadian astrologer predict the outbreak of World War II?

The short answer is: I do not know. The long answer is: perhaps Carl Lewis was the astrologer who predicted the outbreak of World War II, based on the following information.

Axel Harvey is a Montreal-based astrologer and historian of the discipline. He laments the lack of historical interest in the subject in what he wrote in "Postscript: The Rootless Science" included by John McKay-Clements in *The Canadian Astrology Collection: Timed Birth Data of Prominent Canadians* (1998):

> And who was Carl Lewis, "my Canadian contemporary" whom R.H. Naylor put down in 1938 for daring to contradict Britain's leading media astrologers? Lewis had predicted there would soon be a world war pitting the Axis powers against the democracies – something all the mundane heavies knew was impossible! Now here is a role model Canadian astrologers dearly need; but no one I asked has ever heard of him. U.S. people are good at inventing heroes that weren't, like Paul Bunyan and Abner Doubleday. We cancel heroes that really were. A charming habit, but one which our vulnerable country cannot afford.

865. Who is Wiarton Willie?

Wiarton Willie is no ordinary brown groundhog, but an albino groundhog, born in a field on the Bruce Peninsula which sits exactly on the 45th parallel, which lies halfway between the Equator and the North Pole. Since 1956, each February 2nd, Wiarton Willie predicts when spring will arrive. If he sees his shadow, he calls for six more weeks of hard winter. If he does not see his shadow, he predicts the early spring. His annual predictions are part of the Wiarton Willie Groundhog Festival celebrations that see media people and visitors come from far and wide to see Willie at his best.

866. Who first drew a white line along the middle of a highway?

The white line that separates driving lanes is a traffic-control marker that was first devised by J.D. Millar, an engineer with the Ontario Department of Transport. He conceived the idea of dotted white lines in 1930 and so painted a stretch of highway near the Ontario-Quebec border. Within three years there were such lines on highways throughout North America. Laura Penny, "White Lines," *Saturday Night*, February 2000, calls it "the Morse code of the road: double lines, dashed lines, yellow and white slashes on the asphalt, an elaborate choreography of common courtesy, politeness made visible in paint."

867. Have important Canadian events taken place on February 29th?

Every four years is designated a Leap Year when the month of February is 29 rather than 28 days long.

Some 20,000 Canadians were born on February 29, 2000. This means that they will celebrate their birthdays on March 1st for three years running, and then on February 29th for the fourth year.

Hockey star Henri (Pocket) Richard was born on February 29th, 1936. On 29 February 1984, Pierre Elliott Trudeau went for a walk in the Ottawa snow and resolved that he would resign as prime minister.

In Al Capp's once-popular L'il Abner comic strip, February 29 was Sadie Hawkins Day, the one day of the year that a woman could ask a man for his hand in marriage and the man had to accept. Superman, the Man of Steel of the comics, radio, television, and the movies, was "born" on February 29th, presumably on the planet Krypton.

868. Does Canada have a CIA?

Canada does not have a CIA, but it does have a CIIA.

The initials CIA stand for Central Intelligence Agency, the international security agency of the United States government. The Canadian equivalent is CSIS (Canadian Security and Intelligence Service).

The initials CIIA stand for the Canadian Institute of International Affairs, a national, non-partisan, non-profit organization with a mandate to promote the informed discussion, debate, and analysis of foreign policy and international affairs from a Canadian perspective.

869. What is "pegging" a currency?

A country's currency is "pegged" when its value is maintained relative to the currency of another country. The Canadian dollar was pegged to the American dollar at 92.5 cents from 1962 to 1970. In other words, the American dollar was valued at Can $1.07 $^{1/2}$. Except for the interval of pegging, the value of the Canadian dollar "floated" with respect to the American dollar. In 1998 it floated to a low of US $0.64.

870. What is the 1984 Federal Income Tax Return (Simplified)?

There is a piece of urban folklore called the 1984 Federal Income Tax Return (Simplified). It is a brief, brilliant parody of the Income Tax Act of Revenue Canada. In a few words it draws attention to the complexity of the Act's rules and regulations and to the confiscatory nature of all forms of income taxation.

The parody is a photocopied form that appears to emanate from the offices of "Pillage Canada." The full text runs as follows:

> 1984 FEDERAL INCOME TAX RETURN (SIMPLIFIED)
> HOW MUCH DID YOU EARN? $ _____
> SEND IT IN.

The form was collected by the folklorist Jennifer J. Connor in "Parodies of Administrative Communications: Some Canadian Examples," *Culture and Tradition*, No. 10, 1986.

871. Is there a common Indian language?

No. Inuit may speak a common tongue, called Inuktitut, with regional variations, but the Indians speak ten different languages (sucha as Algonkian or Haidan). Language specialists also recognize that the Indians speak fifty-eight dialects across the country.

872. What most accounts for the Indian's loss of cultural identity?

The federal government's suppression of native languages and religious practices in residential schools is frequently cited by aboriginal peoples as the main reason for the Indians facing the loss of their cultural identity and sense of self-worth and well-being.

"Taking away the Indian's religion, and taking away his language," said one elder, "that's how you teach him the white man's way." The notion is mentioned by R.H. Knox in *Indian Conditions: A Survey* (1980), a publication of the Department of Indian and Northern Affairs.

873. Are there Indian Agents today?

Indian Agents were employees of the federal government, invariably non-Indians, who administered Indian bands. Thus the band councils operated more or less under the direction of government officials. The last Indian Agents were removed in 1969, and band councils have assumed increased responsibility for the administration of their bands. Now, depending on the band, band council appointment is arranged either by tradition or by election.

874. When was the first Indian Act passed?

The BNA Act (1867) subjected "Indians and lands reserved for Indians" to federal authority and assigned matters of local or private nature such as "property and civil rights" to provincial authority.

The first Indian Act was passed in 1876 to exercise federal legislative competence by codifying certain rights and obligations of status Indians and setting up a land management system.

Royal proclamations and treaties affected the Indians long before the creation of the Dominion of Canada. The Royal Proclamation (1763) established a framework for the governing of newly acquired territories, thereby nullifying Indian claims to sovereignty and independent status. "Unnumbered treaties" (1871-1921) are recorded agreements made between Indians and the British or Canadian governments to surrender Indian land title to the Crown for expansion and settlement.

875. Do Americans live in fear and dread of an invasion from Canadian vessels on the Great Lakes?

Hardly likely, you say? Consider the fact that the Great Lakes saw a good deal of naval action during the War of 1812. Consider also the fact that the following item (from the 15 April 1890 issue of the *Niagara Falls Advertiser*) originally appeared in the *Rochester Democratic*. It is apparent that three-quarters of a century after the signing of the Rush-Bagot

Agreement of 1817, Americans still lived in fear of British gunboats on the Lakes:

> The construction of the Niagara canal is especially desirable from a military point of view. Without communication between Lakes Ontario and Erie it would be necessary to provide a separate navy to protect the cities of Rochester, Oswego and Ogdensburg. With a ship canal of the capacity provided by the Payne bill, the iron propellers of the upper lakes could be quickly armed with improved steel cannon and sent into Ontario to meet British gunboats sent through the St. Lawrence canals. Under the existing treaty with Great Britain the United States can maintain but one armed vessel on the great lakes. At present our naval power on the lakes is represented by the wheezy old *Michigan*. But there is nothing in the treaty that would prevent the storage of navy guns at Cleveland or Toledo. There is not a vessel on Lake Ontario that could carry a navy gun or that could keep above water ten minutes if confronted by a British gunboat. The Niagara canal ought to be built as quickly as possible. The Canadians are far ahead of us in preparations for offense or defense. It is not necessary for them to maintain a single warship. In a few days twenty British gunboats could pass through the Canadian canals into the great lakes.

876. Only one university in Canada offers sports scholarships. Which one is it?

The awarding of sports scholarships is characteristic of a good many American universities, but only one university in Canada has followed suit. That one is Simon Fraser University in Burnaby, British Columbia, which from its founding in 1965 has promoted an active sports program. Its teams compete on a semi-professional basis in numerous leagues.

877. How many people are there in Canada to "do the work"?

This is a nonsensical question to anyone unfamiliar with a piece of urban folklore popular in the 1960s – and a nonsensical question to anyone familiar with it too! – which explains that only two people in the country "do the work." The rest are incapacitated or otherwise out of the running.

Here is how it goes:

Perspective of the Findings of the Experts, the Following Appears to be Stark Staring Facts Facing You and I.

Population of Canada	20,000,000
People of 65 Years and Over	6,000,000
Balance Left to do the Work	14,000,000
People of 18 Years and Under	10,000,000
Balance Left to do the Work	4,000,000
People in the Armed Forces	1,000,000
Balance Left to do the Work	3,000,000
People in Town Offices	1,000,000
Balance Left to do the Work	2,000,000
People Sick in Hospital	900,000
Balance Left to do the Work	1,100,000
Winos and Others who Won't Work	1,000,000
Balance Left to do the Work	100,000
People in Jail	99,998
Balance Left to do the Work	2
	You and I

And it's about Time You Pulled Your Bloody Socks Up. I'm Fed Up with Running This Place on My <u>Own</u>.

The folklorist Jennifer J. Connor published this piece of light humour in "Parodies of Administrative Communications: Some Canadian Examples," *Culture and Tradition*, No. 10, 1986.

878. Does Canada have a Federal Witness Protection Program?

The Federal Marshal's Office of the U.S. Government operates a program to provide assistance and protection to witnesses who risk their lives to testify against the leaders of organized crime. It makes no difference that many of the witnesses who make use of the Federal Witness Protection Program may themselves be guilty of the crimes they expose. Protection is supplied to all those who assist the police.

As crime reporter James Dubro pointed out in *Mob Mistress* (1988), a book about an informer named Shirley Ryce who turned Crown evidence against a crime family operating in Hamilton, Ontario, Canada has yet to establish a federal witness protection program. Hence assistance and protection to witnesses is often handled in a slipshod or ad hoc fashion.

879. Which Canadian corporation received a special Oscar?

A special Oscar was presented to the National Film Board of Canada at the Academy Awards ceremony in Hollywood in 1989. The special Oscar acknowledged the outstanding contributions made to the motion picture industry by the NFB. Marcel Masse, newly appointed Communications Minister, who was in no way responsible for the creativity of the Board, accepted the Oscar "on behalf of the 26 million people in Canada." Over the years, NFB films were no stranger to the Award. Until 1989, Board films had received 80 nominations and been awarded 52 Oscars.

880. What are firearms?

Firearms are divided into two groups of weapons: handguns; rifles and shotguns. Handguns are divided into revolvers (with chambers) and pistols (with clips). A rifle fires a bullet a considerable distance; a shotgun fires pellets or bee-bee shots a short distance. (Machine guns are not only restricted but prohibited, available only to law-enforcement agencies and the military establishment.)

To purchase a firearm in Canada, an individual must prepare an application for a Firearms Acquisition Certificate. The form must include the details of the weapon. It is presented to "the local constabulary" which passes it on to the Royal Canadian Mounted Police which issues the "permit," a process that takes perhaps six weeks. This F.A.C. permits the individual to purchase a rifle or shotgun, but not a handgun. To purchase a handgun, the individual must fill out both the F.A.C. and appear in person at the headquarters of "the local constabulary" where a C-300 form is filled out. To purchase a handgun it is generally necessary to show proof of membership in a shooting or hunting club or proof of standing as a collector of weaponry.

881. Do the titles "premier" and "prime minister" mean the same thing?

No. Current usage calls for the leader of a provincial government to be known as "premier," and the leader of the federal government to be known as "prime minister." Thus at any time there are ten premiers but only one prime minister. The term "first minister" applies to all eleven.

It was not always so. Earlier in the century the prime ministers of both Canada and Britain were often referred to as "premiers." With the rise of provincial power in the 1960s, the provincial premiers hubristically self-styled themselves prime ministers. Quebec's Jean Lesage referred to himself as "premier ministre," and Ontario's John Robarts and British Columbia's W.A.C. Bennett followed suit with "prime minister." Lesage's successor, Daniel Johnson, went so far as to make it known (according to columnist Charles Lynch) that at press conferences the questions of journalists who addressed him as "Mr. Premier" would go unanswered. Since the 1980s only Quebec's premier calls himself "premier ministre." There is some suggestion that the premiers of the four provinces which united to form Confederation – Nova Scotia, New Brunswick, Quebec, and Ontario – have the constitutional right to the use of the title "prime minister," but this seems an affectation.

882. Is Canada a difficult country to govern?

Canada should be an easy country to govern. After all, Canadians enjoy peace and prosperity as well as a history of democratic government and social stability. Yet the country's governors – or at least its prime ministers – have gone on record as claiming that Canada is bedevilled by politics based on short-term compromises and regional considerations.

Here are the opinions of a number of Prime Ministers:

Sir John A. Macdonald: "Canada is a hard country to govern." Sir Wilfrid Laurier: "Canada is a difficult country to govern." Lester B. Pearson: "Canada is the most difficult country in the world to govern." Pierre Elliott Trudeau: "Canada is a terribly difficult country to govern." Brian Mulroney: "It's a hell of a hard country to govern." Joe Clark, John Turner, and Kim Campbell had such short incumbencies that they must have found it a difficult country to govern as well! Jean Chrétien said, "It's the toughest job in the land."

883. What is the name of the novel James A. Michener set in Canada?

The popular American novelist James A. Michener who died in 1997 was the author of such books as *Tales of the South Pacific, Sayonara, Hawaii,* and *Alaska.* No novel called Canada flowed from his pen, but in 1988 he did publish a short novel set in northern Canada. He might well have called it *Yukon*; instead, it is titled *Journey.*

Journey is a fictionalized account of the true-life adventure of four English aristocrats and their Irish servant who set sail from Liverpool in July 1896, determined to cross Canada to Dawson City. Their destination is the Klondike gold fields, but their dream turns into a nightmare at the booming frontier town of Edmonton, and they face death on the Athabasca and Mackenzie rivers.

This unlikely novel by a master storyteller was originally conceived and written to be so many chapters of the multi-chaptered novel *Alaska* (1987). But the adventures of Lord Evelyn Luton, the veteran explorer, had to be cut from the longer work in the interests of length. Therefore Michener offered it for separate publication to McClelland and Stewart which issued it as *Journey* in 1989. The author donated all earnings from this book to underwrite the costs of offering the Journey Award to the best work of fiction published in the previous year by a Canadian author. *Journey* anthologies of short fiction are published annually by McClelland & Stewart.

884. What was Chief Dan George's prayer?

Chief Dan George was interviewed by Roy Bonisteel on CBC-TV's *Man Alive* in the fall of 1979. When asked if he prayed, Chief Dan George replied, "All tribes in North America used to say this prayer daily, even before Christopher Columbus came to our shore." Here is his prayer:

Oh, Great Spirit, whose voice I hear in the mind, whose breath gives life to the world, hear me!

I come to you as one of your many children. I am small and weak. I need your strength and your wisdom.

May I walk in beauty. Make my eyes ever behold the red and purple sunset. Make my hands respect the things that you have made and my ears sharp to hear your voice.

Make me wise so that I may know the things that you have

taught your children, the lessons you have hidden in every leaf and rock.

Make me strong, not to be superior to my brothers, but to be able to fight my greatest enemy – myself.

Make me ever ready to come to you with straight eyes, so that when my life fades, as the fading sunset, my spirit will come to you without shame.

885. What is the Indian expression about walking in another man's moccasins?

"Oh Great Spirit, help me never to judge another until I have walked two weeks in his moccasins."

No one knows who first recorded this traditional Indian expression, but it appears on posters and on birchbark souvenirs. It also appears in *The Oxford Book of Prayer* (1985) edited by George Appleton.

886. What are June Callwood's Five Steps to Wisdom?

In a manner suggestive of serious fun, the Toronto writer and media personality June Callwood listed her Five Steps to Wisdom for columnist Joey Slinger in *The Toronto Star*, 15 June 1989:

> The first thing is you cannot get red wine stains out with white wine. It just won't work. It is better in that situation to drink the white wine.
>
> The second thing is you cannot solve fundamental problems. The best thing you can do is find some sort of accommodation.
>
> The third thing is you cannot find true peace of mind, and you will not grow up, until you forgive your parents.
>
> The fourth thing is if you go on a canoe trip it will rain every day but the last one. A bicycle trip is the same.
>
> The fifth thing is consider celibacy. If you refuse to consider celibacy, then please remember the latex condom. Anal sex is high-risk.
>
> There, that's everything I know. Except never buy anything that is not assembled. It is difficult enough to assemble a life without having to assemble something from Ikea.

887. Did Pierre Elliott Trudeau compose a Preamble to the Constitution?

Pierre Elliott Trudeau, the Prime Minister responsible for the patriation of the Constitution in 1982, composed its Preamble, as an introductory statement of its principles. But the Preamble was dropped from the text before the Constitution became law.

The Preamble was tabled in the House of Commons and as the prologue to Bill C-60 was published in *Hansard* on 10 June 1980. Although it met a sad fate, Trudeau remained partial to the Preamble and quoted from it when he delivered his address before the Senate Submissions Group on the Meech Lake Constitutional Accord. Here is the text of the Preamble from *With a Bang, Not a Whimper: Pierre Trudeau Speaks Out* (1988) edited by Donald Johnston:

A Statement of Principles for a New Constitution

We, the people of Canada, proudly proclaim that we are and shall always be, with the help of God, a free and self-governing people.

Born of a meeting of the English and French presence on North American soil which had long been the home of our native peoples, and enriched by the contribution of millions of people from the four corners of the earth, we have chosen to create a life together which transcends the differences of blood relationships, language and religion, and willingly accept the experience of sharing our wealth and culture while respecting our diversity.

We have chosen to live together in one sovereign country, a true federation, conceived as a constitutional monarchy and founded on democratic principles.

Faithful to our history....

As Trudeau told the senators, "I think it was pretty hard to beat, but, look, it was panned by the English-speaking columnists, and do you want to know what happened in Quebec? It did not get beyond the fifth word. When we said, 'We, the people of Canada,' one hullabaloo broke out in Quebec."

888. What was the Toronto School of communications theory?

The so-called Toronto School of communications theory flourished in 1962-63, according to the Oxford historian Oswyn Murray. Writing in *The Times Literary Supplement*, 16 June 1989, he explained: "The scene is Toronto, for a brief period the intellectual centre of the world. There, a new theory was born, the theory of the primacy of communication in the structuring of human cultures and the human mind."

Murray had in mind the near simultaneous publication of three texts: Marshall McLuhan's *The Gutenberg Galaxy* (1962), Eric A. Havelock's *Preface to Plato* (1963), and the extended article by Jack Goody and Ian Watt called "The Consequences of Literacy." These texts extended the notions of the Toronto economic historian Harold Adams Innis who in an earlier work, *The Bias of Communication* (1951), explored the relationship between orality and literacy and the interconnection between the carrier and the content.

"Although each work offered its own modifications and developments, the basic theory appeared simple and universal: the most fundamental factor in the cultural progress of man was change in the modes of communication. The crucial question is not what is transmitted but how it is transmitted – in the famous slogan of McLuhan, the Medium is the Message." He went on to note important stages in human history: evolution of speech; development of writing by the Greeks; invention of printing in the Renaissance; appearance of telecommunications in the mid-twentieth century. The result was a new theory of man, history, and society as well as the birth of a new discipline: communications theory.

889. Why was there a censorship fuss over the film *Not a Love Story?*

Not a Love Story: A Film about Pornography is the title of a documentary film produced in 1982 by the National Film Board of Canada. Directed by two women film-makers, Bonnie Sherr Klein and Anne Henderson, the hour-long film takes the form of a freewheeling inquiry into the subject of pornography, highlighting the grubby aspects of the trade in New York City. Not surprisingly for feminists, the producers found pornography to be degrading and dangerous to women.

Curiously, *Not a Love Story* is more visually explicit than most soft-porn features, so it never received commercial exhibition. It was censored in some jurisdictions, including Ontario, where it was shown on a restricted basis only. As the film critic Gerald Pratley noted in *Torn Sprockets: The Uncertain Projection of the Canadian Film* (1987), "Male critics who found the film lacking were severely castigated by women's groups and individuals for not being sympathetic to the way women feel and for exhibiting feelings of male superiority."

890. Did the U.S. Department of Justice restrict the exhibition of three NFB documentary films, designating them "foreign propaganda"?

To everyone's surprise, yes. It all happened in 1983, and it was described by Gerald Pratley in his book *Torn Sprockets: The Uncertain Projection of the Canadian Film* (1987):

> The National Film Board ... was startled to receive unimaginable publicity in the United States (and subsequently in Canada) when the U.S. Department of Justice designated three NFB documentaries, *If You Love This Planet, Acid from Heaven*, and *Acid Rain: Requiem of Recovery*, as being "foreign propaganda" under a wartime ruling that gave the government the power to control films reflecting "a foreign government's point of view." The three films were suspect because of their direct or implied criticism of the way in which the United States is handling the issue of nuclear war, and because its industries are responsible for much of the acid rain falling in Canada and ruining the lakes and forests. Under this order, distributors were required to list the names of persons attending projections of the films. Concerned Americans who were outraged over governmental restraint of freedom of expression, countered this order in the courts with the result that a judge in California declared the Department of Justice ruling to be "unconstitutional." (His decision was later appealed to a higher court and overturned.) The films themselves are simple yet effective, with *If You Love This Planet* being no more than an illustrated lecture by Dr. Helen Caldicott on the need for nuclear disarmament.

891. What was the National Film Board's Unit System?

The National Film Board of Canada evolved a system of specialized production units designated by letters of the alphabet. The system was established by the Film Commissioner John Grierson in 1944, but it became fully operational only in 1950. There were seven units in all – five English-language units and two French-language units – when the system of separate production units was abolished in 1964.

Unit A was responsible for agricultural, French-language, foreign-language, and "interpretive" films. Unit B was concerned with sponsored, scientific, cultural, and animated films. Unit C produced theatrical films, the *Canada Carries On* series, newsreels, and tourist and travel films. Unit D focused on international affairs and special projects. Unit E undertook sponsored projects like the filming of royal tours. Later a specialized unit and a women's production unit were added. As D.B. Jones noted in *Movies and Memoranda: An Interpretive History of the National Film Board of Canada* (1981), "Each unit had its own staff of writers, producers, directors, and editors." The system ensured a degree of autonomy and creativity within the larger Film Board which found itself increasingly under attack by the government of the day.

892. For what NFB film did NASA order at least 300 prints?

The National Film Board's documentary film *Universe* produced in 1960 "became one of the most widely distributed educational films ever made, earning much more than its total production cost in revenues," wrote D.B. Jones in *Movies and Memoranda: An Interpretive History of the National Film Board of Canada* (1981).

The film had special appeal for the U.S.'s National Aeronautics and Space Administration. As Jones noted: "NASA ordered at least 300 prints of the film, which they used for training and for public information. By 1976, the Film Board had sold over 3,100 prints of *Universe*. Stanley Kubrick, when he started work on his *2001: A Space Odyssey*, discussed the project with Colin Low [the producer] and hired Wally Gentleman, the wizard who had achieved the optical effects for *Universe*, to do the same for Kubrick's film. And Kubrick used the voice of Douglas Rain, who spoke the commentary for *Universe* (which Stanley Jackson had written), as the voice of Hal, the computer.

893. Who were the Commissioners of the National Film Board?

Commissioner is the title of the head of the National Film Board of Canada. A Commissioner has the status of a Deputy Minister. Between the time of the appointment of the first Commissioner in 1940 to the present (1 July 1988), there have been ten Commissioners. They are as follows:

John Grierson (1939-45), Ross McLean (1945-50), Arthur Irwin (1950-52), Albert Trueman (1953-57), Guy Roberge (1957-66), Grant McLean (1966-67), Hugo McPherson (1967-70), Sydney Newman (1970-75), André Lamy (1975-79), James de B. Domville (1979-84), François Macerola (1984-88), Joan Pennefather (1989-94), Sandra M. Macdonald (1995-present).

894. What words appear at the entranceway to the Canadian War Museum?

The words that appear at the entranceway to the Canadian War Museum in Ottawa go like this: "Peace is the dream of the wise; / War is the history of man." The remark is attributed to Comte Louis Phillipe de Ségur (1753-1830), French officer, diplomat, and writer, according to Fred Gaffen in his book *In the Eye of the Storm: A History of Canadian Peacekeeping* (1987).

895. Is peacekeeping expensive as military operations go?

The answer to this question is provided by Fred Gaffen, an historian with the Canadian War Museum in Ottawa and the author of *In the Eye of the Storm: A History of Canadian Peacekeeping* (1987): "Professor Albert Legault of the department of political science, Laval University, has estimated the financial outlay by Canada to international peacekeeping (excluding Korea) from 1949 to 1980 at 226 million dollars, less than one-half of one percent of the total budget of the Department of National Defence over that period."

896. What is the legendary Golden Butterfly award?

There is a lot of lore associated with the lot of the Canadian peacekeepers who were members of the International Commission for Control and

Supervision in Indochina in the 1970s. Apparently a select number of servicemen received the Golden Butterfly award – a small gold pin worn discreetly behind the lapel. According to one authority, the award was given not for experience in engaging with the Vietnamese on the battlefield, but rather in the bedroom. The number of Golden Butterflies awarded is unknown.

897. Who is the experimental filmmaker whose total output consists of five short films, the total screening time of which runs 1 hour 2 minutes 22 seconds?

Any fan of experimental films who answers that the experimental filmmaker in question is Norman McLaren is wrong, but the error is excusable. After all, McLaren's work is experimental and his films are brief works. But he produced more than sixty-three films. The complete list – from *Alouette* to *V for Victory* – appears in the Film and Video Catalogue issued by the National Film Board of Canada.

Arthur Lipsett, the filmmaker in question, like McLaren, worked for the NFB. Less prolific a filmmaker than McLaren, his five short films are no less provocative. Lipsett specialized in compilations. Each of his films is a succession of unrelated images and sounds. It is left to the viewer to decide on their "meaning." The best-known Lipsett film is the earliest and also the shortest. *This is Very Nice, Very Nice* (1961) which runs 6" 59' and consists of a cascade of images and a voice repeating the words of the title. It is up to the viewer to decide whether or not there is any organizing principle behind the imagery other than the mood of the moment.

Thereafter Lipsett's films grew longer. *Free Fall* (1964) runs 9" 15' and consists of assembled images without repeated words. His third film, called enigmatically *21-87*, was made in 1964, and runs 9" 33'. It shows views of a passing crowd. *A Trip Down Memory Lane* (1965) at 12" 40' is an anthology of newsreel footage in no apparent order. His fifth and last film, *Fluxes* (1967), runs 23" 55' and captures the awkward and eccentric movements of people.

The total running time of all five films is 1 hour 2 minutes 22 seconds. But few viewers would ever – could ever – watch them in succession. They upset the conventions of filmmaking and the viewer's need for simple narrative or complex continuity.

898. What award-winning film is only 8 minutes 10 seconds long?

Norman McLaren's award-winning film *Neighbours* (NFB, 1952) is only 8 minutes 10 seconds long. Its cast consists of only two actors, Jean-Paul Ladouceur and Grant Munro, who come to blows over the possession of a flower which grows on the boundary line of their lawns. McLaren in *Neighbours* was innovative in the application of the technique of "pixilation" – employing the manner of animating drawings or puppets with live actors – to create slapstick-like movement. The battle of Ladouceur and Munro leads to unimaginable consequences.

899. Why is the sentence for first-degree murder a mandatory twenty-five years of imprisonment?

It is characteristic of the Criminal Code of Canada that the sentence for first-degree murder is the mandatory sentence of twenty-five years of imprisonment.

There is no special wisdom behind the length of the sentence; it is a compromise position reached in the 1960s between those who favoured retention and those who favoured abolition of the death penalty. The compromise position was described by the journalist Mick Lowe in *Conspiracy of Brothers: A True Story of Murder, Bikers and the Law* (1988):

> According to a number of Canadian parliamentarians, the twenty-five year mandatory sentence for first-degree murder was the product, not of some immutable commitment to justice or some careful consideration of right and wrong, but of pure political compromise. There had been, after all, a considerable body of public opinion that strongly supported the retention of the death penalty. As a trade-off for the abolition of hanging, the abolitionists conceded the harshest possible prison sentence for pre-meditated murder, the twenty-five year mandatory.

900. Was there ever a Special Relationship between Canada and the United States?

What was loosely called a Special Relationship was said to exist between Canada and the United States. It commenced with the presidency of

William Howard Taft (1909-1913) and continued through the presidencies of Woodrow Wilson, Warren G. Harding, Calvin Coolidge, Herbert Hoover, Franklin D. Roosevelt, Harry S. Truman, Dwight D. Eisenhower, John F. Kennedy, and Lyndon B. Johnson. It was unceremoniously concluded by Richard M. Nixon (1969-1973).

The Prime Ministers during this period were Sir Wilfrid Laurier, Sir Robert Borden, Arthur Meighen, R.B. Bennett, W.L. Mackenzie King, Louis St. Laurent, John G. Diefenbaker, Lester B. Pearson, and Pierre Elliott Trudeau. The Special Relationship required that the two countries deal with differences on a consultative basis in private rather than on a confrontational basis in public. In this manner, the smaller country could seek exemption from restrictive or protectionist legislation contemplated by the larger country.

The relationship was meaningful to the extent that it was based on mutual trust and shared goals. It was tried and found wanting by Kennedy and Diefenbaker and dismissed by Nixon and Trudeau. It was revived in the sense of continental co-operation by Ronald Reagan and Brian Mulroney.

901. Is Canada a family name?

Not really, except that in Spanish the name Cañadas is not unknown. Here is one instance. Francisca Cañadas Morales was the name of a young Spanish woman who was caught in the centre of a feud waged by her suitors. The incident which took place in rural Andalusia in 1928 inspired Féderico Garcia Lorca's tragic play *Blood Wedding*.

902. What is the origin of the word Cajun?

The word Cajun refers to the society and culture of the French-speaking population of the State of Louisiana, which was a colony first of Spain and then of France. In 1803 Louisiana was acquired by the United States. Cajun is a corruption of Acadien or Acadian.

The Acadians are French-speaking descendants of the original settlers of the French colony of Acadia in present-day Nova Scotia. In 1755, the English sent ten thousand Acadians into exile. Many settled in Louisiana, where the French culture – influenced by Spanish, Indian and Southern American culture – has survived to this day, producing a most distinctive Cajun patois and cuisine.

903. Who speaks Bougalie?

Bougalie is the name of the Cajun dialect spoken in rural areas of the State of Louisiana. The word Bougalie may be derived from "bogue talk" or "bayou talk," the characteristic speech of the Cajun or Acadian settlers of Louisiana. So Bougalie is spoken by the Cajun population of Louisiana.

904. Who speaks Michif Cree?

Michif Cree is the name of the language spoken by the older Métis people of rural Manitoba. The language, a mixture of French and Cree, dates from the first half of the nineteenth century. Although it has survived in rural parts of the province, its existence is threatened by the predominance of the English language. Other names for Michif Cree are "French-Cree" or simply "Cree."

905. How many provinces have names that are derived from native languages?

The names of four of the ten provinces are derived from native languages. The names of the rest of the provinces find their origin in the English language.

The feature that the four, native-derived names have in common is the fact that they refer to bodies of water rather than to areas of land. Quebec is derived through the French from the Algonkian word for "narrow passage" or "strait." Ontario is said to be an Indian (perhaps Iroquois) word for "beautiful lake" or "beautiful waters." Manitoba is probably taken from the Cree word for "strait of the spirit." Saskatchewan is likely borrowed from the Cree for "swift-flowing river."

Close to half the names of the provinces are derived from native sources. It is more than half in the case of the United States. Of the fifty American states, the names of twenty-six are derived from native languages.

906. Is there a distinctive Canadian speech?

"As in so many other aspects of Canadian individuality, you have to look carefully for the subtleties that make Canadian speech distinctive. In language, as in national character, Canadian identity often seems understated and unhistrionic beside the boisterous American giant across the border." So wrote Robert McCrum, William Cran, and Robert MacNeil in their popular study *The Story of English* (1986).

They went on to say, "Canadian English is difficult to distinguish from some other North American varieties without the tools of the phonetician, yet it is instantly recognizable to other Canadians, if not to the rest of the English-speaking world. In a crowd, where the Englishman or the Australian could not, the Canadian with a good ear will easily spot the other Canadian among the North Americans."

The distinctiveness, they noted, lies in the vocabulary and the pronunciation, characterized by a mixture of British and American influences, as well as the presence of ten thousand or so specific Canadian words and expressions. Especially distinctive in Canadian speech is the vowel sound of the diphthong ou, as in the tell-all phrase "out and about in a boat."

907. What is so distinctive about "out and about in a boat"?

It comes as a surprise to English-speaking Canadians to realize that linguists and phoneticians regard as distinctive their way of saying the following words "out and about in a boat."

What is distinctive is the vowel sound. The pronunciation of the dipthong ou results in the phrase sounding (to a non-Canadian at least) like "oat and aboat in a boat." As the linguist Jack Chambers has noted: "The ou in "house" and "about" begins with the vowel sound in hut and but, whereas the ou in "houses" and "bough" begins with the vowel sound in hot and bought. The difference in the two ou sounds is systematic, and known to linguists as Canadian Raising. Because of it, Canadians have a different ou sound in house and houses, and in lout and loud."

908. What was the National Energy Policy?

The National Energy Policy was the attempt of the Trudeau administration and especially of Energy Minister Marc Lalonde to foster the Canadianization of the domestic oil and gas industry, then as now largely owned and controlled by American corporations. The ideal was 50% Canadian ownership and control of the industry by the year 1990.

NEP was announced on 28 October 1980 and formally ended on 25 April 1985. The policy met with great public approval, as shown by opinion polls, but leaders of the industry and some financiers resented the Liberal intrusion – or initiative – particularly the creation of Petro-Canada and the tax incentives and direct grants to Canadian-owned companies. Resistance from the Alberta government, a moratorium on private exploration, the worldwide decline in oil prices, the 1982 recession, and Liberal defeat at the hands of the Conservatives in September 1984 all sealed NEP's fate. Nonetheless, it seems that the industry, even without NEP, is inching toward 50% Canadian ownership and control.

909. Is the membership of the Canadian Parliament about the same size as the membership of the U.S. Congress?

No. The United States, which has about ten times the population of Canada, runs its republican system with about twice the number of representatives as does Canada with its monarchical system.

The Parliament of Canada consists of the Senate with a membership of 104 and the House of Commons with a membership of 282. Thus the total membership of the Canadian Parliament in 1988 was 386. The U.S. Congress consists of the Senate, with 100 seats, and the House of Representatives, with 438 seats. Thus in the same year the total membership of the U.S. Congress was 635.

A good question is the following one: Why does it takes 386 politicians to run a country of 30 million, but only 635 to run a country of 260 million?

910. Do American politicians use the word "caucus" to mean the same thing as Canadian politicians?

No. The words have different meanings and usages in the two political systems. In American politics a caucus is a meeting of members of a political party to select delegates to their party's state convention where the delegates vote for the candidate they want their party to back. In Canadian politics a caucus is a meeting of a political party's elected and appointed members of Parliament. Thus in the United States a caucus selects political candidates; in Canada it determines political procedures and policies.

911. Are Canadian high-school students well-informed about themselves and their country?

Not at all, according to the Canadian Student Awareness Survey undertaken in all the provinces and territories in January and February of 1975 by the Edmonton-based publisher and nationalist Mel Hurtig. The survey found that the younger generation is woefully ignorant of its history, institutions, culture and traditions, and how they affect their everyday lives.

Here are some of the survey's findings: 68% of the students were unable to name the Governor General. 61% were unable to name the BNA Act as the (then) constitution; 89% could not identify Gabriel Dumont, 68% René Lévesque, 96% Emily Murphy, and 92% Norman Bethune. 62% could not identify the conflict between Alberta and the federal government. 59% could not say into which ocean the Mackenzie River flows. Over 60% were unable to list the ten provinces in geographical order, east to west. About 70% had little or no idea what percentage of Canada's population is French Canadian. Given a list of eight names, between 60% and 80% could not select Pauline Julien, Bruce Cockburn, or Robert Charlebois as Canadians. The majority of the students could not name the province or territory in which the Annapolis Valley, Athabasca River, Mackenzie River, or the Klondike are located.

Although the survey is now dated, it is doubtful that today's students would do much, if any, better.

912. What was E.P. Taylor's Three-point Business Philosophy?

E.P. Taylor evolved his Three-point Business Philosophy – others called it his formula for success – in an attempt to account for his phenomenal business successes during the postwar years. It embodied three principles of business.

1. He believed in borrowing money on the principle that companies may be purchased or increased in size through the careful use of the money of others.
2. He believed in bigness because a large operation may be run more efficiently and effectively than several small operations.
3. He believed that one major shareholder, with less than a majority interest in a company, may oversee the operation and may be thrown out by the other shareholders should he fail to do the job.

913. When was simultaneous translation introduced in the House of Commons?

Prime Minister John G. Diefenbaker moved the following motion in the House of Commons on 11 August 1958: "That this House do approve the installation of a simultaneous translation system in this chamber and that Mr. Speaker be authorized to make arrangements necessary to install and operate it." The motion won unanimous approval. The system was installed and officially inaugurated on 16 January 1959. One wonders how unilingual members fared between 1867 and 1959.

914. Was Tuponia seriously offered as a name for the about-to-be-named Dominion of Canada?

Semi-seriously. The Fathers of Confederation deliberated for two years before selecting "Canada" as the name for the new Dominion. Some names that were given consideration during the pre-Confederation debates include Albertoria, Cabotia, Efisga (a contraction of England, France, Ireland, Scotland, Germany, Aborigines), Hochelaga (the original name of Montreal), Norland, Tuponia (a contraction of The United Provinces of North America), Victorialand, and West Britannia.

So many silly names were suggested that the patriot Thomas D'Arcy McGee rose in the legislative Assembly in Ottawa on 9 February 1865 and made the following suggestion: "One individual chooses Tuponia and another Hochelaga, as a suitable name for the new nationality. Now I would ask any honourable member of this House how he would feel if he woke up some fine morning and found himself, instead of a Canadian, a Tuponian or Hochelangander. (Laughter) Now I think, sir, we may safely leave for the present the discussion of the name as well as the origin of the new system...."

915. Whatever became of the Unitarian Service Committee?

It was renamed. The Unitarian Service Committee was once familiar to a generation of Canadians. The Committee was established by the Unitarian Congregation and other interested parties in Ottawa on 10 June 1945 as a voluntary agency to supply refugee relief. Its good works were well publicized but the fact that it became known as "the agency with a heart" is a testimonial to the personal qualities – especially the dynamism – of its Prague-born founder, the social activist Dr. Lotta Hitschmanova. There are Unitarian Service Committees is some twenty other countries. The agency was renamed USC Canada, as noted in *The USC Story: A Quarter Century of Loving Service* (1970) by the Unitarian Service Committee of Canada.

916. Are there references to Canada in Joseph Conrad's novel *Under Western Eyes?*

No, but once there were such references. The Polish novelist published *Under Western Eyes,* his novel about Russian revolutionaries, in 1910. An early draft of the novel was called "Razumov." It was the object of study by Eloise Knapp Hay in *The Political Novels of Joseph Conrad* (1963). She found that there was a section which did not make it into the published version. The narrator mentions receiving a letter from a niece who lives somewhere in Canada and this gives rise to a short aside on the subject of the migration of the Doukhobors from Russia to the Canadian West. The passage begins, "A lot of strange immigrants from Russia had just been landed on the stores of the Dominion...."

917. Who wrote the first "animal stories"?

Stories about wild or domesticated animals have long been popular, especially when they show their love and loyalty to human beings. But the genre of the "animal story" – the drama of a wild animal in a natural setting which has been so described as to satisfy the conflicting demands of the naturalist and the *littérateur* – derives from the prose of two Canadian authors.

The earliest realistic fiction of this type was a story written by Sir Charles G.D. Roberts and published in *Harper's Monthly* in December 1892. It was called "Do Seek Their Meat from God" and was reprinted in Roberts' collection *Earth's Enigmas* (1896). But the vogue for the genre was sparked by the success of *Wild Animals I Have Known* (1898), a collection of such stories written and illustrated by Ernest Thompson Seton. In this genre "the animals do not talk," although quite often they have human qualities other than speech ascribed to them – rudimentary reasoning, sympathetic feelings, etc. At the turn of the century animal stories were particularly appealing to "armchair naturalists." They continue to have appeal today, but largely to young readers.

918. What is the story behind R. Murray Schafer's oddly titled musical composition "No Longer Than Ten (10) Minutes"?

The Toronto Symphony Orchestra offered the innovative composer R. Murray Schafer a commission for a musical composition. The contract read: "It is agreed that the work shall have a minimum duration of approximately seven (7) minutes and no longer than ten (10) minutes." Schafer accepted the commission and its terms and called the composition "No Longer Than Ten (10) Minutes."

As Stephen Adams noted in his study R. Murray Schafer (1983), "Rightly or not, the implication seemed to be that, while the orchestra felt bound by duty (not to mention Canadian-content stipulations attached to government grants) to support Canadian music, no audience could be expected to sit through anything like a major work occupying a high priority position on its concert program." Adams continued: "Schafer retaliated with a piece that assaults the conventions of the standard subscription concert." The piece is scored to begin with the orchestra tuning up. Its finale is as unconventional as its first few notes. The score calls for members of the orchestra to reach a crescendo every time members of the audience began to applaud. Conceptually the crescendo-applause cycle could extend the finale for an indefinite period of time. The composition was premiered in 1971 to the merriment of the Toronto Symphony's audience.

919. What are the titles of some books that have been censored in Canada?

For the purposes of this discussion, a distinction is drawn between censored books and banned books. The former are books that have been denied importation into Canada or publication in whole or in part in Canada. The latter are books that are generally available but have been banned from purchase or use by some body or other – generally a board of school trustees.

The expatriate writer Elizabeth Smart always maintained that her autobiographical novel *By Grand Central Station I Sat Down and Wept*

(1945) was censored in Canada. She was living in Britain at the time of its publication there. An Ottawa bookstore imported and sold six copies. One of these was bought by her socially prominent parents who were scandalized. They complained to their neighbour, who happened to be Prime Minister Mackenzie King, and he obligingly saw to it that the customs authorities seized all further shipments and burnt them. That at least is Smart's story. There is no proof that any of this occurred, although it is true that the book was published and copies of the first edition are scarce in this country. The American paperback edition of 1966 was imported into the country and distributed without hindrance. To coincide with a latter-day interest in Smart's life and writing, *By Grand Central Station I Sat Down and Wept* was issued in Toronto in 1982. The romantic prose poem generated mainly sentimental and nostalgic interest.

Bernard Ostry and H.S. Ferns were young historians when they wrote *The Age of Mackenzie King: The Rise of the Leader* (1955) which was published in England. The two authors claimed that the Liberals in Ottawa inspired a media boycott of the book which took a revisionist look at the late Prime Minister and found him personally corrupt. Certainly it was not widely reviewed or taken very seriously when it was initially published. When it was reprinted in Toronto in 1976, it was treated more as a novelty than as a work of serious scholarship.

One book that was withdrawn by its Canadian publishers within weeks of publication was *Gay Canadian Rogues, Swindlers, Gold-Diggers and Spies* (1958). The publishers were responding to the threat of legal action. The author of the book, journalist Frank Rasky, had devoted one chapter to the career and personality of Igor Gouzenko, the Soviet defector. Gouzenko did not object to the innocent use of the word "gay" in the title – it had yet to take on other connotations – but he did object to being lumped in with rogues, swindlers, and gold-diggers. Once withdrawn from publication, the book was never reprinted. Rasky's next book was *Great Canadian Disasters* (1961) – which might well have been a description of the fate of *Gay Canadian Rogues!*

The Makers of Canada was the overall title of a series of biographical monographs on historical figures published in Toronto between 1903 and 1911 plus a concluding volume issued in 1926. The historian John Macnaughton wrote a study of Lord Strathcona for the series in 1917. It was considered controversial – in modern terms "revisionist" – and members of the railway financier's family took strong exception to some of Macnaughton's statements. Publication of the study was delayed nine years, and when it did appear in 1926, it did so in a truncated, toned-down form, reworked by the series editor, W.L. Grant. In 1948 the literary critic E.K. Brown praised the volume, even in its censored form, as one of the best Canadian books of all time.

920. Is it true that the Governor General is denied a vote in a general election?

No. There is no law that denies the Governor General the right to cast a vote. Excluded by law are the Assistant Chief Electoral Officer, judges appointed by the Governor General in Council, people convicted of corrupt or illegal election practices, and "persons restrained of their liberty of movement or deprived of the management of their property by reason of mental disease" – that is, inmates of penal institutions and the insane. In the 1990s a movement was mounted to extend suffrage to inmates of penal institutions.

921. Have any Canadian authors paid to have their own books published?

A commercial publishing house is expected to pay an author a royalty on the sale of a book. From time to time the arrangement is reversed and the author pays for publication – by picking up the printer's bill or guaranteeing the publishing house against loss. Whether it involves self-printing or an author's subvention, the practice is called "vanity" publishing. Some authors regard it as "sanity" publishing. For a beginning author it might be good business, as Stephen Vizinczey discovered when he self-published the first edition of his novel *In Praise of Older Women* (1965). Dr. Peter G. Hanson did likewise with his self-help book *The Joy of Stress* (1985). Both became outstanding bestsellers. Stephen Leacock launched his own career as a humorist by paying for the printing of *Literary Lapses* (1910). Robert W. Service was all set to bear the printing costs of his first collection of ballads, *The Spell of the Yukon* (1909), when the firm's salesman convinced the firm's editor to take a chance on an unknown bard.

Some other notable Canadian books published with author subvention include the following: Isabella Valancy Crawford's *Malcolm's Katie* (1884), Richard Maurice Bucke's *Cosmic Consciousness* (1901), Germaine Guèvremont's *Le Survenant* (1945), Irving Layton's *Here and Now* (1945), and John Glassco's *A Point of Sky* (1964). An outstanding bestseller was *The Wealthy Barber* (1989) which launched David Chilton's financial-advice career into orbit.

Indeed, it could be said that all the literary and scholarly books published in Canada benefit from direct or indirect subsidy in the form of block or project grants made by governmental bodies to publishing houses. The Internet offers authors on all levels of popularity self-publishing possibilities through the licensing of electronic books known as e-books.

922. What was the newspaperman's Stationery Allowance?

Broadcaster Knowlton Nash recalled the nefarious Stationery Allowance in his book *History on the Run: The Trenchcoat Memoirs of a Foreign Correspondent* (1984). It was the name given by the government in power to newspaper reporters who covered the provincial legislatures in the 1940s and 1950s. Nash wrote: "As I remember it, this was about $50 a year, equal at that time to about three weeks' pay for me. But in fact, in the press gallery we got all our stationery free, so this little bonus was presumably a way of trying to make us less hostile to the government of the day. In Quebec the stationery allowance was substantially more – several hundred dollars."

923. What was the so-called Provisional Government Plot?

During the October Crisis of 1970, with rumours abounding, one whopper was the Provisional Government Plot. Apparently a group of prominent Québécois was planning to replace the newly elected provincial Liberal government of Robert Bourassa with a Committee of Public Safety. The names of René Lévesque, Jacques Parizeau, Marcel Pepin, and Claude Ryan were mentioned as being members of the committee which wished to negotiate with the FLQ kidnappers for the release of the "political prisoners," i.e., the kidnapped hostages Cross and Laporte. Cabinet Minister Marc Lalonde and Prime Minister Pierre Elliott Trudeau encouraged Peter C. Newman, managing editor of *The Toronto Star*, to publish an article on the "takeover plot" to give the rumour substance. An unsigned story with an Ottawa dateline duly appeared beneath a banner headline in the *Star* on 23 October 1970. As Christina McCall Newman noted in *Grits* (1982), it was all speculation and disguised fear. There was not a scintilla of truth to it. It retroactively helped to justify the imposition of the War Measures Act.

924. In the opinion of Northrop Frye, which is "the greatest poem in Canadian literature"?

The eminent literary critic Northrop Frye declared that *The Truant* is "the greatest poem in Canadian literature." The judgement was rendered in a paper delivered on 11 June 1956 and published the following year by the Royal Society of Canada in its Studia Varia series. E.J. Pratt wrote the long poem in June 1942. It examines mankind – "the truant" – from a cosmic perspective.

925. What are Margaret Atwood's four basic "victim positions"?

Margaret Atwood claimed that Canadians suffer a victim complex and want to fail. In her book *Survival* (1972), which studied the victim scenario in the country's literature and psyche, she outlined the following four basic "victim positions":

Position 1. Deny the fact that you are a victim.
Position 2. Acknowledge the fact that you are a victim, but explain this as an act of Fate, the will of God, the dictates of Biology (in the case of women, for instance), the necessity decreed by History, or Economics, or the Unconscious, or any other large general powerful idea.
Position 3. Acknowledge the fact that you are victim but refuse to accept the assumption that the role is inevitable.
Position 4. Be a creative non-victim.

The last line of Atwood's novel *Surfacing*, published in the same year, reads: "This above all, to refuse to be a victim."

926. Who has more shoes than Imelda Marcos?

It is said that in the closets of Imelda Marcos's palace in the Philippines held 5,000 pairs of shoes, sporty walking apparel being the passion of the dictator's wife. Sonja Bata owns more than 10,000 pairs of shoes, that being the number she had collected by 1999, but precisely how many more than that she will acquire is a matter of conjecture. Her collection is on display in the Bata Shoe Museum in Toronto, the world's sole museum devoted to footwear. Sonja Bata comes by her passion honestly. She holds a corporate position in Bata Limited, headed by Thomas Bata whose father established the international shoe manufacturing empire in Czechoslovakia before World War II. It was estimated that one out of every ten persons in the world buys a pair of Bata shoes every year.

927. In which Canadian city in this century was a solar eclipse last seen in North America?

Canadian astronomers were delighted that Winnipeg had clear skies one night in the late winter of 1979. It was perfect viewing weather for the last solar eclipse to be seen in North America this century. The moment of totality lasted almost three minutes.

The occasion was caught on still film by the well-known New York-based photographer Henry Groskinsky. Life in April 1979 carried his multiple-exposure shots of the Sun, gradually being obscured by the Moon. He made exposures every fifteen minutes for more than two hours. Groskinsky's work is reproduced in colour in *Life: Classic Photographs – A Personal Interpretation* (1988) by John Loengard.

928. What are Jerry S. White's Seven Truths about Canadian Business?

Jerry S. White is a Toronto-based management consultant and corporate head. In his book *Intrapreneuring: The Secrets of Corporate Success in Canada* (1988), he discusses the characteristics of corporations and governmental institutions in this country. He does so in a list of the "Seven Truths about Canadian Business:"

1. The Protestant work ethic is paramount: security first, profit later, no risk please.
2. Lip service is paid to innovation and creativity; Canadians prefer change to be evolutionary rather than revolutionary.
3. Institutions are resistant to change so that they can be counted upon to compromise to the point of caution and their detriment.
4. The initiative of entrepreneurs and intrapreneurs is feared.
5. Government exerts an undue influence on business and the economy.

6. Corporations are increasingly concerned with paper shuffling, acquisition, and corporate concentration.
7. Canada is seen as an extension of the United States so that an imported product, service, or idea is preferred to a domestic product, service, or idea.

929. Who is Dr. Tomorrow?

Dr. Tomorrow is the registered trade mark of Frank Ogden, the futurist, who lives and works on his yacht anchored in Vancouver's Coal Harbour. Ogden is a researcher and communicator concerned with change and innovation. He communicates less through the printed word than he does through the distribution of columns on computer discs and through his keynote addresses, seminars, presentations, and lectures. One of his maxims is: "My idea of advance planning is lunch."

930. Who is the author of "Lincoln's Warning"?

"Lincoln's Warning" is an anti-Catholic tirade attributed to U.S. President Abraham Lincoln that circulated in the United States in the late 1880s and thereafter. It turns up from time to time and it runs like this:

> I do not pretend to be a prophet. But though not a prophet, I see a very dark cloud on our horizon. And that dark cloud is coming from Rome. It is filled with tears of blood. It will rise and increase, till its flank will be torn by a flash of lightning, followed by a fearful peal of thunder. Then a cyclone such as the world has never seen, will pass over this country, spreading ruin and desolation from north and south. After it is over, there will be long days of peace and prosperity: for Popery with its Jesuits and merciless Inquisition, will have been swept away from our country. Neither I nor you, but our children, will see those things.

This "warning," according to Paul F. Goller, Jr. and John George, authors of *They Never Said It: A Book of Fake Quotes, Misquotes, and Misleading Attributions* (1989), was written not by Lincoln but by Charles Chiniquy, the Quebec-born former Roman Catholic priest. Chiniquy ascribed these words to "the Great Emancipator," whom he knew personally, in his tract *Fifty Years in the Church of Rome* (1886). In the same book Chiniquy ascribed to Lincoln a belief that differentiates between Jews and Christians: "Moses died for his people's sake, but Christ died for the whole world's sake!" These ideas are foreign to Lincoln's beliefs and feeling for tolerance.

931. Did Sherlock Holmes solve any Canadian cases?

Sir Arthur Conan Doyle did not require his fictional master detective Sherlock Holmes or his sidekick the able Dr. Watson to investigate or solve any Canadian cases, although some references to this country do appear in "the canon," as Holmesians (or fans of the doings of the Great Detective) refer to these novels and stories.

The references are two in number. The trademark "Meyers, Toronto" on a boot is an important clue in the novel *The Hound of the Baskervilles* (1902). (This reference inspired the Canadian Holmesians to name their society The Bootmakers of Toronto.) "Try Canadian Pacific Railway," says Holmes to a fellow investigator who can make no sense of the initials "C.P.R." in the story "Black Peter" collected in *The Return of Sherlock Holmes* (1904).

What Sir Arthur failed to do was done with *éclat* by writer Jack Batten and the historian Michael Bliss who collaborated on "The Adventure of the Annexationist Conspiracy." In this short story, Holmes responds to the urgent request of Prime Minister Sir John A. Macdonald, travels to Ottawa, and deals discreetly with a delicate case involving conspiracy. The story was included in the anthology *Maddened by Mystery* (1982) edited by Michael Richardson.

The Scarlet Claw (1944), the best of the vintage Holmes movies starring Basil Rathbone as Holmes and Nigel Bruce as Watson, is set in the imaginary Quebec rural village called La Morte Rouge. The movie is loosely based on *The Hound of the Baskervilles*, and it finds Holmes solving the problem of "the monster of the marshes." The film was produced during World War II, so it is perhaps understandable that Holmes near the end refers to Canada as "the linch-pin of the English-speaking world"!

One of the best theatrical plays to star the Great Detective is *The Incredible Murder of Cardinal Tosca* which was written by poet Alden Nowlan and theatre director Walter Learning. The three-act comedy-mystery is full of dash, colour, and excitement. It adds a variation on a familiar line to "the canon." The variation runs, "Rudimentary, my dear Watson."

More recently, the scriptwriter Ronald C. Weymna wrote the novel *Sherlock Holmes and the Mark of the Beast* (1989). It explains where Holmes was residing during the years he was "killed off" by Sir Arthur. It seems Holmes was on a mission to Canada to save the visiting Prince of Wales from assassination. Needless to say he succeeded, and the Royal Visit of the Prince was a great success.

Latter-day additions to "the canon" are called "pastiches" by Holmesians. The Canadian pastiches are better than most. In fact, Cameron Hollier, who for many years served as the librarian in charge of the Conan Doyle Room at the Metropolitan Toronto Reference Library, regarded the Nowlan-Learning collaboration as the best of the Holmes plays.

932. Which musical performing artist, as a youth, conceived of the notion of composing an opera about "the ultimate catastrophe of nuclear destruction"?

One of Glenn Gould's unfinished childhood works was an opera that "was to deal with the ultimate catastrophe of nuclear destruction. In Act I the entire human population was to be wiped out and in Act II they were to be replaced by a superior breed of frogs." Gould claimed that he had actually composed "a few bars" of a chorus for frogs in the key of E major, "which I always felt to be a benign and sympathetic key," but he acknowledged that there would have been a "casting problem." Further details appear in Otto Friedrich's *Glenn Gould: A Life and Variations* (1989).

933. Did 'Abdu'l-Bahá compose a prayer for Canada?

'Abdu'l-Bahá, the son of the founder of the Bahá'í Faith, was a religious leader in his own right. He was regarded as "the Servant of God" and the leading, living exemplar of the Bahá'í life. He composed a prayer for Canada.

The Persian religious leader visited Montreal in 1912 and was much impressed with the country's religious tolerance and its system of justice. In 1917, in Haifa, Palestine, he dictated his "Tablets to Canada from The Divine Plan," which depicted Canada as enjoying a glorious future. He charged North American members of the Bahá'í Faith with the responsibility to missionize the rest of the world.

It is assumed that in the same year 'Abdu'l-Bahá composed "A Prayer for Canada." It begins:

> Praise be to Thee, O God! Verily these are Thy servants, who are attracted by the fragrances of Thy mercifulness, enkindled by the ignited fire in the tree of Thy singleness, and their eyes are brightened by beholding the effulgences of the light in the Sinai of Thy oneness!" It begs God to "loosen their tongues ... make them the signs of Thy guidance amongst Thy creatures.

The full prayer runs about 270 words and is printed in English in *'Abdu'l-Bahá in Canada* (1962), a book issued by the National Spiritual Assembly of the Baha'ís of Canada to commemorate the fiftieth anniversary of the Persian religious leader's visit to Canada.

934. Did a Persian religious leader predict the formation of five new Canadian provinces?

As curious as it might seem, yes; in a way, he did.

'Abdu'l-Bahá, the son of the founder of the Bahá'í Faith, was known as "the Servant of God." In the so-called "Tablets to Canada from The Divine Plan," dictated in Haifa, Palestine, 5 April 1916, he wrote the following: "Likewise in the provinces of Canada, such as Newfoundland, Prince Edward Island, Nova Scotia, New Brunswick, Quebec, Ontario, Manitoba, Saskatchewan, Alberta, British Columbia, Ungava, Keewatin, Mackenzie, Yukon, and the Franklin Islands in the Arctic Circle – the believers of God must become self-sacrificing and like unto the candles of guidance become ignited in the provinces of Canada."

Members of the Bahá'í Faith point out that the speaker anticipated by thirty-three years Newfoundland's admission to provincial status, and that there is an implicit prediction that in the fullness of time the northern regions will produce five new provinces called or sited in Ungava, Keewatin, Mackenzie, Yukon, and the Franklin Islands.

935. Who proposes the Finlandization of Canada's defence policies?

The notion that Canada's defence policies should be subjected to Finlandization has been proposed by defence specialist Gwynne Dyer and television producer Tina Viljoen in their book *The Defence of Canada: In the Arms of the Empire, 1760-1939* (1990). In essence, they argued that Canada should withdraw from its current defence alliances, notably with NATO and NORAD, and marshal its defence resources solely for the purpose of self-defence, a policy pursued by Finland which, like Canada, lies alongside one of the world's dominant superpowers.

936. What precedent did royalty set in Ottawa on a Sunday in May?

According to historians, royalty set a precedent in Ottawa on a Sunday afternoon on 21 May 1939. Immediately following the ceremony marking the unveiling of the National War Memorial in Confederation Square, King George VI and Queen Elizabeth departed from tradition. Rather than enter their automobiles and speed off, they remained and mingled with the crowd. In an unscheduled and unprecedented "walkabout," the first on record, they left their bodyguards behind and moved among the large and enthusiastic crowd, shaking hands with the common people. Their security personnel – members of Scotland Yard and the RCMP – were appalled. This spontaneous gesture established the "common touch" of the new and untried monarch and was the first "walkabout." "It was a way of stamping their own style on the monarchy for the first time," explained Tom MacDonnell in *Daylight Upon Magic: The Royal Tour of Canada – 1939* (1989).

937. What is so unusual about "Predicting a Number"?

It is a magical effect that is of Canadian origin. It goes like this:

Write down your year of birth. Add to it the year of a memorable event. Add to it your present age (as of December 31 of the current year). Add to it the number of years since the event occurred. Then the total is twice the current year.

"Predicting a Number" is the common name for this magical effect. Magicians who use it in their magic shows may know it as "The Buddha Prophecy," "20th Century Prophecy," "The Oriental Thought," "Thought Foretold," or "Thought Bender."

Under the latter name it appears in the 992-page tome *Stewart James in Print: The First Fifty Years* (1989), a compilation of the tricks and effects of Stewart James, postman in Courtright, Ontario, originator of magical effects and historian of magic. James attributed the original concept of "Predicting a Number" to another trick-creator: Allan Lambie of White Rock, British Columbia.

938. What is the title of the most mammoth book of magical tricks ever issued?

The most mammoth book of magical tricks and effects ever issued bears an unusual title. It is called *Stewart James in Print: The First Fifty Years*, and it was privately published for use in magical circles by Jogestja Ltd. in Toronto in 1989. The 1025-page volume weighs 7 pounds 10 ounces. Pages measure 8.5 inches by 11 inches and there are numerous illustrations. Some 1800 copies were sold at U.S. $90 apiece.

The volume collects 412 tricks, routines, and effects devised and previously issued by Stewart James, an historian of magic and a retired postman from Courtright, Ontario. The volume was edited and published by Allan Slaight and Howard Lyons, lovers of magic.

It is only the first in a series of volumes. Its successor, *The James File* (2000), contains 800 more of the illusions created by Stewart James.

939. What is the subject of the book titled *Other Losses?*

The subject of *Other Loses* (1989), a controversial book written by the Toronto editor and author James Bacque, is that German prisoners of war, who in 1945 and 1946 found themselves in American and French camps in Europe, were systematically starved, and that more than one million of them died under the direct orders of Allied leader Dwight D. Eisenhower. Bacque broke the story in the article "The Last Dirty Secret of World War Two" in *Saturday Night*, September 1989. Scholars generally dismiss Bacque's thesis and its documentation.

940. Did a Canadian predict the demise or dissolution of Communism four decades before it occurred?

Yes, more or less. Malcolm Lowry, the British-born Canadian novelist and author of *Under the Volcano*, sent a letter to a Canadian friend in December 1950, at the height of the Cold War, in which he discussed the internal contradictions of Communism and anticipated its collapse in four decades. Lowry wrote:

> Even if communism were temporarily victorious it doesn't carry with it such a hopeless teleology of tyranny – even if tyrannical in its present phase – as did Nazism. In short anything [that] is a revolution must keep moving or it doesn't revolute: by its very nature it contains within it the seeds of its own destruction, so by 1989, say, everything ought to be hunky dory, all of which certainly doesn't make it any easier to live in 1950.

The passage is reproduced by Gordon Bowker in "Letters," *The Times Literary Supplement*, 29 June 1990. As Bowker noted, Lowry claimed to have foreseen the effects of the atomic bomb in his novel *Under the Volcano* (1947) but among the apocalyptic imagery of his masterpiece there is little to sustain such a reading.

941. What is the provincial order of precedence?

On official occasions for ceremonial purposes, the premiers of the provinces follow the order of their provinces' entry into Confederation. The prime minister appears first, followed by the premiers of the provinces in the following order (with the year of joining Confederation):

> New Brunswick, Nova Scotia, Ontario, Quebec, 1867; Manitoba, 1870; British Columbia, 1871; Prince Edward Island, 1873; Alberta, Saskatchewan, 1905; Newfoundland, 1949.

942. What were Quebec's five conditions for its acceptance of the revised constitution of 1982?

Quebec was the sole province to withhold provincial assent from the Constitution Act of 1982. Five conditions for Quebec's assent were unveiled by Premier Robert Bourassa at an academic conference held in May 1986 at Mont Gabriel, Quebec. These conditions or proposals became the basis of the Meech Lake Constitutional Accord which was adopted by the eleven First Ministers on 30 April 1987 at Meech Lake, Gatineau Park, subject to ratification within three years by federal and provincial governments. When Prime Minister Brian Mulroney was unable to secure ratification by all the provinces within the set period, or even approval of a "parallel accord," the provisions of the accord lapsed and the five conditions were dismissed.

Quebec's five conditions were as follows: the right to choose judges for the Supreme Court of Canada; increased powers over immigration; veto over constitutional amendments; limitation on federal spending power; and recognition of its status as a "distinct society."

943. How many of the nine judges of the Supreme Court of Canada are by convention "reserved" for Quebec?

Three of the nine judges of the Supreme Court are "reserved for Quebec" or, as it is sometimes expressed, are appointed "from the civil code," Quebec being the sole province to operate using the Civil Code of law. This arrangement follows convention rather than statute, so by tradition at any one time on the bench there will be three judges from the Province of Quebec, appointed by the federal government, presumably with the concurrence of the provincial government of the day.

944. Does any government in Canada recognize the native peoples as being organized into "nations"?

The Province of Quebec formally recognized the native peoples in its jurisdiction as constituting "nations." The Parti Québécois gave such recognition to ten First Nations on 9 February 1983: Abenaki, Algonquin, Attikamek, Cree, Huron-Wendat, Inuit, Micmac, Mohawk, Montagnais, and Naskapi. Similar action has yet to be taken by the federal government and the other provincial governments.

945. Who wrote a best-selling novel at the age of twelve?

Gordon Korman, born in Montreal in 1963, wrote his first book at the age of twelve. It was a grade seven English assignment. He titled it *This Can't Be Happening at Macdonald Hall.* It was published by Scholastic-Tab two years later, in 1977, when he was fourteen years old. It became a bestseller. Since then Korman has written two dozen or more books for young readers.

946. Did Sir Arthur Conan Doyle ever visit Canada?

Sir Arthur Conan Doyle, the famous British author and creator of Sherlock Holmes, came to Canada on four occasions. He did so as a popular lecturer, reader, advocate of British Empire causes, and proponent of Spiritualism. His Canadian visits were made in 1894, 1914, 1922, and 1923. In letters, articles, and books, he reminisced about his visits to various Canadian cities.

On one of his later trips, he visited Niagara Falls with his second wife. He remarked to Lady Doyle that it was here at Niagara Falls, not at Switzerland's Reichenbach Falls, that he should have made Sherlock Holmes plunge to his death. Apparently one witness claimed that Doyle carved Holmes's initials on the rock of Goat Island, according to Christopher Redmond in *Welcome to America, Mr. Sherlock Holmes* (1987).

947. Who is the great linguist who worked for fifteen years in Canada?

One of the world's greatest linguists and anthropologists was Edward Sapir (1884-1939) who was born in Pomerania and educated in the United States. From 1910 to 1925, he resided in Ottawa where he headed the Anthropological Division of the Geological Survey of Canada and studied the aboriginal languages of North America. Then he taught at the University of Chicago and after 1931 at Yale University.

Sapir's theories on language, originally influenced by his mentor the ethnologist Franz Boas, who did pioneering work among the Native population of the West Coast, in turn strongly influenced the theories of members of what is now called the Toronto School of Communications. Sapir evolved the theory that language is what most shapes culture. The Sapir-Wharf Hypothesis, elaborated with Benjamin Lee Whorf, a student of Hopi language and culture, affected such communications theorists as Edmund Carpenter and Marshall McLuhan.

948. What is the story of the Coleman Frog?

The Coleman Frog is a featured display of the York-Sunbury Historical Society Museum, Fredericton, New Brunswick. What is on display is the replica that passes for the real thing. It is said to be a stuffed and mounted frog that in life weighed 42 pounds and measured three feet from nose-tip to rump. The frog was named after Fred Coleman, proprietor of the hotel at Killarney Lake, New Brunswick, who boasted that this frog menaced him. He claimed he caught it and had it stuffed in 1885. The Coleman Frog that is on display is a replica, as Stuart Trueman suggests in *Tall Tales and True Tales from Down East* (1979).

949. Did Federico García Lorca ever visit Canada?

The great Spanish poet and playwright Federico García Lorca spent one year of his life in North America. His stay in the United States and Cuba, principally in New York City and Havana, extended from June 1929 to June 1930. The closest he came to visiting Canada was spending ten days with friends in a Vermont cottage at Montpelier Junction, August 16-26, 1929. And that is pretty far indeed! It is sometimes said that Lorca visited Montreal, yet no mention of any such visit was made by Ian Gibson in his detailed biography, *Federico García Lorca: A Life* (1989).

950. What line from which author's work of fiction did Arthur C. Clarke find to be most awesome?

Arthur C. Clarke, scientist and author, was mightily impressed with the daring imagination of A.E. van Vogt, the Manitoba-born, California-based author of science fiction.

Clarke singled out for praise the final sentence of "The Seasaw," a short story written by A.E. van Vogt that first appeared in *Astounding Science Fiction*, July 1941. The line goes like this:

"He would not witness, but he would cause, the formation of the planets."

Clarke wrote as follows: "*Si monumentum requiris, circumspice* indeed! I defy anyone to find a more awesome last line in the whole of fiction." Clarke's praise appears in *Astounding Days: A Science Fictional Autobiography* (1990).

951. Which science-fiction author is credited with the so-called "alien" patent?

As Arthur C. Clarke, the famous science-fiction novelist, wrote in *Astounding Days: A Science Fictional Autobiography* (1990):

> It is usually impossible to identify the inventor of any major idea in science fiction, because some ink-stained scholar can be relied upon to exhume an earlier example. In my opinion, however, van Vogt is the rightful holder of the "Alien" patent, with a string of stories in which spaceships are threatened by monsters of ever-increasing nastiness and capability.

Clarke singled out A.E. van Vogt's powerful short story "Vault of the Beast," which originally appeared in *Astounding Science Fiction*, August 1940, as one of the thematic classics of the genre.

952. What year is called "the year with no summer"?

Climatologists refer to the year 1816 as "the year with no summer." It seems that exceptionally cold weather was characteristic of all months. Montreal experienced snowfalls in June, frosts in July, and chilly conditions in August and September. Similar weather was experienced across the country and the northern United States. Climatologists suggest that the "summerless year" was caused by severe volcanic action elsewhere in the world the previous year.

953. Did Pope John Paul II recite an Indian prayer and perform a native rite when he visited Fort Simpson?

Pope John Paul II impressed an audience of the native peoples of the North at Fort Simpson, Northwest Territories, on Sunday, 20 September 1987, when he recited an Indian prayer and performed a native rite. The prayer and rite were prepared for him by a local Dene elder. Ron Graham explained in *God's Dominion* (1990) that the prayer contained no references to Jesus Christ, the Gospel, or the Cross. Graham wrote:

> Facing east to the Mackenzie River, he gave thanks for water. "As the waters cleanse and heal and strengthen the air and the land," he prayed to the Creator, "so too let your flowing love cleanse and heal us, bring us together as one people, and strengthen us."

Then he turned north toward the sacred fir burning nearby and said, "We give thanks to you, gentle lover, for this fire, for all home fires where offerings of love and kindness, understanding and caring are made. Let this fire burn all impurities from this land and from our minds and hearts and spirits, and send a pure prayer of love from this land and from each of us to you."

Then he turned to the west and thanked the Great Spirit of life for the air. "As the winds awaken and caress the land in spring and summer, as they prepare the land for rest and sleep in fall and winter, so too let the winds of your spirit awaken our lives so that we may always be as the seasons of your love, constant as the land in our expressions of your great creative power."

Then he turned south toward the magnificent fork, the shape of a divining rod, created by the Liard flowing into the Mackenzie. "We give thanks to you, Creator of all, for this land and all she produces, for the animals of the land and water and sky, for the plants which help us to live healthy lives, for the lives we live in caring for this beautiful land you have given to our care."

954. Is there a holiday in Quebec on November 23rd?

No, or at least not yet. One of the resolutions adopted by the Parti Québécois at its convention in Quebec City in January 1991 was that November the twenty-third be set aside as a "national" (i.e., provincial) holiday to honour those who died in the Rebellion of Lower Canada. The date specifically marks the battle of Saint-Denis, 23 November 1837. Should there ever be a Quebec republic, watch the calendar for special status for November the twenty-third.

955. What is the Baie-Comeau Policy?

The Northern Quebec town of Baie-Comeau, the birthplace of Prime Minister Brian Mulroney, briefly lent its name to the policy of the federal government which required that there be at least 51% Canadian ownership of those book publishing companies which changed ownership through foreign mergers or acquisitions. The policy was evolved on a plane ride between Sept-Iles and Baie-Comeau by former industries minister Sinclair Stevens and communications minister Marcel Masse in 1985. Its provisions were allowed to be overridden by subsequent events with the tacit agreement of subsequent administrations.

956. Did any Canadian city ever appoint a theatre censor?

The City of Montreal created the post of official theatre censor. The position was offered to the respected actor Jean-Paul Filion who accepted it in 1907. It was deemed there was the need for a censor because of clerical attacks on Sunday performances and on the production of plays judged to be immoral.

957. What was the first significant case of censorship in Canada?

The first significant case of censorship in New France arose in 1694. That year, Bishop Saint-Vallier of Quebec City suppressed a proposed production of Molière's *Tartuffe*. The Bishop accused the leading actor of uttering blasphemy, had him excommunicated, and then sent him to prison.

958. Did L.M. Montgomery create an urban legend?

The urban legend known as "Not My Dog" may well have been created by the author L.M. Montgomery. The story goes like this:

A woman is invited to call at the home of a woman who is wealthier than she is (or, in variations, older or socially superior). From the moment she is invited, the caller is unsure about how to behave – how to sit, how to make tea, etc. And matters are made worse when the time of the visit arrives. A large, lively, dirty beast of a dog is sitting in the front yard, and when the hostess welcomes the caller into the house, the dog follows her inside. While the caller tries to respect the social amenities, that darn dog does not. It tracks mud about the room, sniffs the cookies, and paws the furniture. The caller makes small talk, but the conversation becomes strained. Still, both parties keep a stiff upper lip, observing proper etiquette.

Finally the visit comes to an end. As the caller rises to leave, the hostess, with one eye on the wreckage, remarks icily, "And don't forget to take your dog!"

"My dog?" the caller says. "I thought it was yours!"

According to Jan Harold Brunvand, folklorist and specialist in urban legends at the University of Utah, the story first appeared in print in Chapter 22 of the third of the popular "Emily" books. In *Emily Climbs* (1924), young Emily calls on Miss Janet Royal and there is confusion over the ownership of the beast of a dog.

Brunvand, in *Curses! Broiled Again! The Hottest Urban Legends Going* (1989), noted:

> The story may have been a traditional one on Prince Edward Island, Canada, where Montgomery grew up and set most of her fiction. Or it may have become a folktale only later, as a result of its appearance in *Emily Climbs*, which has been read by countless children over the years. Either way, it's now an urban legend.

959. What is Wayne Gretzky's ten-point plan to revamp the NHL?

Ten points to revamp and rejuvenate the National Hockey League were proposed by hockey superstar Wayne Gretzky in *Gretzky: An Autobiography* (1990). Here they are in brief:

> 1. End the fighting. 2. Expand. 3. Rename the conferences. 4. Realign the conferences. 5. Bring on free agency. 6. Institute a week-off plan. 7. Let the players help make the rules. 8. Pay the refs more. 9. Bring back ESPN [the Sports Channel]. 10. Let us play in the Olympics.

960. Which agency is the most secret of all Canadian intelligence-gathering agencies?

The Communications Security Establishment (CSE) is the agency of the government that is even more secret than the Canadian Security Intelligence Service (CSIS). The CSE employs some 2,000 people in Ottawa and elsewhere who operate advanced communications equipment and monitor (or eavesdrop) on foreign embassies and consulates in Canada and on military installations abroad.

According to journalist Richard Cleroux in *Official Secrets: The Story behind the Canadian Security Intelligence Service* (1990), "The CSE functions as a funnel. Everything that is telecommunications in Canada is sucked into it. It needs no judicial warrants because it is part of the military, not part of CSIS.... Officially it answers to the Minister of National Defence, but in practice it answers more frequently to the National Security Agency in Fort Meade, Virginia, which gets about 98 percent of its work."

961. What is the Security Intelligence Review Committee?

The Security Intelligence Review Committee reports to Parliament on all aspects of security intelligence in Canada. It is the watchdog group. "SIRC, as it is called, is made up of five part-time members, trusted men and women, who have already proven their loyalty and dedication to Canada and have been cleared to the highest security rating – 'Top Secret – Special Activities' – obtained, of course, from CSIS ... The SIRC members act as the public's eyes and ears," according to the journalist Richard Cleroux in *Official Secrets: The Story behind the Canadian Security Intelligence Service* (1990).

962. Who may attend the Sir William Stephenson Academy?

The Sir William Stephenson Academy is operated by the Canadian Security Intelligence Service (CSIS) to supply training in intelligence operations matters for its newest members. Established in 1985 and located initially at Camp Borden, Ontario, and thereafter in Ottawa, it bears the name of William Stephenson, the World War II spymaster who is variously known as "the Quiet Canadian" and "the man called Intrepid." The Academy is attended by new members of CSIS (who are known to refer to it affectionately as "Intrepid High").

963. Has a Mountie ever betrayed his country to the Soviet Union?

One member of the RCMP is known to have betrayed his country to the Soviet Union. "He was James Morrison, known as Long Knife, who, in

1955, sold out a Canadian double agent to the Soviets for $3,500 – about a year's wages for a Mountie at the time," wrote journalist Richard Cleroux in *Official Secrets: The Story behind the Canadian Security Intelligence Service* (1990). As Cleroux noted, no other Mountie is known to have betrayed his country.

964. Does CSIS operate abroad?

The Canadian Security Intelligence Service (CSIS) is "a mostly domestic service with extensive powers for collecting intelligence on espionage, terrorism and foreign-influenced activities in Canada," according to the journalist Richard Cleroux in *Official Secrets: The Story behind the Canadian Security Intelligence Service* (1990). "It is also responsible for providing immigration, visa, and public service security-clearance screening, as well as providing advice to the government on possible future terrorist and espionage threats." By statute it is required to limit its activities to Canada but on occasion has been known to operate internationally.

965. What is the Enforcement Information Index?

The Enforcement Information Index (EII) is a computerized list of the names and descriptions of "all known terrorists, crooks and undesirables" maintained by the Department of Immigration. It is the immigration officials' equivalent of the Doomsday Book used by American Immigration and Naturalization officials at border entry points.

966. Does the RCMP engage in intelligence work?

The security intelligence work of the Royal Canadian Mounted Police (RCMP) was transferred to the newly created Canadian Security Intelligence Service (CSIS) in July 1984. Yet within the RCMP a small national security investigation and criminal intelligence unit continues to operate. It is called the National Security Investigation Directorate (NSID).

967. Where outside of Great Britain was responsible government first attained in the British Empire?

Responsible government was attained in the colonial legislature of Nova Scotia with the election of the first executive council whose members were chosen exclusively from elected representatives. The election occurred on 2 February 1848. It marked the first such government responsible to the people in the British Empire outside Great Britain.

968. Which provinces receive equalization payments from the federal government?

Equalization payments are fiscal transfers by the federal government to seven provincial governments. The payments are financed by federal income tax and are distributed on the basis of the fiscal capacity of those provinces to enable them to supply or "equalize" services in such essential areas as health, education, and welfare. Seven of the ten provinces are considered "poor" provinces and receive equalization payments. Alberta, British Columbia, and Ontario are considered "rich" provinces and, hence, help support the seven other provincial governments, including Quebec.

969. Has Canada contributed a moral movement or a moral organization to the world at large?

If a moral movement or a moral organization is defined to be ethical thought in action, then Canada has contributed two moral movements and two moral organizations to the world at large.

The two moral movements are the credit union movement and the co-operative movement. The credit union movement originated in Quebec as the *caisses populaires*. The co-operative or self-help movement, which worked in the Maritimes as the Antigonish Movement and on the Prairies as the Wheat Pools, have both been adapted to meet Third World conditions.

Pugwash and Greenpeace are two organizations that are respected internationally for their contributions to peace and ecology. The Pugwash Conference originated in Nova Scotia and eased Cold War tensions by hosting a series of top-level conferences which were attended by scientists irrespective of their governments. Greenpeace was established in Vancouver (its international headquarters is located in Amsterdam) to take direct action with respect to environmental and ecological needs.

970. What was the Mill Project?

The Mill Project was a major program of textual scholarship that saw the editing and publication of all the published and unpublished writings of the nineteenth-century English philosopher John Stuart Mill. The program was launched by the University of Toronto Press in 1959 and completed in 1991. John M. Robson, the general editor, oversaw the appearance of the thirty-three, green-bound volumes that constitute the *Collected Works of John Stuart Mill* – one of the largest editorial undertakings in Canadian history and a major one by any standard.

971. Was Quebec "humiliated" by the patriation of the Constitution?

Members of the Parti Québécois maintain that Quebec never signed the patriated Constitution Act (1982). That is true. In fact, not only is the signature of Quebec's Premier René Lévesque absent, but also absent are the signatures of the nine other provincial premiers.

   The movement for patriation was led by Prime Minister Pierre Elliott Trudeau. Was Quebec "humiliated" in the process? Andrew Cohen suggested no, not at all. In the first place, the signatures of provincial premiers do not appear on the document. In the second place, from Cohen's book *A Deal Undone: The Making and Breaking of the Meech Lake Accord* (1990), here are reasons why Quebec, whether a signatory or not, was not humiliated:

> The fact is that the "injustice" was undertaken by a Liberal government with overwhelming representation in Quebec. The prime minister was a Quebecker who had been elected with large majorities from his native province since 1968. A third of his cabinet was from Quebec, including senior ministers in finance, health, and justice. Moreover, the Liberals had elected seventy-four of seventy-five M.P.s from Quebec, seventy-one of whom supported the package. A good many provincial Liberals supported it, too. If this was humiliation, it was at the hands of *les Québécois*.

972. Was the Canadian Constitution passed without the ratification of Quebec or Quebeckers?

The Constitution Act (1982), which includes the Charter of Rights and Freedoms, was patriated and passed into Canadian law in 1982. Since then a succession of governments in Quebec has claimed that it was patriated and passed without the ratification of Quebec and Quebeckers because the provincial government never "signed" the document. Hence its provisions may be disallowed at the drop of a hat.

Patriation of the Constitution Act is taken as yet another instance of the "humiliation" of Quebec at the hands of the other provinces and the federal government. The fact of the matter is that Quebec's members in the House of Commons voted 73 to 2 in favour of the patriation agreement. Quebec's National Assembly, led by the separatist government of René Lévesque, voted 70 to 38 against the measure. In the words of one observer, writing in the "Letters to the Editor," *The Toronto Star*, 15 November 1997, "A total of 72 of Quebec's elected representatives were opposed, while 111, a sizable majority, were in favour of patriation."

The Quebec government did not "sign" (presumably "ratify") the document because no provincial government signed (presumably "ratified") the document. Signatures are red-herrings. Curiously, the document bears three signatures and all of them are those of Quebeckers. As constitutional authority Eugene Forsey noted, "The proclamation was signed on 17 April 1982, by Prime Minister Pierre Trudeau, Jean Chrétien, and André Ouelette, all three, incidentally, elected representatives of Quebec constituencies."

Quebec is a signatory to the Constitution Act (1982) and is bound by its provisions. In this instance, at least, constitutional law has nothing to do with political "humiliation."

973. Who originated the notion of a "distinct society"?

At a conference on the subject of the future of Quebec and Canada, held in Quebec City on 9 May 1986, Quebec's Minister of Intergovernmental Affairs, Gil Rémillard, presented the province's five conditions for rejoining the other nine provinces. The first of the five conditions was that Quebec be officially proclaimed a "distinct society." It proved to be the most contentious. "We must be assured that the Canadian constitution will explicitly recognize the unique character of Quebec society and guarantee us the means necessary to insure its full development within the framework of Canadian federalism." So Rémillard might be considered the father of the phrase "distinct society." Researchers, however, have found uses of the phrase with reference to French Canada in documents from the nineteenth century.

974. What is unusual about the word Adanac?

Adanac is both a place name and company name. It was widely used in the 1920s, when it was noted to be the word "Canada" spelt backwards.

975. Is Jack London indebted to a Canadian author's book?

The Call of the Wild is one of Jack London's best books and one of the world's best adventure novels. London based his 1903 account of a dog's devotion to its master on the autobiographical work *My Dogs in the Northland* published in book form in the same year by the Canadian missionary writer, Egerton Ryerson Young. London was never one to fly under false colours; he wrote a letter to Young to set forth his indebtedness to Young's earlier work.

976. What is "asymmetrical federalism"?

The political phrase "asymmetrical federalism" is associated with the Mulroney administration's constitutional initiative following the collapse of the Meech Lake Constitutional Accord in 1990. The initiative was an attempt to shift deliberations from the ill-fated "Quebec Round," which favoured "distinct society" status for Quebec, to the new "Canada Round," which seemed to assume "distinct society" status as an administrative rather than a constitutional arrangement. The idea was that Quebec would be granted more rights and responsibilities that the Canadian Constitution reserved to the federal government than the other provinces. The result would be a form of federalism in which there was a lack of symmetry between relationships – Ottawa's with Quebec City and Ottawa's with, say, Toronto.

977. Has Louis Riel ever been pardoned?

Louis Riel was executed for treason in 1885 and has never been pardoned. Yet the Métis leader was posthumously rehabilitated when the Province of Manitoba celebrated its centenary in 1970. On 10 March 1992, the House of Commons gave unanimous approval to the following motion, introduced by Joe Clark, Minister for Constitutional Affairs:

> That this House 1. Recognize the unique and historic role of Louis Riel as a founder of Manitoba and his contribution in the development of Confederation; and 2. That this House support by its actions the true attainment, both in principle and practice, of the constitutional rights of the Métis people.

In a sense the treasonous Riel is now regarded as a "father" of Confederation. Yet there is considerable debate over whether or not Riel should be pardoned, there being various reasons why and why not and also various types of pardons.

978. Which country was the second to outlaw slavery?

Canada was the second country to pass an act to outlaw slavery. The act was passed on 9 July 1793 under John Graves Simcoe, the first Lieutenant-Governor of Upper Canada. Britain did not pass an anti-slavery act until 1833 and the United States until the American Emancipation Proclamation of 1863. While the Upper Canadian act did not free a single slave, it stopped the further importation of slaves and freed the children of female slaves at the age of twenty-five.

979. What is so unusual about Nancy Huston's fiction?

Nancy Huston is a fiction writer who was born to Anglophone parents in Calgary. She has lived in Paris since the 1970s, where she is married to the Bulgarian-born, French literary critic Tsvetan Todorov. She has written a number of books of fiction and non-fiction, all in French. National attention came to her work in 1993 with the simultaneous publication of one of her novels in both English and French. It was issued in Toronto in English as *Plainsong* and issued in Montreal in French as *Cantique des Plaines* (1993). The English jury for the Governor General's English Fiction Award failed to shortlist the novel, but the French jury selected it to receive the Governor General's Award for French Fiction that year. There were immediate protests that the French edition was a translation and that the author was not a Québécois. Perhaps the protests were a sign of Quebec insularity and hypersensitivity. The issue was discussed by Matthew Manera in "Plainsong and Counterpoint," *The Canadian Forum*, July-August 1994. Manera wrote that *Plainsong* "is the story of a man who lived his life between what he was and what he wanted to be" that covered four generations of life in Alberta and the tragedy of the Native peoples.

980. Do members of the House of Commons recite a prayer?

It has long been the custom for members of the House of Commons to open the day's session with the reading of a prayer. In a unanimous resolve, the members adopted a new and shorter prayer on 18 February 1994. The English text, as reproduced in *The Toronto Star*, replaces a longer prayer that had specific references to Jesus Christ and the Royal Family. The new version is considered more ecumenical and less monarchical:

> Almighty God, we give thanks for the great blessings which have been bestowed on Canada and its citizens, including the gifts of freedom, opportunity and peace that we enjoy.
>
> We pray for our sovereign, Queen Elizabeth, and the Governor General.
>
> Guide us in our deliberations as Members of Parliament and strengthen us in our awareness of our duties and responsibilities as members.
>
> Grant us wisdom, knowledge and understanding to preserve the blessings of the country for the benefit of all and to make good laws and wise decisions.

981. How did Canada become an independent country?

In essence, Canada became an independent country in four phases.

On 1 July 1867, The British North America Act brought about the act of Confederation and created "one Dominion under that Name accordingly," the name being Canada. "Dominion" refers to the type of country – monarchy, republic, dominion, etc. – and not the country's name.

On 11 December 1931, Canada acquired self-government, with the right to declare war, control international trade, etc., through the passage of the Statute of Westminster by the British Parliament.

On 1 January 1947, the Canadian Parliament passed the Canadian Citizenship Act. For the first time Canadian citizens were to be distinguished from other British subjects. (At the same time, the United Kingdom distinguished its own citizens from other British subjects. However, all British subjects resident in Canada retain the right to vote in Canadian elections for the foreseeable future.)

On 17 April 1982, the Constitution Act patriated the Canadian constitution (the BNA Act, 1867) from Britain. Henceforth it may be amended without British involvement. Quebec's government was privy to negotiations leading up to patriation but at the last minute refused to ratify the constitutional change.

982. Is "The Dominion of Canada" still the official name of the country?

It was never the official name of the country. Section 3 of the British North America Act (1867) stated that the provinces "shall form and be One Dominion under that Name accordingly," referring to Canada. This clause has never been repealed, though the BNA act is now part of the Constitution Act. Thus Canada remains a dominion, or Dominion; it is correct to refer to it as the Dominion of Canada. In brief, the official name of the country is "Canada." "Dominion" is a descriptive term which can be applied to this country, but it is not part of its official name.

983. Is Canada a bilingual country?

Canada is officially a bilingual country. Canadians have the right to receive services from the federal government in the official language of their choice. Each province can decide for itself what services it will provide in the minority language. New Brunswick has a broad constitutional guarantee of equality of English and French. In Quebec, there is a constitutional guarantee that both French and English may be used in the legislature and the courts though French predominates. Otherwise, provision of services in the minority language is up to the individual government. The Charter of Rights and Freedoms of the Constitution Act (1982) guarantees minority-language (English in Quebec, French elsewhere) education rights "where numbers warrant."

984. What was the worst electoral showing in Canadian history?

The Progressive Conservative Party of Canada elected only two members to the House of Commons in the federal election of 1993. The party had gone from two successful record majority governments under Prime Minister Brian Mulroney to rump status under Kim Campbell and Jean Charest. It was the worst electoral defeat ever in the annals of federal politics in Canada.

985. Does Canada have something similar to the U.S. Bill of Rights?

It does. The Canadian Charter of Rights and Freedoms, adopted as part of the Constitution Act of 1982, is similar to the U.S. Bill of Rights, an amendment to the U.S. Constitution adopted in 1791, but less powerful. The Charter provides guarantees similar to those provided by the Bill and in general has the same power of precedence over other laws. However, the force of the Charter is limited in two ways. One is a clause that states that the rights and freedoms that it guarantees are subject to "such reasonable limits prescribed by law as can be demonstrably justified in a free and democratic society." In practice this means that rights and freedoms mean only as much or as little as the Supreme Court of Canada decides; this is exactly the situation in the United States, even though the American bill has no such clause.

The second and more important limitation is the so-called "notwithstanding clause." This clause allows any ordinary law to take precedence over the Charter for a period of up to five years (renewable indefinitely), simply by stating that it does so. Thus the Charter fails to provide "checks and balances" against the prospect of a tyrannical government in control of Parliament. It was apparently assumed by the drafters of the Constitution Act that to abuse this override power would be political suicide for a government and therefore none would ever do it.

986. Is it true that it is illegal to post an English-language sign in Quebec?

This was once true for most commercial signs but this is no longer the case. In 1977, the Parti Québécois passed the so-called Charter of the French Language, which among other things changed some of the rules affecting education, business, and public advertising in Quebec. With respect to signs, the Charter specified that all commercial signs in the province (except those on family-owned and operated businesses employing fewer than five people) must be in French only. This provision was challenged by two test cases in Quebec. The first case claimed that businesses had the right to post signs in any language or languages that they wanted. The second case claimed the right to include languages in addition to French.

The Quebec Superior Court, the Quebec Court of Appeal, and the Supreme Court of Canada all ruled that it was a reasonable limit on free speech to require the use of French on signs, but not reasonable to prohibit other languages. However, there is a so-called "notwithstanding clause" in the Charter which allows a legislature to exclude a law from certain provisions of the Charter, and the Quebec government used this clause to maintain the ban on languages other than French. This clause requires the law to be renewed every five years, and the Quebec government decided not to do so. A business, either owned by an individual or a corporation, can in the 1990s post signs in any language it wishes as long as a French version is also present and clearly predominant.

987. Must the Prime Minister be an elected Member of Parliament?

There is no actual legal requirement why the Prime Minister must be an elected Member of Parliament, though it is favoured by all precedent and practice. The Prime Minister may hold office without being a Member of Parliament. Indeed, cabinet ministers need not be M.P.s (though they invariably seek and acquire a seat to continue in government). It is extremely improbable that an unelected person would be in a position to assume the power of the Prime Minister. If he or she did, that person would likely and forthwith find a safe seat.

The Leader of the Opposition must be a Member of Parliament, though the leader of a party need not be an M.P. There have been several times when the Opposition's leader lacked a seat in Parliament; each time its parliamentary caucus had to choose a Member as a temporary leader.

988. In which ways do Canada and the United States differ?

Here is an answer to that question that is available on the Internet's "Frequently Asked Questions about Canada":

> Though Canadian and American societies are in some ways very similar, in other ways they are very different. In a sense, Canada represents a rejection of the ideals of the American Revolution. Most of the early settlement of Ontario and New Brunswick was by Loyalists fleeing the revolution, and there was a significant flow of Loyalists to parts of Quebec and Nova Scotia as well. These were people who rejected the notions of individualism and equality which became the basis of an American ideology, in favour of a more hierarchical, elitist society.
>
> This affected many facets of Canadian life. The dominant religious denominations in Canada, Catholic and Anglican, were much more hierarchical than the main Protestant denominations in the U.S. Though Canada does not have a state church, neither do we have the rigorous separation of Church and State that exists in the U.S. There are state-supported schools with religious affiliations in many Canadian provinces. Perhaps because religion was less of a personal affair in Canada, it seems to have suffered a steeper decline here than in the U.S. Church attendance is significantly lower here, and politicians do not make a show of being publicly pious, as American politicians do.
>
> Though the early settlement of Canada reflected a conservative rejection of the liberal (in the eighteenth century sense) ideals of the American Revolution, this has, paradoxically, made Canada far more receptive to socialist ideas, since both socialism and traditional conservatism both involve a more interventionist, "paternalistic" government than classical liberalism. Thus Canadians are far more accepting of government-run health insurance, or of gun control.
>
> Canadians are much less wedded to the concept of individual liberties, and more accepting of government intervention to maintain an orderly society, than are Americans. (This is a very broad generalization, to which there are countless exceptions.)
>
> The adoption of the Canadian Charter of Rights in 1982 can be seen as a significant step towards a more American philosophy. However, note that the Charter is significantly more limited than the American Bill of Rights. The American system basically sees

government as bad. There is an elaborate system of separation of powers and of checks and balances to ensure that one branch of government does not gain too much power. Much of the U.S. constitution is designed to protect individual citizens from the actions of governments.

In Canada, in contrast, the executive and legislative branches of government are intimately linked. The Charter of Rights is a recent innovation, and its application is tempered by the power of legislators to override it.

989. Can a Canadian hold dual citizenship?

Since the proclamation of the Canadian Citizenship Act of 15 February 1977, the right of a Canadian citizen to hold dual citizenship has been recognized. This means that a Canadian may retain or claim the citizenship of one or more foreign countries with the proviso that those foreign countries do not bar dual citizenship to their citizens. Thus it is possible for a Canadian citizen to be an American citizen (the United States recognizes the principle of dual citizenship) but not a Japanese citizen (Japan does not recognize the principle).

990. Is there an increase in bilingualism among Canadians?

Bilingualism is on the increase among Canadians, both Francophone and Anglophone.

According to the Summer 1989 issue of *Language and Society*, the journal of the Multiculturalism Directorate of the Department of the Secretary of State, the increase may be marked for the years 1971 and 1986. In 1971, the percentage of bilingual Francophones was 34.0%; bilingual Anglophones, 5.5%. In 1986, the percentage of bilingual Francophones was 38.5%; bilingual Anglophones, 8.5%. It is apparent that more Francophones than Anglophones are becoming bilingual.

991. Do Canadians use British or American spelling?

Standard Canadian written English uses characteristic features of both British and American spelling. Most Canadians use "colour" (not "color"), "harbour" (not "harbor"), "cheque" (not "check"), and "centre" (not "center"), but also "specialize" (not "specialise"), "draft" (not "draught"), and "tire" (not "tyre").

Canadian newspapers and magazines have individual spelling standards. *The Globe and Mail* tends to use the above rules, for instance, while *The Montreal Gazette* will use "color" and "harbor" but also "cheque" and "centre." Newspaper practice is somewhat influenced by the desire to run stories originating in the United States with minimal editing.

992. Why do Canadians celebrate Thanksgiving on a different day than do Americans?

Celebrations of thanksgiving to God for the bountiful harvest are customary and draw on three traditions: European peasant harvest celebrations; formal observances like the one celebrated by Martin Frobisher in the Eastern Arctic in 1578, the first such celebration in North America; and the Pilgrim Fathers' celebration of their first harvest in Massachusetts in 1621 involving the uniquely American turkey, squash and pumpkin. The latter celebration was brought to Nova Scotia in the 1750s; the citizens of Halifax commemorated the end of the Seven Years War in 1763 with a day of Thanksgiving. Loyalists brought the celebration to other parts of the country as well.

In 1879, Parliament declared November 6 to be the day of Thanksgiving; it was celebrated as a national rather than a religious holiday. Later and earlier dates were observed, the most popular being the third Monday in October. After World War I, Thanksgiving and Armistice (later Remembrance) Day were celebrated in the same week. It was not until 31 January 1957 that Parliament proclaimed that the observance of Thanksgiving would be held on the second Monday in October Not everyone was happy. E.C. Drury, the former "farmer-Premier" of Ontario, lamented later that "the farmers' own holiday has been stolen by the towns" to give them a long weekend when the weather was better.

993. Which Canadian universities are the best?

There is an old saying, "God has many bests." It is almost an impossible task to rank the quality and variety of education offered by universities. The reputation of a university, or the level of recognition given to its degrees, varies from field to field. A measure of the expertise of a university may be obtained by looking at its research activities (primarily conducted at the graduate level).

Each year *Maclean's* ranks the Canadian universities based on the following considerations: Student Body (entering grade, proportion who graduate, international students, students' awards); Classes (median size, number of classes taught by tenured faculty); Faculty (number with Ph.D., grants obtained, awards); Finances (operating budget, budget for scholarships and bursaries, budget for student services); Library (holdings per student, budget for acquisition and budget of university's expenses for library); Reputation (alumni financial support, reputation survey). The ranking is further divided along undergraduate, graduate, and post-graduate lines.

Generally speaking, the following universities usually receive "top marks" (in no special order): University of Toronto, McGill University, Queen's University, University of Waterloo, McMaster University, University of British Columbia, and Laval University.

994. Is it true that immigrants to Quebec must send their children to French-language schools?

Yes. Historically, a large proportion of immigrants in Quebec wanted to send their children to English schools. This was partly because the immigrants saw English as economically advantageous, partly because the French schools were almost all Catholic, and non-Catholics were not always welcome in these schools. By the late 1960s, with the birth rate rapidly declining, French-speaking Quebeckers became concerned about the survival of their community, and the tendency of many immigrants to assimilate into the English-speaking minority was seen as a threat to the future of French. Laws were therefore adopted to require the children of immigrants to attend French schools. English schools would continue to exist, but they would be only for the existing English community, not for newcomers. There were many exceptions and bureaucratic complications to these rules, but that was the basic idea. This law forced not only immigrants from other countries, but also newcomers to Quebec from other Canadian provinces, to attend French schools. In reaction to this, a clause was inserted in the 1982 Charter of Rights and Freedoms to allow this last group to attend English schools. This clause also guaranteed the right to French-language schools in the other provinces. This is not a blanket guarantee of freedom of linguistic choice in education. Quebec can still, and does, require the children of immigrants to attend French schools.

995. How much does it cost a foreign student to study in Canada?

Education in Canada is highly subsidized. The private sector makes a minor contribution to the maintenance of universities; the major contribution to the educational system is made by various levels of government. A semester can cost a Canadian student between $800 and $1,500, depending on the province where the university is located and the course of study.

Foreign students, called "visa students" because they require a visa to live and study in the country, can expect to pay tuition fees of about $1,000 to $12,000 per semester. Newfoundland, British Columbia, Manitoba, and Alberta typically ask lower tuition fees, while Ontario and Quebec ask much more from international students. Foreign fees for graduate studies are usually less than undergraduate fees. Other student expenses include books, supplies and instruments, housing, food, laundry, transportation, health care, clothing, and entertainment. In addition to tuition fees, students may spend from $7,000 to $10,000 per year.

996. Which universities offer programs in Canadian Studies?

A handful of universities offer undergraduate arts degrees in Canadian Studies. The programs usually include sociology, history, politics, economics, literature, etc. Among the English-language universities that do so are the University of Alberta, Laurentian University, University of Ottawa, and York University.

997. What is the International Council for Canadian Studies?

The International Council for Canadian Studies (ICCS) is a federation of twenty national and multi-national Canadian Studies associations. Close to thirty countries have national Canadian Studies associations with some 6,000 members. Most of these members are foreign academics who teach courses in Canadian literature or head programs or departments devoted to Canadian Studies.

998. What is a Canadianist?

"A Canadianist is a specialist in Canadian studies," according to *The Canadian Oxford Dictionary* (1998) edited by Katherine Barker.

Only lately has the word made it into a dictionary. "Not to be found in any existing dictionary, the term 'Canadianist' refers to academics and others who share a fascination with Canada," wrote editor Ben Viccari in the 16 March 1990 issue of *Canadian Scene*, a news and information service for ethnic minority groups. "Most are university professors involved in the learned study of Canada, including teaching and publication on a wide range of subjects relating to this country."

999. Is there a distinctive Canadian sound?

The characteristic sounds of the acoustical environment are heard by all, but few listen for them. People professionally concerned with sound – musicians, composers, audio technicians, etc. – have interesting ideas about distinctive Canadian sounds.

The pianist Glenn Gould felt that the quintessential Canadian sound was the clickety-clack of a passenger train travelling over a northern terrain. He made use of this sound in his radio documentary *The Idea of North*. The ear of travel writer Kildare Dobbs was turned to the train, but not to the sounds of its rails but to its long, drawn-out mournful whistle through the night. He found it most memorable and expressive.

R. Murray Schafer, the composer and student of sound, expressed strong feelings about the call of the loon. "Its haunting and lonely call strikes right to the soul of every native who has heard it on summer lakes or on the coastal ranges where it winters." He recommended the loon's cry to CBC Radio for a distinctive signature sound – to be heard behind the voice of the announcer intoning "This is the CBC."

Many Northerners feel strongly that there is a sound to the silence of the Arctic. They maintain that the Northern Lights not only shine but also audibly crackle or rustle. If they do, that too is a quintessential Canadian sound.

1000. Do the Northern Lights rustle?

The Aurora Borealis, or the Northern Lights, illuminate the northern skies, especially during long winter nights. They seem to "dance," and at the same time they seem to "rustle."

Observers in the Arctic are on record as describing the sounds of the lights as a "rustle" (like a wind blowing leaves) or a "click" (like the sound of static) or a "whish" (like the escape of air). The sounds seem to accompany the movements of the lights. The colder the weather, the louder the sounds.

Atmospheric scientists have been unable to record these sounds and have no idea of any agency that offers the sound effects that could accompany the light displays.

The aurora display begins about 60 kilometres above the earth's surface and extends for hundreds of miles. Observers in the Arctic claim to have seen the lights playing on ground level but this is unlikely according to atmospheric scientists. It was an Inuit custom in the past to snap one's fingers to draw the lights closer to the earth.

Index

Included in this Index are key words and principal personal and place names. In the book itself the questions and answers are loosely arranged in four categories: People, Places, Things, Ideas. The numbers refer to question numbers, not page numbers.

Indian Act, first, 874
Indian agents, gone, 873
Indian Band, term, 229
Indian identity, loss, 872
Indian prayer, Pope, 953
Indian Reserve, term, 230
Indian, defined, 008
Indian, moccasins, 885
Indians, First Nations, 208
Indians, languages, 871
Indigenous people, term, 209
Information, economy, 624
Inn, oldest, 304
Innis, H.A., school, 888
Insulin, first, 706
Insulin, patient, 622
Insurance, AIDS, 652
Intelligence, security, 961
Intelligence, unit, 654
International Council, 997
International Gathering, 323
International Order, meaning, 820
Internet, CA*net, 658
Internet, Canadians, 697
Internet, licensing, 858
Inuit words, snow, 567
Inuit, defined, 208
Inuit, skraelings, 135
Inuk, word, 008
Inuktitut, language, 673
Ionosphere, named, 798
Iqaluit, Frobisher, 431
Irish Rovers, group, 034
Iroquois prayer, text, 801
Iroquois, long house, 649
Irving, K.C., Buctouche, 358
Irwin, May, actress, 035
Islam, presence, 233
Island, Mahone Bay, 337
Isle Madame, namesake, 325

Israel, Emmaus, 353
Italian, language, 673
Ives, George, Trooper, 207

Jack the Ripper, identity, 190
Jack, Donald Lamont, 816
Jackrabbit, museum, 421
Jacks, Terry, songwriter, 161
James Bay Project, 583
James, M.R., prize, 473
James, Stewart, effect, 937
Japan, Anne, 328
Japan, immigration, 215
Japan, tourists, 329
Jarvis, T.S., novel, 698
Jenkins, Fergison (Fergie), 137
Jenkins, Ferguson, athlete, 141
Jeopardy, show, 067
Jesus of Montreal, film, 653
Jock-strap, inventor, 124
Johanssen, Herman (Jackrabbit), 421
John Paul XXIII, prayer, 953
Johnny Belinda, play, 343
Johnny Canuck, stamp, 714
Johnson, Ben, known, 001
Johnson, Edward, great, 210
Johnson, Pauline, poet, 711
Johnson, Rita, B.C., 116
Johnston, Gary, potato, 627
Johnston, John Lawson, 518
Jones, D.B., film, 892
Jones, D.B., unit, 891
Jonquière, Que., 402
Jonquière, Saguenay, 400
Journey, prize, 883
Joyal, Miguel, statue, 746
Judges, Supreme Court, 943
July the first, Chinese, 740
Junk mail, 581